Les Wright

# The Bear
### Further Readings
### and Evolution of a Gay ... Subculture

*Pre-publication*
REVIEWS,
COMMENTARIES,
EVALUATIONS . . .

"*The Bear Book II* is a buffet with a selection of dishes offering something for every appetite. Some are quick stir-fries, with a certain rawness, yet a tangy taste; others are more laboriously prepared with nuance and esoteric seasonings. Not all the chefs are of conventional or equal training. But no reader will go hungry. Where else can one feast on references to Esau in the Old Testament, Longus' pastoral romances, or Said's Orientalism, and revel (or wallow) in that memorable line, 'Do you think those pipes will hold the sling?'

It is as much a tribute to self-creation as the anthropological classic, *Man Makes Himself,* by Gordon Childe. And it shares with this unlikely sibling an iconoclastic text and the spirit of a rough and ready pioneer—imperfect, often premature, but begging further study and research. Something indeed is going on and it is worthy of serious study. Great food for the new millennium."

**J. H. Sibal, MA**
Lecturer,
Interdisciplinary Studies,
New York University Continuing
and Professional Studies,
New York

*More pre-publication*
*REVIEWS, COMMENTARIES, EVALUATIONS . . .*

"**A** second outstanding collection of essays on the bear phenomenon. Alternately sexy, smart, and warmhearted, much like the men who make up bear communities. Celebrations of the successes of the bear movement intersect with honest examinations of drawbacks and ongoing struggles. Of particular interest are essays suggesting that bear culture now has its own center and margins, both in terms of who is included and who is left out, and important topics that sometimes go undiscussed. This is required reading for anyone interested in insider ethnographies that examine the ways queer subcultures renegotiate changing constructions of gender, sexuality, race, class, and mainstream-outsider dynamics at the turn of the century."

**Pete Chvany, PhD**
Activist,
Bisexual Resource Center

"**E**veryone knows that bears like to frolic with their furry friends, but Les Wright has once again shown that bears have a serious side, too. Pulling together a diverse array of contributors, *The Bear Book II* opens up the intellectual and political issues that often remain unexamined about this gay male subculture—from health concerns to cultural tensions to media portrayals. This smart and complicated collection will open the eyes of many gay men to the reality of the bears in their midst—and give the bears themselves some food for thought, as well."

**Wayne Hoffman**
Managing Editor,
*New York Blade*

Harrington Park Press®
An Imprint of The Haworth Press, Inc.

## NOTES FOR PROFESSIONAL LIBRARIANS AND LIBRARY USERS

This is an original book title published by Harrington Park Press®, an imprint of The Haworth Press, Inc. Unless otherwise noted in specific chapters with attribution, materials in this book have not been previously published elsewhere in any format or language.

## CONSERVATION AND PRESERVATION NOTES

All books published by The Haworth Press, Inc. and its imprints are printed on certified pH neutral, acid free book grade paper. This paper meets the minimum requirements of American National Standard for Information Sciences-Permanence of Paper for Printed Material, ANSI Z39.48-1984.

# The Bear Book II
*Further Readings
in the History and Evolution
of a Gay Male Subculture*

## *HAWORTH* Gay & Lesbian Studies
John P. De Cecco, PhD
Editor in Chief

*A Consumer's Guide to Male Hustlers* by Joseph Itiel

*Trailblazers: Profiles of America's Gay and Lesbian Elected Officials* by Kenneth E. Yeager

*Rarely Pure and Never Simple: Selected Essays* by Scott O'Hara

*Navigating Differences: Friendships Between Gay and Straight Men* by Jammie Price

*In the Pink: The Making of Successful Gay- and Lesbian-Owned Businesses* by Sue Levin

*Behold the Man: The Hype and Selling of Male Beauty in Media and Culture* by Edisol Wayne Dotson

*Untold Millions: Secret Truths About Marketing to Gay and Lesbian Consumers* by Grant Lukenbill

*It's a Queer World: Deviant Adventures in Pop Culture* by Mark Simpson

*In Your Face: Stories from the Lives of Queer Youth* by Mary L. Gray

*Military Trade* by Steven Zeeland

*Longtime Companions: Autobiographies of Gay Male Fidelity* by Alfred Lees and Ronald Nelson

*From Toads to Queens: Transvestism in a Latin American Setting* by Jacobo Schifter

*The Construction of Attitudes Toward Lesbians and Gay Men* edited by Lynn Pardie and Tracy Luchetta

*Lesbian Epiphanies: Women Coming Out in Later Life* by Karol L. Jensen

*Smearing the Queer: Medical Bias in the Health Care of Gay Men* by Michael Scarce

*Macho Love: Sex Behind Bars in Central America* by Jacobo Schifter

*When It's Time to Leave Your Lover: A Guide for Gay Men* by Neil Kaminsky

*Strategic Sex: Why They Won't Keep It in the Bedroom* edited by D. Travers Scott

*One of the Boys: Masculinity, Homophobia, and Modern Manhood* by David Plummer

*Homosexual Rites of Passage: A Road to Visibility and Validation* by Marie Mohler

*Male Lust: Pleasure, Power, and Transformation* edited by Kerwin Kay, Jill Nagle, and Baruch Gould

*Tricks and Treats: Sex Workers Write About Their Clients* edited by Matt Bernstein Sycamore

*A Sea of Stories: The Shaping Power of Narrative in Gay and Lesbian Cultures—A Festschrift for John P. De Cecco* edited by Sonya Jones

*Out of the Twilight: Fathers of Gay Men Speak* by Andrew R. Gottlieb

*The Mentor: A Memoir of Friendship and Gay Identity* by Jay Quinn

*Male to Male: Sexual Feeling Across the Boundaries of Identity* by Edward J. Tejirian

*Straight Talk About Gays in the Workplace, Second Edition* by Liz Winfeld and Susan Spielman

*The Bear Book II: Further Readings in the History and Evolution of a Gay Male Subculture* edited by Les Wright

*Gay Men at Midlife: Age Before Beauty* by Alan L. Ellis

*Being Gay and Lesbian in a Catholic High School: Beyond the Uniform* by Michael Maher

# The Bear Book II
*Further Readings
in the History and Evolution
of a Gay Male Subculture*

Les K. Wright
Editor

Harrington Park Press®
An Imprint of The Haworth Press, Inc.
New York • London • Oxford

© 2001 by The Haworth Press, Inc. All rights reserved. No part of this work may be reproduced or utilized in any form or by any means, electronic or mechanical, including photocopying, microfilm, and recording, or by any information storage and retrieval system, without permission in writing from the publisher. Printed in the United States of America.

The Haworth Press, Inc., 10 Alice Street, Binghamton, NY 13904-1580

Cover design by Monica L. Seifert.

Foreword © JackFritscher.com.

**Library of Congress Cataloging-in-Publication Data**

Wright, Les K.
   The bear book II : further readings in the history and evolution of a gay male subculture / Les K. Wright.
      p.   cm.
   Includes bibliographical references and index.
   ISBN 0-7890-0636-7 (alk. paper).—ISBN 1-56023-165-3 (pbk. : alk. paper)
     1. Gays—Identity. 2. Gay men—Attitudes. 3. Gay men—Psychology. 4. Gender identity. 5. Group identity. 6. Masculinity (Psychology) 7. Body image. I. Title.
HQ76.W75   1997
305.38'9664—dc21                                              96-46281
                                                                              CIP

This volume is dedicated to my faithful editor, Bill Palmer, the whole Monty Bears gang, my beloved "mama bear," Tanya Gardiner-Scott, and my loving life partner, Dale Wehrle.

# CONTENTS

**About the Editor** — xiii

**Contributors** — xv

**Foreword** — xxiii
    *Jack Fritscher*

**Acknowledgments** — lxiii

**Introduction** — 1
    *Les Wright*

## PART I: BEAR BODIES

**Chapter 1. Bears and Health** — 15
    *Lawrence D. Mass*

| | |
|---|---|
| Sleep Apnea | 21 |
| Arteriosclerotic Cardiovascular Disease (ASCVD) | 22 |
| Arteriosclerotic Peripheral Vascular Disease | 23 |
| Arthritis | 23 |
| Cancers | 23 |
| Cholecystitis and Cholelithiasis | 24 |
| Diabetes Mellitus | 24 |
| Duodenal Ulcer | 25 |
| Gastroesophageal Reflux Disease | 26 |
| Heart Attack | 26 |
| Hiatal Hernia | 26 |
| Hyperlipidemia | 27 |
| Hypertension | 27 |
| Pediculosis (Body Lice) | 27 |
| Pilonidal Sinus and Cyst | 28 |
| Sexually Transmitted Diseases | 28 |
| Two Postscripts | 32 |

**Chapter 2. Fat Is a Bearish Issue**     **39**
    *Laurence Brown*

    Journey into the Psyche of a Chubby-Chaser     40
    Bearstory/Chubstory     43
    Fat Theory     44
    Icons and Images of Fat-Desire     46
    Gripes About Beardom     53

**Chapter 3. Bear Youth: An Interview with Brian Kearns, Bear Youth Webmaster**     **55**

**Chapter 4. By Any Otter Name: The Negative Space of the Bear**     **65**
    *John Milton Hendricks*

    Bears in Space     67
    Neighborhood Clans     72
    The Otter Questionnaire     77
    Responses     79
    Inconclusions     90

**Chapter 5. The Beard of Joseph Palmer**     **95**
    *Stewart Holbrook*

**PART II: BEAR TESTIMONIES**

**Chapter 6. A Bear Admirer's (Subjective, Fluffy, and Totally Honest) Point of View**     **105**
    *Ned Wilkinson*

**Chapter 7. A Puerto Rican Bear in the USA**     **109**
    *Ali Lopez*

    Family Background     111
    Breaking Out of Captivity     116

**Chapter 8. One Black Bear Speaks**     **125**
    *Jason R. Clark*

**Chapter 9. An Asian Bear in Minnesota**      129
    *Dave Gan*

**Chapter 10. The Ephebe Is Dead—Long Live the Bear**      135
    *David Greig*

**Chapter 11. Parlaying Playmates into Lasting Friendships**      137
    *John R. Yoakam*

**PART III: MORE BEAR SPACES**

**Chapter 12. Theorizing Bearspace**      147
    *Alex G. Papadopoulos*

  Bear Bodies in Space      147
  Bearspace and Theory      149
  Bearspace Exposed      155
  Skepsis/Bears and Globalization      155
  Bearspaces of Subjectivity and Fantasy      159

**Chapter 13. Paws Between Two Worlds: Bears and the Leather Community**      163
    *Robert B. Marks Ridinger*

**Chapter 14. Gen-X Bears International**      169
    *John-Paul Patrick Kucera*

**Chapter 15. The Bear-A-Tones: An Interview with David Salinas**      175

**Chapter 16. East Coast Bear Hugz**      185
    *Tim Goecke*

**Chapter 17. The Bears Mailing List, Part 2: Interview with Henry Mensch**      191
    *Transcribed by Dale Wehrle*

**PART IV: BEAR CLUB SCENE**

**Chapter 18. A Bear's Autobiography**      205
    *Jim Parton*

**Chapter 19. Bear Contests** 211
    *Les Wright*

**Chapter 20. A Short History of Bear Clubs in Iowa: The Bear Paws of Iowa and The Ursine Group** 215
    *Larry Toothman*

  First Meeting 216
  Issues and Feedback Raised in Articles in *The Bear Facts* 221
  The Creation of The Ursine Group 227

**Chapter 21. Houston Area Bears** 233
    *Mitch Froehlich*

**Chapter 22. The Bears Come to Rochester** 243
    *John O. Noble*

**Chapter 23. A Short History of the Brisbears** 249
    *Peter Sharman*

**PART V: MORE BEARS ABROAD**

**Chapter 24. A Bear Voice from Turkey** 253
    *Mehmet Ali Sahin*

**Chapter 25. Falstaff's Legacy: The Bears of Albion** 263
    *Howard Watson*

**Chapter 26. The Rise of the Australian Bear Community Since 1995** 269
    *Seumas Hyslop*

  June 1995: The Death of Ozbears 269
  August 1995: The Birth of Harbour City Bears 270
  April 1996: The Birth of VicBears (Originally Melbourne Ozbears) 272
  February 1997: Bear Essentials '97 and the Sydney Gay and Lesbian Mardi Gras 272
  May 1997: The Melbourne Bear and Cub Competition 274
  Mid-1997: Brisbears Voted Best Male Club in Brisbane 275
  Late 1997: New Bear Club in Canberra 276

| | |
|---|---|
| January 1998: The Second Bear Club in Sydney | 277 |
| February 1998: BEAR ESSENTIALS '98 and Sydne Gay and Lesbian Mardi Gras Become the Biggest Bear Festival in Australia at the Time | 277 |
| June 1998: Southern Hibearnation '98 and the Mr. Australian Bear and Cub Competition Become the Second Flagship Event for the Australian Bear Community | 279 |
| Late 1998: Cougar Leather Club Caters to Bears in Southern Australia | 280 |
| BearsPerth (Formerly WOMBATS) and Ozbears South Australia | 281 |
| 1999: Further Developments | 281 |
| The Future of Bears in Australia | 282 |
| Acknowledgments | 283 |

## PART VI: BEARS IN MEDIA

### Chapter 27. You Can Lead a Bear to Culture, but ... or Bears in Literature and Culture: A Discussion with David Bergman and Michael Bronski — 287
*Ron Suresha*

### Chapter 28. Laid Bear: Masculinity with All the Trappings — 305
*Thomas McCann*

| | |
|---|---|
| Methodology | 306 |
| Bear Erotica | 307 |
| Mainstream Gay Erotica | 315 |
| Leather/SM Erotica | 317 |
| Discussion | 319 |

### Chapter 29. In Goldilocks's Footsteps: Exploring the Discursive Construction of Gay Masculinity in Bear Magazines — 327
*Elizabeth A. Kelly*
*Kate Kane*

| | |
|---|---|
| We Come Upon This Project | 327 |
| Configuring Gay Masculinity/Desire: The Bare/Bear Body | 336 |

**Appendix: Early Published Writings on Bears
by Les Wright** **351**

Exploring the "Bear" Phenomena (*Seattle Gay News*,
   August 3, 1990, pp. 20-21) 351
In the Company of Bears: Finding My Way to the Bear
   Hugs/Leather Bears (*Bear Fax* 6, 1990, pp. 10-11) 357
Sex and the Immutable Laws of Reciprocity (Having Fun
   at Bear Parties, and More) (*Bear Fax* 7, 1991, p. 10) 359
Bear Sex and Hero Worship (*Bear Fax* 8, 1991, p. 10) 361
Bears Go for Each Other (*Bear Fax* 9, 1991, p. 10) 362
What Is a Bear? Further Reflections (*Bear Fax* 13,
   1992, p. 13) 364

**Index** **367**

# ABOUT THE EDITOR

**Dr. Les Wright** was recently tenured at Mount Ida College, where he is Associate Professor of Humanities. He recently completed a Certificate of Thanatology at the National Center for Death Education, and presented a meta-analysis entitled "Trauma Theory and Homophobia: Toward a New Understanding of Alcoholism in Gay Men" at the Boulder Summit (a national gay men's health conference). He continues to publish original research, most recently on the history of gay San Francisco as well as queer New German cinema and is now researching a history of "queer masculinities" and blue-collar male homosexualities.

# CONTRIBUTORS

**David Bergman** is author or editor of a dozen books, including *Cracking the Code*, which won the George Elliston Poetry Prize, *Heroic Measures*, and *Gaiety Transfigured: Gay Self-Representations in American Literature*. His work has also appeared in *The Harvard Gay and Lesbian Review, The Kenyon Review, Men's Style, The New Republic*, and *The Paris Review*. He also edits the biennial series *Men on Men: Best New Gay Fiction* and, with Joan Larkin, the book series *Out Lives: Lesbian and Gay Autobiographies*. He teaches at Towson University.

**Michael Bronski** is author of *Culture Clash: The Making of Gay Sensibility* and *The Pleasure Principle: Sex, Backlash, and the Struggle for Gay Freedom*, and editor of *Taking Liberties: Gay Men's Essays on Sex, Politics, and Culture* and *Flashpoint: Gay Male Sexual Writing*. His writing has appeared in *The Los Angeles Times, The Village Voice, Z Magazine, OUT*, and *Gay Community News*, as well as in the anthologies *Gay Spirit, Friends and Lovers, Home Towns: Gay Men Write About Where They Belong, Acting on AIDS*, and volumes 2, 3, and 4 of the *Flesh and the Word* series. He has been involved in the gay liberation movement for thirty years.

**Laurence Brown,** an otter with attitude, lives in London with George, his huscub of over five years. Laurence has been involved in adult education for a very long time, but is hoping for a pardon from Queen Elizabeth. He wrote widely for the gay press until it went out of fashion. They are both active (and passive) in the big and bear scene in Europe; they also sing in the highly acclaimed London Gay Men's Chorus. Laurence's first novel, *Addictions*, a powerful tale of intrigue, homoerotic desire, and opera, will be published by Gay Men's Press in spring 2000.

**Jason R. Clark** resides in Connecticut as a visual artist, independent filmmaker, and unregistered film historian. Though not embellished in fame and fortune, most of his work has been done in donation (two communal paintings). As a Black Bear in New England, Jason has experienced bear dens and functions in many states and finds most welcoming those without steel traps and nooses. Currently, Jason is working on an independent film, *Broken,* and a book—compiling cult film reviews by nonconformist video store clerks. His chapter in this book is designed to open the doors of curiosity among bears and leathermen worldwide.

**Jack Fritscher, PhD,** is the author of the nonfiction memoir, *Mapplethorpe: Assault with a Deadly Camera;* the gay history novel, *Some Dance to Remember;* and the British photo-book, *Jack Fritscher's American Men.* Research gay history and gay pop culture at <www.PalmDriveVideo.com> and <www.JackFritscher.com>.

**Mitch Froehlich** is originally from Wisconsin, now transplanted to Houston, Texas, where he lives with his partner Ken, dog Freddie, and cats Isis and Cleopatra. He was among the group of men who were at the first meeting of the Houston Area Bears (né Gulf Coast Bears) and served as a Triad member for the first two years. He would like to thank those at that meeting who helped clarify his fading memory of that time. He would also like to thank his partner, Ken, for being supportive of his bear activities and helping to exemplify the best of being a bear.

**Dave Gan** has done time in the recording industry in Baltimore and as a freelance producer and computer consultant in the multimedia industry in San Francisco. In 1995 he moved to Minneapolis to dabble in Internet marketing and communications. He also enjoys music, and is a Concertmaster Emeritus of the Minnesota Philharmonic Orchestra, the first GLBT-sensitive community orchestra. David currently lives in the Bay Area with his partner and spends most of his time working with a cool Internet startup venture.

**Tim Goecke** has designed sets for theater, film, and television, as well as exhibits for museums and galleries. His credits include work for the Smithsonian Institution, the Baltimore Museum of Art, the Civil Rights Museum, and Maryland Public Television. He has exhibited drawings and sculptures in the Baltimore/Washington area. Tim resides in Baltimore with his partner, Perry Cooper, and currently is working on final designs for the Delta Cultural Center in Arkansas. His graphic work is included in the Bear Icons art exhibition.

Contributors xvii

**David Greig** is a Toronto artist and writer whose poetry, fiction, editorials, illustration, and artwork have appeared in *Waves: Fine Canadian Writing, Quickies: Short, Short Fiction On Gay Male Desire* and *Quickies 2* (Arsenal Pulp Press), *The Day We Met* (Alyson Publications), "Showing Our Face" group exhibit, "Collective Stroke" group exhibit, Gallery 76 (solo show), Del Bello Gallery group exhibits, *RFD* magazine (issues 66, 82, 89, and 94), *Canadian Book Review, Up Front, Yukon Violation, The U of T Review, Lines, Orchid Mouth* 'zine, Station Gallery group exhibit, *Xtra* magazine, *The Globe & Mail,* and elsewhere. His poetry chapbook, *Bone Meal,* was shortlisted in the League of Canadian Poets' 1999 Canadian Poetry Chapbook Manuscript Competition. He was the media columnist for the Toronto gay magazine *Xtra* for three years. He is also the author of numerous books on adult literacy.

**John Milton Hendricks,** former resident of Cincinnati, Pittsburgh, Atlanta, Madison, Wisconsin, and a couple other places, is currently a librarian writing in Chicago. A wistful outsider to the bear community (if not all communities), he would like to assure readers that he has no credentials whatsoever. He did think he was an otter for a while, but now even that tentative identity seems to have been thrown into question.

**Seumas Hyslop** is an ex-committee member of Harbour City Bears, and partner of David Coburn. Having met most of the presidents and committee members of the Australian Bear Clubs, he has remained friends with them throughout the last two to three years.

**Brian Kearns** lives in Canada.

**John-Paul Patrick Kucera** was born on August 2, 1974, in Annapolis, Maryland, and grew up in the Dominican Republic, the Bahamas, Maryland, and Maine. He received his BS in Materials Science and Engineering as well as a minor in East Asian Studies from the Massachusetts Institute of Technology in 1996. He began his involvement with Gen-X Bears International during his studies for his Master's at Pennsylvania State University. Currently serving as the Council Moderator for Gen-X Bears International, he is the elected spokesperson for the organization. J. P. resides in State College, Pennsylvania, with his husbear, and both are actively involved with the Keystone chapter there. He enjoys the outdoors, sci-fi films and books, Japanese culture, glass-blowing, and trying to occupy his time with anything and everything that catches a bear's curiosity.

**Ali Lopez** grew up in the small coastal town of Dorado, Puerto Rico, where he began to draw in his early teens by looking at comic books. At age seventeen, he joined the U.S. Army and was stationed at Fort Riley, Kansas, where he became a staff sergeant. After six and a half years in the military, he moved to the DC/Baltimore area where he became involved in the bear and leather communities. He now lives in Southern California. He has been a featured artist in *Daddybear, In Uniform, BEAR, German BEAR,* and *Bulk Male,* and has created comic serials for *American Grizzly* and *Bulk Male.* His graphic work is included in the Bear Icons art exhibition.

**Lawrence D. Mass, MD,** is a cofounder of Gay Men's Health Crisis and the first journalist to write about AIDS in any press. He is the author of a memoir, *Confessions of a Jewish Wagnerite: Being Gay and Jewish in America,* and is author/editor of three collections: *Homosexuality and Sexuality: Dialogues of the Sexual Revolution, Volume I; Homosexuality As Behavior and Identity: Dialogues of the Sexual Revolution, Volume II;* and *We Must Love One Another or Die: The Life and Legacies of Larry Kramer.* Dr. Mass is a unit director of addiction treatment programs at Beth Israel Medical Center and Greenwich House, Inc. in New York City, where he lives with his life partner Arnie Kantrowitz.

**Thomas McCann** lives and works in Berlin. His writings have been published in *The Bear Book* and in *Quickies* and *Quickies 2.* He spends much of his time listening to opera and hanging out with his husbear of five years, Bob.

**Henry Mensch** was born and raised in the Bronx, New York, and now lives with his two cats, Marcus and Natasha, in San Francisco, California. He is currently a student at the Rochester Institute of Technology, and is also employed with an Internet marketing start-up firm in San Francisco. Henry is a former moderator of the Bears Mailing List, and a founding member of the Bears of San Francisco.

**John O. Noble, PhD, CA,** presently lives and works in Rochester, New York, where he has been the Archivist and Records Manager for the City of Rochester since 1977. He obtained his BA from the State University of New York College at Geneseo, his MA and PhD from the University of Maine at York, and is a former adjunct faculty member at the State University of New York College at Brockport and the University of Maine. In addition to being a Certified Archivist, John is a longtime gay community activist, has served on the boards of various state and local organizations, and is a founding member of Empire Bears (incorporated in 1995). He served as club president from November 1996 to December 1999.

**Alex G. Papadopoulos** is Chairperson and Associate Professor of Geography at DePaul University. Although he usually writes about European urbanization, he decided to stick his neck out with his very first queer studies piece in *The Bear Book II*. He lives in Chicago with his partner Stephen, whom he met at a charity bear event in 1996.

**Jim Parton** was born in Duncan, Oklahoma, in 1954, graduated from Oklahoma State University (1976), and married the following year. He divorced and came out in 1991. He has three adopted children (from Korea), and currently lives with his partner Richard Smith in Ventura, California. Jim is a cofounder of Bears Ventura (1995), and has been a title holder twice over—as Mr. Southern California Bear 1997 and Mr. International Bear 1997, and remains active in local, state, and national bear events. He teaches secondary level Continuation High School.

**Robert B. Marks Ridinger,** librarian, was born in the bear-infested hills of western Pennsylvania, has been engaged in gay- and lesbian-related research since 1982 at Northern Illinois University, and contributed the essay "Bearaphernalia" to *The Bear Book*. An active member of the library, bear, and leather communities, his research interests include the history of American leather culture, working with the Leather Archives in Chicago, the Midwest gay and lesbian past, and pelt grooming.

**Mehmet Ali ("Mali") Sahin** was born May 7, 1968, in Ankara, Turkey. While a student he pursued his personal interest in two-dimensional surfaces and glazes. His artwork and ceramic tile designs appeared in four mixed exhibitions, and he held a seminar on organizations and ceramic artists. He graduated from Hacettepe University, Faculty of Arts, Ceramics and Glass Department in 1993, and after graduation worked for a few months in different industries. In 1994 he turned his computer and graphics interests into a profession. He has worked on different projects including posters, postcards, point of information systems, and educational projects. He is currently working as a professional graphics/interaction designer and a manager in the multimedia industry. After meeting bears on the Internet in 1997, Mali decided to start a bear group in Turkey. Currently he's the chairman, organizer, spokesman, and Webmaster of the "group of friends" who call themselves the Bears of Turkey.

**David Salinas** received his training in acting, voice, speech, and dance at the American Musical and Dramatic Academy in New York City, has appeared in numerous stage and television productions, and is the founder, director, and featured vocalist with the Bearatones, the bear a capella group based in San Francisco.

**Peter Sharman** is a past president of Brisbears and has been involved with the bear community in Brisbane for the past six years. In that time he has seen Brisbears grow from a small fledgling club to one of the largest in the country.

**Ron Suresha** has edited several alternative publications and was involved with the early San Francisco Bears. He produced promotional pieces for the Lone Star Saloon during its first three years while also working at odd jobs as a gardener, plumber's assistant, proofreader, and calligrapher. *The Bear Book* included two of his essays, "Bear Roots" and "Bear Mecca: The Lone Star Saloon Revisited." His work has appeared in *The Harvard Gay and Lesbian Review* and *Visionary*.

**Larry Toothman** writes, "I have been aware of a 'bear identity' since I first got my paws on an early issue of *BEAR* magazine (issue 5 or 6). I have been a cofounder and contributor to both the Bear Paws of Iowa and The Ursine Group as well as editor for *The Bear Facts*, the newsletter of the Bear Paws. I am a happy transplant from St. Louis, Missouri, to Iowa City, Iowa, where both my huscub and I work for a software development company."

**Howard Watson** is a thirty-something freelance writer, although his background is mainly in publishing. He writes, "I used to be Permissions Controller for Random House UK Ltd, until they sacked me!" He acted as consultant to David Thomas on his profile of Simon Raven, which was broadcast on *The South Bank Show* (carried on the Bravo cable channel in the United States). He also writes film treatments and the odd script. Presently, he is trying to raise funds for a short film which he has written and also hopes to direct. He hails from South Tyneside in Northeast England.

**Dale Wehrle** was born in New York City in 1963, and was raised in a small town in Piscataquis County, Maine. He received his BA in German in 1986 from the University of Maine at Orono. He lived abroad for several years, in Bergisch-Gladbach and Altenstieg, Germany, and Salzburg, Austria. He has had several different careers, from teacher to retail to buyer, from software technical support to software QA manager. A lover of languages and travel, he met his husbear, Les Wright, in 1994 over the Bears Mailing List, shortly after moving to the Boston area to facilitate a much-needed career change. He now lives happily with Les and their two cats in northern Worcester County, Massachusetts. He enjoys riding his motorcycle and playing with the latest useless electronic gadgets, in addition to seeing how long he can get his beard to grow.

**Ned Wilkinson** holds a BA in commercial arranging from the Berklee College of Music in Boston, Massachusetts. He currently produces soundtracks and jingles, teaches music, and performs on various instruments in the Springfield/Branson, Missouri, area. He resides there with husbear Christopher Leavy and James the Raging Kitty. Ned and Chris still find it amusing to be the only out-of-the-closet male couple known to many native Ozarkians, who seem, for the most part, delightfully scandalized. Ned tried growing a beard early in 1999, but is still among that tiniest percentage of men for whom whiskers just don't work all that well.

**John R. Yoakam** served as the president of the Minnesota Bears from 1995 through 1997. John has worked for AIDS prevention and service programs in Minneapolis since 1987. He is completing a PhD in social work at the University of Minnesota. He enjoys tending a sixteen-acre hobby farm in Wisconsin where bears have been known to camp and forage for wild berries.

# Foreword

by www. JackFritscher.com

Belly up to the bar, boys, and reset your time lines, 'cuz Papa Bear's back in town and has been asked to "fess up the facts o' life: about your bearstreaming 'Bear Roots.'" Complementing Les Wright's analytical and anecdotal *Bear Book II* in your hand, this pioneer informant, like Michael Bronski, has "been there/done that *dolce vita*" in gay popular culture as well as in gay liberation, in gay writing (fiction and feature articles), and in gay video and photography. Les Wright asked me to be keynote speaker at the Bear History Project Conference 2000, because my street credential—6,000 gay pages in print—is one of the keystone voices in the creation of the species bear. This turnkey information, the thirty-five years of acts, facts, and personalities detailed in this foreword, is not postfactum academic theory, but is the witness of one writer in the right place at the right time doing the right stuff to define the "species bear" within the "genus homosexuality" from the first days of gay liberation through the millennium. Once, in early 1993, I was actually on *Oprah* talking about women's blue-collar husbands and their taste for bearish gay sex!

### *MAPPING THE GENOME*
### *FOR* **THE BEAR BOOK II**

As the most published author in *BEAR* magazine, I can write channeling the "bear voice" as demonstrated in the first line in this foreword, as well as in three of the five *Bear Annuals, 1997, 1999, 2000;* or I can write as a university professor with a PhD in literature and criticism, channeling the academic voice of the "discursive entropy of blah blah." Because, in 1967, I was a founding member of the legit American Popular Culture Association, I had two years' head start in pop-culture analysis before Stonewall; I was prepared to anticipate queers, leather, bears, whatever, as the phenoms appeared, particularly in Chicago, San Francisco, and New York. Taking a cue from Les Wright's *Bear Book II,* whose poignancy and character rises from people's voices detailing autobiographical facts of politics and art, my documented life—vetted reportedly by no less than the Mapplethorpe Foundation—details pre-Stonewall education, experience, and politics typical of the pioneers who molded gay lib after June 1969.

During the long hot civil rights summer of 1962, I worked with people of color as an activist Catholic seminarian in the projects on the South Side of Chicago with labor organizer Saul Alinsky, once marching with Martin Luther King Jr., and once carried bodily out of Mayor Daley's office by the Chicago police whose touch turned me on, although I was not out until May 15, 1967, when I came out officially with a hairy Greek named John Constant from the old Gold Coast, 501 Clark Street. In autumn 1967, I was a university professor graduated from the Summer of Love, with a doctorate from Loyola University of Chicago, the "heartland home of leather." In May 1968, in the balcony of the Biltmore Theatre, New York, I sat as a critic on assignment for the *Journal of Popular Culture* witnessing one of the opening performances of the all-important period musical, *Hair: The American Tribal Love Rock Musical,* whose fetish-empowered title song every bear, particularly *The Bear Book II's* Bear-A-Tones (Chapter 15), might study, adopt, and sing as the bear anthem.

## "GIMME DOWN TO THERE, HAIR!"

In August 1968, when cops were "pigs" not "bears," I was in Chicago's Lincoln Park working the anti-Vietnam protests during the police riot at the Democratic Convention. In May 1969, in Paris still smoldering with student revolution, then in Amsterdam, I was swept up, like Vanessa Redgrave's *Isadora* (1969), by a lovely, bearded, revolutionary boy named Nick Perrenet, straight out of the leathery Argos bar (the world's finest leather bar) and into the chair-throwing, shouting maelstrom of students taking over a Dutch university. I didn't understand Dutch, but the choreography of revolution was absolutely familiar from my campus experiences in the United States. In June 1969, I exited a Janis Joplin concert, stoned, to hear that Judy Garland had died. (One person's history is coathook to everybody's history.) Earlier that same June, tripping with iconic leather-priest Jim Kane on two Harley-Davidsons through the mountains—and the mountain men—from Denver to Taos and Santa Fe, I ritually wore, for one glorious evening, Ken Kesey's brown leather jacket—with all that particular fetish implies—while floating in a desert pond.

### *GAY RENAISSANCE 1969-1982: EMERGING BEARS*

On July 4, 1969, I met my first of three significant-other bears in Chuck Renslow's new Gold Coast bar. He was a six-foot-two-inch, 190-pound, twenty-three-year-old cub with a strawberry-blond crew cut and moustache. I marched straight up to him and spit in his face. His name was David Sparrow and we became wild, passionate leather-lovers for eight years, shooting together the earliest bearstream covers of *Drummer 21, 25,* and *30.* (See David Sparrow in bondage in "Honeymoon" photograph, *American Men,* p. 37.) Dr. Thomas McCann (Chapter 28) characterizes latter-day nineties' bear fiction out of what are seventies' early themes, vocabulary, and physical attributes. In 1972, inspired by five years of S&M experience and playing with Male Hide Leather's Bob Maddox at the first Chicago Hellfire Club Inferno runs, I wrote one of the first S&M novels, *Leather Blues,* featuring two bear-themed scenes: a hair fuck of a biker and a mountain man getting fist-fucked. (*Leather Blues* appeared again, serially spreading bearishness in *Son of Drummer* [June 1978], *Stroke* [1985], and full length in *MAN2MAN* [1980-1982]. Click on Les Wright: "Appendix. Early Published Writings on Bears." Surf to <www.BearHistoryProject.com>).

Fritscher Principle: the concept of "bear" is blank enough to absorb countless male identities and fantasies. Thus, inclusively, in 1970, David Sparrow and I lived triangularly between New York, Chicago, and San Francisco where—as cameras investigated gay identity—we were hired as bearded photo models for *Whipcrack,* the first West Coast leather-themed magazine published as a one-issue trial balloon years before *Drummer,* which appeared June 21, 1975. At the same time, in 1970, I interviewed the very straight (and interestingly bearish) Pope of the Church of Satan, the head-shaved and goateed Anton LaVey, for my book *Popular Witchcraft: Straight from the Witch's Mouth,* which in 1971 was the first detailing of gay wicca and gay spirituality, particularly as practiced by Gay High Priest Frederick de Arechaga of Chicago. This gay wicca and leather volume brought *Advocate* editor Mark Thompson to my kitchen table in 1978 when I was editing *Drummer.* Thompson was—like Candide—collecting his studies for the leatherstream of *Leatherfolk* and the radical fairy/bearstream of *RFD.*

When *The Bear Book II*'s Alex Papadopoulos, in Chapter 12, "Theorizing Bearspace," writes about the varieties of "bearspace," consider this historical byte: The urban legend that AIDS was brought to the United States by an airplane steward in 1982 puts an ironic frame to the fact that it was only in May 1969, a month before Stonewall, that the first jumbo jet was introduced, enabling much of early gay liberation to be globalized on the mile-high "gay space" of planes connecting the dots of fabled gay cities. Also feeding the bearstream, on June 26, 1964, five years before Stonewall, was that famous *Life* magazine feature article on San Francisco's Tool Box bar, which pictured artist Chuck Arnett's leatherstream-into-bearstream drawings that fueled gay consciousness from Arnett's High Concept Tool Box to his actual advertising graphics for the Slot Hotel and Barracks Baths and the Red Star Saloon and the Ambush bar. Searching for the book *Leatherfolk.* Scroll down to "Arnett."

## *THE FIRST BEARISH BAR: RAINBOW MC*

By 1972, the world's first bar to turn not-yet literally "bear," but spinning on the cusp of "bearish" in the bearstream, was San Francisco's The No Name (later aka The Brig, and The Powerhouse), run by the redheaded poet and cookbook author Ron Johnson and bearded photographer Mario Pirami who, together in 1971, were the founders of the Rainbow Motorcycle Club (RMC). The original-recipe Rainbows, still existing, including this old Rainbow fuck, were the avant garde of the bearish dirty-biker look. (See *The*

*Bear Cult: Photographs by Chris Nelson,* pp. 19, 22, 40.) Like in the movies, the boiling clouds of time-lapse creation hovered over us all as gay life invented itself first as *gay,* second as *leather,* third as *twinkie/clone,* fourth as *bear.* (Gay culture thrives on "makeovers.") To clarify the gayspeak spoken then: on Castro, homomasculine men used *twinkie* and *Castro Clone* as synonyms. Yet, by some ironic twist of gay DNA, the clones' exact style of flannel shirts, bandannas, boots, etc., evolved into "bear wear" first at the Ambush bar, South of Market, and later, out of the Castro bar, Bear Hollow, riding through the millennium at the second Lone Star bar across the street from the closed Ambush bar. (Alan Lowery, founder and owner of the 1970s' Leatherneck bar, and I had in 1974 tried to buy what is now the Lone Star space, but the large extended Mexican family who owned it as a cantina wanted to keep it for their family weekends.)

At that time, Joan Didion wrote in her seminal 1960s' novel, *Play It As It Lays,* people (and facts) are swept up into history, and can be swept away by history (and by politically correct revisionists) if they don't write notes, take pictures, collect drawings, and shoot movies—all of which pop-culture scholars do, so that bearstream efforts like Les Wright's Bear History Project and books like *The Bear Book I* and *II* can exist accurately, and the contributors—such as David Bergman, Ron Suresha (Chapter 27), Elizabeth Kelly, and Kate Kane (Chapter 29)—can keep gay life from slipping through the cracks of history.

## *UNIFORM BEARS:*
## *"PADDING OUT" WITH THE PDP*

Pertinent to Robert B. Marks Ridinger's Chapter 13, which depicts how the paws of bears straddle diverse worlds, and paralleling Larry Toothman's Chapter 20, a history of localized bears, a prefatory note needs to be made of a pioneering bear(ish) club. In 1972, a gentlemanly gang of men fronted by 250-pound Ursus Ed Linotti, Tony Perles (both Harley-Davidson owners), Frank Gonchar, Bob Cato—all-told nearly twenty of us—founded the first San Francisco uniform club, the Pacific Drill Patrol (PDP). In the 1970s' grooming style of cops, football pros (Terry Bradshaw, John Matuszak), and bodybuilders (like Ur-Bear bodybuilding brothers, the heavily moustached Mike Mentzer and Ray Mentzer), the PDP featured moustaches for all members and favored members genetically endowed with body size and body hair, particularly the kind "that grows up thick around the neck of a white teeshirt," as in one of the first bear stories coded in a nonbear magazine, "Officer Mike: SFPD's Finest," a hairy Italian cop with illustration by REX, in *Skin,* Vol. 2 #2, November 1980, and again in *Just Men,* Vol. 1 #4, May 1984.

Foreshadowing Laurence Brown (Chapter 2, "Fat Is a Bearish Issue"), the Pacific Drill Patrol practiced a bearstream fetish we called "Padding Out" whereby average-sized guys, inventing "prosthetic makeovers," tied sleeping bags around their waists and torsos with rope strategically placed to define the mass; adding red rubber hot-water bottles and canvas bags of water over pecs and shoulders so the bulk would move realistically; wrapping foam rubber around forearms and thighs; then climbing into huge-sized cop uniforms, fishing waders, construction jackets, rubber raincoats, heading out to walk through the midways of county fairs, biker bars, and even McDonalds (where, one time, when Linotti, his 250 pounds padded out to 600 pounds, ordered french fries, the counter waitress took one look at him, sized him up, turned around, and—no kidding—lifted the dripping wire basket of hot fries and dumped the whole load on his tray, so awesome did his size make his appetite seem to be). One of the only prosthetic makeovers to turn "ugly-sexy" erotic on screen is the redheaded "Fat Bastard" in *Austin Powers: The Spy Who Shagged Me.* The rockstar actor, Meat Loaf, turned another "padded out" performance in the man's movie, *Fight Club,* with a beefy Brad Pitt. As a coordinate erotic exercise, a twenty-first-century bear could pad himself out with rolled-up bath towels under latex and leather, topped by flannel, to, say, 400 pounds and go to Home Depot for some quality tool time and ask an actual bear questions about plumbing. "Padding Out," obviously, also puts one bear paw inside a bondage trip, and another inside the latex/rubber/leather scene.

## TWO ESSENTIAL BEAR PHOTO BOOKS

Fulfilling Les Wright's Bear History Project quest for bearstream artifacts, the Pacific Drill Patrol legal charter and bearish PDP photographs, taken in 1974 near the Russian River (which has become the idyllic retreat space of bears), will be available soon online at www.BearArchives.com. Characteristic Pacific Drill Patrol photographs of PDP uniform picnics can be sampled (on pp. 16 and 34) in the coffee-table photo book, *Jack Fritscher's American Men,* published by Gay Men's Press (GMP), London, 1995.

So tied together in creating High Male Concept are Les Wright's *Bear Book I* and *Jack Fritscher's American Men* that the two books were reviewed together in *Lambda Book Report,* May 1997. Reviewer William J. Mann wrote, "It's that celebration of masculinity in its rawest manifestations that is celebrated here in Les Wright's *Bear Book* and *Jack Fritscher's American Men . . .* these are images that could redefine what male beauty is supposed to be."

GMP, now part of Millivres-Prowler, London, intended *American Men* as a kind of *Bear Cult 2* to continue the archetypes of beardom's first photographer, Chris Nelson, in his seminal bear photo book, *The Bear Cult,* GMP, 1991. The pair of books, *The Bear Cult* and *American Men,* are so absolutely important to the photographic genesis of the bear image that each is graced with an introduction written by world-renowned British art critic, photographer, and bear lover, Edward Lucie-Smith. History, even here, too quickly jumps from the 1970s to the late 1980s and 1990s, but only at the expense of early bear culture. *The Bear Cult, American Men,* and all the bear magazines and near-bear magazines, as well as *The Bear Book I* and *II,* and probably bear culture as a distinct entity, might never have emerged, or emerged so distinctly, without the humanist men who nursed the bear roots in early gay culture.

Fortunately, with notebook and camera, I have publicly lived—with other artists—an artist's life in gay culture and media. Personal photographs seem like public snapshots of history. Memoir seems often the autobiography of that culture, written as a primary witness, as well as written as a professionally trained critic and scholar of history. Celebrate! It is exactly that sense of the *personal,* that appreciation of personal oral history and personal identity that makes bear culture different from depersonalized gay culture with its hired, nameless models, and slick magazines reflecting advertisers' censorship, and awards corrupted by the fascists of the politically correct. (Dr. Lawrence Mass, Chapter 1: "Bears and Health," reveals his insights into how the obstructionism of the politically correct can injure bears' health.) Rejoice! The average gay bear probably feels more like a person than the average gay man. (See John R. Yoakam, Chapter 11, "Parlaying Playmates into Lasting Friendships.")

## FROM STEVE REEVES TO BEAR

"Bears," Michael Bronski tells Ron Suresha in *The Bear Book II,* "did not come out of nowhere." The men who created the magazines, photographs, writing, and culture of the first wave of gay lib in the 1970s grew up on the happy post-World War II pop culture of athletic, can-do masculinity. MGM's 1953 spectacle *Quo Vadis* featured a huge, half-naked bear-man named Ursus in the Coliseum. Producer Joe Levine downloaded *Quo Vadis, Ben Hur,* and *Demetrius and the Gladiators* into low-budget "gladiator movies" shot in Italy and spun out of Steve Reeves' beard, hair, and muscles usually opposed by an antagonist bear of thicker proportion and shaggier of chest and head (*Drummer #19,* December 1977). In American homes for eight years on the television series *Cheyenne* (1955-1963), the square-jawed and shirtless Clint Walker weekly bared his hairy chest, furry belly, and upholstered shoulders to mesmerized adolescent boys who were about to come out in the Gay Renaissance of the 1970s. See *Drummer #27,* February 1978, and Clint Walker's bank-heist movie, *The Great Train Robbery* (1969), which shows the True North where gay bears were about to head after Stonewall.

As genome tributary to the bearstream, Bob Mizer's AMG studios in Los Angeles shot many returning soldiers, smooth to hairy, from World War II, Korea, and Vietnam, publishing them in *Physique Pictorial.* Chuck Renslow's Kris Studios in Chicago featured handsome, dark, brooding men so nonsissy, so masculine, that the reader at that time wondered specifically, "Do these straight guys know what the photographer is doing with their pictures, putting them in magazines where other guys get hard looking at them?" In 1965, Avery Willard at Guild Press in Washington, DC, published a seventy-page, hand-sized photo book titled *Leather!* which featured hairy men and used key bearstream totem words, "lumberjacks," "Davey Crockett," "Daniel Boone," and hyper "masculinity at a full

6 on the Kinsey scale." As a footnote, the opening model, nonbear Gary Adams, is the actor Gary Lockwood who starred in *2001: A Space Odyssey* (1968) and in *Kit Carson and the Mountain Men* (1977).

Complementing Ned Wilkinson's Chapter 6, "A Bear Admirer's Point of View," *Bear Classic 5,* March 2000, in the story "Mapping the Genome of Bear" invented a woof-way to judge a guy's essential bearness as a bear. *URSUS* is the unit of measurement of BEAR the way *RICHTER* measures EARTHQUAKES. So: judge a BEAR on a one to ten URSUS SCALE. HALF-URSUS (five). FULL-URSUS (ten).

## *THE FIRST BEAR: LEDERMEISTER, FULL URSUS*

In 1961, in San Francisco, in North Beach, at the beatnik bookstores, I used to stand, wearing my big-kid first beard, awestruck looking at the athletic masculinity of lifeguards in *Young Physique* in color, and the muscular sailors in *Tomorrow's Man* in black and white. By the mid to late 1960s, Colt Studios, first in New York, shooting naturally masculine muscle men, with Clint Walker as the platen, struck on the hairy model Ledermeister (Leathermaster) who was in fact the muscular, very upholstered archetype of bear, Paul Garrior, from whom all later bears descend.

Paul Garrior/Ledermeister is the Ur-Daddy Bear who in real life was a lineman for a San Francisco utility company. He appeared Full Ursus in Colt's *Gallery 5,* 1971, and *Manpower 5,* 1972. Rip Colt/Jim French wrote in 1971: "Ledermeister is the Colt prototype . . . quiet but extremely powerful. He works outdoors, lives simply . . . is very rugged and prefers surroundings that reflect that quality . . . a loner who shuns parties and is happier on his motorcycle. He showers daily, disapproves of deodorants and colognes and sleeps nude. If it's masculinity that turns you on, Ledermeister has it in spades."

In 1972, in San Francisco, I shot two reels of Super-8 film of Paul Garrior sitting, boots down in a manhole in the street, splicing cable with his gloved hands between his denim thighs. I consider that bearish two-reel movie to be the first motion picture shot by Palm Drive Video (then called Spitting Image, with David Sparrow) which used Super-8 film for fifteen years until 1982 when video became possible. Paul Garrior was a god, an archetype, the Platonic Ideal of masculinity. In media, he was virtually the first gay man to look like a man. He was a human rebuttal to the straight stereotype of powerless effeminacy.

Digital bears looking back at history's search for the genesis of the "Bear Face" can note the second official Palm Drive movie, *Cop Faces*. Shot during the 1972 gay parade, *Cop Faces* consists of tight close-ups of SFPD cops *(faces only* featuring *big moustaches)* standing on guard along the route of the parade which continues on around them. I stood in front of each cop and held the camera on his face as long as it took for him to break his official middistance stare and glance with personal "fuck-off" attitude at the camera; now that's radical filmmaking that breaks the public mask down to the personal face.

Actually, history's memory of the 1970s would be quite different if video-with-sound had been the medium of a decade that was shot on silent Super-8 film on four-minute reels! Not long ago, a young lesbian asked me to show her on demand the video of the Stonewall riots. She was quite disturbed to find out that video did not then exist. Her point of view shows the necessity of tracing bear roots in the fashion of *The Bear Book I* and *II*, in order to point out the flawed principle that most people think the world began to exist the day they first noticed it.

When Paul Garrior finally exited my bed in 1980, after a four-way with his lover and mine, the hairy bodybuilder, Jim Enger, I saved the designer sheets, tan with two stripes, red and green, and three years later, nearing the end of the shelf-life of fetish items, I brewed the sheets into tea, and the PDP, at a formal supper, toasted and drank the essence of uniform-leather-muscle-bear masculinity: Garrior and Enger. (*Mea culpa:* "I am like so totally dedicated to masculinity.") Every tribe eats the god they desire. I confess: History for me is fetish; accuracy is obsession. Also early on in the 1970s, Colt hit on the ethnicity of Italian bear Bruno who was a man adored on the streets of Greenwich Village. (Palm Drive Video revived Colt's Bruno in *Big Hairy Bruno, American Men,* p. 52.) With the commanding Ledermeister and the cuddly Bruno, Colt launched its alternately bearish-and-shaved history that by the millennium had landed Full Ursus on Colt's major-money bearstream stars, Steve Kelso, Carl Hardwick, and Pete Kuzak. (Bearophiles: Ledermeister, *Best of Colt Films 7;* Bruno, *Best of Colt Films 8.* All Colt films are silent movies.)

### *COLT THROUGH A LENS DARKLY: TARGET*

Les Wright's *Bear Book* theme pursuing "the History and Evolution of a Gay Male Subculture" evokes this oral history of the New York to Los Angeles bicoastal dawn of bears as icons. When Colt, in the early 1970s, left the dark lofts and cellars of Manhattan for the sunny gyms and beaches of Los Angeles (1974), photographer Jim French created the decade's hairiest icons in Dan Pace (Dan Padilla) who was the real life partner of Colt model Clint Lockner (Chuck Romanski), an actual LAPD officer, who was the former lover of my hairy muscle lover, Jim Enger. In the words of Jacques Maritain, we were all friends together. In the 1970s, life was a cabaret, ol' chum, and even the orchestra was beautiful! (Bruno starred with Clint Lockner in the famous uniform-bear *pas de deux, Lockner's Key, Best of Colt Films 12.*) When Jim French split New York, his former Colt partner, Lou Thomas/Jon Target, started Target Studios, and Lou's own beautiful, cliché-breaking, bearish photographs ruled out of New York. Thumbnail: Check the drawings of Rip Colt. The parting was so amicable that Colt mailed Target's first brochure.

So powerful are Lou Thomas' leather and western images that his pictures still appear regularly in magazines. Unlike Jim French's wisely guarded copyright to Colt images, most often Lou Thomas's work is not credited either "Lou Thomas" or "Target Studio." (Bearophile hint: When a magazine credits a photo as "From the 'Its-Own-Name' Archive," it is virtually stolen, or appropriated by a lazy editor who fails to research ownership.) Lou Thomas is a world-class example that every artist's identity so violated is lost to history. Note that even Richard Bulger, who founded *BEAR* magazine, found his intellectual property "appropriated" against his will by other well-intentioned bears. Click on *Caveat:* The only "gay community" that exists is the one that thinks all gay artists' and gay writers' and gay photographers' work is community property to be used despite copyright, credit, and permission. This year, for example, a bear image might be new to the reader but it was actually created between 1970 and 1985 by Lou Thomas/Target. Because so many of the authors in *The Bear Book II* write about the personal moment they woke up in midbearstream and discovered "bearness," remember what they're discovering was produced previously by someone else, upstream, working out universal male archetypes in writing, drawing, photography, and video.

### CAMERAS: HUNTING BEAR VS. WYSIWYG

As *The Bear Book II* traces the origins of bears, remember that "gay men" per se weren't even invented as an object of desire in anyone's head until about 1972. No man had ever "come out" to bed another gay man until gay media made "gay men" an attractive category. The gay ideal had always been "straight," even straighter than the present, when gay personals ads still insist on "seeking straight-acting, straight-appearing." (See David Greig, Chapter 10, "The Ephebe Is Dead.") Gay male identity did not burst full-blown out of Stonewall. The first liberated queers had no idea such diverse ways of being gay would soon come out of the closet. The big surprise was that not every homosexual was a sissy, a drag, or a sweater queen. We all walked around a bit dazed and confused, asking, *Is that hairy, six-foot-three-inch, 250-pound, bearded hippie man over there . . . gay?*

The way fashion designers mimic the streets, gay media aborning reflected the street of Christopher and Castro. Early gay media was clogged with **WYSIWYG** gay stereotypes, because the gay media, before *Drummer* went "grassroots," saw only gay stereotypes of homosexuality and not gay archetypes of homomasculinity. The gay stereotype managed to butch itself up in leather, but the leather seemed on some an accessory. The more subtle flavors of homomasculinity came out simmering slower in the hot boil of gay lib. Word was out: there were "men's men" who were gay. But, like bird-watchers wondered about their subjects, how to spot them? How to get them into magazines? Cameras were the weapons of vice cops. Cameras at the first gay parades were a hot debate. Cameras at the first gay rodeos caused some cowboys to wear an orange patch that meant "No Photos." The day after the gay rodeo in Reno, which I covered as a photographer with reporter Randy Shilts for the Associated Press, newspapers across America published for the first time (August 6, 1979) a mass media image introducing a "new" concept to straight American popular culture: The gay cowboy (*San Francisco Chronicle,* First Section, page 3, column 1). The cowboy, who had consented to the photography, immediately lost his job on a ranch in Wyoming; a second cowboy ended up on the cover of *MAN2MAN* as well as the cover of the fiction anthology, *Rainbow Country.* Up until the 1990s, cameras were *verboten* in a gay bar.

## *THE FIRST BEAR CONTEST*

Bearstream note to Les Wright's Chapter 19, "Bear Contests." In February 1987, Palm Drive Video's Mark Hemry and Jack Fritscher shot the first-ever video of the first-ever bear contest, hosted by bear John Muir, and sponsored by Richard Bulger at the Pilsner Inn bar on Church Street near Market. The paranoia about the video camera ran high despite the fact that since ten years before I was the well-known and trusted editor of *Drummer.* No patrons could be photographed. The lights and camera could only be aimed at the stage, and only on the contestants who had agreed beforehand to be taped. It's a wonder any tangible history of early bear culture exists at all. Such attitudes, based on fear of persecution, hampered the emergence of bears, and have caused many digital cubs to think bears were invented in the 1990s when bears finally became camera-ready. (Afterword: No bears were harmed during filming!)

## *1989 EARTHQUAKE TOPPLES DOMINANT* **DRUMMER**

Also, for years, much like Stewart Holbrook's charming Chapter 5, "The Beard of Joseph Palmer," bears had been censored as "undesirable images" by the twinkie/clone media, and as too "oppressively masculine" for the politically correct "revolutionaries" who took control of the gay male press during the decimation by plague that left empty offices with empty chairs and empty tables. Bear men also hardly helped the photographic advent of bear culture by being shier themselves than groundhogs. It took an earthquake, in October 1989, to shoot bears publicly in the street. Chris Nelson snapped a group photograph in front of the original Lone Star bar the morning after the Loma Prieta quake. So historically important is the photograph that it is the first photo in *The Bear Cult.*

Of the eleven men standing against the ruins of the Lone Star, three faces are basically hidden or purposely deleted. That's nearly 30 percent obscuring their faces in 1989. On the other hand, eight men boldly give "Bear Face," with the most assertive being the Black Bear. *Now Loading:* Jason Clark, Chapter 8, "One Black Bear Speaks," and Dave Gan, Chapter 9, "An Asian Bear in Minnesota." On the 2089 centennial of the Loma Prieta earthquake, that Chris Nelson photograph of bears standing in the ruins of the Lone Star will be displayed as a historical artifact. (This from a professional analyst of gay pop culture.) That same earthquake's damage brought down the San Francisco house of *Drummer.* Publisher Anthony DeBlase put *Drummer* up for sale, and the magazine, quintessentially American, was sold to the Dutch in Amsterdam and lost the American sex appeal that so seduced the world—an appeal so strong that years before even Tom left Finland behind for the United States. *Original Fritscher Analysis:* The sudden exit of dominant *Drummer* from the San Francisco magazine scene set the stage for the newcomer rise of Richard Bulger's *BEAR* magazine, started in 1987, and the bear-based publishing empire of Brush Creek Media.

## *ANTHROPOMORPHS: MEN AS ANIMALS*

Lou Thomas's personal interest in the darker side of leather and fur found expression in his Target take on what had been Colt territory. The Roman Catholic S&M priest, Jim Kane, had introduced me to the hairy Lebanese hunk, Lou Thomas, in 1969, and we played together regularly in Manhattan until about 1975, but I only modeled for Target once (1970) in a set of black-and-white stills with a 42nd Street/Times Square hustler. I suggested themes to Lou Thomas, which later, as founding San Francisco editor of *Drummer,* I was finally able to develop. These leatherstream themes (e.g., cigars) became the first articulation of archetypical gay themes that continue to this day, some directly into the Bear Culture. In the early 1970s, at Target I suggest pairings, such as "Tokers and Takers," which was to be openly gay "Marlboro" men smoking cigarettes as aggressive tops, as well as "Bulls and Bears," an obvious pairing, I suppose now, because of Wall Street, but I wanted to apply the anthropomorphism to strong masculine role models to balance the anthropomorphism of the guy in the butterfly costume so loved by CNN at pride parades.

In *The Target Album #3* magazine (1982), Lou Thomas printed a new overt bearstream story titled, "Dirtiest Blond Contractor in Texas," which he had illustrated specifically to the text by Etienne. The story featured the hairy bodybuilder god, Kick, who was the primary bear-man of desire in *Some Dance to Remember*, the 1990 novel of gay history, 1970-1982, that *The Atlantic Monthly* reviewed as a "classic," and critic Michael Bronski called: "A mammoth saga of gay life . . . the erotic psychology of how gay men (leather men, muscle men, pornographers) live and love" (*Firsthand*, January 1991). Completed in 1984, *Some Dance to Remember* fought for six years to be published, because the book was not about a sensitive soul coming out politically correct and dying of HIV. Much more satiric, muscular, and bearish than that genre, *Some Dance to Remember* is a fast read with fifteen principal characters and eight story lines. The protagonist is pointedly named after the Ursa Major Bear Constellation, Orion: Ryan O'Hara. His first lover is named "Teddy" and his physical description resembles biker-bear David Sparrow. One main theme is what happens to an extremely handsome, extremely hairy, drop-dead blond bodybuilder who grooms his fur and grows himself so big, so huge, that he wonders if his human soul can fill so much new manimal flesh. Thumbnail: Go to www.BeefyBoyz.com and click on "Wanna Get BIG?" Link to THE FIRST BEAR ARTISTS: NYS'S A. JAY & DOMINO.

At the dawn of the 1970s, the very furry artist A. Jay (Al Shapiro) was art director for *Queen's Quarterly* in New York. A. Jay featured fur in his very popular cartoon strip, "The Adventures of Hairy Chess," which moved from *QQ* when A. Jay moved to San Francisco to start up art direction on *Drummer*, which had also moved to San Francisco, escaping Los Angeles after the Great Slave Auction Raid. The arrests that night at the *Drummer* fundraiser put Los Angeles leather's leading artists, writers, photographers, and players behind LAPD bars. Fred Halsted, whose leather films are in MOMA, quipped in his column in *Drummer,* "That crowded jail cell holding tank looked like Los Angeles' hottest leather bar."

Influentially, in the mid-1970s, before artists like *BEAR* magazine's incredible H. K. Tuttle, the first and original heavy-duty bear artist, Domino, was—like the martyrologist photographer Arthur Tress (*Drummer* #30)—working the piers and streets of New York. Domino drew hundreds of pictures of men now defined as bears doing bear activities wearing bear-associated gear in bear-identified spaces. Domino's context for his ursine men (hunting cabins, manholes, toilets, Latin boxing gyms) is the First Defining Look at "bearspace" as theorized in *The Bear Book II* by Alex G. Papadopoulos, Chapter 12. Back then, before "gay space" was commercialized into designer playrooms, Fred Halsted marveled at how easily gay men made do: "A garage with the light on is just a garage. With the light out, it's a fuckspace" (*Drummer* #20).

Domino's first bearstream drawings were completed in 1975. His earliest shows, "Domino: Original Drawings and Prints," were exhibited at Stompers, New York, December 15, 1978, and at the opening of Robert Opel's Fey Way Gallery, San Francisco, March 25 through April 2, 1979. Robert Opel, who was a photographer of nasty bikers and a writer for *Drummer,* is most famously remembered as the naked man who streaked the 1974 Oscars. He was murdered, July 9, 1979, in his gallery, 1287 Howard Street, in a plot that spun out of the assassination of Harvey Milk and Mayor George Moscone, but that's a private story not appropriate for *The Bear Book II.*

## *ROBERT MAPPLETHORPE SHOOTS BEARS*

Click on Kelly and Kane's, Chapter 29, "Discursive Construction of Gay Masculinity." That March 25, 1979, opening at Fey Way also exhibited Robert Mapplethorpe and several of his San Francisco photographs of leather and mouth-pissing that later were put on trial in a First Amendment battle about gay culture's freedom of expression. Page through any of Mapplethorpe's beautiful coffee-table photo books as part of any study of the emergence of bear culture, because, legend that he himself was, Mapplethorpe found time to formalize a few bearstream men. Click on *Mapplethorpe: Assault with a Deadly Camera,* whose title is a twisted homage to Christopher Isherwood's I-Am-a-Camera memoirs of decadent Berlin; the nonfiction book is a memoir not only of Robert Mapplethorpe, but of the wildly decadent times in which we conducted our bicoastal affair.

Historians may note: *Mapplethorpe: Assault* is the nonfiction companion volume to the novel, *Some Dance to Remember,* which is dedicated to Mapplethorpe. Unlike the present when everyone is taking pictures, writing, and publishing off their desktop, in the 1970s, few were doing anything but sex, so it was not easy to fill a magazine off a manual typewriter. Under such circumstances, actually, I wrote and shot virtually twelve whole issues of *Drummer* to fill its pages from October 1977 through December 31, 1979. Particularly, *Drummer* needed covers: hot, real, truthful! I wanted the face on the magazine to reflect not models but the faces of the grassroots readership. For *Drummer* #24, I sketched the posture and cast the model, my bearish NYC S&M pal Elliot Siegal, who Mapplethorpe then shot in New York. So, on *Drummer* #24, I produced Mapplethorpe's first magazine cover, September 1978, the bearstream icon, "Authentic Biker for Hire." The cover copy over the Mapplethorpe photograph reads "Sexstar Richard Locke."

## LORD OF THE BEARS

So far, so good. Thinking I'd put my two best lovers together, I scheduled Mapplethorpe to shoot the blond bodybuilder, Jim Enger, who looked like a man's man version of the very bearish young Robert Redford who himself was so hairy of chest and torso he was featured in *Drummer* #1, June 1975, playing the biker-bear title role in *Little Faus and Big Halsey*. Jim Enger, with his CHP moustache, grooming, and physique, was the Lord of the Bears. (There is a California Golden Bear Physique Contest at the California State Fair each year.) Jim Enger had grown his golden body fur to its full one-and-one-half- to two-inch length. What a scene! My two friends: One was a star in front of the camera; the other was a star behind the camera. Papal diplomats never performed better than I did that day! The shoot turned out glorious black-and-white as well as color photographs, because the voyeur Mapplethorpe needed the exhibitionist Enger, and vice versa, therein rose my power as producer to get them beyond personality and into the work.

Jim Enger—when Jim French of Colt shot him—posed frontal. However, Jim Enger refused to sign a frontal release, even though he had a large national endowment. Enger's vascularity, definition, and sheer muscle mass looked so good stuffed into a pair of two-ounce nylon posing briefs, who of the judges and audience ever noticed the cockring pushing his full monty toward the footlights? The *demanding* Mapplethorpe, pleased by the full frontal photographs, but ticked a bit by the *commanding* Enger's reluctance to sign a model release before he had seen the actual resultant photographs, soon published a four-color greeting card of Jim Enger's big dick and massive furry blond torso, neck to things, *head cut off*. Perfectly spinning, the perfect moment of that Mapplethorpe image of Jim Enger is the First Formal Bear Photograph, 1980, seven years before the first appearance of *BEAR* magazine. Robert gave me a number of the large black-and-white photographs; they are perfection.

## *JIM ENGER, TOM OF FINLAND, DOMINO, AND RICHARD LOCKE*

When CHP/USMC doppelganger Jim Enger was still the lover of actual LAPD cop, Chuck Romanski (Clint Lockner), Tom of Finland made a drawing based on the two of them together in uniform—so absolutely *iconic* did Tom of Finland judge Romanski and Enger, who were the toast of El Lay and the height of the Platonic Ideal during the Gay Renaissance, 1970-1982. Tom of Finland confirmed my written and photographic takes on Enger as the most desired man on Castro. (See *American Men,* p. 12, Enger Winning Contest.) So did Domino, who, in 1981, in my bedroom in San Francisco, drew Jim Enger in CHP uniform seated smoldering on a portable toilet chair. In that fit, nonfat era, Jim Enger was the

First Muscle Bear. In association with *Drummer,* Domino also drew gay porno's First Daddy Bear, Richard Locke, star of the Gage Brothers hirsute blue-collar Super-8 double feature which, featured in the pages of *Drummer,* influenced hugely the emerging homomasculine consciousness. See *Kansas City Trucking Company* and *El Paso Wrecking Company,* which in 2000 begat *Big Bear Trucking Company.* Type in www.ToughCustomers.com: Click on the bears of *The Domino Video Gallery,* 2000.

### OLD RELIABLE: BLUE-COLLAR EROS

Early on, Jim Stewart, who had moved out from the Midwest with David Sparrow and me to our 25th Street commune, began shooting his Folsom photographs documenting "Men South of Market." I produced his first leatherstream photographs in *Drummer* #14 (May 1977), *Drummer* #16, and *Drummer* #18. In June 1975, Jim Stewart introduced me to David Hurles, Old Reliable. A versatile entrepreneur, David Hurles shot a museum's worth of black-and-white photographs, color transparencies, Super-8 films, and taped audio recordings of backstreet boys working out of the Old Crow hustler bar on Market Street and the Tenderloin. His young, tough-guy cons—way harder than Bob Mizer's at AMG—were graduates of trailer parks, carnival midways, and juvenile halls of the American South. Gay magazines totally rejected Old Reliable's work, but I saw genius that I pasted directly into perhaps the best-ever single issue of *Drummer* #21, March 1978. Old Reliable was a hit. Readers ate him up. His photographs in 1977 created more sensation than Mapplethorpe, who wasn't famous until the late 1980s. His outlaw boys scared men into orgasm. "Never invite them," Old Reliable warned, "into your lovely home." As a man and an artist, he himself confessed about his tattooed scooter trash and bearded ex-cons, "Terror is my only hard-on."

Old Reliable photographed, and employed for cash money, literally thousands of homeless street people in this order: straight, bi, and gay. He shot men of all types as long as they were tough, had attitude, could smoke cigars, and knew choke holds. Old Reliable's gift to nascent bear culture was that his bearded, hairy men introduced hillbilly blue-color glamour into the homomasculinity of the bearstream. David Hurles still is Old Reliable. His legend was made when, in 1983, as David said, "The French are coming with a camera crew to interview me about my work." From *Drummer,* David Hurles' Old Reliable photos for years filled complete issues of magazines titled *Skin, Just Men,* and *Inches,* often with my homomasculine stories printed alongside his photographs.

   Bearstream Guide: Look for the bear roots of images and stories in the diversity of vanilla gaystream magazines that began appearing in 1981. In the 1970s, photographer Crawford Barton shot the occasional fat hairy hippie man as published in *Drummer* sibling, *The Alternate* #8, January 1979. Leatherbear Cigar photographer Greg Day has long featured hypermasculine men including Castro Street shots of his once-upon-a-time college roommate, Jim Enger. Click on Greg Day's photographs at <www.ManDreams.com>. Also, the diversifying photographers, Kirsten Bjorn, who appeared in *BEAR* as early as the first six issues, and Max Julien of Marcostudio, have for years specialized in importing uncut Latin musclebear images from Brazil.

## *NAME THE LOVE THAT DARE NOT . . .*

   All these Ur-springs of the bearstream trickled along because in the invention of "gaymen" and "gay culture," ideas and concepts required the invention of a new vocabulary to describe categories and subcategories inside the love that so long had dared not speak its name. Writing *Drummer* was an exercise in creating words (vocabulary) to describe what never had been written or even spoken before, but that's what pioneers do, just as Adam, in the archetypal story of Bible folklore, woke up and found his job was to name everything. Suddenly in charge of the most original and powerful grassroots magazine in gay history to date, I had to create words and concepts: *homomasculinity, sensualist,* and *mutualist, man* as a prefix, *Second Coming Out:* into fetish, etc. In the same way, Les Wright commissioned the authors in *The Bear Book II* to invent words, such as I coined originally for this analytic history: *bearstream, leatherstream, gaystream, manstream,* the *Ursus Scale, Anthro-Morph,* and *morph* as a new category of live bear.

## MAGS, BOOKS, AND 'ZINES, OH MY!

In the 1970s, magazines ruled gay culture. Confer *The Bear Book II*, Chapter 27, "Bears in Literature and Culture." Most publishers of gay books emerged only after HIV, later in the mid-1980s, as if suddenly there was time to read more than a magazine. Also, because books carry *gravitas* in American culture, lesbigay historians, themselves writing in the genre "books," often ignore the vital importance of the genre "gay magazines," as if magisterial books last forever, and a dirty magazine only thirty days. Ironically, gay culture's literary awards fail to even have categories for magazine literary excellence. Sociologically, there is more gay *verite* for the researcher in the features, photos, and personals of gay magazines than in all the gay coming-of-age books in the world. I champion gay magazines because magazines traditionally responded more quickly than books to pop-culture mood swings. Long before the first book on bears, there were bears in magazines. Magazines are *radical* in the literal sense of the word *radix*, which means *root*, because magazines show the grass roots of what actual people think and desire. Actually, exactly like the first gay magazines (handmade, folded, stapled), personal Web pages, or home pages on the Internet, have become the new gay magazines of grassroots identity and desire: do-it-yourself photo layouts, fantasy fiction, true confession, even banner advertising. Overnight, www.BearStream.com sites and links infinitely outnumbered the dinosaurs of tree-pulp magazines and books. Click on www.HuzBears.com.

By *Drummer* #30, the fourth anniversary issue, I had included a High Concept on the masthead. Because I believe you can make Tinker Bell live, I stretched the *Drummer* in the Gay Renaissance of the 1970s in ways that cannot be overestimated. *Drummer*, with no competition, was the Bible of gay culture at the time, with a press run, according to publisher John Embry, of 42,000 copies each issue in 1979. Consider that the average year-2000 press run of the very successful *BEAR* magazine, competing in a crowded bear market, was 20,000 plus copies. Most gay books have press runs of 2,000 to 5,000 copies total. Casting about for themes, verbal and visual, I wrote the first article ever on cigars (*Drummer* #22, May 1978) as a gay erotic fetish—and then watched cigars come out in gay public spaces where no cigar had gone before. Twinkies ran. Cigars were a way to separate the men from the boys. Cigars have become an accessory of bears. That's how the mix of fetish works. For the sake of Dr. Lawrence Mass, Chapter 1, in that first article on cigars, I defined the difference in tobacco use between a fetish (cool) and a habit (not cool).

## *SIZE RULES*

Click on Laurence Brown, Chapter 2, "Fat Is a Bearish Issue." In the 1970s the most used gay drug was actually steroids. They were new. They were sexy. Huge bodybuilders like Arnold appeared in *Pumping Iron* (1977). American men, straight and gay, all want to grow bigger. American parents always describe their sons by height and weight, as if being eighteen, six feet, two inches, and 200 pounds is a way, like money, of keeping score in America! In 1979, a man pumped up at the gym all week, because come Saturday night without pecs you were dead. First came the oral steroids, then the injectable, which, along with speed, suggests that needles, more than sex, killed off the drop-dead A-Group. (Bummer!) The lust for body size was so huge that the "pursuit of bigness" is the seminal plot line in *Some Dance to Remember.* In fact, the main bear theme, and musclebear theme, in the novel is the ordinary gay man's pursuit of physical identity—bigness—which has become the homomasculinist signature of bear culture, and masculinist American pop culture of WWF, NFL, and *Sex in the City*'s Mr. Big. In the musical play *The Full Monty,* based on the movie and written by gay playwright Terrence McNally, the loveable "bear" character, "Dave," sings in the first act, "You Rule My World," to his tummy. *The Full Monty* is about men with ordinary physiques who gain self-esteem through feel-good masculine exhibition.

"Dick size" is absolute: even with a vacuum pump, a man has what he has. Body size is relative along the genetic lines of Sheldon's somatotyping: ectomorph (lean), endomorph (medium), and every bear's favorite, mesomorph (just right). Bearophile Note: While a man can't make his dick bigger, he can make it smaller. Every thirty pounds of fat (not muscle) over normal body weight takes a half-inch off one's dick.

"Body size" to contemporary bears is a huge fantasy on the Internet, where any number of bear-linked Web sites actually "morph" photographs digitally to add huge shoulders, massive pecs, tiny waists, giant quads, and big guns. (Interestingly, the heads all stay the same size.) Click on Greg's "Morphs" at www.BeefyBoyz.com. Try to translate the twenty-first century shorthand of size rules, reminiscent of the arcane symbols in *Physique Pictorial*, that reps a young fireplug of a player making himself available first by e-mail at www.MuscleBear.com: 5-6, 195, 48c, 34w, 18a, 25q, 16c, 18.5n, 14fa. He doesn't need morphing. He's a live "morph," like the live "morphs" seen at bear gatherings. The Hun is the leather-bearstream artist most noted for "morphing" men in his hand drawings into huge lumberjacks and musclebears long before e-morphs existed. See Hun books and *Hun Video Gallery: Rainy Night in Georgia*. Early on, Britain's Bill Ward, cartoonist for *Drummer*, caught the wave and made his leather bikers increasingly bear, all the way to Full Ursus appearing in *BEAR* itself. The Los Angeles artist, Jakal, from the early 1970s on always drew his men, especially his handballers, as hairy beasts. REX drew the very polished poster and advertisement for the new Lone Star, the saloon of choice for bears.

## *BLUE-COLLAR BLUES*

Les Wright's *Bear Book II* dives to the heart of the politically correct controversy about bears who, by nature and humanist philosophy, are not usually politically correct. Les Wright himself backs out of political infighting at www.BearHistoryProject.com, where he writes that ideally bears are *apolitical* and *human, humanist*. Many latter-day saints of the politically correct condemn all words and images of bears and of the 1970s as being authoritarian and oppressive. Not! Those words of the first wave of gay liberation were offered as trial balloons attempting to invent gay identities. No one got authoritarian until the PC eighties when, to justify their jealous politics, they failed Logic 101, made the *post-hoc-ergo-propter-hoc* fallacy (what-came-before-this-caused-this), and claimed that 1970s culture caused AIDS. A virus caused AIDS. Not *Drummer*. Not sex. Not the innocent men on the streets of New York City, San Francisco, or Los Angeles. After 2,000 years of being in the closet, a decade of celebration really doesn't seem like indulgence! Except maybe to the New Puritans: the politically correct. Intellectually, the lesbigay fundamentalist politically correct connection of HIV to gay culture is wrong in the same way that Right Wing Republican fundamentalists are wrong about gay culture. Period. Burn me at the fucking stake, but the politically correct are mortal enemies foisting the agenda of failed Marxism/communism on lesbigays living in a capitalist society that gives everyone a chance. No less a bear and gay culture maven than Richard La Bonté wrote in *The Advocate* #599, February 17, 1992: "Political correctness is an over-the-top attitude any au courant cartoonist is duty-bound to skewer." *Cartoonist* rhymes with *humanist.*

The politically correct make this "thing" out of "working class" which is a reverse bragging that bears have to think about in fetishizing working-class men, jobs, and gear. Actually, when watching whining politically correct faces on PBS claiming they themselves are working class ("because they collect unemployment"), I think: "Who doesn't work? Who isn't working class?" Many people believe this ironic stereotype that gay men don't work at the same time that gay men's archetypes of desire are working men. What if a man gets a job doing his fetish? Paul Garrior, Colt model, was a real lineman. While there are "professional homosexuals," it nevertheless remains difficult to get a job as a bear.

A uniform bear could be an actual cop, deputy, or at least security guard, like the famous redhead Bob Cato, who trained many a San Francisco bear out of the Pacific Drill Patrol. Once, leaving my leatherbear ranch, Cato drove his van straight into a taxi carrying actresses Mary Martin and Janet Gaynor, killing Gaynor's press agent. For crashing into Peter Pan (Mary Martin) and Janet Gaynor, winner of the first Oscar ever for Best Actress, Cato, the cop groupie, did his time in the penitentiary, living the other side of his wild desire for cops, in cages with biker bears and convicts and big beefy guards. Be careful what you jerk off to; you may get it. (An orgasm is a wish your heart makes.) Cato wins the award for most living his bear fantasies in the history of bear culture, and I got to live it too, visiting him Sundays at the prison, which, for all gay fantasy, is no place anyone should ever want to be.

## *BEARSPACE TRAINING CENTER*

In terms of bearspace, Cato's kind of bearish cop-prisoner fantasy is best played out at the Academy Training Center outside Atlanta where bodyguards will imprison you in a private prison with real cops and real pro-wrestlers as guards who will turn bear-baiting inside out through bondage, breath control, cigars, and "no-sex" that is so totally erotic you can jerk off to it for years. See *Drummer* #145, December 1990, "The Academy: Incarceration for Pleasure." In 1989, I coaxed Chip Weichelt into editing his first videos out of his cells' security cameras which I named at the time a whole new genre. That style finally arrived overground as the netcam genre on the Internet. In fact, I titled the Training Center's first video feature *Atlanta Knights* and changed the lead cop's grooming from nonbear to bear, making sure he grew a moustache and showed his torso hair, which he had to stop shaving. As a bear, Dave Munroe grew to be so popular a star in a nonsexual role, he was hiring himself out in almost full-page *Frontiers* ads as a dominant no-sex bear cop with uniform and gun in Los Angeles to gentlemen of appreciation. That raises a couple of questions. What's a live bear model worth in dollars, yen, marks, and pounds? And if you see a terrific bear for hire, why shouldn't you rent him? The 1990s' porn model Tom Katt first appeared clean shaven, and then renewed his career with one of the most marvelous pelts ever seen on screen in *Leather Obsession*, but did that make him a "bear"? On the other hand, Donnie Russo, who shaves what fur he has, seems a "bear" to many.

## *BEAR DADDY: MAKING A VIRTUE OF NECESSITY*

In 1978, impressed with a foreign film titled *In Praise of Older Women*, I made a fetish of the older men in the pages of *Drummer* who would reflect the gay population as it grew older. I produced Richard Locke's interview in *Drummer* #24, because, as the breakout star of the Gage films, Locke was a personality to hang a concept on. I remember the interview started, "Now that you're all of thirty-seven, what's going to happen to you and your film career?" Richard Locke's frame of reference was "bear." He termed *Kansas City Trucking* costar

Fred Halsted a "teddy bear." Locke went on to success after success, moving up to the Russian River, which is sacred bear territory ritualized each year by any number of bear weekends. When Richard Locke wrote his autobiography, he gave me the manuscript to read and I sent him along to Winston Leyland at Gay Sunshine Press. Richard Locke, the people's bear, became an AIDS activist, sometimes videotaped and broadcast on network television crossing back and forth across the Mexican border loaded with anti-HIV drugs for distribution in San Francisco. That pretty much describes the true heart of a bear.

Just as Dr. Thomas McCann, Chapter 28, "Laid Bear," describes bearish details in fiction in a variety of gay magazines, *Drummer* continued the Whitmanian drumbeat rhythms of American masculinity and homomasculinity that would eventually allow bear and bearness to merge as shield emblems and totems of gay masculine-identified homosexuality. As Les Wright says in *The Bear Book II*, I wrote in *Drummer*, "A homomasculine man has more in common with a straight man than he does with a female-identified/Streisand-identified homosexual." You can do your "mother's act," or you can do your "father's act." Bear identity is a celebration of the best things in masculine identity: archetypes of strength and warmth; not stereotypes of stone-cold violence. Bearness is nothing more or less than actual male bonding. Attempts to categorize bearness are interesting academic exercises, and worthwhile, but bears are really like "How Do You Solve a Problem Like Maria?"

## MAN2MAN *SETS TONE FOR BEARISH 1980s*

By the time 1979 turned into 1980, I wanted to exit the decade dropping stereotyped ideas in media of what homosexuals are, and move into the archetypes of how homosexuals see themselves personally. I moved my *Drummer* work into new magazines, specifically *MAN2MAN*, which, as it turned out almost as a masculine manifesto, set the tone of masculinity and bearishness for the 1980s. *MAN2MAN* was an international quarterly that lasted eight issues from 1980 to 1982. I wrote it. Mark Hemry published it. Mark Hemry is the blond bear with Buffalo Bill hair I met under the marquee of the Castro Theatre at Harvey Milk's birthday party, Tuesday, May 22, 1979, the night after the White Night Riots set five to fifteen police cars outside City Hall. We have been married bears since, living in the woods for twenty years, with beards like ZZ Top. *MAN2MAN* was first mentioned in *Drummer* #30, June 1979, p. 18. *In Touch* immediately reviewed *MAN2MAN* as a major masculine event in gay publishing.

For Father's Day, the June 1981 *In Touch* #56 published the first article on "The Daddy Mystique" in which my column headline reads: "In Praise of Mature Gay Daddy Bears. Gay men use their sex lives to fill in the blanks of their backgrounds. As the Baby Boom grows older, lots of Gay Babies have reached their own maturity. To make a come-on out of necessity, the bar-street concept of Daddy Bear/Baby Bear cruising makes a match on both generational sides of the Daddy Trip." This June 1981 use of the terms "Daddy Bear" and "Baby Bear," as well as the psychocultural analysis of the phenomenon, was a first in mainstream gaystream culture, and a hard sell to the editor, because *In Touch* has a demographic different from *MAN2MAN* and the bearstream.

But is was a lonely time: *Drummer* in 1980 dropped into a six-year coma, repeating themes from my issues 19-33. (In October 1986, new publisher Anthony DeBlase resurrected *Drummer* with issue 100, two months before the debut of *BEAR* magazine.) Mark Hemry and I were like monks illuminating manuscripts. *MAN2MAN* was created on an electric typewriter on a kitchen table in the last two years before computers and video. Physically, cut-and-paste production was an enormous labor in addition to the writing and design. Magazine distributors refused to handle *MAN2MAN,* not because of content or pictures, but because—get this—it was the wrong size to fit the magazine racks in book stores. Distribution of *MAN2MAN* was very grass roots: subscriptions by mail and distribution in major cities by friends and fans who sweet-talked local bookstores into racking the hand-sized 'zine as a favor. The rest is history.

To this day, as an ongoing homage to *BEAR* magazine's primal roots in *MAN2MAN,* the personals in *BEAR* magazine are called "Man-to-Man Personals," continuing the rhetoric written in *MAN2MAN's* "Manimals." Brush Creek Media's other magazine, *Leatherman,* acknowledged on the masthead of *Leatherman* #2 (June 1994) that its title came from the novel *Some Dance to Re-*

*member.* So, seven years before *BEAR* magazine, and six years before *Drummer* revived, "*MAN2MAN:* The Journal of Homomasculine Popular Culture" was a cult hit. The cover of the premier issue of *MAN2MAN* featured the hairy torso of Jim Enger—*plus his head,* with CHP blond moustache. That first issue also coined the anthropomorphism of "Manimals" for the classifieds in every issue. A featured erotic article was titled, "Dogmaster." Animal references to *chicken* and *hawks* and *sexpigs* evolved to the Anthro-Morphs of the bearstream slowly. *MAN2MAN* #1 printed the word *mountain-man* for the first time, and—perhaps for the first time ever in a classified ad—the word *bear* was used as a discrete category all its own on page 9: "BIG BEAR. Male, shaved head, hairy, masculine, open to spontaneous, inventive, experimental scenes where all goes with sensuality and mutuality moving beyond labels. Possible threesome with bearded, well-built lover. Bay Area." *MAN2MAN* #3 featured a cover shot by Mario Pirami of hairy bear Clay Russell who is still very much a bear porn star.

## THE FIRST MAG COVER TO HEADLINE "BEARS"

For four years, Mark Hemry and I had total custody of bear incubation. One cannot know the bearstream of bear without considering the impact of *MAN2MAN* internationally and the *California Action Guide* in San Francisco. Michael Bronski is correct in pinpointing bears beginning in San Francisco. In fact, in the BEAR VS. BEAR Copyright War of 1987, when bears started fighting other bears over the word *bear* as a trademark, I was called upon to point out that as founding editor of the *California Action Guide*, I went on record as the first editor/writer to spit out in print the actual word *bear* as a category name on a gay magazine cover. Go to <www.Advocate.com> and click on *The Advocate* #596, February 17, 1992.

## WAKE-UP CALL: THE BIRTH OF BEAR RHETORIC

Five years before the first issue of *BEAR* magazine, the first magazine cover using the word "bear" was the November 1982

*California Action Guide:* "BEARS: HAIR FETISH RANCH!" The High Concept of bear headlines appeared on that newspaper, sized the same as the *Bay Area Reporter,* over a cover photo of film director Wakefield Poole's hairy model, Roger. On the same cover, another High Concept headline read: BEYOND GAY: HOMO-MASCULINITY FOR THE 80'S!" My lead cover feature article was titled "Ambushed in Manbush: Hair Fetish Confidential, 'Hair-Balling'!"

This November 1982 *California Action Guide* article is to bears and bearstream development the clarion equivalent of what the June 25, 1964, *Life* magazine article was to leathermen. The pioneering column lines read exactly in bold capitals: "HAIRY BEARS AND BEAR-CHASERS: HUNTING IN THE TRUE HOMOMASCU-LINE PRESS."

As a gay pop culturalist, I wanted to alert readers by promoting "The Hirsute Club" also known as the "Hair Club" created by Daly City Bob, age twenty-eight, who sold his early Bearstream business to my friend, Veet Manu (a Sanskrit name he took in India, meaning "Beyond Mind"). SoMa leatherman/biker Veet Manu published *The Hirsute Stud Ranch Newsletter,* whose tag line was "The Club for Hairy Men Who Love Hairy Men." In a personal letter, dated November 10, 1982, Veet Manu wrote to me: "I'm still operating in the red, but I have big plans and want to see the club really expand.... So many hunky guys belong. I think you're right about throwing big open parties... to recruit new blood." In another personal letter, dated May 23, 1983, Veet Manu wrote: "The first Hirsute J/O parties begin this summer. Thanks for help with graphics and promotion."

To publicize those parties in summer 1983, I published six photographs in the *California Action Guide,* featuring Ledermeister, two leatherbears from Target, and my "moustache" shot of the Pacific Drill Patrol's ultimate bear, the Sacramento cop, Clay Stacey. The three highly refined, beautiful drawings were by the Hirsute Club's artist "KA." The Hirsute Club's photographer and pencil artist was Joe Lembo with whom Palm Drive Video shared a very hairy model, Chuck Longone, in the video *A Man's Man: See Dick Cum,* with John Muir. The *Hirsute* "personals ads" use the same rhetoric written in all "bear personals" to date: *bear, bear-*

*gorilla, mountainman,* etc. The *California Action Guide* article teaser, "Ambushed in Manbush" pun, was homage to the hippie-bear Ambush bar, whose owner, the Full Ursus David Delay, appeared in the Palm Drive Video, *Daddy's Beerbelly in Bondage,* under the screen name of "Sam Bush."

My article was very progressive in its opening endorsement: "This *Hirsute Newsletter* of fair-haired boys and dark, furry men is a fetish idea whose time has come." The classifieds in that same issue of the *California Action Guide* carried the bold ad: "HAIRY BEARS WANTED FOR JO POSING. I'm good-looking, hot, horny, and VERY INTO MEN who dig their FUR and want to share it." A Bear Demographic First: Nearly twenty bears "bears ISO bears" personals ad appeared in that 1983 article! Bearophile News Flash: Previously, on the cover of the September 1982 *California Action Guide,* I featured a special bear photograph of the hairy Hulk Hogan who was so brand new he had not yet shaved off his thick curling pelt of dark-blond chest and belly fur. Woof! Inside, with Hulk's photos appeared another photographic study of facial hair: twenty-four photographs of cowboys with moustaches. To study how the gay male image was changing toward bearish homomasculinity, and how the early classified personals led to Chapter 17, "The Bear Mailing List: Interview with Henry Mensch," see "Those Dirty Classifieds" in *Just Men,* Vol. 3 #1, January 1984.

MAN2MAN, the *California Action Guide,* and the *Hirsute Club Newsletter* all happened in 1979 and 1980 through 1983, and crashed with the plague, four years before *BEAR* magazine rode to the rescue of the bearstream in 1987. This is not to piss on territory, but is to give a time line from both witness and causality. This historicity is one of the reasons publisher Anthony F. DeBlase, after he resurrected *Drummer,* asked me in the summer of 1988 to "anchor" the first leather history column in *Drummer* titled, "Rear-View Mirror." Click on *Drummer* #125, February 1989, p. 82. Additionally, in the creation of bears, Palm Drive Video, coming up in 1982 with the tag line, "Masculine Videos for Men Who Like Men Masculine," was shooting hairy, bearish cowboys at the Cowboy Poetry Festival in Elko, Wyoming, in documentaries titled, *Cowboy Beards and Moustaches* (1986).

## THE BEAR BOOK II *THEORY: SHOW YOUR FACES*

In November 1982, in the early rush of the bearstream, the handsomely upholstered and moustached Tom Selleck tangled with "Bear Art" in the pages of the *National Enquirer*. Selleck was the very popular star of *Magnum P.I.*, a television series that was watched to see bear/beefcake Selleck—not plot. According to the *Enquirer*, Selleck filed an $8 million lawsuit against artist Timothy Anderson whose obviously come-hither "bear" drawing of Selleck had been published as a poster which the straight-laced actor rightly found too titillating: shirt open to below hairy navel, one shoulder exposed with hairy pecs and furry abdominals, all topped by that big famous moustache, that hair, those eyes, the lips that sound out that endearing voice that ultimately played comedy so well in the Paul Rudnick film *In & Out* (1997). Selleck illustrates the quandary some gorgeous straight men must deal with: gay sex appeal, bear sex appeal. He has all the secondary male sex characteristics that cause throbs to throb. In my treasure trove of hot stuff, I have a copy of the forbidden poster by Timothy Anderson whose work, interestingly, seems identifiable as a well-known bear artist.

Quintessential bear point: bearness is less about the genital sex act and more about the celebration of secondary male sex characteristics on a social level that leads to sex. My career as a photographer has been devoted to shooting beef, bulls, and bears, because these are the "Anthro-Morphs" that most resemble mature masculinity and assert positive body types like those grassroots bears exposing their bodies and faces at Internet sites like <www.MuscleBears.com>, <www.MuscleBearz.com>, <www.BeefyBoyz.com>, and all the bear Web ring links. The world was not always so liberated.

In 1978, in *Drummer*, I invented a High Concept page called "Tough Customers" which invited men to send in photos of themselves with their personal ads, because I wanted to create a magazine that reflected the readers to themselves. Even before the advent of gay porn studios flooding all the gay rags with models who do not reflect the readers, but potentially make the readers feel bad about themselves, I thought the most powerful force in gay culture would be actually real masculine faces, masculine bodies, masculine trips, because the masculinity factor is what is missing in heterosexual society's judgment and treatment of homosexuals who are, by definition, men seeking men. At first, I had to berate the guys who sent in their photos with their heads cut off or with faces masked. (Remember, the "gay thing" about cameras lasted well into gay lib.) The concept was revolutionary: homosexual outlaws printing their own faces in a perversely new kind of "Wanted" poster! (Stuff like that—the ability to "spin everything," even the word *queer*—is why homophobes absolutely fume at us.)

Historically, the first place ordinary, normal gay men showed their personal faces in print was in *Drummer.* (All the other magazines used models.) This liberation opened up the possibility of grassroots magazines like *BEAR* whose heart and soul had always been the personal faces of actual guys and not models. "Personality" is a key quality in the incredible lightness of being bear. As David Bergman in *The Bear Book II* makes a good and fair assessment of photographer Tom Bianchi's "look," I don't exclude photography that turns a man into a svelte model posing in deep shadows holding a hula hoop, but such "glamour fotos" seem a pretentious parody against male nature. My "Tough Customers" was successful enough to spin out as a magazine in its own right. There was a time, before video and before the Internet, when a direct lineage of gay magazines actually propelled bear culture, *Physique Pictorial + Drummer + MAN2MAN + California Action Guide* leads directly to *BEAR.*

### *RICHARD BULGER: ENTER, PURSUING A BEAR*

Edward Lucie-Smith's 1991 introduction to the photo book, *The Bear Cult,* begins with *BEAR* magazine. By 1995, Lucie-Smith deepened his first sense of bear roots in his introduction to *The Bear Cult* sequel photo book, *American Men.* As a player and scholar, sometimes I smile, because I try to be neither ironic nor cynical. I read lines in *The Bear Book II* like, "I began to read Foucault in 1979." Well, I first tortured Foucault in 1976. Postmodernly, of course. Life is more than unraveling six degrees of separation, but here's one story line of *BEAR* magazine.

In 1987, when marketing genius Richard Bulger contacted us, Mark Hemry recalls Richard's first words, "I'm modeling *BEAR* on

*MAN2MAN.*" What a compliment! *MAN2MAN* had been off the stands for five years. The Macintosh computer had arrived, empowering small publishing. Richard Bulger's "revival" was the start of *compadre* days at the salon that floated back and forth from early *BEAR* to Palm Drive Video. Richard Bulger was also a legit agent for video actors. Most of the first *BEAR* models in his *Live Bear* series were also Palm Drive models who, because Palm Drive also shot much still photography, began to appear in other magazines, even crossing over to many of the late 1980s and 1990s *Drummer* covers, centerfolds, and photo spreads. The bearstream began to flow.

Within six months of *BEAR's* 1987 debut, *Drummer* #119, July 1988, with an issue titled in large print, "FETISH FEATURE: BEARS & MOUNTAIN MEN," displayed Bulger/*BEAR* discovery, John Muir, using seventeen Palm Drive photographs to illustrate my lead feature article, "How to Hunt Buckskin Leather Mountain Men and Live Among the Bear." Again, we were all friends together. Two years later, in June 1990, the cover and centerfold of *Drummer* #140 featured the video bear from *Daddy's Tools,* shot by Jack Fritscher to cover the lead feature article by Les Wright, "The Sociology of the Modern Bear."

The premier issue of *BEAR* #1 looked exactly like *MAN2MAN*. The first and only advertiser supporting the new magazine was Palm Drive Video and Fantasy Men phone sex. The cover model and centerfold of the twenty-four-page *BEAR* #1 was John Muir, the archetype of bear, titled "Best Bear," as picked by Richard Bulger and shot by Chris Nelson, with additional photography by David Grant Smith. The three videos advertised, shot immediately before there was a *BEAR* magazine, were John Muir/Mike Kloubec in *A Man's Man,* Chuck Longone in *See Dick Cum,* and Big Bruno in *Big Bruno.*

Richard Bulger, cueing himself off my coinage, *homomasculinity,* said in his own words:

> I've been doing a lot of thinking about the roots of *BEAR*—its growth, its visuals, its focus. I didn't start *BEAR* to exclusively be a listing of personals for guys that like hairy/bearded men . . . that's not what the original image of *BEAR* was. I also

didn't start *BEAR* to exclusively be a showcase for great photos of naked, bearded men. . . . I guess I started *BEAR* because there was no media product out there which addresses my sexual needs and interests as a hairy, bearded, masculine guy who likes similar men. There was nothing out there with personality. . . . I don't look like the guys in *GQ, Advocate Men, Honcho* . . . I am a man-loving man. There's another side to gay media: the side which *Drummer, RFD* . . . among others capture. You can feel the homomasculinity in these publications *[MAN2MAN]* . . . where we have seen the promotion and development of sexual icons for a gay culture . . . : leather, spirituality, metal, fur, sweat, piss, respect for nature. I'm not a fairy. I'm not a leatherman. I'm not a fashion follower . . . something's happening. . . . My friend Al said, "Richard, it's the Bear Experience and it's as real as any other movement in gay men's history. You just happen to be documenting it and putting it together at the cutting edge." The Bear Experience? It's the lifestyle and choices of not buying into the gay media role models, because we have bought the wider cultural identification of maleness.

Also, see *BEAR,* Vol. 2, Issue 6, p. 23 as well as p. 46 where my satiric piece, "Bear Deteriorata," set out to define "the Bearness of Being Bear" in this issue questioning, "Who or what is a bear?"

As quickly as Richard Bulger conceptualized the 'zine of *BEAR,* imitators—also empowered on new computers—flattered his genius in producing their own 'zines like *Husky, GRUF,* and *Southern Cumfort.* Mentioned earlier, the artist, the Hun, who had been around in the 1970s, caught the wave of *BEAR* which matured his drawings by giving him the bear archetype. No longer was "bear" suggested. The Hun drew hairy men who actually looked like bears. Fur and cigars ruled at the Hun's Shadnook Prison. The Hun's work exists on page and screen in books and tapes like the *Hun Video Gallery 1* and *2.* Oftentimes gay art looks like the therapy of mental patients, but the Hun paved the way for the gorgeous drawings of artists whose work is legendary in *BEAR:* Fran Frisch (no relation), Steve Stafford, Dade Ursus, T. C., Rolando Merida, and Douglas, to note a few. Richard Bulger was the best kind of friend: he did real business as opposed to gay business; that is, he kept his word, he paid his bills, he treated the first nominated bears as people. His salon reflected his personality: fun, easy-going, productive. Balancing Bear with Brahma, Richard Bulger and his partner, Chris Nelson, resuscitate the mid-1980s collapsed under the tragedy of AIDS, through the publication of Richard Bulger's *BEAR* magazine and photographer Chris Nelson's Brahma Studios. Richard Bulger sold *BEAR* magazine in December 1994 to Beardog Hoffman and Joseph Bean.

## CHRIS NELSON: FIRST BEAR *MAG PHOTOGRAPHER*

In 1987, Chris Nelson shot the prototypical archetype of bear, John Muir, whose beard, hair, body, and manly beauty define bear masculinity in the first solo photograph—after Chris Nelson's own self-photograph—in the diversely cast *Bear Cult*. The photograph was so perfect that Palm Drive received permission to print it on brochures to cross-promote John Muir's Palm Drive Video. Like genius Robert Mapplethorpe who spoke very little, Chris Nelson let his photographs speak volumes. His photography was the first to introduce a real range of race and age and look. He took homomasculinity, ignored by the gay mainstream, and turned it into the *manstream* (no "i") that is now known as *BEAR*. Without photographs, there would have been no *BEAR* magazine.

In 1987, Chris Nelson shot me with my ZZ Top beard and a cigar (*The Bear Cult,* p. 87), and Richard Bulger, who often listed me on the masthead as a contributor writing for *BEAR,* dropped me in my mountain man gear into one of the first *BEAR* centerfolds. Fast forward here over the fifteen years that Mark Hemry and I spent in summer encampments reenacting the Indian and mountain man period of 1780-1820 with straight blue-collar men in buckskins, and their hatchet-throwing wives, and all of us living happily in teepees, swimming in the creek, and singing under the moon, so we could bring back the words, photographs, and mountain man culture to gay magazines. (Little things say a lot: Rick Redewill, when he was opening the postquake new Lone Star, called Palm Drive Video, because he wanted to order the same Mason jars with glass handles that we had featured in our videos from our mountain man rendezvous.) Our aim was to conquer the gay world's heterophobia by showing how much masculine-identified gay men have in common with masculine-identified straight men—as opposed to those two new politically correct breeds I've dubbed the male lesbian man and the straight male queen.

Chris Nelson during the shoot worked as smoothly as Mapplethorpe, and with his professional equipment created his own "perfect moment" frame to frame. He worked silently, nondirectively, having me move about, or simply "be," while he climbed up a huge scaffold to shoot down at my reclining body. I remember, when he was directly in front of me, kneeling between my legs, bearing down for a close-up with cigar, he spoke two words, "More smoke." Like Mapplethorpe, he was also very generous with his work, giving his models large-sized fine art prints of photographs other than the photographs printed in *The Bear Cult*. The list of models shared between *BEAR* and Palm Drive includes: John Muir (Mike Kloubec), Sonny Butts, Randy Rann, Jason Steele, Vigilante, Russ Wade, Tex Waco, and Mike Cox.

Interestingly, Chris Nelson discovered the young Jack Radcliffe in 1989 (*The Bear Cult,* p. 13). Jack Radcliffe remains *BEAR* magazine/Brush Creek Media's top icon and box office star, followed by the Palm Drive bear who went to Brush Creek, Tom Howard, who at the millennium was bear #2 in sales reflecting popular taste. By 1983, and continuing, venues like Palm Drive Video *verite* and subsequently in 1987 *BEAR* magazine with its *Live Bear* video line, had become safe-sex substitutes for actual sex, because safe sex was not that easily invented or practiced. All sex was said to be dangerous. The camera for Bulger, Nelson, and Fritscher, as well as for many of the models, was in many ways an erotic continuum that kept sex going through the safety of the lens. Richard Bulger created *BEAR* on a desktop Macintosh, which allowed him facility of production that had not been available to *MAN2MAN* seven years before. The electronic world had changed. The sexual world had changed. The gay male image had changed.

## *LES WRIGHT ASKS: DAVID GRANT SMITH?*

All around the lifeboat of *BEAR* was the titanic wreckage of AIDS and the arrival of the technology of rescue: video and computer. Richard Bulger, with an open-door policy, was in a very cordial sense a friend of the arts and artists as well as models. In his left-bankish studio, which was his home in a remodeled storefront, he displayed many photographs. One was a black-and-white picture of a muscular blond man sitting right-profile behind a military foot-locker trunk. Mark Hemry and I admired the photo so particularly that Richard Bulger arranged to introduce us to the photographer, David Grant Smith, who is rightly of so much interest to Les Wright, because David Grant Smith was a purely homomasculinist photographer, a street hunter capturing the "genus bear."

The clock was ticking. David Grant Smith was dying, yet he welcomed the three of us to his tiny apartment ablaze with sunlight so bright I've never forgotten how blinding it was and how I feared the UV might be damaging to the photographic prints sitting about. Richard helped guide us through David's work. Hundreds of photographic prints appeared from drawers and files and closets, all of hot bearish blue-collar men shot beautifully, but no "Blond-Behind-Trunk." In the course of tea and the afternoon, we picked out fifteen black-and-white five-by-seven-inch photographs of men displaying the burly new look emerging after the first shock of AIDS. Even shooting guys dropping their pants impromptu in alleyways, David Grant Smith was a genius at casting, at composition, and at lighting mostly with dazzling sunlight. I wanted to telephone Robert Mapplethorpe who with Sam Wagstaff had pronounced male photography collectible and respectable in the 1970s; but, in San Francisco, Mapplethorpe's "Manhattanization" raid of the city was unfortunately not remembered kindly by any local photographers, including David Grant Smith.

Finally, Richard Bulger said, "David! The blond-behind-the-trunk." David who had been observantly silent as his work spoke for itself, said, "There's only three prints of that photograph, Richard. I have one. You have one...." He hesitated as if in some great pain of parting. We, open wide as history, looked at him who was dying. What our genuine interest promised moved David to say, "They can have one. No one else. These will be the only three prints." These were the days when madness reigned because of anxiety, suffering, and death. David Grant Smith reached into a large folder and pulled out the "Blond-Behind-Trunk."

We urged him to sign it; he hesitated; then he smiled, still reluctant, and with his weak, shaky hand, wrote his signature as "David Smith" in red ink as we wrote the check as if beauty somehow has a price. One of the fifteen photographs was printed as a sepia of a cowboy sitting in a chair in a fancy old-time brothel, looking down at his rising dick. The photo could have been taken a hundred years before. Those David Grant Smith photographs were so seminal to the genome of bear that several men shot by him later turned up, coincidentally, without our ever seeking them out, in Palm Drive Videos: for instance, Jack Husky, *Nasty Blond Carpenter* video, *American Men* (p. 58, opposite John Muir), *A Man's Man* video, "American Bear," *American Men* (p. 59). Jack Husky made several videos for Palm Drive before he proved bears die. He was accidentally poisoned by a batch of bad medicine that hit San Francisco one weekend, killing him while he slept over at Bob Cato's house above Castro. So also passed David Grant Smith. In a 1988 personal letter, Richard Bulger wrote: "Dear Jack, Here you are [your photographs] as well as the rest of *BEAR* #4. Crazy times. This move upstairs (469 Fillmore)! David died . . . and orders as well as magazine production seem overwhelming. . . . Need a vacation. I'll talk to you soon . . . wish to talk longer. Thanks for all your help. XXOO, Richard."

## *CHICKEN HAWKS ENDANGER BEARS*

Someone should write all this down. I can only connect some of the dots. The mainstream gay media tried to stop the emergence of bearish diversity. For instance, in the annals of antibear villainy, the hands-down winner as the bear movement struggled to begin was magazine packager John W. Rowberry who was a video critic the minute gay video appeared. Dedicated to chicken, Rowberry refused to give any bear-themed, mature-male video a good review because it wasn't stereotype girly-boy gay. I was longtime friends with Rowberry from his first days as office "boy" at *Drummer.* I told him, "You like 'em so young, if sperm could act, they'd get a good review." Single-handedly, Rowberry resisted the tide of the bearstream as I arm wrestled him all the way through the pages of *Skin, Skinflicks, Inches,* and *Uncut,* where he continued to print the bearish homomasculine fiction I wrote for him, at his request, to fill his mags. I wonder: Did he read it or only look at the column inches of text between his chickie photographs? Historically, many gay magazines have been controlled by straight men who prefer young blond girls and their transference in managing their packagers figures that gay men coordinately prefer smooth, young blond boys. The concept of bearish men was a joke.

I once handed Rowberry in his office above the fetish clothes resale shop, Worn Out West, on Folsom, a set of my photographs of Jack Husky who was so drop-dead sexy at the time he couldn't walk down the street without men biting at the cuffs of his jeans. The imperial Rowberry looked at the photos, and said—a line I've never forgotten—"I can't give a good review to a balding, bearded, construction worker with a beer belly." He wouldn't even look at the video, *Nasty Blond Carpenter,* which has gone on to sell thousands of copies to Jack Husky fans. Rowberry equally tried to stiff the very bearish, strutting Police Olympics video series because it was full of "the enemy": real cops, sheriffs, and deputies in documentary features titled, *Cop Wrestling, Cop Powerlifting: Bears and Bulls, Cop Boxing,* and *Cop Tug-of-War.* Gay criticism, gay reviews, gay politics, gay exclusiveness often are reduced down to just so much "sour grapes" because "somebody else was the homecoming king!"

Richard Bulger himself experienced the Full Rowberry who was indignant about what he called "sexually excessive pornography on video." He meant bears "getting down." Richard ignored Rowberry, but Rowberry—bound to more commercial and elitist gaystream video studios—was determined to stop the bear movement's video rise. He loathed the *video verite* of grassroots artists with personal visions putting diverse and real men on screen. Rowberry's choke hold on video impeded the ability to do business for Richard Bulger's COA Films, Adam and Company, Altomar Video, SIRCO Video, and Palm Drive Video. Rowberry's passing opened the floodgates for bear videos that support the bear magazines, which, because they are print in a video age, cannot support themselves in a culture that views but does not read, valuing an eighty-minute bear video at $60 and an eighty-page bear magazine at $7.95.

## *FULL-BODY ROGAINE*™

*The Bear Book II* references the diversity of the bearstream and bear magazine publishing. Curiously, bear publishing is all magazines; there is no particular bear-committed small press publishing bear books. Les Wright and his Bear History Project point out the importance to gay male popular culture of archiving and studying the bearstream of such grassroots *verite* magazines as *American Bear, Daddy, American Grizzly, GRUF, Southern Cumfort, German Bear,* as well as the bear stories in *MR (Manifest Reader,* which is *Drummer's* successor), *Big AD, Girth and Mirth, Bulk Male, TRASH,* etc. Will the plurality of bears go on forever? What could possibly be "postbear"?

This digital millennium time predicts—yeah, yeah, yeah—that soon, all three-based magazines will exist only online except, of course, for some future young radical boy-cub who decides to go back to the kitchen table, type up his erotic masculine thoughts, fold the pages in half, staple them, and . . .

*©JackFritscher.com*
*<jack@JackFritscher.com>*
*June 20, 2000, San Francisco*

# Acknowledgments

I owe a great deal of thanks for the cooperation and support of too many individuals and groups in the bear community to list here, both for their ongoing contributions to the Bear History Project's archives, for spreading the word of the call for contributors for *The Bear Book II*, and for being a thousand eyes and ears in cyberspace. My thanks to Phi Beta Kappa and New York University Press for granting reprint permissions, to my partner Dale Wehrle for taking time out of his insanely busy schedule to transcribe the last oral interviews at the eleventh hour of production, and to Jim Sibal and Trish Kerlé, whose efforts on behalf of the Bear Icons portion of the Bear History Project also contributed to the development of this volume.

My thanks for acts of kindness and generosity to Mali Sahin, Steve Albert, Bob MacIlwain, Jack Fritscher, Van Lynn Floyd and Ron Triplett, Steve Heyl and John Griffin, Larry Mass, John Noble, Jim Alexander, TJ Norris, Eric Rofes, Bill Benemann, to longtime friends Dave Thompson, Sam Ganczaruk, Billie Aul, Steve Klein, and to my sister Lauren Wright. And grateful acknowledgment to Mount Ida College for a faculty development grant to cover reprint fees.

# Introduction

## Les Wright

The assassinations of Robert Kennedy and Martin Luther King, the invasion of Czechoslovakia in 1968 (I was fifteen at the time), the annual, almost ritualistic summer race riots in American cities, and the mounting frustration with the endless nightly news reports of body counts from the war front in Vietnam had a deep *emotional* impact on me. However, my own coming to political consciousness emerged gradually in the aftermath of two pivotal moments, separated by more than an ocean—the brief appearance of the Gay Liberation Front (GLF, Gay Activist Alliance [GAA], and Maoist Gay chapters had already organized when I arrived on the SUNY Albany campus in 1971[1]) and the spirit of May 1968 (the Paris student strikes which spawned an international New Left, parallel to but very different from the American civil rights-oriented movement)—which I absorbed in my university years in Germany. My first activist involvement was in the leftist camp of the *schwulene-manzipatorische Bewegung* (gay liberation movement) in Germany, at the universities of Würzburg (1974-1975) and Tübingen (1975-1979).

Since that time, my sense of gay activism has been a hybrid between the American vision of utopian communitarianism of that peculiarly American 1960s incarnation and the Hegel-and-Marx-inflected politics of German idealism. I first read Foucault in 1976 (various pieces in German and English translations), along with Guy Hocquenghem (*Le désir homosexuel* in German translation); *Der gewöhnliche Homosexuelle* (The average homosexual), a sociological study by Martin Dannecker and Reimut Reiche (1976); and the materialist critique *Unfähig zur Emanzipation? Homosexuelle zwischen Getto und Befreiung* (Incapable of emancipation? Homosexuals between ghetto and liberation) (1978) by Udo Hoffmüller and Stephan Neuer. Such analyses offered me Foucaultshaded insights into how restructuring social perception can reshape social reality.

I was active in the local student gay activist group in both university towns, traveled to the leather bars in the capital cities, and attempted to pursue a committed life that was both conscious, deliberate, and ideologically grounded (how un-American!) and fun (how un-German!)—and which grew messy and chaotic, as I began my descent into alcoholism.[2] In Germany, I had kept abreast of gay social developments in the United States, reading every gay publication I could lay hands on printed in Germany, the Netherlands, Britain, and Sweden, as well as (the earlier version of) *The Advocate*. I picked up on the new clone style in America, began daily compulsive workouts, became anorexic, and went on periodic fluids-only fasts (of fruit juices, beer, and wine). For five years I tried to sweat and starve myself down to a twenty-eight-inch waist, before I realized one day my pelvic bone's circumference was twenty-nine inches and, even as a skeletal corpse, I would *still* never get down to twenty-eight inches. Here, I believe, is where the seeds for my bear values were sown. Imagine my surprise—extreme reverse cultural shock, in fact—when, in 1979, I abandoned my life as an American expatriate in Germany to join the great experiment in gay community building in a San Francisco neighborhood called the Castro.

The Castro was, in fact, a gay commercial and residential district, unique in its existence, but far removed from what I considered serious politics. Like every American utopian community ideal before it, the gay communes following the Summer of Love were rapidly fading. Most of the organized gay politics in San Francisco (and indeed all across America) had been pursued along the traditional "two-party one-party system" of the United States. The Castro was a psychological never-never land, befitting Lewis Carroll. I arrived in San Francisco a year after the assassination of Harvey Milk and the White Night riots. The community was in a state of shock, rage, fear, and renewed activism; we experienced everyday life in the Castro with a heightened sense that each day was another day of gay history in the making; and every day and night on Castro Street was a Mardi Gras-like festival. I immediately disappeared in the apolitical maelstrom of the bars-bathhouse-disco-drug subculture.

Today, I can admit to having seen—and wanting desperately to see—a reawakening of these old sexual liberationist values in the burgeoning bear movement of the 1980s. The bear movement has grown into something much larger than anyone expected, and different from anything I had hoped for it. For all that, many positive, even idealistic changes have emerged. Parts of the bear community have merged with or established themselves as social trendsetters and generators of popular values; parts of the community have persisted in that indomitable, at times irascible, spirit of independent-mindedness. And a good deal of old-fashioned hypocrisy—preaching "inclusivity" while practicing exclusionary behaviors—has muddied the waters as much as the "appearance versus attitude" camps of defining a bear.

Since the appearance of *The Bear Book* in 1997, many more bear clubs have sprung up in North America, bear-identifying individuals, groups, and events have appeared all across the globe, and are spreading further and further afield from the original American and Anglo-Saxon-based societies. Bear community seems to be at least as big in Australia as in the United States (no doubt in part due to the nature of Aussie "mateship"). Do a "bear" basic keyword online search, and you will be overwhelmed. The bear community is, arguably, the first Internet-generated global community.

This raises some interesting questions—about social class, about race, ethnicity, and nationality, about the degree to which American-style gay (and bear) identity is a cultural export from America, along with fast-food franchising, rock music, Hollywood movies, and shopping malls. Bearfolk have created personal, social, and sexual networks on the local level through bear-oriented print media, organized bear clubs and events, and the Internet. Since gay-mainstream print media in America was extremely slow, and by and large *remains* reluctant, to generate copy addressing bear audiences, it becomes clear how vital and vast a role the Internet has played in spreading the gospel of bears. In much of the world, most Internet use is restricted to that infrastructure (e.g., the bear from El Salvador, the bear admirer from Malaysia) of high enough social class and income to afford this expensive technology.

In the United States and other postmodern societies, the distinction between blue- and white-collar classes has become blurred. Manual labor typically pays (often *much*) better than service-industry jobs. A bear electrician, a bear plumber, even that rare creature, a bear factory worker, is likely to have as much—or significantly more—disposable income than the bear bank teller, the bear waiter, or the bear bus driver.[3] To some degree, the lust for blue-collar men-as-bears may be a part of a national nostalgia for the moribund industrial society and imagined simpler values of simpler times. And yet, blue-collar values, as lived by blue-collar bears—and perceived as natural, normal, typical by them—live on. While television continues to spin out tales of upper-middle-class fantasy, most bears, like most Americans, seem to live out messy, half-organized, mundane lives, modestly happy or in quiet desperation. Bears' homes often seemed to be filled with bearapherenalia—tchotchkes, souvenirs, and other memorabilia—the way my grandmothers' homes were filled with ceramic knickknacks, homemade doilies, and midway game prizes, where keeping up with the Joneses means getting Poppa Bear Jones to show you how to download some free shareware, and *not* about getting a bigger SUV than him. As Eric Rofes outlined in his essay in *The Bear Book*, some bears may be professional/managerial class men in pursuit of their fantasy of blue-collar bodies and values. With the rise of glamour bears and some of the muscle bear crowd, we find, at worst, a case of the "higher" bear classes slumming with the hoi polloi—in most cases, perhaps, seeking enough sexual (domestic exotic) difference to spice up their sex lives.

Bears have moved beyond the race/ethnic divide at its simplest level. In theory, anyone who self-identifies as a bear *is* one ipso facto. In practice, in the United States the vast majority of bears are "white." (The term is oversimplistic and implicitly racist—not all "white folks" are the same. In fact, hardly anyone is "white," just as hardly anyone is simplistically "Asian," "Hispanic," or "black." Indeed, these are terms which have meaning only in U.S. American culture, and become meaningless, absurd, even incomprehensible in other cultures.) This hegemonic categorization system becomes apparent if you consider self-identifying bears from non-Anglo-Saxon-derived cultures.[4]

This debacle of ethnicity poses two significant questions: To what extent is the notion of a "gay"—and "bear"—social identity the product of middle-class Western philosophy, a specifically American sociological worldview? In other words, to what degree is a gay or bear social identity part of a "white" social value system? To what degree might the absence of "ethnic" (non-"white") participation in the bear tribe be due to something as simple as the fact that many African American or Hispanic MSM (men who engage in sex with men) do not identify with a white, middle-class concept of social identity?

Some men of color do identify as gay, even as bear. All the bears of color I know personally seem to identify with middle-class values (or their gay community interpretations). The second question is the problem of putting "inclusivity" in the bear community into practice. What bear of color is *not* self-conscious of being perceived as (racially) different, just as what gay man does not experience a self-conscious awareness of being gay in a heterosexist society? How do we, and how is it even possible to, transcend the racist society from which we have all emerged?

For *The Bear Book II*, I strove to include as many divergent bear voices as possible. In particular I sought to create an entire section by African-American, or black bears. The frustrating part of putting this volume together was my mixed success in locating divergent bear voices—key bear leaders of (several) colors bowed out in the end. I was somewhat more successful in the inclusion of others on the margins of beardom—disabled bears, otters, Gen-X voices, bear youth, and one non-Western cultural voice. Certain individuals refused to acknowledge, let alone respond to, my requests to contribute to *The Bear Book I* or *II*. In short, what was potential, but has not materialized, would create another volume in itself. Indeed, the inclusivity/diversity questions would have been answered in a very different fashion from what emerges from this volume.

Also missing from this volume are several key voices from the early San Francisco days of beardom. My interview with Lurch can be found in *American Bear* (2:5 [February-March 1996] 32-33). Among my repeated requests to other Bay Area bears, the standing invitation to the original owner-publisher of Brush Creek Media was never accepted. Another correction to information contained in

*The Bear Book:* "There is no Bart Thomas. That was a pen name used by Richard Bulger."[5]

My opinions about organized bear clubs—as in some way anti-bear in spirit—have been ameliorated over time. When I moved from San Francisco to Boston in 1993, my initial encounters, or rather attempts to encounter, the local New England Bear group bore out all my misgivings about bear clubs, organized social hierarchies, and rigid clique structures. I am happy to report that this was at another time and under very different club leadership. The NEB is a much different animal now, though it still copes with the legacy of its past negative reputation. That old reputation became one factor in the subsequent organizing of other bear clubs throughout New England. Perhaps the largest and most visible group is the Northeast Ursamen (Connecticut), noted as a very active social group. The Berkshire Bears (western Massachusetts) maintains a staunch commitment to blue-collar sensibilities. For a wild weekend in New York City, join the Ursamen; for a lumberjack festival in the Adirondacks, join the Berkshire Bears. The Rhode Island Grizzlies (Providence), the Mainely Bears (down east) and the Bare Bears (Portland-based, nudist bears), a short-lived New Hampshire bear club, two New England-based Generation-X clubs, no formal organization in the mountain hamlets of Vermont, and our local Monty Bears Group round out the current New England scene. Nine clubs for a regional population of a little over 13 million.[6]

This brings me back to the question of bear clubs and the differing roles they fill, depending upon local circumstances. My partner Dale and I moved to north central Massachusetts, a.k.a. the Montachusett region, in 1997, partly to escape the escalating Boston real estate market, partly to escape the ubiquitous Boston cold-shoulder attitude. One cannot run *from* something without having something to run *to*: Fitchburg is both currently the cheapest real estate market within an hour's commute of Boston and is an old blue-collar mill town with a legacy of nineteenth-century entrepreneurial largesse to the community. The city is built on hills along the narrow Nashua River valley, the old downtown mostly a ghost town of unaltered monumental architecture from an era long gone, surrounded by old-fashioned wood tenements, triple-deckers, and early twentieth-century suburban single-family houses. The local folks are pretty straightforward, no-nonsense types, quick to take the wind out of the sails of a pompous Bostonian. It remains an immigrant city and thus it is not so surprising that in the middle of rural central New England you find generation after generation of immigrant populations, each acculturating into the fabric of the city as newer waves of immigrants arrive. Among other things, this makes for an interestingly tolerant social atmosphere. Queer folks have lived quietly throughout the area, and over the last five years, a new, visible gay community is emerging. The Monty Bears Group has played no small part in that process.[7]

In January 1998 I sent out a call to form a new bear group in the Montachusett area. Don Robichaud, a local gay activist, advised me the *Fitchburg Sentinel and Enterprise* would have no problem running such a public service announcement, and so it was added to the list of Boston gay bar rags and the local edition of the alternative newspaper, the *Worcester Phoenix*. Fitchburg already had a de facto gay center on Main Street, the PMAP (Peers Mobilized Against AIDS) office directed by Gary Comeau and the site for several local groups' meetings (Common Ground, LOMA [Lesbians of the Montachusett Area], MAGMA, [Montachusett Area Gay Men's Association], and a drop-in center during the day for street addicts. The local Unitarian Universalist church on the Upper Common hosts PFLAG meetings, Father Rich Lewinowski of St. Camillus Parish runs an AIDS outreach, Burbank Hospital has an HIV/AIDS clinic,[8] and both local colleges have a GLBT student organization. The nearest gay bars are out of the area—thirty minutes to Worcester, sixty minutes to Brattleboro, Vermont, seventy-five minutes to Boston proper, and ninety minutes to Springfield. By Midwest standards, I realize we must seem to be tripping all over each other in our relatively thronging crowds here. But remember that winter driving conditions and the threat of a fast-approaching blizzard is a perpetual problem—do you risk that thirty-minute drive over lightly traveled highways from which you may never arrive?

The group settled on the name the Monty Bears Group, to identify and promote our location in probably the most overlooked corner of Massachusetts. The frequently hiked Mount Monadnock, just over the border in New Hampshire, is the most recognizable name. Lesser known are the facts that our twin city, Leominster, is the birthplace of both Johnny Appleseed and the plastic pink flamingo lawn ornament. The group has grown to an active core of fifteen to twenty men, with a total paid membership of thirty-five. It is a mix of rural and small-town local natives and transplants as far away as Ohio and North Dakota. Monthly gatherings will typically see one or two new faces. The group serves as a loosely-knit community, a nexus for social and sexual networking, and a definite gay presence in the mainstream community. Our members range from old pros who have been around the block more than a few times (and I *don't* mean *just me!*) to men scarcely out of the closet, for whom the Monty group may be their only connection to anything gay. I have come to understand that much of non-Boston queer New England consists of married fathers, "bi curious" singles, and other MSMs, who do not identify as gay and desire contact with gay men only for sex. For me, this raises again the question of cultural differences between working-class and middle-class gay men, rural and urban gay spaces, and whether this new idea of self-identifying bears has created an alternative path to a gay identity for nonidentifying MSM. It also offers me a perspective, very different from gay San Francisco, on the progress of the gay movement.

The one consistent criticism I heard about *The Bear Book* was the frequent and arguably reckless use of the term "twink" by several contributors. The adoption of the term twink (various other ones were and are used as well) became a political act, to invert the paradigm of the gay social hierarchy. The term was intended at times to be pejorative, at times to be merely descriptive. In the early days of beardom, coming out as a bear meant, among other things, rejecting the negative labels and the imposition of social and sexual invisibility thrust upon us by the gay-mainstream upholders of an impossible ideal of youth and fitness (the American ephebe, as portrayed in most gay pornography) and advertising. Its use is analogous to the gay term for heterosexuals ("breeders"), the black term for whites ("crackers"), or the old feminist term for men ("male chauvinist pig")—the disempowered inventing a counter-discriminatory vocabulary, which most likely has only the power of private cold comfort rather than effecting any real shift in power dynamics. Of course it is not nice to call people names, and bears using the term twink makes us no better than the young or youthful, buffed, pretty gay men who have called us "trolls," "fat slobs," "icky hairy beasts," "gross," "old," and a host of other names intended pejoratively, for which no one ever thought they should apologize, and who typically barred bears entry to sex clubs and certain bars during the hedonistic and narcissistic gay male culture of the 1970s and early 1980s. In discussions of social prejudices in the gay male community, it is interesting to note how looks- or ageism has rarely been mentioned, let alone analyzed. It's one thing to be outraged over barring a beautiful black man from a bar, but quite another to keep the fat fairies outside on the street "where they belong!"

In terms of class, "twink" has also been used in response to a long tradition of contemptuous dismissal by A-list gays and the socially aspiring (e.g., recent notable comments in print by Daniel Harris and Wayne Koestenbaum) of beefy or heavyset, hirsute gay men as lower class, unkempt, inarticulate, gluttonous, and stupid. When the gay crowd of the rich, the beautiful, and the power-wielding begin whining they are being mistreated by (in their eyes) their social inferiors, it reminds me of nothing so much as the Reagan-era ploy that demonized Republican detractors by claiming that they—an abused and misunderstood minority—were being victimized by the dark, dangerous, and evil forces of political correctness, while they continued to shake down the American public in what has been the most enormous upward transference of wealth in American history.

So, in certain small ways, the hegemony of high-fashion beauty is being altered. Space for more kinds of gay men to be socially and sexually visible, and viable, continues to open up. Through the Bear History Project I have continued to explore the visual realms of beardom. Out of an Internet connection with Jim Sibal grew a multimedia panel presentation and discussion of "Bear Icons," held January 4, 1999, at the Lesbian and Gay Community Services Center on Little West 12th Street in Manhattan. It became the kickoff event to the still-evolving Bear Icons project. This project came into being when I tried to resolve the problem of including an array of visual materials to accompany *The Bear Book*. I hit upon creating a virtual art show, to be published in book form as Bear Icons. As I put out calls to artists and researched the history of images of masculinity, an actual art show came into being. Through Jim Sibal's introduction and the active support and encouragement of Trish Kerle, director of cultural events at the Center, the first installation of "Bear Icons: Collective Artists' Work, 1984-1999—Gay Male Masculinity in Two-Dimensional Art Forms" ran for the month of April 1999 in a bright, medium-sized gallery space at the Center. The show was popular and has been followed up with numerous requests (by other gallery owners, fellow bears, other friends, and myself) to expand and create additional installations of the original exhibition. "Bear Icons: Art and Artifacts," the second incarnation of the exhibition, was held at Mount Ida College, March 6-19, 2000; a serious venue has been offered in San Francisco; other requests have come from Toronto, Milwaukee, and Los Angeles. As that project develops, I consider it an extension of the project contained in the two *Bear Book* volumes.

Two works have been particularly illuminating to my understanding of what the transgression of beardom is—Naomi Wolf's *The Beauty Myth* (1992) and Susan Bordo's *The Male Body* (1999). As gay men have been granted increasing validity as human beings in American society, advertising has discovered a new consumer population with seemingly deeper pockets and an eager willingness to fall in line with advertising's manipulations of concepts of beauty—primarily for the profit of corporations, often to the physical and psychological detriment of the gay male consumer. Since Stonewall, beautiful, often (nearly) naked young men appear with as much frequency as the female beauties from whom their iconic language has been borrowed. Gay men have been taught, even compelled by the media, to objectify themselves exactly as women have traditionally been forced to do. The pressure to conform, to measure up to impossible standards is greater than ever, so much of it is unconsciously absorbed as simply the way things are.

In the wake of lethal school violence and the media's discovery that increasingly bulky musculature is eclipsing the slender surfer look, America is finding itself in the midst of a crisis of masculinity—heterosexual America is raising its boys to try and fit into the bodies and psyches of ideal men, beyond the remotest resemblance to feasible reality. In Littleton, Colorado, a pair of male high-school social outsiders "crack" and take out their frustration and rage by assassinating the jocks and other popular clique members. In Laramie, Wyoming, a young and handsome gay male college student buys drinks for a pair of poor local straight boys, unwittingly sealing his own fate—to be crucified and murdered by frustrated and enraged social outsiders from the same hometown. What's going on here? In our increasingly cutthroat winner-take-all society, the "losers" are beginning to revolt. By contemporary norms, even the second-place race winner (who lost by a fraction of a second) becomes another loser in the crowd of all those who ran the race.

I see the bear movement as a spontaneous, evolving response to such inhumane social dynamics. Rather than becoming leaders to some brave new utopian future, bears, to some degree, offer alternative ways beyond the insanity of all this, at least within the microcosm of the gay community. We are living at a time when social class differences are greater than ever, yet our society as a whole pretends we're all still "middle class." As homosexuality becomes less demonized in many realms of our society, we nonetheless go on demonizing each other; and "faggot" or "gay" remain the only terms of opprobrium with which kids can taunt each other with impunity. Recently, I was privileged to participate in the Boulder Summit—Launching a Multi-Issue, Multicultural Gay Men's Health Movement—as a presence on behalf of gay bears and societal abuse of male children. For me, it was a reenergizing experience, to see and take part in a renewed movement toward a broad-based, progressive, grassroots gay men's movement, one organized around our health and all that implies. The conference conveners intentionally sought to foreground gay youth, rethinking gay male social identity beyond the AIDS crisis, and health issues specific to today's generation (barebacking, drug circuit parties, and the entire reinvention of the 1970s). The express commitment to urge a new and younger generation into leadership is exactly the mentoring the moment calls for, given the loss of much of the Stonewall and ACT UP generations to AIDS. I must admit, however, to having noticed that only fellow bears attended sessions addressing bear-related issues (weight, aging, looks-ism, and bear history), and—while bears are happily among the "politically correct," progressive strands of today's gay movement—the vast majority of today's activists seem to be as youth-and-beauty-struck as ever. We bears were not invisible to other conference-goers, but bear-related issues still are. Wherever the queer movement goes from here, the bears will become an increasingly large presence—may this all be for the good.

## NOTES

1. In my freshman year, I had a brief romance with Young Republicans. I knew nothing of their political values; I was in love with a certain Tom Smith, who *was* a believing YR. By second semester I had become involved with student protests at the state capitol, a few miles down the road, to fight tuition increases. At the time, I was more enamored of the rococo architecture of the state capitol building.

2. I discovered the joys of getting drunk and getting high at about the same time. Jack Kerouac, Charles Bukowski, and other writers and intellectuals who romanticized alcoholism spoke to me like the fabled siren Lorelei along the banks of the Rhine River. I drank and smoked hashish on a daily basis to the point of blacking out or passing out for ten years. The last two years of my career as an addict/alcoholic accelerated my near-demise when I arrived in the Castro in 1979 and found myself a kid let loose in a candy shop of drugs of every sort. Terrifying as it was at the time, I am grateful that this acceleration brought me to my "bottom" and into recovery at the age of twenty-eight.. I have remained continuously clean and sober ever since.

3. I choose these professions because I know actual bears holding down exactly these positions.

4. In the United Kingdom, some English still do not consider the Irish to be "white."

5. Anonymous source.

6. Vermont has 500,000 and Rhode Island less than a million (roughly the population of Greater New York or Greater Los Angeles), but at 66,672 square miles New England is no bigger than the state of Wisconsin—all six New England states together make up an average east-of-the-Mississippi-sized state. Most of the population lives along the coast, from the outer suburbs (in the broadest sense) of Boston (e.g., Portland, Maine, and coastal New Hampshire to Providence, Rhode Island) and along the Connecticut coast—most of New England is relatively empty, much like Pennsylvania and New York State.

7. See two articles in the local daily newspaper. "Out of Hibernation Emerging from a Decade of Loss, 'Bears' Seek New Connection for Gay Men" by Emily Van Hazinga, *Fitchburg Sentinel and Enterprise* (January 11, 1998): B3 and "Support System Growing for Region's Gays, Lesbians" by Margaret Smith, *Fitchburg Sentinel and Enterprise* (August 26, 1999): A1, A7.

8. A satellite of the University of Massachusetts Medical Center in Worcester.

## *PART I: BEAR BODIES*

Chapter 1

# Bears and Health

Lawrence D. Mass

[In "Books This Fall," October 12, 1997, *Lesbian and Gay New York (LGNY)* published a review by Lawrence D. Mass of *The Bear Book: Readings in the History and Evolution of a Gay Male Subculture* (Harrington Park Press), edited by Les Wright, in which Mass criticized the collection for not dealing with what he saw to be distinctive health issues emerging within this community. When plans came together for a sequel to *The Bear Book*, Mass decided to take on that challenge himself. An abridged version of Mass's review of *The Bear Book* first appeared in the Fall 1997 issue of the *Harvard Gay and Lesbian Review*. While written expressly for *The Bear Book II*, this chapter has also been serialized in three parts in *American Bear*, Vol. 5, Issue 4, December 1998/January 1999, pp. 21, 23; Vol. 5, Issue 5, February/March 1999, pp. 37-38; and Vol. 5, Issue 6, April/May 1999, pp. 38, 40. The chapter was also adapted and appeared in *Lesbian and Gay New York*, October 22, 1998, and has also been presented at the Gay Men's Health Summit conference in Boulder, Colorado, July 1999.]

Before the advent of the bears, most of us who later came to self- or group-identify as bears hung out on the fringes of the leather world, never quite fitting in. Though I was never myself into leather per se, I identified most with the frankness and openness and adventurousness about sex that characterized this community and branded it as outlaw, even within the greater, more mainstream, gay movement.

It was there, as a regular—however outsiderly a regular—at leather bars and sex clubs that I found myself, as a physician who had begun writing about health issues in the gay community, making somewhat modest observations about health vis-à-vis the worlds of leather and S&M. During that time period, three pieces emerged. One was a sprawling overview for *The Advocate* of the tug-of-war that was going on between older psychiatric theories and newer sex research perspectives on sadomasochism. It was called "Coming to Grips with Sadomasochism: Psychiatry vs. Sex Research." A second piece, called "Handballing: High Risk Sport," was about the health hazards of "brachiopractic eroticism," otherwise known as fist-fucking, and was published in the *New York Native*. Torn rectums were turning up in emergency rooms with enough frequency to arouse concern. But such were the political sensitivities of the community in those days, when the word "promiscuity" had to be put in quotes, that editors eliminated my last line as too provocative: "If you're going to be forearmed," I had written, "be forewarned." A third piece was a call for greater scrutiny of and within the leather world for health issues, very analogous to the inquiry I'm pursuing regarding health issues and concerns among bears.

Again, at that time, civil liberty issues were so sensitive, and criticism of gay people was considered so politically incorrect, that these writings elicited considerable hostility. It wasn't simply that I was an outsider to most leatherfolk. It's that I was raising critical concerns. When anthologies about leatherfolk and issues finally began to be published, I was not invited to contribute (though *the Advocate* piece did appear in what was the first such anthology of academic and scholarly pieces); but neither, so far as I could glean, was anyone else with critical perspectives. One prominent member of the leather community, for example, sensing or projecting condemnation from my work, asked defensively why fisting injuries should be regarded any differently from those resulting from sports.

Actually, I was and remain in complete agreement with her, and this gets to the nub of the role I have seen myself trying to play, however primitively or unsuccessfully. Where there are health issues pertinent to our subcultures or communities, we need to continue to try to characterize and address them, regardless of their timing, political correctness, or the observer's credentials as a member or nonmember of the group being scrutinized.

In the early 1980s, at the start of the AIDS epidemic, during a time when our civil liberties were still very precarious, and the possibility of some extreme right-wing reprisal against gays was more than paranoia, discussing our vulnerabilities, our health issues, seemed provocative and controversial. In larger perspective, it's the reaction elicited by Larry Kramer when he seemed to be so dangerously and vindictively airing all our dirty laundry in public, when he seemed to be giving ammunition to the enemy. Though social and political danger are far from vanquished, I think we have now reached a point in the development of our aggregate communities of gay culture, that we *can* brook criticism, even from outsiders.

Today, more than fifteen years later, talking about bears and health is more likely to elicit support than defensiveness and hostility, and that has in fact been the case. I have gotten only positive feedback. Is the same now true of the worlds of leather and S&M? I'm not sure, though surely that level of defensiveness must be at least diminished. Meanwhile, I don't recall seeing an anthology on leatherfolk that includes a solid piece on medical and health issues and concerns.

So, with this background of my experience trying to write about health issues for other gay community subcultures, let's move on to the subject of this chapter: bears and health.

One evening at Bear Pride 98 in Chicago, about eight of us were flopped about on the big, comfortable sofas in one of the secluded lounge areas of the Marriott Hotel that was our host. An impressive amount of hugging and caressing—physical communing—goes on at these events. It's no coincidence that so many bears sign off literally (online and in letters), as we do in person, with HUGS. More than sex, I think, the camaraderie is really what it's all about, what most gay events are all about—and this grouping was typical in this regard. Heads were on shoulders and chests, arms were rubbing knees and massaging backs and necks; our entwinings probably deconstructed what was happening better than anything that was being said. But on this occasion, the conversation that developed was also worth noting for its absence in bear discourse—at bear gatherings, meetings, and in bear magazines and literature.

The subject we found ourselves talking about, at my initiative, was bears and health.

By now we all know that there is no specific definition of a bear, and this fact will be important to return to in the later stages of this discussion, when I am talking about future directions. Meanwhile, I am a stereotypical bear in that I am a burly, bearded, hairy, middle-aged daddy-type and attracted to the same and to "cubs." Despite many exceptions, I continue to be drawn, more than to anything else, to bigness in men (height and weight, to the extent of fat). As a physician, however, I have long been aware of the health hazards attendant to bigness—in myself and others. And I would propose that the bear subculture has reached a level of development at which the time is more than due to take a look at this aspect of ourselves.

So there we were on the couch. With my right hand, I was massaging the thick, meaty leg of an exceedingly handsome sex educator from San Francisco. With the left, as he lay on my lap, I was caressing a regional Mr. Bear who has done some original design work for the greater bear community. The subject got onto defining bears, and the sex educator, so typically San Franciscan in the pride with which he carries himself, and who had one intelligent insight after another, gave his own, provisional definition: "For me," he said, "a bear is just a man who is comfortable with himself." Certainly that's who he is. But what about the question of bulk and hirsuteness that are such commonalties, if not absolutes, of bear preference, I found myself asking. Everyone more or less agreed, including the sex educator and the bald, virile, *suthun*-accented riverboat operator from Nashville, whom I'll call Tennessee, who was laying in the lap of his close friend, who happened to be a thin and hairless bear lover. The conversation then reverted to its characteristic fragmentation with people variously introducing themselves, interrupting each other, talking about this and that in bits and pieces.

When I explained that I was a physician, Tennessee's antennae immediately perked and he wanted to tell us about his recent health crisis. He had been hospitalized with a life-threatening condition called (deep vein) thrombophlebitis. Folks like him who are on their feet all day probably have a greater tendency to develop this affliction, as do those who are overweight, I explained. In fact, I continued, I think the whole subject of bears and health is worth looking at. Thrombophlebitis is a condition I'd never thought of before as perhaps being more common among bears, but there are others that can be comparably serious—major, life-threatening—and that are unquestionably more common among us: hypertension (high blood pressure, HBP, HTN), diabetes mellitus (DM), arteriosclerotic cardiovascular disease (ASCVD) with stroke and MI (myocardial infarction, otherwise known as heart attack), arthritis, duodenal ulcer, hiatal hernia (HH), gastroesophageal reflux disease (GERD), gallstones, cholecystitis, some cancers (e.g., colorectal and prostate), and sleep apnea. When I mentioned this last, which I myself suffer from along with hypertension and arthritis, a fellow from the adjacent lounge area came over to join us, saying he'd overheard our conversation and wanted to second our observations. After years of exhaustion, falling asleep on the job, at the wheel, and other inappropriate and dangerous places, he finally underwent a sleep study, was diagnosed with sleep apnea, and now uses "the machine" (which will be discussed later) with excellent results. He feels that his life has been transformed. How many other bears are there out there, I found myself asking, who have no idea that they have this condition or what they might do about it?

Hirsuteness is likewise a consideration. When I said what so many of us have already learned firsthand, the hard way, that body lice (crabs and scabies) are common among bears, the regional Mr. Bear on my lap casually explained his home-remedy approach: on the last day of whatever bear event he's attending, he treats himself with Kwell lotion, not so much unlike the way gay men who still have unprotected oral sex with multiple partners at the baths and other communal environments use prophylactic antibiotics as "morning-after" pills.

Before I get into more detail on some of the specific conditions that bears should be on the lookout for, let me first address the issue of weight in broadest, contemporary perspective. Many were confused when a major medical study was published suggesting that people who have always been heavyset and who have managed to avoid common, anticipated complications of being overweight into their elder years are probably at no more at risk of morbidity and mortality (sickness and death) from these conditions than those who are not overweight (on the basis of widely accepted ideal body/weight guidelines).[1] While this may be true, and may mean that some of us who are heavyset will have no worse health than those with more "ideal" weight, it will not be true for the majority of us. For the majority of us, the health risks of being overweight will remain considerable.

The most recent estimate of the might of the diet industry in America, as cited by Jane Brody in *The New York Times*, is $33 billion a year.[2] If there is excess anywhere, certainly it abounds within the endless, ubiquitous, manic, patently dollar-minded programs and guides and television shows that urge us to shed what some of us see as our glory, that would have us look skinny, like the gym-body types we tend to find as unattractive as they do us (though, of course, opposites also attract). That society does not recognize and affirm that diversity of physicality and desire is itself a problem. For now, let's just say that there can be no doubt of the narrowness of America's preoccupation with leanness, of its relegation or even exclusion of what it sees as less desirable body types. All this is also taking place unquestionably within an appropriate context of affirming optimum health.

Some of this came to a head recently, when the National Institutes of Health released its latest findings and recommendations. According to their statistics, an unprecedented 55 percent of Americans are currently overweight.[3] This prompted an immediate response from the National Association to Advance Fat Acceptance. Appropriately, the association is worried that the new information and guidelines will result in a lot more negative energies and pressures being directed at overweight people, will drive them to repeat on-and-off diet patterns that studies have demonstrated achieve little over time, and to even be counterproductive in terms of the burden of stress they augment. But as Brody points out, however sympathetic these perspectives and claims, the fact remains that being trim is enormously more healthy, and we cannot fault the medical allied health professions and leading American spokespersons and organizations for emphasizing optimum health. Although the public needs to be more tolerant and respectful of overweight people, it is not under any obligation to endorse the false concept that fat is healthy. According to the National Institutes of Health, obesity-related illnesses are costing the nation in the range of $100 billion per year. In this sense, obesity can be seen as comparable to smoking as a costly health hazard. In fact, obesity is now cited, after smoking, as the second leading cause of preventable death in the United States.

So what is the so-called ideal body weight? As you may have guessed correctly, there is no such absolute. Currently, the terminology most commonly used by health professionals centers on BMI, the body mass index (replacing the older height/weight charts), which takes into account waist size as a separate risk factor. For those of you who want to calculate your BMI, Brody includes the rather complex formula in her discussion.[4]

Let me now proceed to some of the specific health consequences of being overweight or obese. Though these conditions are found throughout the population, they are notably common among those who are overweight. The following are the most common.

## *SLEEP APNEA*

The whole field of what we call sleep disorders is relatively new. It is only with the publication in recent years of major studies demonstrating the commonness of serious sleep disorders and their health consequences that sleep-disorder centers, evaluations, and guidelines have begun to proliferate. By far the most common sufferers are those who are overweight or obese. The principal symptom of sleep apnea is loud snoring. This is something I have been living with all my life. Ever since I was in my late teens and early twenties I have been told by those I have slept with or near that my snoring is formidable. Richard Dyer, music critic of the *Boston Globe* (my close friend during the years of my medical training in Boston), once likened my snoring to "a buzz saw." On closer inspection, many of us loud snorers are obstructed (the literal cause for the snoring) as we breathe, and may even enter periods when the obstruction is total and we stop breathing air altogether (hence the term apnea). What results is a night during which quality sleep is fitful, when one awakens from time to time sweating and breathing heavily. The most serious long-term consequences of sleep apnea are high blood pressure, chronic exhaustion and associated psychological and psychiatric problems, and premature death from stroke or heart attack—the likelihood of which is enhanced by inebriation with alcohol or sedation with tranquilizers or combinations thereof—or from an accident resulting from falling asleep while driving a motor vehicle or operating dangerous machinery. Recent studies suggest that a significant percentage of accidents involving drivers are due to their suffering from sleep apnea.

What can we do? There are treatments for sleep apnea. One approach is to lose a lot of weight. In my own case, I feel fairly certain that significant weight loss improves my breathing, and this has kept me from pursuing more certain treatments, such as prosthetic devices worn during sleep, that reshape the mouth so that air can be exchanged with less obstruction; and (most successful), CPAP. Continuous positive airway pressure (CPAP) is applied from a machine that costs $1,000-$2,000 and which exerts its effect through a nasal mask with cloth strips worn during sleep. It is somewhat cumbersome (and retaliation is the treatment of choice when cruel friends tell you that the mask makes you look like Hannibal Lecter), but is by far the most effective treatment to date. If you think you have sleep apnea—and I have no doubt that a significant percentage of us bears do—you must first be evaluated by a sleep disorders clinic, which, for those of you who have health insurance, would be arranged via your carrier and primary physician. (A personal postscript: After seven years of unsuccessful, up-and-down dieting I took the plunge and ordered "the machine.")

## *ARTERIOSCLEROTIC CARDIOVASCULAR DISEASE (ASCVD)*

Also known as "hardening of the arteries," ASCVD is the phenomenon of plaque buildup in the arteries, the principal contributors to which are cholesterol and other fats. ASCVD is ubiquitous, since most folks have it in greater or lesser degree but it is most common and serious in overweight adults, among whom it too often eventually exacts a heavy toll in early death from the principal complications of ASCVD: heart attack (myocardial infarction) and stroke. Various cholesterol and lipid-lowering medications can be helpful, but weight reduction remains the bottom-line treatment.

## *ARTERIOSCLEROTIC PERIPHERAL VASCULAR DISEASE*

ASCPVD is a hardening of the arteries, as it applies, primarily, to the extremities (arms and legs). The principal manifestation of this disease is a symptom called claudication, whereby the legs don't get enough blood and begin to ache from a lack of oxygen, sometimes with even minimal physical activity. Other symptoms include tingling and numbness and a sense of having, literally, cold feet.

## *ARTHRITIS*

Arthritis or osteoarthritis is just what most of you know it to be—an inflammation of the joints and bones that is painful and that can even be deforming, and that seems to be more common as we get older. That's all true, but it is also more common among overweight folk. Arthritis can be caused by or associated with other diseases. In most sufferers, however, its etiology (why it develops) is not well understood. And there are no definitive treatments. For many arthritics, losing weight unquestionably helps. Anti-inflammatory agents like aspirin, ibuprofen (Motrin), naproxen, and others can limit inflammation and ease pain; in more severe cases, more powerful medications with serious side effects and even surgery may be necessary. Though there are no known cures for arthritis, several experimental medications show considerable promise for more sustained relief of symptoms with fewer or no side effects.

## *CANCERS*

Cancers, like many other diseases, are often statistically associated with such factors as age, gender, ethnicity, and location. Weight is another. Although none of these factors is actually causative, they may be associated with increased risk and are thus called "risk factors." Cancer of the bladder, stomach, and lung are more commonly associated with leanness. Two cancers that have been statistically associated with being overweight are two of the most commonly diagnosed in older men—prostate and colorectal. Digital (finger) examination of the prostate gland and a stool test for occult blood should be a part of your annual physical examination. Additional tests, such as the PSA (prostate specific antigen), may also be conducted, depending on your age and symptomatology.

## *CHOLECYSTITIS AND CHOLELITHIASIS*

Cholecystitis, an inflammation of the bile duct often associated with cholelithiasis (gallstones), is most often diagnosed in those who are overweight. The pain, characteristically precipitated by large, fatty meals, is usually felt in the right mid-abdominal area but can be variable, vague, and felt in other areas such as the back (what we call "referred pain"). Diagnosis is made with a combination of laboratory, X-ray, and dye and sonographic tests, in association with the clinical history and presentation. Treatment can range from conservative dietary recommendations to surgery—cholecystectomy (removal of the bile duct and the stones it invariably contains), lithotripsy (a sound wave breaking up the stones into dust in a procedure that is noninvasive, i.e., that doesn't involve surgery).

## *DIABETES MELLITUS*

There are two broad categories of diabetes, a disorder of blood sugar metabolism. The first is the kind one is born with or develops in early childhood, adolescence, or young adulthood. This type, type I, is not caused by obesity and is often familial. Type II is far more common and typically develops in midlife and in the elderly. It is invariably precipitated by, and very closely associated with, overeating and being overweight. So common and consistent is this association that it can be said that anyone who is middle-aged and significantly overweight, especially as they advance in years beyond their twenties, runs a high risk of developing type II diabetes. Once this disease develops, it can then be controlled or eliminated (in the majority of cases) by weight loss and diet regulation. The disease itself, diabetes, can be very serious and cause progressive damage to various organs and tissues. Among the more common conditions it can lead to: peripheral neuropathy—a progressive numbing of the nerves in the arms and legs, which can in turn lead to sores and ulcers that heal poorly. This consequence of diabetes is likewise common and can lead to the eventual loss of limbs (amputation of the feet or legs). Other, similarly serious complications of diabetes include kidney damage and failure, blindness, and impotence. Symptoms of diabetes include polyuria (having to pee a lot more than normally), polydipsia (excessive thirst, because of all the peeing), and blurring of vision. Even where there are no such symptoms, if you are significantly overweight, the risk of diabetes is so high that you are advised to have your blood sugar checked regularly, at least annually. If you do develop type II diabetes, it can be brought under control with dieting—with successful dieting, blood sugar returns to normal—and/or medications. Keeping blood sugars as close to normal as possible does not guarantee that complications won't develop, but the likelihood of their developing is reduced.

## *DUODENAL ULCER*

The symptoms of duodenal ulcer (DU) classically begin as heartburn, an acidy kind of pain in the mid-stomach area that can seem to be brought on by stress and certain foods, especially those that are greasy or fatty and spicy, that often comes and goes in relation to eating, and that can seem to be relieved by antacids and dairy products. In recent years, our understanding of duodenal ulcer has been revolutionized by the finding of an associated bacteria (called *H. pylori*) that causes a lot of the damage. Once diagnosed, DU is often treated with antibiotics as well as medications that decrease acid and give symptomatic relief, e.g., Tagamet, Zantac, Prilosec, Pepcid, and others. In many instances, treatment of the bacteria will result in complete relief and the need for these other medications will be eliminated. Because of the recently discovered bacteria, it is imperative that those with symptoms of duodenal ulcer be evaluated medically rather than just self-treating symptoms with over-the-counter remedies, which now include Tagamet, Zantac, and others. Untreated duodenal ulcer can lead to bleeding, which is not uncommon, and perforation, a life-threatening emergency requiring surgical intervention. Although duodenal ulcer is common among those who are overweight, it is also a condition found among the general population.

## *GASTROESOPHAGEAL REFLUX DISEASE*

Here, too large a meal, especially a fatty one, can result in the reflux of the partially digested and very acidic stomach contents back into the espophagus, and from there back up into the mouth. This problem primarily manifests itself during sleep, when muscles are relaxed and the backup of abdominal contents is experienced as a kind of passive regurgitation. So you wake up, if not with actual vomitus in your mouth, with a terrible, acidic taste. Antacids and other medications can help, as can sleeping with the thorax elevated (your head and trunk elevated to a 45 degree angle or greater), but significant weight reduction will usually have more impact than any other measure.

## *HEART ATTACK*

Heart attack can result from any excessive strain on the heart. For our purposes, it should be noted that it is far more common in those who are overweight or obese. A heart attack, which results from the heart not getting adequate blood supply or oxygen, which in turn usually results from ASCVD, is a life-threatening emergency that is often fatal, or that can leave the heart permanently damaged. The extent of heart disease and risk of heart attack can be gauged by a (cardiac) stress test.

## *HIATAL HERNIA*

In this condition, the pressure from the abdomen, because of obesity and/or the intake of a large amount of food, is such that the abdomen gets pushed up through the diaphragm that normally separates the abdomen from the esophagus, and the abdomen from the chest. What results is a deep pain in the chest and upper abdomen and sometimes mid-back from that extrusion and GERD. Again, the principal treatment is weight reduction. In the absence or failure of that measure, and the failure of symptomatic treatment with medications, surgery can be undertaken.

## *HYPERLIPIDEMIA*

Hyperlipidemia refers to elevated cholesterol and/or other lipids (triglycerides) that are, like ASCVD, hypertension, and diabetes, commonly associated with obesity. Hyperlipidemia is part of the process of plaque formation in ASCVD and is considered a risk factor for all the complications of ASCVD. It can be treated with cholesterol and lipid-lowering medications.

## *HYPERTENSION*

High blood pressure (HBP) or hypertension (HTN) is probably the most common side effect of being overweight. Like diabetes, it is so common that it must be continually looked for in those who are overweight, especially as they enter their middle years. Hypertension is the principal risk factor for heart attack and stroke. It is often silent, without symptoms, until very late in its development, when it has already caused a good deal of heart damage. Therefore, people must have their blood pressure checked regularly, even if they feel fine. If hypertension is present, it is very important that it be treated, which can be done with an array of different medications, some of which have side effects. In general, antihypertensive medications are very well tolerated.

## *PEDICULOSIS (BODY LICE)*

Talk to any bear who is in frequent intimate contact with other bears, in bars, at meetings, or regional gatherings, especially if there is sexual contact with multiple partners, and you will appreciate the common consensus that body lice (crabs, scabies) are more common in this population. Treatment regimens for pediculosis—Kwell lotion, pyridine A200, Elimite—vary, and the bear movement raises the question of prophylactic treatment, e.g., at the conclusion of regional gatherings where a lot of intimate contact has taken place (see Sexually Transmitted Diseases).

## *PILONIDAL SINUS AND CYST*

In addition to pediculosis, hirsute men are prone to another ailment that is not uncommon—an infection of the hair follicles in the small of the back (the sexy spot where loin meets crack). These infections seem more common in truck or bus drivers (!) because they are sitting for extended periods during which there is repeated minor trauma (bumps) to that area. These infections are sometimes easily treated and recurrences prevented by avoiding aggravating circumstances (extended motorbike or other driving). Not uncommonly, however, they must be surgically excised. Likewise not so uncommonly, these surgical procedures have to be repeated.

## *SEXUALLY TRANSMITTED DISEASES*

I have this gut sense, which may be erroneous, that there is less drug use and unsafe sex among bears than in other circuit subcultures—in part, because bear culture is less youth-oriented and boasts significantly greater numbers of middle-aged men. Nevertheless, regional pride events, such as the big Chicago gathering I attended, present lots of opportunities for unsafe sex, even as the extent to which we refrain from such may be otherwise or in aggregate impressive. For those who do still have unsafe sex, the same diseases are still out there: HIV, syphilis, gonorrhea, herpes, hepatitis, and others. In the contemporary debates about the relative safety of oral sex for HIV, the risk of acquiring and transmitting *other* sexually transmitted diseases (STDs)—e.g., herpes, gonorrhea, syphilis, hepatitis A and B—tends to be overlooked or underemphasized. Rimming, as you already know, poses risks for parasites and hepatitis A and B. In a small percentage of cases, hepatitis B will become chronic and lead to serious, sometimes fatal, liver disease. Hepatitis C, which seems to be less sexually transmissible than HIV or hepatitis B, has a higher rate of progression to chronicity with serious complications. (The extent to which hepatitis C is a sexually transmitted disease remains unknown. Hopefully, this urgent question will be answered by studies in the next few years. Meanwhile, gay men who have been sexually active with multiple partners should be tested for hepatitis C, notwithstanding the continuing disagreement on this recommendation among health care professionals.)

Other areas of health are probably pertinent to bears. Les Wright, for example, wonders about depression and anxiety. While there are no hard statistics on bears and these disorders, they are common throughout the general population. It should be noted that depression, often bound up with anxiety, is much more readily treated today, with the advent of safer, more effective medications, and with the decrease in stigma associated with their usage. The medications that have revolutionized the treatment of depression are in a category known as the SRIs (serotonin reuptake inhibitors), better known to the public as the Prozac family of antidepressants (Prozac, Zoloft, Effexor, Paxil). Most of these have the side effect of quieting sexual drive. It has been hoped that by treating depression there will be an impact on the craving that is the driving force in compulsions and addictions, e.g., substance abuse, overeating, and sexual compulsivity. Although individuals anecdotally report that these antidepressants seem, generally speaking, to help them with their various compulsions and addictions, there are not as yet any studies demonstrating clear effectiveness in eliminating or even reducing craving. If and when an antidepressant or any other pill comes along that is clearly, demonstrably effective for treating overeating or any other form of compulsion or addiction (other than OCD, obsessive-compulsive disorder, a very specific psychiatric syndrome that is amenable to treatment), it will be very big news. Meanwhile, there are no known diet pills that do not have serious side effects and their own risks of addiction, e.g., the amphetamines and their relatives.

An area of mental health pertinence and concern I would add here is sexual compulsion. This is a very controversial area of discussion. Many people feel that it is a pejorative and stigmatizing misnomer, as indeed it can be when misused, much the way the word "promiscuity" can be. But what I propose is that just as we no longer feel compelled today to put promiscuity in quotations, we should no longer feel so inhibited in talking about sexual compulsion, a phenomenon that is really worth looking at in our lives and communities. There is no absolute definition of too much sex or of sexual compulsion, of course, but recovery programs emphasize that you define it as such yourself, if and when you feel or recognize that your own sexual drive and behavior are really interfering with your life. If you know that you wanted to get some work done, read a book, have dinner with a friend, go to a play or movie that you missed because you are so locked into patterns of getting off—going to sex places such as the baths, masturbating with pornography, running up high bills with phone sex—that would be the kind of thing to look at in this context. When sex has become a kind of drug to medicate any kind of feeling—boredom, depression, anxiety—and seems to be taking up more space and energy than you want it to, there may be cause for reflection. The most extensive thinking in this area has been developed around Sexual Compulsives Anonymous (SCA), a twelve-step recovery group. Its ideas and principles are summarized in a book called *Out of the Shadows* by Patrick Carnes.[5] Whatever one's preconceptions about this subject or about 12-step recovery programs, it is worth a real effort on anyone's part to take a look at the "characteristics" of sexual compulsion, as they are spelled out in one of the SCA's principal leaflets.

And last, of real importance to our population with its large numbers of middle-aged men, is the use of Viagra. As most of you already know, it works and works well, and it is not known to have any serious or common side effects, though it could be dangerous if one takes more than the recommended dosages and it is dangerous when used in combination with inhalant nitrites (poppers). The main point to make about Viagra is that it is not an aphrodisiac. Rather, it will significantly enhance erection (it will augment hardness) for a majority of users who have erectile insufficiency when and where there is already arousal. It will not create an erection by itself, nor does it enhance sexual orgasm or pleasure per se. If you are not genuinely aroused in a situation, it's very likely that nothing will happen. *Repeat warning: do not use poppers if you have taken Viagra.*

So, where does all this leave us? If optimum health stresses weight reduction, where does this leave those of us who are heavyset and attracted to such? This is a difficult question and goes to the heart of the bear movement, which has always been a haven for us. As we have noted earlier, there is no absolute definition of being a bear; weight is not a requirement, but it's such a commonality that if we gave weight reduction any kind of high visibility or emphasis—say, in our magazines, at meetings or regional gatherings—it would likely be controversial. In the greater and pressing interest of our health, however, that is precisely what I would propose: a cautious advancement of this agenda. That is, start raising the subject in talks, in presentations, in articles; consider having a medical health booth at regional events where literature could be passed out and information exchanged. (For example, Steve Albert, director of HIV services for the Callen-Lorde Clinic and a former Mr. New York Bear, has begun a health column for the New York Metorbears newsletter.)

As for dieting, I have no magic formula or solution. As we all know, there are thousands of diets, many of them genuinely effective, but none has emerged as significantly better, healthier, more effective, more enduring. The main thing about a diet is to reduce fats and sugars and increase raw vegetables, fat-free or very lean meats, fish, and fruits. And to accompany that reduction with physical exercise, which, in the case of middle-aged men who are seriously overweight, should be commenced slowly.

Especially as I get older, the issue of dieting becomes increasingly pertinent and urgent. Much as I enjoy being heavyset and having people respond to me as such, I am determined to make a greater effort to lose weight. Some readers may think I'm some kind of traitor for raising this unpleasant and inconvenient subject, but the truth should not be negotiable for any cause, and certainly not for any true scientist or physician. The truth is that I love us all too much and I'm too much a bear—in the Native American Indian sense of the bear as healer, as physician—not to press ahead.

## TWO POSTSCRIPTS

### The First Bears and Health Survey

[first published in *American Bear*, September 1999]

Around the time I wrote my "Bears and Health" chapter for this anthology, I discovered that I had a colleague who was doing complementary and groundbreaking work in the same area. In fact, Steve Albert, who I mentioned earlier in this chapter, had begun writing his own column on bears and health for the newsletter of Manhattan's Metrobears. But Albert's column was a first not only for the Metrobears and bear organization newsletters, it was also pioneering in its approach. Having recently completed his master's degree in public health, Albert did what was doubtless the first health survey ever conducted of a bear community. And what he discovered is eye-opening.

This premiere survey consisted of a checklist of medical problems that people might be concerned about—e.g., diabetes, high blood pressure, asthma, arthritis—but it also included other health issues, such as drug use (with listings of specific drugs, e.g., alcohol and marijuana), as well as such other conditions and circumstances as unemployment, stress, poverty, loss/bereavement, aging, domestic violence, eating disorders, and depression. Although the sample of readers he drew from was small (fewer than 100), here's what he found:

As published in *Metropolitan Bear* November 1998, the NYC Metrobears newsletter, Albert found that the greatest overall health concerns were as follows: (1) eating disorders (compulsive overeating), (2) depression, (3) HIV/AIDS, (4) health insurance (un- or underinsured), and (5) stress. In further musings in that issue of the newsletter and in conversations with me subsequently, Albert indicated his surprise that there was so little concern about drug use, which confirmed my suspicion that because bears tend to be a somewhat older community we see less drug use than other circuit subcultures. That's not to say that drug abuse, especially alcoholism (even if it's mostly "just beer"), isn't a presence among us. But we probably score better than the Chelsea circuit party boys.

In subsequent columns, Albert began looking at the five categories. Noting that overeating and weight gain are almost bear pastimes, and that anyone attempting to pathologize them was in for sexual politics trouble, he nonetheless opened up the subjects of diet and exercise. The other subject he began to explore before leaving for Provincetown this summer was depression. To what extent is depression bound up with eating disorders? What can we do about it?

Although it must be emphasized that Albert's sample of bears was very limited and by no means representative, it is certainly worth pondering that we ourselves cite an eating disorder—compulsive overeating—as our number one concern. That's what we ourselves are admitting, even if we also feel that heavyset or even overtly fat people are attractive, in contrast to those who are thin; even if we also agree that overweight folk are often subject to prejudice.

### *Bears: Icons of Gay Male Masculinity?*
### *Weight and Fat As Masculine Drag*

(Adapted from a bear panel presentation for the Sexuality Series at the Lesbian and Gay Community Services Center in New York City [December 4, 1998])

A book by Daniel Harris called *The Rise and Fall of Gay Culture*[6] takes a very jaundiced look at every aspect of gay male culture, including the bears. In a one-sentence dismissal, not so different from his single observation/single dimension put-downs of everyone and everything else, he snips: "Just as the tattoo has become a brooch, so the bear's fur is really a mink stole." Probably the best revenge on someone whose outlook is so invested in being so literally cutting-edge is to point out that it is not. In fact, with comparable acidity and regality, Wayne Koestenbaum in his book about the world of opera queenery, *The Queen's Throat*,[7] had already dismissed the bears with even shorter shrift as "the fat ghetto."

Now, as I have written in my review of *The Bear Book*, Les Wright's pioneering anthology about the bear movement, I think that the bear movement is fascinating and complex and bears scrutiny from many different angles. The angle I myself have been most preoccupied with is the question of health in this community. As we have already noted, even though many who define themselves and are integrated into the community as bears are not in fact overweight, weight is such a commonality among us that it is easily our biggest health concern, encompassing a number of specific illnesses and conditions that can ensue from or are facilitated by being overweight.

So here's how I'd like to tie all this together as a subject we might open up for discussion. We bears all know that the bear movement is about more than weight and gender and we are used to snideness from those who don't identify. At worst, we practice the same contempt on them. In fact, one of the bigger problems with Les's *Bear Book* is the extent to which contributors are careless with the use of epithets such as "twink." But what I want to bring up, to explore, is not how and why Harris and Koestenbaum are all wrong, but the extent to which they are in fact hitting upon something real. At the risk of buying into the self-hatred that their put-downs invite, *is* there a real basis for Harris's implication that bearness is really a new form of what might be called "masculine drag"? Am I the only one whose mind this thought has crossed?

I have a close friend, Melanie, who is an FTM (female-to-male) transsexual. She never had the surgery or hormones and feels she probably never will, but she's most comfortable in her masculine identity. When I told Mel, as she prefers to be called, my wonderings about weight as masculine drag among bears, she told me she'd often wondered the same thing about heavyset or overweight lesbians as well as bears. Some of that may be eating disorders, which in turn may be related to other disorders such as depression, as we have already speculated, but isn't some of it the same phenomenon—bulk as masculine accoutrement? In many of these instances, as my life-partner Arnie Kantrowitz has put it, has fat become surrogate for muscle?

Certainly, the connection of bulk to sexuality and desire is by no means limited to bears and lesbians! Or, for that matter, to specific cultures, times, or places. Consider the phenomenon of Sumo wrestlers or power lifters. There's now a sitcom called *King of Queens* in which a big bear who worries about being fat is obviously a big sex object, presumably primarily for heterosexual women. Of course, we all know that the bear community includes otters, wolves, bear-lovers, many body types, so that any generalization will eventually, at whatever level, especially in changing time frames and perspectives, prove to be erroneous. In fact, we need to say a little more about this. When I reviewed *The Queen's Throat*, I noted that the biggest conceptual problem Koestenbaum had was in his belief in an entity, a being, "the opera queen." My point was that it's like the legendary "gay sensibility" or "the sexual revolution" or "the fag hag." Or even "the gay community." The moment you begin a hands-on examination of these elusive terms, the moment you try to precisely define them, they disintegrate. Ultimately, there is no such thing as "the bear," just as there is no such single, circumscribable entity you can capture as "the fag hag" or "the opera queen" or "the Castro Street clone." And as former New York Metrobears President John Outcalt has pointed out, the business of gaining weight can be a whole subcultural world unto itself, much less about gender than about eroticization of certain body parts—our bellies—and functions—eating. In a similar vein of speculation, some have suggested that the bear movement, in coinciding with the AIDS epidemic, represents a move toward a physical appearance that should in theory seem safer, healthier, more attractive; if your partner is heavy, so the simplistic logic would go, he's less likely to have AIDS.

Notwithstanding all these exceptions, is there something here about bears and weight and sexuality and gender to try to articulate? Instead of trying to come up with some sweeping formula or theory, I think what's needed is a lot more discussion. In the interests of furthering that process, I'm going to go out on the honesty limb a little further and tell you a little bit more about my own subjective experience. For me, bulk, heft, is definitely a feature—somehow with the appearance and visceral appeal—of "masculinity." It has happened to me many times in the past that upon gaining weight, an individual suddenly becomes attractive, or more attractive, who never was before. Conversely, if someone I find attractive suddenly loses weight, especially if it's a lot of weight, I tend to find him less attractive. And what I'm attracted to, intangibly, is what I call, in my own perception, "masculinity," "virility." Although patently ridiculous in terms of the fluidity of these sociocultural constructions, my perceptions of gender, and my sexual desire, do happen to be, at the most visceral level, cloaked in weight, heft, bulk. In the

Stonewall era, I would have been dubbed a chubby-chaser, even though I'm less hypnotized by overt fat than by huskiness, stockiness, burliness. (For me, massive obesity is a boundary.) And as *The Bear Book* points out, one of the earliest bear groups did originate as an offshoot of Girth and Mirth.

Still, even with these real limitations as givens, I can't help wondering to what extent my experience is common among us. The question that most intrigues me is really rather in synch with Harris's: To what extent is the bear movement a genuine exploration and celebration of "masculinity" versus a new set of pathways and mechanisms of masculine drag, of hiding our "femininity"? To what extent is bearness more about fashion than substance? If you change the fashion of what used to be called "the Castro Street clone," is there anything left that can really be subculturally distinguished or otherwise identified? Likewise, with bears, if you remove the buzz cuts and flat tops, goatees and stubble beards, tight shirts, bulk, and body hair, is there anything more elemental and uniting that can be identified? For my other half, Arnie, a de facto bear, there are tangential questions: for example and especially, to what extent has the bear subculture arisen in response to the "twink" predominance of greater gay culture?

I will end this with my own answer about what the bear movement is: it's all of these things and others we can't yet see. The bear movement is really this ragtag composite of all these different types and fashions and preferences, intersecting with larger social and cultural and political and historical trends that aren't yet in focus. There are many whose exploration and celebration of their "masculinity" seems healthy and natural. There are others in and with whom it seems more cosmetic, forced, compensatory. And there are others for whom bearness has little or nothing to do with gender. Can we make any even tentative generalizations? We can, but few or even none will endure. Time will keep revising them.

## NOTES

1. Stevens, June, et al., "The Effect of Age on the Association Between Body Mass Index and Mortality," *The New England Journal of Medicine* 338:1 (January 1, 1998): 1-53.

2. Jane Brody, "New Guide Puts Most Americans on the Fat Side," *The New York Times*, June 9, 1998, p. F7.

3. Shute, Nancy, et al., "The New Truth About Fat," cover story, *U.S. News and World Report*, January 12, 1998, pp. 9-21.

4. Brody, op cit. See also Willett, Walter C., et al., "Primary Care: Guidelines for Weight," *New England Journal of Medicine* 341:6 (August 5, 1999): 427-434.

5. Patrick Carnes, *Out of the Shadows*, Center City, MN: Hazelden, 1992.

6. Daniel Harris, *The Rise and Fall of Gay Culture*, New York: Hyperion, 1997.

7. Wayne Koestenbaum, *The Queen's Throat: Opera, Homosexuality, and the Mystery of Desire*, New York: Random House, 1994.

## Chapter 2

# Fat Is a Bearish Issue

### Laurence Brown

Like all texts that break new ground, that gem of bearology *The Bear Book* left certain key areas for future exploration. I want to meditate upon two of those areas in this chapter: the huge question (pun fully intended) of fat and size as an issue within gay culture and its interaction with the parameters of beardom; and, more prosaic, to bring in a British, and specifically London-oriented perspective on this whole relationship as I have seen it develop over the last twenty years. Too much theory is dreary and denies the erotic which "gay liberation" sought to find in everyday life; but a certain amount, enlivened with history—*bearstory*—and a touch of raunch is good for the mind and does no harm to the soul. So what follows is a combination of three elements: my personal erotic history—not blow by blow (too pornographic) but in terms of confronting forbidden desire; an outline history—as far as I can piece it together—of chubby (and bear) groups in England (Scotland is, as they say, another country); and some discussion and theory of bears, sizeism, and the beauty of big men. I want to say something about the eroticization of the male body and, in particular, the voluptuous and fleshy male body of forbidden desire. Why are chunky men so desirable yet the desire so forbidden? A few gripes about bearworld are thrown in for good measure.

One of my aims is to get back to some of the roots of gay liberation and reexamine them and, as the gay pioneers used to say, the personal is political. I take that as justification for giving you my take on beardom. Let me say at once that I am quite a small man: about five-feet-six-inches tall and around 140 pounds. Not chubby

I; but a bear? I guess so, being dark and rather hairy. An American once described me as a "stoat," which I find laughable. I prefer to say: a medium-sized bear. But I digress. My entry into the bear world was from a particular angle. Back in the mid-1980s I first identified as a "chubby-chaser": a man who, whatever his own size, feels desire for men who are defined by our culture (both mainstream and gay) as fat, "overweight," "chubby," or (most insultingly) "obese." This realization dawned upon me gradually as a kind of second coming out. It was only through attending a chubby and chubby-chasers group in London that I met people who used the term "bear" and began to have some comprehension of its meaning and usage. At that stage, chubbies, chasers, and bears met indiscriminately (promiscuously?) in a couple of chubby-friendly pubs (one of which is best known for the older age-range of its clientele). Only later did I learn of the existence of bear groups, bear magazines, and the whole panoply of beardom. And, in the final stage, I joined the London group called Bearhug jointly with my lover (a beautiful, chubby young man) about two years ago. To understand and explain this development, we need to regress still further, like Freudians, into childhood.

## *JOURNEY INTO THE PSYCHE OF A CHUBBY-CHASER*

When I was a small child I would sometimes stay at home on a Saturday afternoon and, while Mum was in the kitchen and Dad was at work, I would be watching TV. The usual Saturday fare was sports, but there is only one sport I recollect watching: wrestling. I would be transfixed at the sight of two big, fat, magnificent men grunting, sweating, and throwing each other around that ring. I'm sure you can picture the seven-year-old boy kneeling on a back-to-front armchair, rubbing up against the broad chair-back fascinated by the sight of these powerful, manly giants as he breathlessly experiences all sorts of novel sensations. These were among my earliest erotic experiences. The point is that my gay sexuality and an attraction to big men emerged hand in hand while I was little more than a toddler.

Becoming aware of my gay sexuality as a growing teenager was not a problem as it enabled me and my flamboyant best chum, Nicholas, to consider ourselves part of a misunderstood elite. No, the problem lay in discovering that Nic and apparently all other normal queers (yes, we used the word back then in England in the late 1960s) lusted after slender younger boys while my desires were set on chunky older youths and men. A rotund, baby-faced English teacher who used to take us swimming gave rise to many fantasies of shared cubicles at the baths; another fine figure of a man who would appear in school in his sports kit, rugby ball beneath his arm, meaty thighs chafing under tight-fitting shorts, was the only attraction I could see in that sport. But even hinting at these desires was to invite gentle ridicule from Nic and Co. And my reading of my authors, Oscar Wilde and the Greek classics, made it abundantly clear that a slender, hairless youth is the proper object of homosexual love. Already conventional cultural assumptions had begun to bite. It was all too clear: I was the queerest of the queer.

Cut to Boston 1980. In my twenties, I am wide-eyed and full of excitement visiting the United States for the first time. My friends, a gay couple, Hal and Kris, have brought me to a huge Sunday night disco called Boston Boston. What was big in discos back in the heady pre-AIDS days of 1980? Grace Jones singing "I Need a Man"? Whatever. Some such glorious torch song is pumping out as I spot a man I think staggeringly beautiful. Dry-mouthed, I confide to one of my pals, "That's the kind of guy I really fancy." He looks at me open-mouthed and calls over to his boyfriend, "Hey, Kris, see that enormous fuckin' guy over there? *That's* what Laurence likes." And they both regard me with a kind of horrified awe. My confidence feels betrayed. Here I am among my own kind, having only struggled out two or three years before—and they are ridiculing me in their ignorance, unable to accept the object of my desire. As the song says, "Love don't need a reason."

In the early 1980s, concepts such as "chubby-chasers" or "bears" were, to my knowledge, totally unheard-of here. In fact, we were, like all gay communities, struggling to come to terms with the terrors of the epidemic that had suddenly hit our liberated young world of hedonism. The region I gravitated toward in my search for a comfortable berth within our community (and, small as it was, it did feel more like a community then) was of course the land of leather. The leathermen's world, in London centered round the famous Coleherne pub in Earl's Court and the Cellar Bar at Heaven, was redolent with images of manliness and power, where big-bellied or hairy or older guys and rough-looking men with tattoos or a hippie look could feel reasonably at ease, and so could those like me who desired them. The look and smell of leather and rubber began to appeal to me. And I teetered on the brink of the fascinating, if zany, world of SM. But I never really liked pain or submitting my will to another's for more than five minutes. The recurring feature in my sex life was always my love for big men, men of size, men with big bellies and broad shoulders and open, baby faces, whether hairy, bearded, or not, I really didn't mind. And like the reverse of the coin, with it came the astonished reactions of certain "friends" to the objects of my affection. Instance: quite a close friend saying, "Do you really fancy these fat men you go for, Laurence, or are they all you can get?" With friends like that, who needs homophobes? Interesting, isn't it, how we all tend to assume that the objects of our desire are intrinsically and objectively beautiful and that others who cannot see the attraction are weird or lacking in aesthetic sense?

But mine is not a nature to be oppressed by such attitudes for long. I began to feel that identifying as a leatherman was not only restrictive (not that I don't still crave and enjoy the feel of leather and rubber from time to time) but also in some sense a kind of closet, a skin within which to hide another skin. At some point in the mid-1980s, a point I cannot exactly locate, I became aware that there was a group called cryptically "C. and C.C.s" meeting weekly upstairs in an otherwise straight pub in Notting Hill Gate, a trendy area of West London, not so far from Earl's Court. Those initials (standing for "Chubbies and Chubby-Chasers") appeared chalked on a blackboard at the foot of the stairs of a side entrance of the pub. The upstairs room was like a friendly old-fashioned drinking club, and the clientele could hardly have been more different from the appearance-conscious attitudinizing crowd of leather bars I was used to. So it was friendly and welcoming, though for me far from raunchy. Most of the men were overweight, middle-aged to elderly, and unfashionably dressed. Personal presentation was not at a premium, probably because these were guys who had been made to feel unwanted and undesirable on the "scene." Some of them might have been highly presentable if groomed, e.g., for the leather scene, but they mostly lacked the self-confidence or desire to try it. On my first visit I met a friendly and charming writer with whom I became friends, and who has sadly since died. But I never picked anyone up there. The ambience was, in British camp jargon, decidedly "naff." If I wanted sex—and boy, did I want sex!—I went back to the leather scene, to bars like the Block and the Coleherne pub. There were always fat and/or hairy men in leather who looked raunchy and confident and were fully integrated into the leather scene.

Then in 1987 I came out, as a chaser. *Gay Times,* both then and now the leading monthly magazine for our community in Britain, published a two-page feature by me titled *Talking Big* and using as its epigraph Julius Caesar's words as written by the Bard, "Let me have men about me that are fat." To my knowledge, it was the first time the subject had been broached in the British gay press. It was fairly lighthearted but made serious points about sizeism (and that period was the high point of "isms") and the wide variety of sexual desire. But although I pointed out that "it's not fatness that's the problem but prejudice against fatness" the two illustrations provided by the magazine were drawings of a group of fat guys looking mostly cheery and pretty ugly. The culture continues to see fat men as funny, happy souls to be laughed at, or at best *with*—but never desired.

## *BEARSTORY/CHUBSTORY*

And then from 1990 slowly, almost imperceptibly, the ice began to melt. The first Girth and Mirth U.K. newsletter appeared that year, advertising regular Wednesday evening socials of the group for "bears, chasers, and friends" at a pub hidden in a little alleyway in London's West End called The Empire. I have good memories of those Wednesdays and Saturdays, which were a transitional stage from the naffness that was passing to the glorious raunchiness to come.

And then came Bulk. Around the middle of 1992 a new club was started in London which revolutionized the whole chubs and bears scene. Instead of a pub evening this was a late-night raunchy disco club with its own mascot, a drawing of a chubby, sexy young man called Bumper, and its own newsletter, *Bulk Delivery*. At its Thursday evening club nights in a large murky club in Islington there were good, up-to-date DJs, video screens showing Sumo wrestling and the world's strongest man competition (have you seen those gorgeous hulks?), and with good looking sexy fat guys in leather or rubber on the door and the coat check. Later, there was also a backroom area. The result was that when chubbies or chasers came into the club they at once felt wanted and desirable. This was progress. Despite several moves and a change of ownership, Bulk is still big in London and attracts huge numbers of all types of guys, but especially the big and horny. Needless to say, it's my favorite club, and the one where I met my lover. Doesn't life constantly surprise us?

In April 1993, *Him* magazine, *G.T.*'s raunchier sister, brought out a special issue (which I treasure) called "Double the Fun," on which I am proud to have collaborated. Its cover showed a pair of sexy, chubby twins, sweet-faced, tattooed guys in their twenties, back to back and wearing smiles and rubber. There were more pictures of them together inside in various raunchy poses, with articles on the beauty of fat men. My own piece was "A Chubbies Lexicon," from A for "abnormal load" to Z for "zeppelin." And just as in the 1980s almost everyone seemed to be into leather, thanks to Bulk in the 1990s being big and bearish became fashionable on the London gay scene. A little quarterly magazine from 1995 called *Big Boys and Buddies* shows that "chubbies and teds" were meeting at the Empire pub, and advertised meetings of Bear Club U.K. and Bearhug as well as Bulk. Meanwhile we were becoming more aware of the wider European scene with the indomitable Girth and Mirth Belgium club having been founded mid-1990, publishing its lively, often sexy A5 [roughly equivalent to U.S. 8.5″ × 11″ format, *LKW*] newsletter *The Fat Angel Times* from November of that year. The chubby had landed.

## *FAT THEORY*

Fat is not only a bear's issue; it is a queer issue. If the significance of queer, as distinct from gay, is its inclusiveness, its broader radicality, its aim to spread the aura of our community over wider issues of gender and cross-sexuality, then it must surely also embrace the issue of size and the prejudices against it. If to be fat is (sometimes) to be made a "figure" of fun, then to be a chaser is to have your deepest sexual desires ridiculed, when that which you find awesomely beautiful is dismissed as pathetically ugly, sweaty, smelly, untouchable. While muscle is taken as a sign of power, an enhancement of masculinity, fat is considered a signifier of ridicule, asexuality, and lack of self-discipline and self-respect.

However, as I am well qualified to state as a chaser, there is rarely any lack of competition for the attentions of self-confident chubbies in most settings. Moreover, when the lights go down in the back room, many of those who have avoided or even ridiculed big men suddenly sense an irresistible attraction to the object of their "official" distaste. There are several reasons for this: (a) gay men, especially when young, are loath to admit to any attraction or desire which may be risible to their friends, so hold back their true needs until they believe themselves to be out of sight; (b) such men are often hiding their true feelings even from themselves and find their inhibitions released only within back rooms and in open air nighttime cruising; and (c) there are chasers whose major thrill is derived from a sadistic desire to humiliate the fat objects of their desire, presumably due to an unresolved self-hatred ("You're so fat and unattractive you should be honored to take whatever I choose to impose on you"). This appalling attitude is, needless to say, extremely destructive to the self-esteem of those big men who unfortunately lay themselves open to it and is another aspect of the two-faced "backroom-chaser." No doubt this unacceptable behavior can be partly attributed to the conformist and oppressive attitudes of society.

But this very oppression, as all queers instinctively know, creates its own aura, its own mystique. There is a unique and powerful excitement about forbidden, transgressive desires and behavior, dreams, and longings that transgress the strongly-policed bounds of the known, the acceptable, the conventionally doable in our society. Dreaming beyond those bounds is itself an aphrodisiac; acting beyond them is liberation. All the theorizing of Dennis Altman[1] and Guy Hocqenghem[2] in those heady early 1970s days of gay liberation can equally be applied to the bear cult and fat-desire. Loving men beyond the boundaries of conventional stereotypes—*because* rather than in spite of it—is an aspect of our liberation, of finding and celebrating ourselves. But what is it that makes fat men suckable, fuckable, beautiful? What particular aspects and characteristics can we isolate and drool over lubriciously?

## ICONS AND IMAGES OF FAT-DESIRE

### The Fat Bastard

This is a very British phrase which will not, I suspect, travel transatlantically. [Since the commercial success of the film *Austin Powers: The Spy Who Shagged Me* (1999), Americans have become very familiar with this, as a concept of ridicule, *LKW.*] But it's a phrase that certainly turns me on. What is a fat bastard? A beer-swilling, working-class lad (blue collar to you), probably skinhead, who wears Ben Sherman shirts and weighs at least sixteen stone (multiply that by fourteen to know the number of pounds). He has a cockney or other regional accent and a very cheeky grin. He has a hard stare but, like all chubbies, soft contours. He loves football and going out with his mates. This type is partially culturally specific, but there are American equivalents (I speak from experience). Of course, when you see a man who perfectly meets this image and speak to him, he may reply in a high, camp voice or in a register that speaks of Oxford or Harvard. But life is a series of compromises between icons and realities and we are speaking here only of the former.

### The Adult Baby

This has nothing to do with age but is about shape and smoothness. This is a man whose rounded chubbiness, large shaven head, and smooth skin have a babylike quality. There is clearly some overlap here with the previous image. Such a look has a certain innocence and freshness which is very appealing, even touching. One imagines the personality to be open, honest, even naive. While showing babylike properties one knows this is very much a man with youthful adult potency and testosterone in abundance. (Excuse me while I take a short break for relief.) Being smooth-skinned and largely hairless, this icon is the furthest removed from bear images, but there are many gradations falling between the two.

## The Chubby, Furry Bear

At the other end of the spectrum, being abundantly hairy, big-bodied, and weighty, this image is the perfect crossover, straddling both camps Girth and Mirth and beardom. He would be considered too overweight to be one of the new, somewhat suspect breed of glamour bears[3] but his furry cuddliness would appeal to a broad cross section and such men frequently appear in the pages of both bears' and big men's magazines.

## The Big-Bellied Daddy

This is an older man, at least forty and probably over fifty—mature, fatherly, heavily built, often balding, ripe with experience and paternal care. He may or may not be hairy, but his substantial size, like his age, indicate strength and reliability. As a daddy figure, he tends to appeal in particular to younger men in search of the fantasy father who loves and chastises with kindness and strength. This is a remarkably potent icon which seems to possess an almost spiritual intensity. It is also a healthy counterbalance to the ludicrous cult of youth with which Western society is obsessed.

## The Heavy Hippie

I use the term "hippie" very loosely. This type is unkempt or wild looking, probably bearded, close to one of the frequent images of bearishness (at least before glamour bears became all the rage). He's fat because he's natural, unconcerned about conventional standards of body image. He'll probably have an unusual hairstyle (unusual for a contemporary gay man, that is), long, 1970s style or shaven with a topknot; its very unconventionality carries a sexual charge. He may well have tattoos and piercings also, and is probably in his forties, so he's a kind of uncle to the Tattooed Fat-Boy archetype (described later). In the dreamworld of archetypes, he's a truck driver or an ex-con who does odd jobs and cultivates an allotment or even a poet (in fact, he bears a distinct resemblance to the great Walt Whitman). In real life, he might be an academic, but it's unlikely that he could be in one of the status-driven professions. He's an oddball, with hidden masculine power, though sexually he might be quite passive, an image of that which is desired and made love to. A potent stereotype.

## *The Bulky Leatherman*

This image of a mighty masculine man in full leathers, big belly peeping out though the zip of his black leather jacket, suggesting shades of SM mastery, is a hangover from the now rather dated world of leather/SM from which many of us emerged (largely unscathed) in the last decade. When bears were but cubs in their den and Girth and Mirth was a rhyme yet unsung, the leather world permitted and acknowledged the attraction and potency of men of size and weight, hairiness and, indeed, maturity. We should not forget our debt to the leathermen, even if like former devotees we are now amused by their quaint antics and costumes.

## *The Enormous Softie*

This is a huge, cuddly blancmange-like chubby, something like the Michelin man made of tires (called "Bibendum" in some European countries), sometimes with features that would be considered conventionally plain or even ugly. Culturally, in Western society, this figure is considered at best laughable, at worst grotesque; Sergeant Bilko's best pal is a case in point. He's assumed to be greasy and unattractive, but why shouldn't he be considered cute? The French have the apt term *beau-laid,* which I free translate as "ugly-sexy." In Japanese culture, the Sumo wrestler, who has much in common with this stereotype, is exalted and admired as a symbol of purity and strength. Again shades of the Adult Baby arise. The attraction seems to come from the contradiction between enormous physical power and a look of childlike innocence. Interestingly, in an interview, Phil Silvers (who played Sergeant Bilko) has commented on an instance when, to his astonishment, an attractive young woman was drawn to his very fat colleague. Sumo wrestlers, on the other hand, are expected to live in a monastic community. One can therefore only speculate upon their sex lives, and readers so inclined are free to spend some happy hours doing so.

### The Tattooed Fat Boy

I have adapted this rubric from the phrase "tattooed lover boy" which has been used for a (nonchubbies) club night in London. I use it as an indication of "pervy" body decoration of all types, which have recently become super cool among younger people in Britain and Europe, especially tattoos and body piercings. While ten years ago only guys heavily into SM would dream of having a pierced tongue or a Prince Albert, these accoutrements are now almost fashionable. The fat young stud with tattoos and piercings became a symbol in the early days of the Bulk club in London, epitomized by the cartoon character Bumper. This interlinking of fat with diverse, slightly risqué sexualities certainly helped to make big men raunchy. It also plugs into the underlying linkage between fat-desire and transgressive needs and behavior. If what you desire is considered forbidden anyway, why not go for broke by doubling the perversity?

### The Bulky Muscleman

This is an icon that verges on cheating as it idolizes an ideal of masculine super strength which would not necessarily be ridiculed or condemned (if only through physical fear!) by conventional society. Here a large proportion of body weight is in the form of muscle, not fat; but sheer immensity brings these guys into our orbit. When they are hairy also, they are known to my lover and me as muscle bearies, and are a species of glamour bear, usually considering themselves too grand to condescend to consort with mere mortal bears and chasers. But that's where you belong, baby! The *locus classicus* of such types, and something surely most chubby-chasers/bear-lovers love to watch, is the "World's Strongest Man Competition," involving (mostly) blond Scandinavian demigods of enormous bulk and magnificent musculature. Their sweating and straining as they drag a truck single-handed, attached to them by a leather harness, has powerfully erotic overtones. It is interesting how the televised competition always emphasizes the presence and support of these men's long-suffering wives and girlfriends in case the viewer might assume that such an obsession with the strength and grandeur of men's bodies might be linked to homoerotic desire. And where masculinity is stretched to such beauteous extremes can that be wrong?

## *The Male/Female Body of Voluptuousness*

The fat male body possesses a voluptuous sensuality which, in the Western cultural tradition, can only be compared with the fleshy sensuousness of Peter Paul Rubens' women. Why is our age and culture so frightened of fat? Is it because fat *is* in fact sensuous, voluptuous, desirable? Straight men are clearly afraid of big women because they are more powerful, more confident, and more sensual; hence the popularity of painfully skinny super models. But why should gay culture follow the images of beauty and desirability portrayed and pushed by the straight media? We should not, but we cannot help but be influenced by them. Which brings me back to the voluptuous male body. It's invidious to pick out any particular body parts—all are beautiful as parts of the whole—but there are two particular features of the sensual male form which are especially relevant to our analysis of fat-attraction. These are: (a) *the breasts and nipples of desire* and (b) *the sensuous belly of pregnancy*. I pick out these features, rather than gorgeous upper arms and glorious tree-trunk thighs, much as I adore them both, because they are crossovers from the more usual images of the female form and point to a possible theory that in its massive sensuality the body of the fat man combines the traditional strengths of the male form with certain voluptuous features associated in our subconscious with the female. Nothing is more sexually arousing to a chaser than the fleshy tits and darkly-aureoled nipples of a full-figured chubby and nothing is more characteristic of such a man than his well-rounded and pregnant-seeming tummy.

## Chubbies, Bears, and Leathermen

These, then, are my ten archetypal icons of fat desire, which I should love to see illustrated by any bear artists of distinction. There is clearly a considerable overlap between these images and other archetypes of both bears and leathermen, this last being the world from which many of us have emerged during the last decade. In fact, the three zones might be depicted as three overlapping circles, like the circles of the Olympic games, with a small area shared by all three.

The area of overlap and of identification between fat boys and bears is debatable. They are clearly not identical, or as English lawyers say, "on all fours" (appealing as such an image of a bear might be). In fact most of the above icons, apart from the Chubby, Furry Bear and the Heavy Hippie, can easily be unbearish in the sense of lacking beards and body hair. Then again, all could comfortably fit Les Wright's definition of a bear in his introduction to *The Bear Book* as "a gay man who is as comfortable being a man as he is being gay." To some extent, the historical development of the bear movement and of the big men's movement has been separate, as a longer, historical study would show. Bears groups can develop a kind of cliquishness that tends to exclude the clean-shaven or nonhairy and, falling back on those social prejudices we are trying to get beyond, may also exclude the very fat (those condemned by society as "obese"). Indeed, having just attended a Big and Bear Weekend in Amsterdam I am aware of the relativity of size and of how easy it is to say, "I love fat men. Ah, but not as fat as *that*," partly under the influence of social disapproval. A man perceived as a chubby in one context may be a medium-sized bear in another. In the same way, some chubbies may be seen as too camp or "fem" to be accepted as bears. Yet this is paradoxical, as many bearish characteristics, nurturing/nourishing qualities and loyalty, for example, have traditionally been regarded as female (as has been pointed out before).

Another point of contrast between the two movements may lie in the nature of desire. Among bears, desire tends to follow the *twin model* of attraction, i.e., bears (typically though not always) are drawn to each other as twins or long-lost brothers, like attracting like, to form a double image of beardom. In the realms of Girth and Mirth, a convenient and widely utilized term despite its possibly patronizing connotations of fatness equalling jollity, the common usage of the terms "chubby" and "chaser" demonstrates the *magnetic model* of attraction whereby the slim-to-medium-build chaser is drawn ineluctably to the man of weight and vice versa, thus completing a complementary whole. Thus fat-desire is seen as based in the attraction of opposites and bear-desire in the attraction of likes.

But in real life neither of these models holds very much water. Bears come in all sorts of shapes and sizes with every permutation of interest between them. And in the world of Girth and Mirth there are many chubby chubby-chasers, i.e., fat guys who are mainly or wholly attracted to other fat guys, as I (a smallish chaser) have good reason to know. There is also in existence, in the United States, if not in Europe, a movement based on "gain/encouragement" consisting of slim men ("gainers") who wish to become fat, and partners ("encouragers") whose task and pleasure is to feed them and develop their bellies. This is a movement which it is tempting for me as a European to dismiss as an American fad, disturbing and even health-threatening in its aims. Nonetheless it indicates how some slim chasers wish to emulate the objects of their desire and thus illustrates the age-old paradox of attraction as it moves between *to have* and *to be*. Having been irritated in past years by being called "skinny," I now revel in having put on some weight, and thus, feeling a little more similar to the objects of my desires, I can appreciate to a small extent the nature of the "gain" movement.

Despite these areas of potential conflict between beardom and Girth and Mirth, the two can and should coexist and mingle. In the contemporary London scene there is very considerable overlap in membership between Bulk and Bearhug (the two major relevant clubs), and the annual Big and Bear Weekend which my partner/husbear and I have just attended in Amsterdam was an excellent example of camaraderie between big men, chasers, and bears.

Many of us owe a debt to the leather world, which provided a haven before we discovered bears/chubbydom. The two worlds have something else in common, an ease shared by leathermen and bears in relation to their sexuality and a lack of hang-ups around jealousy and possessiveness which are much harder to find in other areas of the gay world. There may be a lot the straight world too can learn from us about the nature of relationships; in particular about how to combine emotional loyalty with a negotiated degree of sexual freedom—but here I embark on another topic that requires an essay of its own.

With regard to the leather world now, there is considerable variation between European cities. In Amsterdam, for example, there is still a lot of interaction between bears, chubbies, and leather simply because the leather scene makes up a large proportion of the gay world (the famous Warmoesstraat alone has at least five leather bars). But in London, where the realm of leather shrank substantially to a committed nucleus during the 1990s, it is less common to see men in leather at Bulk or Bearhug events. Indeed, while the leatherman/clone remains the major archetype of the Amsterdam gay scene and the handsome/pretty boy seems predominant in Paris, in London, due to the success of these clubs and to the ever-changing nature of this city in general as the "style capital" of Europe, bears and men of (moderate) weight are now becoming increasingly fashionable and desirable, especially in the shapes of fat bastards and tattooed fat boys. Perhaps we are beginning to win the fight against fat discrimination and sizeism. But if and when the struggle has been won, will fat-desire still be as strong when it is no longer transgressive?

## *GRIPES ABOUT BEARDOM*

As I near the end of this piece, in which I realize I have concentrated far more on fat issues than on British bear history (which will have to await another time), I want to briefly raise a few gripes and grumbles about the world of bears so as not to end on a complacent note.

1. Why do we see so few black and Asian bears and chubbies? This is certainly true of events in England and I suspect it is true throughout Europe and, possibly, the United States. Could it be that the racism existing in the wider society is reflected in our own worlds? And, if so, what can we do about it? Do our definitions of bears, chubbies, and chasers need to be broadened?

2. What is the relationship between our worlds and dykedom, the world of (gay/lesbian) women? Sometimes I have detected a degree of sexism, even misogyny, among some bears—hardly surprising as it exists in the wider world, but it is still something we need to address. How?

3. Body fascism, that dreadful obsession of our culture with the slim, hard, usually hairless, young body as the image of (male/female) beauty, is something we are proud to be fighting against, but it takes many forms. As a small man I have sometimes felt excluded from big men's groups and, as mentioned above, often bear groups exclude or marginalize those who are hairless or perceived as too fat. We should aim for inclusiveness, for that brotherliness which is the essence of beardom, which recognizes the beauty of the male not only in glamour bears but in the male body in all its shapes and sizes. Which is why, as I said before, fat is a bearish issue.

*Postscript:* This chapter has raised many more issues than it can answer. Do we need a further sequel to *The Bear Book* to explore these and related questions of size and sizeism in the gay world, perhaps with a title like *Girth, Mirth, and Meaning*? Think about it.

## NOTES

1. See, in particular, Dennis Altman: *Homosexual Oppression and Liberation,* published 1971 (New York: Avon), a powerful exposition of the liberationist politics of the time.

2. Guy Hocquenghem: *Homosexual Desire,* published in French in 1972 and in English by Duke University Press (Durham, NC), 1993; a highly intellectual Gallic interpretation which I confess I find practically unreadable.

3. "Glamor bears" are described by Les Wright in *The Bear Book,* pages 8 and 9.

Chapter 3

# Bear Youth: An Interview with Brian Kearns, Bear Youth Webmaster

**Les:** I find it always best to begin at the beginning. Could you tell me a few basic statistics—your name, place of residence, age, profession, and the like?

**Brian:** My name is Brian Kearns. I'm from Whitby, Ontario (less than an hour's drive east of Toronto), will be living in Toronto to begin studying interior design in the fall, and am currently staying in Toronto while I work. I'm nineteen years old and I work in retail (a dollar store), not too exciting. Other than being the Webmaster for Bear Youth [www.bearyouth.org] I'm not currently involved with any gay or bear groups or clubs.

**Les:** You are based in Canada. What is life like where you live as an openly gay man?

**Brian:** Well, growing up in Whitby there was a small gay community in the area, enough for a gay youth group to form, and a couple of gay bars. However, in high school I didn't have any gay friends, but I was out during my last two years of school, twelve to thirteen (OAC—university prep year). Being out in school was all right. I can't say I was harassed but I still ran into homophobia, and some people had a difficult time believing I'm gay. I got involved with a gay youth group when I was seventeen—the LGBYD (Lesbian Gay Bisexual Youth of Durham Region). However, the group was not very well organized, and it collapsed from a lack of management. Local gay bars have always been good about letting younger people in, most of the time, since there is no place else outside the big cities for gays. Of course even in places like Toronto most of the gay teens I know always did end up getting into the gay bars and clubs. Most everyone from the main Toronto Gay Youth Group had fake ID. Simply, gay teens don't have many places to go, and few places cater to the crowd. The youth groups that exist usually don't keep many permanent members as they tend to form their own smaller group of friends and get bored of the discussions about coming out and other repetitive topics. I don't have to worry about ID now that I'm of age, but it would be nice all the same to have had someplace to go where ID wasn't an issue when I was younger. Now, of course, the only gay bar in town is a lesbian bar and it's not very popular with the younger crowd. I guess that happens in smaller cities and towns. Of course those who have cars and the money do go into Toronto as much as they can. It beats sticking around in the suburbs where there's little to do and only one good, small, barely decent club that's in the middle of practically nowhere. In case I sound confusing, there is one gay bar and one gay club near where I live outside of Toronto. In Toronto, of course, there is a lot more to do, and even bear clubs. The Gen-X bear club is rather nice—it draws on younger members while still including the older ones when possible. I haven't had the chance to participate much with the Toronto bear community, but I'm only nineteen and I'm sure that will probably change soon.

**Les:** When, where, how did you first come out as a gay man?

**Brian:** I came out to myself in the middle of elementary school. By grade four I was sure I had feelings for guys, but it wasn't until grade five that I could accept that I didn't have any for girls. Once I came to terms with the fact that I couldn't be straight I was fully accepting of my sexuality, but became really frustrated feeling like I couldn't come out until I had some independence and security in my life. It made school more difficult knowing I was gay, especially when all my friends started dating and talking about girls. I got through it, but not without some suspicion along the way. During high school I tried to get in contact with a local youth group, but I found it difficult (as I mentioned the group was badly managed) and it wasn't until a year later that I went to a meeting (that was in May of 1997). Fortunately, I had finally gotten on the Internet, found out more info about the local gay community and the youth group that was difficult to get any other way. Of course earlier that year I had come out to one other person in a bizarre "I know you know that I know you're gay" manner, which was interesting to say the least. That person was a friend of the family who was around nineteen or twenty and was staying at my parents' place and liked to monopolize the computer (which was frustrating) and found some gay material on it. I cannot say it went bad, he kept it to himself, and from then on I started coming out to other family members. Of course, I might also mention that before I even came out to myself, I remember when I was six thinking that I sure liked bears (my teddy bears anyhow, I had a few) more than girls. I was not sure about boys then, but I guess that is because I didn't have anyone to point out to me how some guys are bearish and that it was okay, normal, and safe to like boys. I was too young to understand what being gay or sexuality was all about, and how it could eventually override my socialization to like girls. I feel that I have always been gay, but just did not know I was not straight. That was something I had to realize on my own.

**Les:** I found you while surfing the Net via the Bear Youth site. How and when did it come into existence?

**Brian:** I first heard about bears by searching the Internet for a description of the type of man I admired. (Yes, I found out about bears from an adult site.) Much to my surprise I discovered that I was not alone in liking beards and body hair and even bigger built guys, bears existing as a gay subculture. It was sure enlightening, as I had not really allowed myself to believe that nonstereotypical gay images of men existed. As I seemed to fit into most of the stereotypes myself, and that I could actually have a chance at finding a guy who I was sexually attracted to, was relieving and rewarding. It was strange growing up with the idea I might not be able to find sexual satisfaction, being gay or straight, if I could not find a gay guy that was my type.

Not being a bear myself, and only being a teenager, I did not feel like I fit into the traditional bear culture. Nor did I feel like my tastes fit into traditional gay culture. I was too far away from Toronto to enjoy what the gay community had to offer, and too young to get involved with the bear community. I wanted to find someplace where I could fit in—when I couldn't do that, I created one. That's when I opened a free Web page account and starting making a personal page including a section on bears, which later grew into a separate page which I called Bear Youth. That would have been in 1997. I tried to bring some supportive resources and some basic Net communications to the site, along with some info on what bears were about, and provide some basic resources. In mid-1998 I became frustrated with the limitations of the Web hosting service for Bear Youth and posted a request on the Bear Youth page for hosting assistance. To my luck, Rick A. Clark of CCubed Webhosting and design (www.ccubed.net) (his personal page is <www.desertbear.com>) replied and set up (<www.bearyouth.org>), all expenses paid. I owe him a lot of thanks for that because he allowed me to improve the Bear Youth site and its visibility on the Net.

**Les:** What work, activities, connections are involved with your being the Bear Youth Webmaster? (Are you a strict or a gentle Webmaster?!)

**Brian:** I've set up a lot of different features and track down information links and all sorts of things for the site. I've learned a great deal about the Internet and html being a Webmaster. I try to make sure the page looks good while not overextending myself. I've been limited at times by school and now by work as to how much I can put into the site. However, I work on it now and then, to ensure that it is always up to date, and bug free. I always have some plans as to how to improve and build new parts to the site. The galleries take up a lot of time. I've only added them within the last few months, and they've proven to be popular, as has the Yahoo club which is an easier means to chat and message than the mailing list I also created, which is used mostly just for announcing site updates. The message board is also popular and to a lesser degree the ICQ list, which allows fellow bear youth to display ICQ info. I like to think I'm doing a good job. I earned a lot of praise for the site, which makes it all worth the effort. Of course, what I enjoy the most is seeing other young people finding the bear youth resources helpful, and seeing them enjoy the page.

**Les:** The bear youth of today would represent the third generation of bears (following the 1980s convergence and the rise of Generation X-ers). How do bear youth of today identify as bears, particularly in a gay subculture which, like earlier generations of the leather community, tended to attract over-thirty-fives?

**Brian:** One thing I find with young bear culture is we haven't yet started any large-scale clubs. To me, I'm not a true bear, at least in the physical sense. But I do indeed fit into the bear community in my own way. I cannot say I can speak for everyone who's under twenty and identifies with the community, but I can give you my view on it. I find bears in general just trying to find an identity, and more people being attracted to bear ideas than the identity that bears are trying to create. Every group of friends and every group of bears seems to have its own unique set of issues and things it identifies with. Running a Web site just for bear youth, I really can focus my own bear ideas to a more specific group of people; of course, I can't control who actually does and doesn't visit the site. Like many other young people, we are going through the tribulations of school, coming out, and some of us moving out and becoming adults. It's difficult and confusing—a time when you find yourself, and gain a better sense of your individuality. Perhaps it's bizarre to find a common identity or to try and fit into one when we are all individuals. Of course, not everyone has the same interests. We don't even all have the same sense of what it means to be a bear, yet want to retain a sense of masculinity (or perhaps not trying to deny what is to be a man while still being gay) and be able to be accepted for the characteristics that set us apart from the general gay community. A lot of what happens among my generation is far from unique and certainly much of what the youth of today are going through has happened to the earlier generation of bears. The Gen-Xers have played a big part in influencing me and, I suppose, others of my generation—the supposed "Echo Generation," or whatever else they like to call us. A lot of young bears of my age have Gen-X friends and certainly share some of their taste in music. We're not that far apart, but what separates us most is the impact of the changes in politics and the media that are the result of decades of struggle for freedom and gay rights. Such change has sparked a growing movement toward acceptance of homosexuality and against tolerating homophobia. I sincerely hope that such movements get stronger and I hope to do what I can to help along the way. Certainly you don't need to be political to be gay, but it is what gives an identity and visibility to the community. Of course, there are things in the gay community that revolve only around sex, but it's far from the only thing. There is the fight against AIDS, social groups, parades, clubs, teams, history, stories, common experiences, and the friendships that are also part of the gay community. Hopefully, youth will be able to find these positive things out in the gay community and hopefully their only exposure to gay culture won't be in gay bars. Thank the Internet god, wherever he is, for at least giving us the Internet.

**Les:** What are some of the problems or issues gay youths—bear youths in their teens or early twenties—face today: in general, in the gay community, in the bear community?

**Brian:** As with the Gen-Xers, I find it is relationships that most people are looking for on the Net. Of course, there are exceptions, but it can be said that young people are more accepting now of their sexuality than ever before, given the higher visibility and acceptance of gays and lesbians. Just trying to decide whether you're straight, bi, or gay is difficult. Accepting your true nature, and not hiding behind a false image that society might have led you to believe is better than being yourself, is difficult. (That's one concept my mom just doesn't understand.) Having a negative body image, or feeling as though you won't be able to find an attractive partner, or that others around you might find your idea of a good-looking partner revolting, is frustrating. One of the interesting things about body image is that if resources like Bear Youth can help promote the idea that body and facial hair is acceptable and even considered sexy, then this will surely have a positive impact on youth who exhibit such characteristics. This could lead to more young men having warmer thoughts about growing a beard and not detesting their body hair.

Some of the more important gay teen issues, of course, are suicide and STDs, topics most gay men are fairly familiar with, as stats have shown that gay teens are more likely to be suicidal. A survey done recently in California suggests that one of the greatest risk factors for STDs in younger men is related to the age of their partner since, for example, men over thirty have a greater chance of having the AIDS virus. This leads into another somewhat controversial issue of young men and teens being attracted to older men. This seems to be more common among bears, as many older men exhibit more dominant bearish features. Of course, this gets more complicated as relationships with large age differences can be difficult—especially since the older generations of gay men have had more difficulty accepting their sexuality and handling relationships. Just trying to sort out what kind of relationship you want to pursue and how open or closed it should be is difficult for gay men, especially us younger guys who haven't had that many relationships, if any at all.

**Les:** I was struck by the fact that there are several "underage" (i.e., under eighteen) self-identifying gay bears who post on the site. What problems and what new avenues of communication and connection have you seen come into existence—by creating a space for bears who otherwise have no voice in their community?

**Brian:** The more people under eighteen who visit Bear Youth, the better. They are the people who I'd most like to bring to this site. I know what it's like to not be out to others and to feel like you do not have a place where you can fit in. The sooner kids, teens, youths, whatever, can find a place where they can be themselves, the better. I've made sure for the sake of the young visitors to include as much information as possible geared primarily to them every step of the way, while still trying to appeal to the slightly older audience. That is why with many of the site's user areas I try to impose age restrictions to keep the site youth-oriented, ages thirteen to twenty-five. I don't mind older people participating in the site user functions, but it can disrupt the atmosphere of the site if I allow older men to try and pick up teens on the message board or in other user feature areas. So, as a youth forum, the youth have to be protected. I know some youth have an interest in older men, however I try to point out to these youth that many of the features they find appealing about older men are common to younger guys too, and that they will probably prefer, in the long run, other younger guys. Of course, deciding what age limit, if any, a teen or man should impose is often difficult and must be determined individually.

I also know that youths are exploring their sexual identity to a large degree at a young age, so I make it a point not to try and hide material that could help them. I agreed with Rick Clark not to put any adult content on the Bear Youth site, and that's fine by me, and safer for teens. After all, most other bear sites do have that type of material anyhow. Adding links to sites that lead to bear magazines, and sites like Bearpress has been questionable, but I believe links to such sites are necessary for anyone who wants to know more about the bear community. Teens are going to find that material anyhow, so I'm not going to compromise all potentially good links because of some questionable material. I shouldn't be the one to control or mediate what youth have access to, that's up to them and their parents. In addition, it is up to the visitor, no matter what their age, to decide what material is appropriate. In some cases, their parents decide for them. For that reason, any site that may not be suitable for minors is identified as such by its link—a red paw if it may have adult material and a blue paw if it does not.

Opening up lines of communication between teens has been important to Bear Youth, and many teens have issues that may not be dealt with elsewhere which they want to use the Bear Youth forum to discuss. For the purpose of being anonymous in such matters, I like to keep Bear Youth open enough for anyone to participate in user features. The site allows for young bears and admirers to get in contact with one another; certainly various visitors have been able to make friends and maybe more. Just making friends with someone who has the same taste, or with whom you share the same issues and problems, is rewarding for a lot of the youth who visit Bear Youth. It's difficult to open yourself up to strangers at first, but the Net tends to be helpful for a lot of people.

**Les:** Could you share a particularly enlightening story (positive or negative) from your experiences on the Bear Youth Web site?

**Brian:** I'm not much for stories, but I have enjoyed getting Bear Youth connected with various Web rings and sites on the Net. I've run into many a snag with some bad Webmasters and met my share of good ones. Of course, I never can seem to keep all the bear youth

Web rings in order, as they just keep growing of their own accord, and sometimes just disappear completely. One of my most favorite Web rings, of course, is the bear ring [<http://www.bearring.org/>] for obvious reasons. One site for youth that I think is phenomenal is the youth resource [<http://www.youthresource.com>], which has lots of great resources and even featured me as one of the "Top 100 Most Influential Gay Teens of 1998," which was great, and a title I hope I can live up to. Even though I never started a gay youth group in my high school, they included me for creating Bear Youth and helping to fill the gap between youth and bears.

**Les:** Is there anything you would like to add?

**Brian:** Hmm. . . . Oh, yes, I have made a personal vow to myself that I'll never do drag, no matter who begs me to. I just like my men's clothing too much to wear something I'm not comfortable with, even if it's just role play. I'm not comfortable with the idea of rejecting my masculinity or pretending to be something I'm not. I hate people assuming I'm straight. I don't want them to assume I'm a transvestite—I don't know how I'd deal with that. I just like being me. I don't know why I added that in, but, oh well. . . . All right, that said, I'd like to thank you for your time and for coming to me with your questions.

## Chapter 4

# By Any Otter Name: The Negative Space of the Bear

### John Milton Hendricks

In issue number 52 of *BEAR* magazine, reader "P.G." from New York shared the following in a letter to the editor:

> Here's my problem: I was in the Dugout bar last Sunday night for the usual six o'clock rowdiness—a bunch of hairy bears in cutoffs and ball caps throwing back beer and cruising the hell out of each other. . . . So, I'm in there trying to join in on the fun with my cutoffs and my ball cap and my beer, and I can't help but notice that I'm registering a big fat nothing on the bear-o-meter. Nobody's slapping my back or cruising the hell out of me or grabbing my ass, and just as I'm wondering what the hell is the deal, my bear-friend Adam, the one taking the motorcycle lessons, tells me that my problem is that I'm not actually a bear, but, rather, an otter.
> An otter?
> Who the hell wants to be an otter? (P.G., *BEAR*, 1998)

P.G. went on to lament the "not very sexy, much less hot!" image of the "frolicsome, waterlogged cowards" in comparison to that of the "dangerous and aggressive" bears. He then asked why there wasn't a magazine for otters, and his friend replied that there was one: "It's just called *National Geographic*." *BEAR* illustrated the joke with a small graphic of its own cover, changing the title from BEAR to OTTER and showing a photograph of an actual sea otter floating on its back. In the place of its classic slogan "Masculinity . . . without the trappings," it now read "Masculinity . . . with a smaller trap." P.G. concluded his letter (headlined "Bitter Otter") as follows:

> I suddenly realized that I was on the outside of the den locking in. So I need some help here. I need to raise my otter awareness. Do Otters belong in Bear clubs? Is there such a thing as an Otter club? Are there special Otter groups and Otter weekends and Mr. Otter Contests? Are there Otter T-shirts and ball caps and coffee mugs and, well, Otter-related products that I can buy? Is there an *OTTER* Magazine? It took me forever to find my group and I don't want to waste any more time finding my sub-group? If I've gotta be an otter, I wanna be on the inside track.

Despite the comic illustration, the editor responded kindly enough, stating that he was "not much on the definitions thing" and that he knew "plenty of bears who spend a good deal of time on their backs, too." He added, "Let's face it—I'm still tryin' to figure out the . . . what the heck's it called . . . 'bear code.' " But *this* reader had a different reaction: I thought I had found my identity in relation to the bears.

It was six years earlier, in 1992, when I picked up my first copy of *BEAR* and was dumbfounded to see portrayed—finally—a physical type of man to which I had long been attracted. A friend and witness of mine calls them "fireplugs" and he's not far wrong: I have often preferred the gut over the muscle, the stocky over the lean, the hirsute over the shaven, the regular guy over the boy next door. Larger, hairier men, particularly those older than thirty, were given little attention in gay media at that time, and I was excited to learn that these men actually gathered in groups and supported each other socially. I wanted to join, and yet I suspected that I didn't really belong: I'm scarcely taller than five feet six inches and presently weigh in at 130 pounds; at best, my body hair could be called visible. I have always prided myself on possessing a casual, individualistic, and friendly masculinity that didn't seem far different from the bear "attitude" I'd heard about. But I feared rejection from the bear clubs, and as for the bars, my reserved character rarely compensated for any apparent physical shortcomings.

Despairing of ever being invited into the clan, I resigned myself to the lonesome roles of secret bear admirer and closet *BEAR* reader for several years—until I saw P.G.'s letter. Ignoring any latent sarcasm or suggestions of undesirability, I immediately embraced the identity of otter. The totem fit easily enough as I had felt a deep, quiet connection with the animal since childhood: its lithe and independent spirit, its crossing of borders both elemental and social, its sense of play, its intelligence and adaptability. But on the tail of this revitalized identification followed the question as to whether there were others who *willingly* identified as otters—physically, spiritually, or what. That, and the related question of how the bear community responded to them. Inspired by the possibilities of this new perspective on the bears, I decided that I would search for the otters. First, I would take a closer look at bear-oriented media; second, I would contact the local bear groups of Chicago; and third, I would join the Bears Mailing List (BML) discussion group on the Internet, to which I could submit my freshly drafted Otter Questionnaire.

Merely the simple curiosity of the wistful outsider. . . . Little did I know that this was to plunge me into disagreements about identity and belonging that have been plaguing the bear community for years, if not since the earliest moments of its consciousness.

## *BEARS IN SPACE*

Judy Martin defines *negative space* as "an area in composition, either painting or sculpture, that surrounds or penetrates the main forms and thus contributes to the overall image without itself having a positive form" (Martin, 1986, p. 137). The concept of negative space struck me as relevant as I began first to explore bear-oriented media. Bears, of course, are the "positive space" or central object of their magazines, newsletters, Web sites, erotica, and events. This is to be expected: it was not so long ago that bears had to depend on mainstream gay and heterosexual-oriented media for rare, and often unflattering (see Locke, 1997) representations of the larger, hairier, and more "naturally masculine" man. In other words, it was not so long ago that bears were lost or invisible in the negative space of mainstream gay and heterosexual media. It took groundbreaking publications such as *BEAR* and *Bear Fax* to place this type of man front and center, a direct result of which was the fostering of a community beyond that of one's local leather bar. Not only were initially isolated (or "hibernating") bears transformed by these positive depictions (e.g., Mauerman, 1997; Rand, 1997), but in addition they were provided a sense of belonging to a wide and growing circle of like-minded (and -bodied) individuals. (For more developed discussions of "bear roots," see Wright, 1997b; Suresha, 1997.)

While I certainly enjoyed encountering fine specimens of bears in their own media, I could not ignore the fact that they were occupying almost all of the positive space. Indeed, representations of nonbears, not-exactly-bears, and other bear admirers were few and far between. Some might argue that this shouldn't be surprising, and yet I *was* a bit surprised as I was simultaneously encountering strong assertions of inclusivity (e.g., Hill, 1997, p. 76; Ridinger, 1997, pp. 86-87). The membership policies of many bear clubs insist on the acceptance of bear admirers; the long-running and prominent BML states that it also invites "those who enjoy the company of bears" (Bears Mailing List, 1999). But if this were so, then where were they depicted? Not in the erotic fiction of the magazines nor the bear-oriented videos of Brush Creek Media; most decidedly not in the contests nor the celebratory Web sites. Were bear admirers only participating as spectators and consumers? As for the otter, *my* idea of that type seemed more likely to surface in *RFD* and *Honcho* than *BEAR* and *American Bear*. Were otters now lost or invisible in the negative space of the bears?

My suspicions were further corroborated by criticisms being voiced within the bear community itself. Locke, who performed a detailed content analysis of male images in bear-oriented magazines, warned of the increasing prominence of a "superbear stereotype" in its media. He asked,

> What are the psychological consequences of joining the Bear community to feel included, only to turn around and feel as though one somehow does not measure up physically as a Bear? Men in this position have now been doubly wounded—they did not measure up to the ideal of male beauty repre-

sented in traditional gay media, and now they feel inferior within the Bear community. (Locke, 1997, p. 133)

Webster, in describing the Kiwi Bears of New Zealand, had this to say about the characteristics of its members:

> There is some bulk among members, but also a leanness, an attribute which has caused on the very odd occasion the remarks—what is a Bear? What is a Bear admirer? Are you a Bear, or a cub? Cubs, apparently, are thought by some to be admirers without the hair, bulk, and other attributes considered necessary to qualify as a Bear. This analytical reasoning has raised a question posed here and overseas, namely, by insisting on certain criteria are we not establishing the very same restrictions imposed by other gay septs that we have rebelled against?" (Webster, 1997, p. 247)

Above all, the BML was my most direct initiation to the passionate and intelligent debates occurring in the bear community about such issues. At the time of my joining the discussion group (July 1999), submissions to the daily Bears Digest of the BML were arguing over the existence of "A-Bears"—bears privileged with popularity in the bear clubs and contests by virtue of their appearance if not other attributes. That month also featured a stirring account from "BuckcuB," a longtime member of the bear community, who described his recent rejection from a bear event "because I was *(now considered)* too slim and too short and too smooth." He concluded:

> Beardom used to be accepting; I know from personal experience. But when someone . . . writes in, almost apologetically, about losing weight, maybe it's time Beardom took a good long look at itself. Do you want to just be the Hairy Fat Boy's Club? ("Skinny smooth guys, Keep Out!") Or are some bears going to take a stand and prevent Beardom from falling completely into the snooty prejudice of mainstream-gay twinkdom? (BuckcuB, 1999)

Still unsure, I wondered if my lack of a definition of the otter was the real problem—perhaps I was not seeing the otter because I was following the wrong tracks. Could bear-oriented discourse at least provide me with a working definition? After all, P.G. was labeled an otter by a self-defined bear, so from where was the term originating? This line of inquiry led me to the (in)famous Natural Bears Classification System, created by Bob Donahue and Jeff Stoner "while eating lunch at a Boulder, Colorado, Wendy's on Thanksgiving weekend, 1989" (Donahue and Stoner, 1997, p. 149). Purportedly conceived as a joke regarding the "objective" definition and description of bears, the Classification System regardless has been widely adopted by many bears as an efficient tool for quickly pinpointing one's physical traits and sexual tastes. It is not uncommon to find a string of letters, plus signs, and minus signs attached to a bear's personal ad or e-mail message, determining factors such as height, kinkiness, muscle, hairiness, and degree of non/monogamous behavior. And it was here, in Version 1.10 of the code, under "The Weight Factor" (w) that I found the following delineation 9 (p. 152, emphasis added):

| | |
|---|---|
| w++ | a round bear or *big* teddy bear |
| w+ | a big-boned bear |
| w | bear with a tummy |
| (none) | average weight for frame |
| w − | a thin bear (aka, **otter**) |
| w − − | a bony bear |

On finally spotting the word I felt an initial rush of inclusion, of verified belonging, of *proof*. I was a member of the bear clan after all: an otter, a "thin bear" (w −) if not a bony one (w − −). Well, wait a minute. I have a small frame for which my weight would seem more or less average (none). I was beginning to get the joke: here I was trying to locate a definition of the otter in relation to the bear, when the bear itself had no agreed-upon definition!

This realization, like that concerning the problem of inclusion, was easily supported in myriad contexts by contributors to *The Bear Book* (Wright, 1997a) and discussions on the BML, but Rofes summarized the issue best:

The pages of *BEAR* magazine and other discursive materials focused on Bearish men have been filled with editorial commentary and letters to the editor debating questions related to Bear identity, definition, and representation. Key points of controversy have fallen into three broad categories: (1) *Questions of core identity:* Is a Bear defined through appearance or spirit? (2) *Issues of definition:* Must all Bears have a beard? Body hair? Hefty body weight? and (3) *Representational matters:* Do Bear texts (magazines, newsletters, flyers, social events, sex parties) conflate Bears with chubs? Is the Girth and Mirth crowd a subset of Bears? How do we fit men without facial or body hair into the "Bear community?" (Rofes, 1997, p. 92)

Thus, it finally became clear to this newcomer that, not only was the otter absent from the positive space of the bear, but, in addition, the positive space of the bear had no clear borders or edges separating it from its own negative space—not to mention other types of men. It was as if someone inked a portrait of a bear in the woods with smaller animals dotting the background, and then accidentally smeared the bear's outline so that it blended in confusion with those of the other species. Indeed, this was exactly the case in one of the oldest known portraits of the "bear" in gay media: George Mazzei's 1979 *Advocate* article, "Who's Who in the Zoo? A Glossary of Gay Animals," in which Mazzei humorously caricatured seven types of homosexuals as owls, bears, gazelles, cygnet swans, pussycats, marmosets, and pekes/afghans. While the description of the bear is fun enough (and not much different from beareotypes today!), what is even more interesting is how four of the other six animals are described *in the context of the bear.* The gazelles "sometimes like to play Bear." Pekes and afghans "have excellent taste in Bears." Marmosets "look like small, manicured Bears." And pussycats "have the Bear look down pat. But where Bears are somewhat shy, Pussycats have a dry wit. Also Bears are naturally rumpled while Pussycats keep their workshirts neatly tucked . . ." (Mazzei, 1979, pp. 42-43).

In 1979, it was apparent at least to Mazzei (however playfully) that, while the bear had a visible identity, it was also *already* a problematic identity in that it shared characteristics with "other woodland creatures," it could be appropriated or imitated by other creatures, and it could, evidently, be willingly mated with them as well. In 2000, the bear identity continues to be problematic in the ways noted by Rofes above, but with the additional, specific (and for some, painfully real) social issues of exclusion and discrimination—this can only be due to the development of the self-consciousness of the bears and the growth and elaboration of the bear community internationally. Hence, the great bearadox of body versus spirit, or physical appearance versus "attitude," in the bear community (see, for one example, Wright, 1997c). If one prioritizes appearance, particularly in terms of his or anyone's own definitions of attractiveness, he inevitably risks excluding those he does not find "sufficiently" bearish; if one focuses on attitude, particularly in terms of his or anyone's own sense of self, he inevitably risks including so many people that the point of having a distinguishable bear community is nullified. I had to admit: it's certainly *easier* to measure a man's beard than his masculinity.

After crossing this mire of exclusionary politics and identity confusion, contained within the discourse and media of the bear, I was still no closer to the otter. Nor did I know where the positive space of the bear finally ended and where its negative space began—and in which did the otter belong?

It was time to consult with my local bear leaders.

## *NEIGHBORHOOD CLANS*

My primary reasons for approaching Chicago's two major bear groups—the Great Lakes Bears-Chicago (GLB) and the Chicago chapter of the Gen-X Bears (GXBC)—were simply to (1) learn the official stance of each club regarding its membership and sense of purpose, and (2) ascertain the existence of any otters in the clubs. As an outsider unfamiliar with the goings-on of such organizations, my approach might seem naive to most organized bears. However, I was already confused at the idea of there being two bear groups in one city—were there that many bears to go around? I also wondered if the clubs supported a political agenda, or mainly focused on events and activities, or simply met at a bar once a month. . . . And would the leaders have opinions about the definitions of the bear, the bear admirer, and even the otter?

I met with Tim, vice president of GLB, at the North End bar before the start of GLB's monthly meeting in July 1999. He was very gracious about taking time out to talk, as my arrival was unexpected—after not getting responses to messages I had left with the club about my intent, I decided just to show up. Tim struck me as a responsible and gentle man at twenty-six years old; he had been with GLB for two years.

I first put forth questions about the group, and Tim offered the following. GLB has been around for about ten years, having been started by a core group of guys who wanted to meet more men like themselves. The goal has always been social, and pointedly not political nor intentionally class-distinguished: a way "for like-minded individuals to meet each other" in a setting "where someone feels more comfortable." The sole criterion for membership is the annual dues of $20, and Tim estimated that GLB currently has about 170 paying members. Though regional in scope and having some members scattered across the nation, GLB chiefly comprises Greater Chicago-area men ranging in age between the mid-twenties and the sixties. Tim believed that the group may have been generally older in its composition in its beginning, but has since attracted more and more younger members; he thought this was due to increasing awareness and publicity of the bears as a community and movement. When I asked if all of the members were bears, he asked me to clarify, and I said, "What I mean is, do all of the members identify themselves as bears?" and he said yes. Typical activities of GLB are social, with the biggest event being the sponsoring of the annual Run—Tim figured that about 1,000 bears attended it this year. I asked if there was anything unique about GLB in comparison to other bear groups across America, and Tim said he felt that GLB managed to attract a wide range of people, both urban and rural, due to its placement in the Midwest. In terms of external perceptions of GLB, Tim noted that there was a time in the past when bears (in general) were looked down upon, but that GLB experienced mostly positive interactions within the gay Chicago community—not counting the "occasional disgruntled individual."

I then moved the interview toward more theoretical questions about the bear community and belonging. Tim agreed with the common perception that bears first organized in a conscious attempt to provide an alternative to the gay culture of the 1980s. He added that bears "show everyone else that you don't have to fit the media-perpetuated stereotype. . . . Being a normal, average, everyday guy who happens to be gay is all right." He went on to say that many bears, when first coming out, deeply resent the gay community at large for making them feel unwanted. Thus, an important function of bear groups has been to help these men feel accepted within a group; by doing so, the new bears can ultimately find peace with the gay community.

Tim made it clear that, while bears may tend to share some physical attributes, "attitude and behavior supercede the physical." I asked what a bear admirer was, and Tim wagered that bear admirers "don't see themselves as fitting in with the physical characteristics of the bears." Did he know any otters? He said he thought he might by physical appearance, though he admitted that those few people "probably would not call themselves otters." He explained that the concept of "bear" was all-encompassing, while the otter and the cub were just subcategories applied only for physical description: otters as slimmer bears, cubs as younger or boyish bears. "You wouldn't have a cub club or an otter club." I finally had to ask, a bit red in the face: "Would you say that I'm an otter?" Tim hemmed and hawed a little and screwed up an eye, but finally concluded, "Yeah, I guess I would call you an otter, I think so." A perfect gentlebear.

Afterward, I reflected on some of the suppositions gathered from the conversation. If the otter was merely a slimmer bear—a subspecies—then why would those few, apparently slimmer bears of GLB hesitate to call themselves otters? It seemed clear that the descriptive term "otter" must possess some pejorative connotation to those slimmer bears, and it certainly didn't seem implausible that the absence of "thin" and "bony" bears in the conceptual positive space might have something to do with it. In my case, I originally felt inadequate because, as an outsider, I could only see the physical discrepancy between me and representative examples of the bear; I was unaware of the bear community's postulation of attitude and self-definition as being equal to (or, to Tim, "superceding") the physical traits in importance. But to have an insider possibly feeling some inadequacy is different. I have no opinion nor experience regarding the inclusivity of GLB; this is not my concern. What I am interested in is the possibility of a shared aversion to the idea of being an otter: "shared" at this point being between a few Chicago bears and our reluctant prototype of the otter, P.G. from New York (who, it should be noted, gave no physical nor personal self-description in his letter!).

So, while preparing to meet next with GXBC, I was thrilled to discover that its "lair leader," Tom, identified as an otter—and with no reluctance whatsoever. This information headlined the Web page of the GXBC ("He's an Otter") along with Tom's classification of himself à la the bear code highlighted above (w−). A picture of a shirtless Tom mounted on the site thus provided me with my first look at one self-identified otter: a fleshy but generally lean build; not much noticeable fur on the chest and arms (though the quality of the scanned photo may have been misleading); a trim goatee; a ball cap (Gen-X Bears-Chicago, 1999). He later described himself to me as "6 feet tall and barely weigh[ing] 160 soaking wet." Tom, twenty-five, was personable and communicative in our e-mails and phone conversations preceding our meeting, which we arranged to hold at Touché, tavern and gathering space for GXBC.

Gen-X Bears International, according to the membership coordinator Benny Chan, is "a social organization to give support and have fun in a more social atmosphere and [a less] cruisy atmosphere. We are open to everyone including but not limited to big guys, small guys, women, straight folks, all races, and all ages eighteen and over" (Chan, 1999). A strictly social group could hardly attempt to be more inclusive, and the Chicago chapter apparently has lived up to some of the claim: Tom's predecessor was a bisexual woman. (She has since left GXBC due to increased involvement in the leather community.) In our discussion, Tom confirmed the primary importance placed on inclusivity by the organization, as well as its firm stance against any kind of membership dues. The sole criterion that Tom could come up with for belonging is to "be open-minded."

I asked questions about the chapter. Tom thought it had been around for two or three years; at present, forty-four people subscribe to the mailing list—Tom's benchmark for a membership count. Members are mostly between the late twenties and early thirties, mostly gay men, and mostly residents of Greater Chicago. Many in the group identify as bears though "bear chasers" are not uncommon. Regular events consist of the monthly gathering at Touché and semimonthly brunches, and all members are encouraged to suggest and plan any other activities. Tom mentioned that some GXB chapters, such as one in Indianapolis, are "thriving" in comparison to GXBC. I wondered what, if any, roles GXBC has been filling that GLB has not been, and Tom conceded that GXBC has simply offered "another social outlet" for bears: this is because GLB has made distinctive and admirable efforts toward getting younger bears interested in the group. According to Tom, this has not been the case in many other cities which tend to have older bear collectives, and hence a lack of avenues for younger bears searching for belonging (particularly among their peers). A friend of Tom's was sitting with us, whom I asked why he was a member of both groups. "The more the merrier," he smiled.

Tom felt very strongly about the inclusivity of GLB and the bear community as a whole, especially in contrast to the exclusionary attitude of the "twinks" populating Chicago's gay neighborhoods. To him, the bears value the person and the personality foremost. It occurred to me that this conviction might explain Tom's comfortableness with the self-applied label of otter. As a respondent to the Otter Questionnaire (discussed below), Tom had this to say: "[Otters] are bears. We're simply another stripe in the flag. The term otter is simply a description, like cub or daddy. . . . In my experience, bears accept the slimmer members of the community just as readily as they do behrs (hairless bears—yes, they are included too) and bear lovers." But he also echoed Tim when he wrote the following about how bears and otters relate socially: "I haven't seen any difference in the groups that I've been in. Though I also notice I don't see a lot of otters. There are maybe one or two others who fit the otter description, and they often don't call themselves otters."

Was it possible that the degree of acceptance a slimmer and/or less hairy man felt among the bears might directly correlate with that man's willingness to be called an otter? In Tom's case, this seemed so: for him there was nothing problematic about being an otter or "thin bear," not even with his awareness that other otter types might choose not to put the label on themselves. To keep with the conceptual metaphor, it could be said that Tom felt secure in his sense of placement in the positive space of the Chicago bears; he could be a self-identified otter as well as the leader of a bear club that prioritized inclusion—i.e., the erasure of negative space.

A hypothesis was starting to take form. Any interpretations of the identity of the otter by a member of the bear community must be shaped by that member's personal experiences in the bear community. These members, lutrine or not, could be categorized in one of three ways: (1) Those with a strong aversion to the *distinction* of the otter would insist on community definition as, basically, bear or nonbear/bear admirer. This could be due to any number of reasons, such as: a lack of awareness of the label; a disinterest in creating further subdivisions within the subculture of the bear; or, as suggested above, a sense of inadequacy or undesirability in regard to the distinction, perhaps especially held by those with an intense need to share the identity of bear—in a word, to belong. (2) Those with the perception of "otter" as simply a descriptive physical label would view the otter as an unproblematic subspecies within the bear family. These members would consider slimmer, less hairy men still to be members of the bear community *as* bears, based on the experience that these less prototypically bearish types were nonetheless fully accepted in the community. (3) Those who felt that otter types were essentially different from the bears would visualize the otter as its own separate species, not just a subspecies of the bear. This could be due to any number of reasons, such as: an appreciation of a uniqueness as sensed in the totemic concept of otter; an interest in creating further descriptive subdivisions within the subculture of the bear; or a sense of difference based on experiences in the bear community in which otter types have been ignored or excluded. In terms of space: (3) would view the otter as existing in the negative space of the bear (i.e., otter as what the bear is not); (2) would view the otter as sharing the positive space of the bear (i.e., otter as type of bear); and (1) would view the otter as nonexistent, period.

To this outside otter, already questioning his newfound identity in relation to the bears, it was a hypothesis worth exploring. As I had tracked down as many self-defined otters as I was able to find at this point in the local woods (one), it was time to broaden the search. I submitted a call to the otters and their admirers on the BML.

## THE OTTER QUESTIONNAIRE

When I subscribed to the BML, I had no guess as to how many of the 2,700+ listserv members would identify as otters, not to mention would even be interested in participating in the questionnaire. I sensed that twenty-five respondents to the questionnaire (via e-mail) would be very fortunate, and made that my goal. The first of the three types of members noted above, of course, would not respond at all, and surely certain members of the second and third type would not respond for whatever reasons. During the weeks following my subscription, for example, I noticed that several writers in the Bears Digest sported addresses and signatures with "otter" in the moniker, but did not respond to my initial call (July 8, 1999—Vol. 10 #268) nor to my last call (July 22, 1999—Vol. 10 #284). At any rate, I felt strongly about including "otter admirers" in the survey, as these particular bears inevitably play as much of a role in the identification and experiences of otters as the otters themselves; in addition, there might be something to learn from possible similarities and disparities in perception between the otters and their admirers.

In both calls I briefly explained that I was looking for otters and their admirers to answer questions regarding issues that would be addressed in the creation of this chapter. Upon receiving an e-mail message of interest, I then sent the potential participant the questionnaire. In its introduction I described its purpose as being "to find out what you think an 'otter' might be, particularly in relation to bears." I also assured the participant of anonymity if desired, and encouraged him to "Have fun!" Below is the text of the questionnaire in a slightly condensed format:

1. First Name
2. Age
3. Sexual Orientation
4. Race
5. Single? Got partner/s? Play the field?
6. City or suburban or small town or rural dweller?
7. How do you participate in the bear community? (e.g., clubs, online, bars, events, magazines, friends/partners, not at all . . .)
8. What other communities, interest/activist groups, and subcultures do you belong to or participate in?
9. Do you or would you call yourself an otter? (yes? no? jokingly? "sure, why not"? whole-heartedly?) Any special reasons?

10. Did you formerly perceive yourself as (write yes or no where applicable): a bear; a cub; a daddy; a top; a bottom; other (please specify)?
11. Do you still perceive yourself as (write yes or no where applicable): a bear; a cub; a daddy; a top; a bottom; other (please specify)?
12. Describe the physique and appearance of a man you would identify as an otter (include clothes, hair, build, posture, age, whatever you wish).
13. What in particular would distinguish the otter from the bear?
14. Have you heard the word "otter" used by others in the bear community or in the gay community at large? Was the context positive, negative, or neutral? Was it explained?
15. Many bears claim that a certain "attitude" is what, above all, makes them true bears. What "attitude" (or approach to life) would you imagine otters having?
16. Would you mate, date, and/or pal around with an/other otter? Would you prefer a bear?
17. How do otters and bears that you know relate socially?
18. Finish these sentences:
    a. A bear is to beer as an otter is to . . .
    b. Bears cuddle; otters . . .
    c. If bears are big-hearted and easy-going, otters are . . .
    d. If bears are naturally masculine, otters are . . .
19. (You're almost done!) Here is where you can add whatever else you wish to say about: otters; bears; the gay community at large; this questionnaire.

## *RESPONSES*

Of twenty-six potential participants who responded to the calls, twenty-three ultimately returned answers to the questionnaire by the deadline; Tom, of GXBC, to whom I submitted the questionnaire personally, brought the number of respondents to twenty-four. Responses varied widely in tone, length, and degree of completion, and all were considered valid in regard to the purpose of the questionnaire.

Results have been classified into several focus areas which I feel are of most interest and relevance to the concerns of this chapter. Attempting to quantify and compare the mostly verbal responses, largely qualitative in nature, was difficult. Thus, in the following discussion I will often quote from responses that represent the most common opinion gathered on an issue, or, in the event of major disagreement, represent the degree and type of the disagreement. However, I did manage to place most responses into one of two categories for four major factors:

    A. Otter—Otter admirer
    B. Physical prioritized—Attitude prioritized
    C. Otter as subspecies of bear—Otter as own species
    D. Socializing as fine—Socializing as in need of change

As will be shown, some responses simply could not be categorized for some of the factors, usually due to vagueness or incompletion of the questionnaire. I would like to stress here that determining (B) was an especially tricky balancing act for some of the responses: essentially I had to weigh comments across several questions and trust my judgment of whether the body or the spirit carried more heft in terms of overall importance. These factors will be discussed in greater detail below, with occasional references made to the letters (A, B, C, and D).

## *Otter Demographics*

This focus considers the quantifiable responses of the otters (not the admirers) to Questions 2-8 and 10-11. Sixteen of the twenty-four respondents identified themselves as otters and fit into the following age ranges: twenty-one to twenty-five (2); twenty-six to thirty (1); thirty-one to thirty-five (6); thirty-six to forty (4); forty-six to fifty (1); and sixty-six to seventy-two (2). Fourteen were gay and two were bisexual; all identified as Caucasian or white. Three were single; two were single and "played the field"; eight had a partner; and three had a partner and were nonmonogamous. Twelve lived in a city; three in the suburbs of a city; and one in a small town.

Otter participation in the bear community manifested itself in the following areas (participation online was of course shared by all of the respondents as they subscribed to the BML, except Tom who at that time was not a subscriber, but maintained the GXBC Web page): clubs (10); bars (9); magazines (8); events (7); friends/partners (7); or minimally/not at all (2). Participation in other communities included: specifically gay-oriented activities and groups (7— e.g., gay journalists association, leather club, pridefest organizing); religious organizations (3); other online cultures (2); miscellaneous ventures (4—e.g., music, sports, disability work); or not at all (5).

Past and present identification with other labels familiar to the bear community was influenced in part by whether or not the otter viewed himself as a subspecies of the bear (C): ten of the sixteen otters held this view. However, it must be understood that a few otters who did view the otter as a subspecies (determined elsewhere in the responses) did *not* select the bear label in their responses to Questions 10 and/or 11; this was either due to strict identification as a cub or to a change in one's usage of labels. While "versatile" was not listed in the questions, enough respondents specified this as "other" so that I have included it here:

|           | Formerly | Now |                                                                    |
|-----------|----------|-----|--------------------------------------------------------------------|
| Bear      | 7        | 7   |                                                                    |
| Cub       | 8        | 6   |                                                                    |
| Daddy     | 0        | 0   | (2 specified increased/future leanings toward this identification) |
| Top       | 3        | 1   |                                                                    |
| Bottom    | 4        | 2   |                                                                    |
| Versatile | 5        | 6   |                                                                    |

Other former identifications included "misfit," "just a queer who didn't seem to identify with the other queers wandering around," and "a cute LGB (little guy with beard)." Some current identifications included "ferret (hyperactive otter)," "son in need of a daddy bear," and "definitely OTHER!" (Please see Otter Identifications below for further discussion of these findings.)

## *Otter Admirer Demographics*

While not central to the purpose of the questionnaire and the concerns of this chapter, a summary of the demographics of the handful of non-otters might be of interest. Six respondents were otter admirers. The remaining two respondents of the twenty-four could not in all honesty be determined as either otter or otter admirer; at best they can be described in this context as interested in the otter concept. One was currently dating a bear and seemed open to self-identification as otter, perhaps with the concept's increase in usage in the bear community. The other identified with numerous totemic animals and spiritualities, including those of bear and cub, but had not previously considered the otter. While I found their answers useful regarding other foci in the questionnaire, I have not included them in the demographics of the otter admirer. However, I would like to note that these two respondents were the only nonwhites to participate.

Age ranges were as follows: twenty-six to thirty (2); thirty-six to forty (1); forty-one to forty-five (2); and fifty-one to fifty-five (1). All identified as gay white men. Three were single; one was single and nonmonogamous; and two had a partner and were nonmonogamous. Five lived in a city and one in a suburban village.

Otter admirer participation in the bear community subdivided this way: clubs (2); bars (2); magazines (2); events (3); friends/partners (4); or minimally/not at all (1). Participation in other communities included: specifically gay-oriented activities and groups (4—e.g., political concerns, Gay Men's Chorus); other online cultures (1); and miscellaneous ventures (3—e.g., music, the gym, social work).

Past and present identification with other labels familiar to the bear community broke down as follows:

|        | Formerly | Now |                                                                        |
|--------|----------|-----|------------------------------------------------------------------------|
| Bear   | 3        | 4   |                                                                        |
| Cub    | 2        | 2   |                                                                        |
| Daddy  | 1        | 1   | (1 specified increased/future leanings toward this identification)     |
| Top    | 2        | 2   |                                                                        |
| Bottom | 2        | 2   |                                                                        |

Other identifications, like those noted above, tended to remain the same over time for the otter admirers, two of whom specifically mentioned being "oral," and one who described himself as "a smooth man (with the heart/attitude of a bear) . . . [and] follower of furry men."

## Otter Physique

Question 12 asked respondents to specify aspects of the physique and appearance of the otter; on occasion some answers to other questions such as 9, 13, and 19 also contributed to this focus. In terms of (B), thirteen respondents prioritized physique while ten prioritized attitude.

### Hair and Hairiness

Opinions on the degree of hairiness of the otter ranged widely, but with the majority of respondents emphasizing at least some notable amount of hairiness. "Irrelevant," "no restrictions," and "slight or no body hair" marked one end of the spectrum, while "furry, long hair," "definitely hairy," and "almost always have facial hair, and are likely hairy elsewhere, too" marked the other.

### Age

For those who remarked on this aspect, age was usually considered irrelevant ("doesn't matter") or to span across so broad a range of years ("from early twenties through late fifties") as to seem indistinctive. However, specific stipulations included "in their thirties at least . . . mainly older men," "upper thirties, low forties," and "young."

### Build

Respondents were in more agreement on this aspect than on any other—indeed, than on any other issue broached by the questionnaire. Almost all felt that the otter possesses a slim build, and most worded this in comparison to that of the bear, e.g., "not as husky as bear," "merely *narrow bears* . . . a lithe luscious cousin," and a "small, slim, hairy guy who has all bear characteristics and appearance." Three specified a tallness of the otter; a few made mention that otters would not be overtly muscular.

For the most part, other aspects such as clothes and posture were rarely remarked upon or deemed irrelevant.

### Otter Attitude

Questions 15, 18, and 19 stimulated commentary about the possible existence and nature of an otter attitude or "approach to life." Question 18 was playfully designed to fish out ideas held by the respondents regarding otter personality, especially in contrast to what I consider to be pervasive notions or stereotypes within the community and media regarding bear attitude and behavior. Two concepts rose above all others:

*Playfulness*

Variations on the word "playful" were invoked often, and more so than any other concept, throughout most of the responses.

*Masculinity*

Particularly in response to Question 18 ("If bears are naturally masculine, otters are . . . "), the majority of respondents insisted that otters are equally masculine to the bears. Twelve respondents specifically answered "too" or "the same" or "naturally masculine" to the last part of Question 18, and several others expressed this idea elsewhere in their responses.

Variations or disagreements in regard to the existence of a distinctive otter attitude, however, did appear. One end of the spectrum voiced the absence of such, e.g., "none (otters *are* bears)," "the same as a bear's," and "the same as bears, at least on paper . . . friendly disposition, optimistic outlook, generous, introspective." Still, approximately half of the respondents *to this topic* fell toward the other end of the spectrum of perceiving or even advocating a marked distinction from the bears in attitude. Some examples:

- "more of an adventurous nature with the otter—not quite as settled into patterns . . . a desire to perform and serve more than watch and be served . . . avoid some of the mental bear traps"

- "helpful, helping and assisting . . . the active group organizers, busy as an 'otter' "
- "self-assured, quick to smile and laugh, open and approachable, playful, mischievous, sexy!"

## *Distinction of the Otter from the Bear*

This focus directly stems from the previous two, but aims to highlight the distinctions made by the respondents in Question 13, and also in the word associations of Question 18. As noted above, "build" or size was the foremost physical aspect that distinguished the otter from the bear. Nineteen respondents noted build while three explicitly stated "weight"; three also specified body hair; two, age; and one, metabolism. Some variety of playfulness was the foremost personality aspect for the eleven respondents who envisioned any distinction in attitude.

I believe that as much can be learned from the inherent silliness of Question 18 as from the neutrality or seriousness of any of the other questions. Preconceptions and stereotypes of the bear are perpetuated by bears in their own discourse and media, especially when linked to claims of a "like-minded" attitude or personality and shared communal behaviors. The playfulness of these word associations loosened up some of the more reticent respondents as well as a few of those who otherwise insisted on otters as being indistinguishable from bears in any way aside from build. What follows are samples of the responses, with totals following those mentioned by more than one respondent. (Note: assertions of the prominence of the concepts of playfulness and masculinity were based on responses to the questionnaire as a whole, not just to the following word associations.)

- *A bear is to beer as an otter is to . . .* beer (3); lite beer (2); wine (2); soda (2); shots (smaller container, still a lot of punch!); fruit juice; cider; Snapple; Yoo-Hoo; Old Milwaukee . . . just a more specific type of the same thing.
- *Bears cuddle; otters . . .* cuddle (4); snuggle (3); play/are playful (2); enjoy being cuddled; are *all that* and then some; wrestle; suck; wrap; scamper; rock your world!; play Shostakovich?; totally overwhelm you; are just cute.

- *If bears are big-hearted and easy-going, otters are* . . . big-hearted and easy-going (6); playful (5); mischievous (2); soft-hearted and receptive; lithe and handsome; just hard-going? ;-); lucky if they can find a big-hearted, easy-going bear; magical and able to turn a situation on its ear; big-hearted, organizing, and compulsive!; in need of constant reassurance; big-dicked; and hard-fucking.
- *If bears are naturally masculine, otters are* . . . naturally masculine/the same/too (12); masculine too, just not as cultic about it; slightly less so; often butch, but at times stand like girls; easy on the eye, a king-size bed is not a *must;* a little androgynous at times but fascinating!; naturally hairy; naturally neutral in demeanor.

### *Otter Identifications*

The intent of this focus is to provide further illustration to the quantified, categorical breakdown of past and present identifications shown in the Otter Demographics. Identifications and self-labeling were chiefly addressed in responses to Questions 9 to 11, though responses to Questions 13 and 19 occasionally provided additional information. I asked these questions as I was curious in regard to: how many otters also considered themselves bears; how many shifted from the bear and/or cub identity to the otter identity over time; if any otters perceived themselves as daddies; and if there was any correlation between identification as an otter and identification as a sexual type (top or bottom).

The numerical totals displayed in the Otter Demographics table can be somewhat misleading, as they do not reveal particular transitions in some of the otters' self-identification. For example, three otters with former identifications (e.g., cub, bottom) now identify solely as otter: in addition, one of them views the otter as a subspecies, one of them views the otter as its own species, and one of them expressed no view on that matter. Despite such interpretive complications, a few patterns are discernible:

- Ten of the sixteen otter respondents consider the otter to be a subspecies of the bear.
- Seven of that ten did not change in their identifications over time, while five of the remaining six otters did change.

- Six of the seven otters who formerly identified as bears continue to do so now.
- Six of the eight otters who formerly identified as cubs continue to do so now; no otters "later" adopted the label of cub.
- No otters formerly identified as daddies but at least two may do so in the future.
- More otters labeled themselves as versatile than as top or bottom.
- Fewer otters continued to identify as tops or bottoms over time.

Some words from the otters themselves (not the admirers) will help illustrate the issues involved:

- "I see an Otter as a subclass of a Bear. I've always viewed a Bear as being a masculine GAY man. . . . An Otter I see as a Thinner Masculine Gay Man."
- "Otters aren't relationship labels like daddy or son. . . . There CAN be otter cubs, even otter daddies (which I find delish!), which is for some guys just way too pigeonholing, but again, it's not social or sexual role assigning, it's physically descriptive. . . . I see such descriptions as terms of endearment . . . "
- "I think a lot of [otters] . . . started by self-identifying as 'gay.' Then they switched to 'bear,' then to 'otter.' [ . . . ] They also seem more likely to be at *ease* with these uncertain labels and definitions, and perhaps less constricted by them. On the other hand, I sense less a sense of 'community' among otters."
- "I define myself more as an ottercub, I have been told I am 'too thin to be a bear' by some and gotten snubbed by some for not being 'enough of a bear.' But to others I AM a bear. So go figure."
- "Otter Nationalist and Proud!!! (Now if I could just find at least one other otter who didn't think he was a 'cub' or didn't resist labels . . . )"
- "The only thing Bears as a breed have going for them is the Hair. Take that away and what do you have—A fat man with an attitude."

## Socializing

### Usage of the Term "Otter"

This is the first of three foci concerned with the social experiences of otters as perceived by all of the respondents. These foci do not deal with specific ways of participating in the bear community, the numbers for which are self-explanatory and presented above in Otter Demographics. In Question 14, I asked if respondents had encountered the term "otter" in either the bear or gay community, if they had a sense of positive or negative usage of the word in those instances, and if the term was explained. Nine respondents viewed the usage they encountered as positive, nine viewed the usage as neutral, and one viewed the usage as occasionally negative. Some comments:

- "just a simple label."
- "Heard it once in a bar, but figured it out myself (what was meant)."
- "I had to figure out what BMLers meant by 'otter.'"
- "Hardly ever. There is a lot of confusion of otters with cubs."
- "Community prefers 'cub,' I think. I received some negative responses as well as positive. Some love otters, some think they're just 'wannabes.'"
- "A couple times was deemed too confusing and oversubdividing of the bears."

### Preferences

Question 5 (highlighted in Otter Demographics) requested information on the respondents' current partnership status, the results of which revealed no significant patterns (except, perhaps, that all six otter admirers are potentially on the prowl). The purpose of Question 16 was simply to determine the social preferences of the respondents. Due in part to my poor wording of the question, it was occasionally difficult to determine if the respondents were referring to friendship or partnering; regardless, I could at least determine the general "preference" (more often sexual than social) of many of the respondents. Ten otters preferred a bear, though half of them noted they would consider another otter. Four otters preferred their own, and the final two had no real preference (e.g., one of them was fifty-fifty regarding "otter daddies and tough cubs"). As for the eight non-otters: two bears preferred an otter; one bear and all three cubs (two otter admirers and one undefined) had no real preference; one "smooth guy" otter admirer preferred an otter; and the other one undefined preferred a bear.

*Bears and Otters Together*

In Question 17, I asked, "How do otters and bears that you know relate socially?" From responses to this and occasionally to Question 19 if not elsewhere, I determined whether a respondent perceived socializing in the bear community to be "fine," or to be in need of change (D). Of the eighteen respondents for whom I felt I could determine this, ten fit the former and eight the latter. The ten who felt that the socializing was fine consisted of six otters and four non-otters. The eight who felt that the socializing was in need of change consisted of five otters and three non-otters. The sides of such a split are best illustrated by a sample of commentary:

- "Friendly, overall nice, and good company with each other."
- "I didn't really feel truly accepted in the gay community until I started hanging out with bears."
- "I have on occasion run into bears that have shunned me for being 'too thin/not hairy enough.' But that is why it is called a sexual preference."
- "Bears should concentrate on being more inclusive so maybe subcategories, like otter, fox, polar bear, would only exist if those people wanted to identify with them. . . . I would hope otters exist because they feel otterish rather than feeling rejected by beardom."
- "Not real well. Most bears are interested in other bears and ignore the otters, and vice versa."
- "Uncomfortable—most of the time—just as the *old* with the *young*."

- "Bears should not be so snotty or feel as if their masculinity is threatened by an iota of slender/slightly effeminate men in their presence."

## The Gay Community at Large

Though essentially beyond the scope of my concerns, Question 19 invited any remarks on the gay community beyond that of the bears. It is simply worth noting that the solid majority of responses to that question were critical, and most others were ambivalent at best.

## Further Research?

Question 19 finally, if unexpectedly, triggered some comment along the lines of recommendations. Overall, these included various ways in which the bears could improve (e.g., see "Bears should" quotations under Bears and Otters Together), and possible "next steps" for the otters, such as organizing and creating otter-based Web sites. "Courage—" one respondent wrote, "maybe the Otters will multiply and become a community."

## INCONCLUSIONS

At the beginning of the previous section I outlined four quantitative factors, for each of which a response might be categorized as one or the other. Below I have featured the totals (as determined to the best of my ability and only when deemed applicable to the response):

    A. Otter (16)—Otter admirer (6 + 2 undefined)
    B. Physical prioritized (13)—Attitude prioritized (10)
    C. Otter as subspecies of bear (11)—Otter as own species (7)
    D. Socializing as fine (10)—Socializing as in need of change (8)

For (B), eight otters and five non-otters prioritized the physical; seven otters and three non-otters prioritized attitude. For (C), ten otters and one non-otter specified the otter as a subspecies of the bear; five otters and two non-otters expressed the idea of the otter being a different animal altogether. And for (D), six otters and four non-otters seemed to view socializing in the bear community as fine; five otters and three non-otters noticed problems or a need for change.

As must be apparent to most readers by now, the painting of some collective portrait of the otter by these numbers—indeed, by much of the quantitative and qualitative data discussed in this chapter—would be no easy task if not almost impossible. If we focused only on potential areas of "agreement" in the responses, we might attempt to claim the following. Of otters: "Otters tend to be gay white males in their thirties, urban residents and possibly mated with a bear, and involved in multiple ways in the bear community if not in other gay-oriented activities (despite being critical of the gay community at large). They are more likely to view the otter as a subspecies of the bear and less likely over time to adopt other labels besides 'bear' or 'otter.'" Of otterishness: "Otters are almost universally perceived as slimmer than bears. They are probably supposed to possess a playfulness in contrast to bears but also a masculinity equal to that of the bears." And of socializing in the bear community: "Most members of the bear community found usage of the term 'otter' to be either neutral or positive (though not necessarily clarifiable)."

A vastly different image would develop if we focused only on potential areas of disagreement. Of otters: "Otters are known to be as young as the early twenties and as old as the late sixties, with no particular degree of hairiness but probably slimmer than the average bear. They can be diverse in mating habits and may participate in a wide range of activities outside of the bear community, some of which are gay-oriented (despite being critical of the gay community at large). They may or may not change in personal identification over time, having varied opinions about self-labeling and categorization in general, and may or may not share an interest in the development of otter awareness." Of otterishness: "Otters are not perceived to be physically definable in terms of hairiness nor age, and may be mistaken for cubs. As for attitude, there is much disagreement on its distinctiveness in comparison to that of the bear, and little shared vision on any other qualities besides a playful masculinity. It's almost fifty-fifty as to whether a member of the bear community would consider the physique or the attitude of the otter more central to its definition." And of socializing in the bear community: "There is near-total division in perceptions of any harmony or disharmony between the otters and the bears."

Thus, little can honestly be asserted regarding these conflicted results, aside from possibly two things: the fact that twice as many otters viewed the otter as a subspecies (any concerned bears can breathe a sigh of relief in that otters have yet to border on *total* secession); and the fact that otters are slimmer than bears. At this point we have hardly taken one step beyond the original classification of the otter as a "thin bear" (w − ). However, if we glance at the combination of factors (C) and (D) across the fourteen respondents for whom this is possible, one small but sturdy pattern does emerge:

- Six otters: view otter as subspecies *and* socializing as fine
- One non-otter: views otter as own species *and* socializing as fine.
- One otter + one non-otter: view otter as subspecies *and* socializing as in need of change.
- Four otters + one non-otter: view otter as own species *and* socializing as in need of change.

My hypothesis, as developed in the section Neighborhood Clans, was that "any interpretations of the identity of the otter by a member of the bear community must be shaped by that member's personal experiences in the bear community." I had suspected that respondents who considered harmony to be reigning in Bearland would consider the otter to be an unproblematic subspecies of the bear—i.e., sharing the positive space. In turn, I suspected that respondents who perceived disharmony would envision the otter as separate from the bear—i.e., placed in the negative space. Although I can hardly pronounce confirmation given the nature of the questionnaire and the range and variety of responses, I do believe a possible correlation exists in the numbers.

As for assuredly existing in reality, further research *would* be necessary. For if there is one set of voices absent in this study, it is that of both the former members who abandoned the bear community, and the potential, lost "brothers" who never even joined. In other words: those who aren't in the picture *at all*. One respondent half-joked: "Many otters date and marry outside the religion entirely and are seen with twinks or un-typable guys." But is it still funny when someone like BuckcuB shaves his beard in anger and despair over mounting incidents of exclusion?

The questionnaire failed to locate substantial agreement on the many issues and ideas represented by the otter. Truly, this makes perfect sense, given the disagreements of identity and belonging at the heart of the bears—could I really have expected the otter to have any clearer definition? But in this failure—these disagreements—I find great hope. I would wager that the endurance of the bears lies less in identity politics and "organization," and more in the creation of inclusive and dynamic social spaces, whether down the block, in the woods, or on the Web (but, please, not *only* on the Web). Even now, at the beginning of the twenty-first century, I doubt we can afford to factionalize in a still homophobic and increasingly controlled society.

Many thanks to everyone who participated.

## REFERENCES

Bears Mailing List. 1999. "Semi-Monthly Administrative Reminder." E-mail to the author, July 5.
BuckcuB. 1999. "Thinner . . . " Bears Digest 10: (July 28) 290.
Chan, Benny. 1999. "Re: Joining." E-mail to the author, July 6.
Donahue, Bob and Jeff Stoner. 1997. "The Natural Bears Classification System: A Classification System for Bears and Bearlike Men: Version 1.10." In *The Bear Book*. Ed. Les Wright. Binghamton, NY: Harrington Park Press, pp. 149-156.
Gen-X Bears-Chicago. 1999. Web site <http://www.genxbears.org/~genxchicago/>, July 5.
Hill, Scott. 1997. "Aroused from Hibernation." In *The Bear Book*. Ed. Les Wright. Binghamton, NY: Harrington Park Press, pp. 65-82.
Locke, Philip. 1997. "Male Images in the Gay Mass Media and Bear-Oriented Magazines: Analysis and Contrast." In *The Bear Book*. Ed. Les Wright. Binghamton, NY: Harrington Park Press, pp. 103-140.
Martin, Judy. 1986. *Longman Dictionary of Art*. Essex, UK: Longman Group.
Mauerman, Luke. 1997. "*BEAR* Magazine." In *The Bear Book*. Ed. Les Wright. Binghamton, NY: Harrington Park Press, pp. 207-217.
Mazzei, George. 1979. "Who's Who in the Zoo? A Glossary of Gay Animals." *The Advocate,* July 26, 42-43.

P.G., 1998. "Bitter Otter." Letter to the Editor. *BEAR,* no. 52: 13-14.

Rand, John. 1997. "John Rand, Photographer: An Interview with Les Wright." Transcription by Dale Wehrle. In *The Bear Book.* Ed. Les Wright. Binghamton, NY: Harrington Park Press, pp. 157-166.

Ridinger, Robert B. Marks. 1997. "Bearaphernalia: An Exercise in Social Definition." In *The Bear Book.* Ed. Les Wright. Binghamton, NY: Harrington Park Press, pp. 83-88.

Rofes, Eric. "Academics as Bears: Thoughts on Middle-Class Eroticization of Workingmen's Bodies." In *The Bear Book.* Ed. Les Wright. Binghamton, NY: Harrington Park Press, pp. 89-99.

Suresha, Ron. 1997. "Bear Roots." In *The Bear Book.* Ed. Les Wright. Binghamton, NY: Harrington Park Press, pp. 41-49.

Webster, John. 1997. "Kiwi Bears." In *The Bear Book.* Ed. Les Wright. Binghamton, NY: Harrington Park Press, pp. 239-250.

Wright, Les, Ed. 1997a. *The Bear Book.* Binghamton, NY: Harrington Park Press.

Wright, Les. 1997b. "A Concise History of Self-Identifying Bears." In *The Bear Book.* Ed. Les Wright. Binghamton, NY: Harrington Park Press, pp. 21-39.

Wright, Les. 1997c. "Introduction: Theoretical Bears." In *The Bear Book.* Ed. Les Wright. Binghamton, NY: Harrington Park Press, pp. 1-17.

# Chapter 5

# The Beard of Joseph Palmer

## Stewart Holbrook

### *I*

One of the unsung but really great individualists who helped to make the United States a better and a safer place to live was Joseph Palmer of Fitchburg and Harvard, Massachusetts, a man to be reckoned with in any discussion of the Bill of Rights. He is forgotten now, and this is bad forgetting, for Palmer was of a race of men that is now all but extinct. And his story, I think, is as heartwarming as it is improbable.

Palmer came to national attention because he was the victim of one of the strangest persecutions in history. Neither race nor religion played a part in Palmer's case, which with some reason might otherwise be termed *l'affaire Dreyfus* of Fitchburg. It was brought about by the fact that Joe Palmer liked to wear a beard, one of the most magnificent growths ever seen in New England or, for that matter, in the United States; and what made this beard particularly heinous was that it was almost if not quite the only beard east of the Rocky Mountains, and possibly beyond.

One lone set of whiskers amid millions of smooth-shaven faces *is* something to contemplate, and Palmer paid dearly for his eccentricity. Indeed, one might say, with but little stretch of imagination and metaphor, that it was Joe Palmer who carried the Knowledge of

---

This chapter is reprinted with permission from *The American Scholar* 13:4 (Autumn 1944) 455-458. Copyright ©1994 by the Phi Beta Kappa Society. Many thanks to Steve Klein, who rediscovered this historical gem, *LKW*.

Whiskers through the dark ages of beardless America. He was born almost a century too late and seventy-five years too soon to wear whiskers with impunity. He was forty-two years old in 1830, when he moved from his nearby farm into the bustling village of Fitchburg. He came of sturdy old Yankee stock. His father had served in the Revolution, and Joe himself had carried a musket in 1812. He was married and had one son, Thomas.

When the beard first made its appearance isn't of record, but Joe was wearing it when he came to Fitchburg, and here, because of it, he immediately became the butt of cruel jokes and derision and, in time, the victim of downright persecution. But before relating the violence caused by Palmer's famous beard, it is imperative—if one is to comprehend the proceedings at all—to trace briefly the history of whiskers in America up to the time of the Palmer beard.

This continent was explored by men of many nationalities, almost all of them wearing whiskers. About Columbus and Amerigo Vespucci we are uncertain, since there are no authenticated contemporary portraits of them. But after them came a host of beards. Cortes, Ponce de Leon, Cartier, Champlain, Drake, Raleigh, Captain John Smith, De Soto—all sported whiskers of varying length and style. Little wonder the Indians thought them gods.

Then came the Pilgrims and the Puritans, bearded almost to a man when they arrived at The Rock and elsewhere. But the beards of the first settlers didn't last. American whiskers were reduced gradually in size until they were scarcely more than mild goatees, and soon disappeared entirely. By 1720 at the latest, American colonists were wholly free of facial hair. Try to find a Copley portrait, or a Ralph Earle, with a whisker in it. And the fighting men of the Revolution were beardless. Not a moustache or a suspicion of a mutton-chop appeared on the faces of Washington, Gates, Greene, Knox. Even old John Stark and Israel Putnam were smooth-shaven, and so was the backwoods general, Ethan Allen. It was the same with the other Patriots, and with the British also—Cornwallis, the Howes, Burgoyne. No signer of the Declaration had either beard or moustache.

And so it continued down the years. No president before Lincoln had any hair on his face. Until 1858 the cartoonists' conception of their own creature, Uncle Sam—otherwise much as he is today—

was of a tall and lanky but smooth-shaven man. America did not really go hairy until the Civil War was well under way.

Thus when Joe Palmer came to town wearing a beard in 1830, whiskers had been virtually nonexistent for at least a hundred years. In spite of his hirsute oddity, Palmer was an honest, kindly man and a good citizen, deeply religious but tolerant, and a man of many intellectual interests. He was also quite immovable when it came to principles, which in his case included the right to wear a full flowing beard.

Everywhere he went small boys threw stones and shouted "Old Jew Palmer," and made life miserable for his son Tom. Women sniffed and crossed to the other side of the street when they saw him coming. Often the windows of his modest home were broken by unknown rowdies. Grown men jeered at him openly. The Reverend George Trask, local pastor, took him to task for his eccentricity, but Joe replied with exact Scriptural reasons—nay, commands—for beard-wearing. Old Doctor Williams told Joe to his face that he should "be prosecuted for wearing such a monstrosity." And, when Joe went to Boston to attend literary and reform meetings, huge crowds "followed him the length of Tremont Street, jeering." He was present at the celebrated Chardon Street Convention in 1840, and one has no difficulty locating him in Emerson's comment on that gathering:

> If the assembly was disorderly, it was picturesque. Madmen, madwomen, men with beards, Dunkers, Muggletonians, Come-outers, Groaners, Agrarians, Seventh-Day Baptists, Quakers, Abolitionists, Calvinists, Unitarians, and Philosophers—all came successively to the top, and seized their moment, if not their hour, wherein to chide, or pray, or preach, or protest. (Works, X: 3S2)

By the time of this Convention, Joe Palmer was a national character, made so by two events that had happened in quick succession in his home town of Fitchburg. In spite of the snubs of the congregation, Joe never missed a church service, but one Sunday he quite justifiably lost his usually serene temper. It was a Communion Sunday in 1830. Joe knelt with the rest, only to be publicly humiliated when the officiating clergyman ignored him, "passed him by with the communion bread and wine." Joe was cut to the quick. He rose up and strode to the communion table. He lifted the cup to his lips and took a mighty swig. Then: "I love my Jesus," he shouted in a voice loud with hurt and anger, "as well, and better, than any of you!" Then he went home.

A few days later, as he was coming out of the Fitchburg Hotel, he was seized by four men armed with shears, brush, soap, and razor. They told him that the sentiment of the town was that his beard should come off and they were going to do the job there and then. When Joe started to struggle, the four men threw him violently to the ground, seriously injuring his back and head. But Joe had just begun to fight. When they were about to apply the shears, he managed to get an old jackknife out of his pocket. He laid about him wildly, cutting two of his assailants in their legs, not seriously but sufficiently to discourage any barber work. When Joe stood up, hurt and bleeding, his gorgeous beard was intact.

Presently he was arrested, charged with "an unprovoked assault." Fined by Justice Brigham, he refused to pay. Matter of principle, he said. He was put in the city jail at Worcester and there he remained for more than a year, part of the time in solitary confinement. Even here he had to fight for his whiskers, for once Jailor Bellows came with several men with the idea of removing the now famous beard. Joe threw himself at them and fought so furiously that the mob retreated without a hair. He also successfully repulsed at least two attempts by prisoners to shave him.

In the jail Joe wrote letters which he smuggled out a window to his son, who took them to the *Worcester Spy*. They were published and soon were being widely copied by other newspapers. In his letters the bearded prisoner stated that he was in jail not for assault but because he chose to wear whiskers—which was unquestionably the case. He complained of the food, of the quarters, and of the lack of any religious life behind the bars. People all over Massachusetts read these letters. They began to talk and even to reflect. It wasn't long before the sheriff came to realize that he had a Tartar and possibly a martyr on his hands. He went to Joe and told him to run along home and forget it—the fine and everything. No, said Joe. The jailor urged him to leave. His aged mother wrote him to come home. All in vain. Nothing could move the man who was now known as The Bearded Prisoner of Worcester.

Day after day he sat in his limbo, keeping an elaborate and pathetic journal of his persecutions. And time after time he told officers and worried magistrates that they had put him there, and they would have to take him out. "I won't walk one single step toward freedom!" he roared through the bars. Nor did he. He sat there in a chair like a whiskered Buddha until the desperate sheriff and jailors picked him up in his chair and carried him to the street.

## II

Never again was violence attempted on Joe Palmer's beard, which by the time of his release, or rather his eviction, from jail, was a beard famous as far away as New York and Philadelphia. Free now, he soon became a minor figure in New England's intellectual ferment. A hater of slavery, he went to Boston often for the meetings of Parker and Garrison, contributing both time and money to the movement for Abolition. He met Emerson, Thoreau, Alcott, Channing, and these men found him an odd but staunch character, the possessor of much good sense. He loathed liquor as much as he did slavery and was active at Temperance meetings. He visited the communities at Brook Farm and Hopedale.

When Bronson Alcott and family, with Charles Lane and a few others, bought a farm in Harvard, near Fitchburg, named it Fruitlands and attempted to found the Con-Sociate Family, Joe Palmer was vastly interested. He donated a lot of fine old furniture and up-to-date farm implements to the colony. When he saw that Alcott's idiotic ideas about farming were going to bring famine to the group, he brought his own team and plow and turned up the soil. He was, in fact, the only sensible male in that wondrous experiment. (Joe Palmer appears in Louisa May Alcott's *Transcendental Wild Oats* as Moses White.)

Fruitlands had the distinction of being the worst-managed and shortest-lived of all American colonies. When the half-starved Alcotts and the others had moved away, Joe Palmer bought the farm and moved there with his wife and family. Here for more than twenty years he carried on a strange sort of community life of his own devising. He was widely known now and never lacked for company. Emerson and Thoreau visited him, and so did every reformer who passed through or operated in New England. The merely curious came to see the famous beard. The Palmers always had a pot of beans on the stove, plenty of bread in the butt'ry. All were welcome to come and to stay, so long as they had no trace of liquor about them.

In place of persecution, Joe now found himself something of a hero. The years crept on and with them his great beard grew even more famously, spreading like a willow. A photograph taken at about this time shows a growth that makes Walt Whitman seem a beardless youth in comparison. And at last, many years before he died, the whiskers of all America came into their fullest glory. This Second Coming of the beard was sudden, an almost instantaneous wilderness of hair that covered the face of male America.

One cannot know with certainty the reason for this sudden era of Whiskers; it can only be recorded. Lincoln, when elected, was smooth-shaven, but when inaugurated wore a beard. Grant, the lieutenant, had worn a tiny moustache; Grant, the general, had a full beard. Robert E. Lee went smooth of face to war, and was presently full-bearded. In 1860 Jeff Davis was clean of chin. He was soon wearing whiskers longer than Lincoln's. Nearly all of the generals of the Civil War, on both sides, were peering out of whiskers by 1862, and so were their men. Stonewall Jackson grew a mighty beard. Custer grew a unique combination beard and moustache, but it was General Ambrose E. Burnside who gave his name to a special type of whiskers.

The baseball players of the [Eighteen-] Sixties and Seventies, as depicted by the careful Currier & Ives, had whiskers. Bankers grew a style all their own. Razors went into the discard and vendors of quack beard-growers swarmed into the new market. The proper gift to a male was an elegant moustache cup. Manufacturers of soap, patent medicines, and cough drops—notably cough drops—came out with one or more bearded faces on their labels. [The bearded Smith Brothers' cough drops have lasted into the twenty-first century, *LKW.*] Whiskers, through some odd turn of the folkways, now were a sign of solid worth, a badge of integrity in every line of endeavor. If the poor barbers thought the end of things had arrived, it is easy to understand why.

As for old Joe Palmer, he was immensely happy, a true prophet who had lived to see his justification. Few prophets have been so fortunate. All over America, Joe Palmer knew, were now full beards, Van Dykes, goatees, galways, dundrearys, muttonchops, burnsides, fringe beards, and millions of stupendous moustaches of the over-Niagara type. Aye, the prophet had come into his own. Yet Joe was no gloater. He seems to have remarked only once on the greatly changed styles of what men wore on their faces. That was when he met the same Reverend Trask who had so churlishly upbraided him many years before for wearing his beard. Trask himself was now wearing a luxuriant growth. Meeting him on a Fitchburg street one day, Joe stroked his own beard and remarked: "Knowest thou that thy redeemer liveth?"

## *III*

Joe Palmer died in 1875 when beards were at their fullest, and was thus spared the dreadful sight of their withering and final disappearance. What happened during the thirty-five years following Joe's death would certainly have saddened him.

The whisker debacle of the last quarter of the nineteenth century has engrossed only a few of us minor social historians, but Mr. Lewis Gannett has charted the decline so graphically that little more research needs to be done. He used his alma mater, Harvard University, to demonstrate the mysterious rises and falls of male American hair; and his studies show that graduating classes of the 1860s were hairy as goats. The Class of 1870 had four beards. Two years later a good majority were wearing not beards but moustaches and burnsides. By 1880 beards and burnsides (sideburns are the same thing, only there isn't quite so much to them) were distinctly obsolete, and the moustache was at or nearing its peak.

Decline now followed with tragic speed. The Class of 1900 was without one beard, the first such crowd of sissies since the Mexican War. The last Harvard football moustache appeared in 1901, Mr. Gannett's chart shows, and the last Harvard baseball moustache in 1905.

Since then Harvard men—except for a few professors—have been mostly smooth of chin and lip.

The White House witnessed a similar decline of hair. From Lincoln to Wilson only one man without at least a moustache was elected to the Presidency. Grant had a beard, Hayes was positively hairy. Garfield fairly burgeoned with whiskers. Cleveland had a sizable moustache, Harrison a flowing beard, and both Theodore Roosevelt and Taft had moustaches. The lone smooth-shaven president during this entire period was McKinley.

Beginning with Wilson in 1912 and continuing to the present, no President has worn hair on his face. Many thought it was his beard that defeated Hughes, and his was for years the only honest beard to wag on the once heavily whiskered Supreme Court.

Old Joe Palmer, then, died at exactly the right time, and he took some pains to make certain, no matter what styles frivolous men might adopt, that he was not wholly forgotten. In the old cemetery in North Leominster, not far from Fitchburg, is his monument, a rugged square stone as tall as a man; and on its front is an excellent medallion carving of Joe's head, with its noble beard flowing and rippling in white marble. Below the head appears a simple legend: "Persecuted for Wearing the Beard."

Joe Palmer's last home, the celebrated Fruitlands in nearby Harvard, has been restored with loving care as an historical showplace by Clara Endicott Sears—not so much in memory of Palmer as of the Alcotts. In this charming house, however, one may see old Joe's beautiful furniture, and a good photograph of the kindly yet determined old gentleman who wished to be remembered only as the Redeemer of The Beard.

## NOTE

Author and journalist, Stewart Holbrook makes his second appearance this year [1944] in *The American Scholar*. (His article, "The Peshtigo Fire," was published in the Spring 1944 issue.) Mr. Holbrook edited the daily column "Books and Things" in *The New York Herald Tribune* during the month of July.

# PART II:
# BEAR TESTIMONIES

## Chapter 6

# A Bear Admirer's (Subjective, Fluffy, and Totally Honest) Point of View

Ned Wilkinson

Boston, mid-1980s: While taking breaks from college classes, I began writing chapters of a story, as a creative writing exercise or perhaps as a bit of therapy for a malaise I hadn't become aware of yet. One of the main characters, named "Bear," was distinguished by his height, bulk, and what would later be known as "fur factor." He was the most quiet, polite, and self-effacing character in the story, and kept the others from becoming victims of their own indulgences. "Bear" was always my favorite, and the spiral notebooks are still tucked away somewhere, full of what I would later recognize as love letters to a love I thought could only exist on paper.

Somewhere in the Ozarks, September 1990: I hurried out to my car in the post office parking lot, nervously looking around to make sure no one was coming close, grasping the manila envelope with white knuckles. I sat in the driver's seat, shaking like a kid at his first piano recital, trying to get up the nerve to open that package. My life seemed ready to change forever, and my fear pounded in my chest. My longing and curiosity won out over the temporary paranoia, and, holding my breath, I ripped open the envelope. There, on the cover of this *BEAR* magazine sent to me by a new online friend, was a half-smiling, half-scowling Joe Thomas giving me a look that said, "Heh . . . caught you lookin', funboy. Welcome to the club." The universe pretty much collapsed at that moment.

Or so I thought. Most of that particular chapter of my life didn't turn out to be nearly as original and unique as I imagined at the time. I was actually somewhat disappointed to find out that many of us do our best to construct ill-fated heterosexual identities before figuring out we'd do better on the other team. Some men figure it out much later than their midtwenties, so I was not a hopelessly late bloomer. It's simply that I didn't see anything in gay culture as it had been presented to me which was all that compelling, so there was no reason to check it out—that is, until the day I learned that someone had stolen my "bear" idea. To my deep surprise, there were other men in the world who were just as fascinated as I was with hairy, bearded men, and had taken it further than I'd ever imagined. *How did they read my mind?* I wondered.

Obviously, it was merely another privately held conceit that made me imagine that I had discovered bears all by myself. But I *did* discover them; it's just that others had done the same years before, and had not had the courtesy to inform me. To make matters worse, writing about "Bear" all those years did not give me a bit of insight as to how I could meet him in real life. I had found him—or, more correctly, those like him—lurking around in the still-underground cyber culture of 1990, and now I had photographic evidence of him in *BEAR* 12. Clearly, I could not resist him. I'd do just about anything to meet up with him. But there was one huge hurdle to overcome.

The initial thrill of learning that there was an entire subculture devoted to men that I considered to be strikingly handsome was tempered by the fact that, physically, I'm one of the least ursine specimens you'll ever meet. You will never see my baby-smooth chest and beardless face in any bear iconography. I'm never going to win the title and leather sash at any bear events. No, if I were to get anywhere in this new bear subculture, it would have to be on the strength of my admiration for bears, rather than my identification with them. Fortunately for all involved, it worked.

It worked partly because of something I managed to understand correctly from the start; bears, as we think of them, don't actually exist. Men with qualities we consider "ursine" do exist. The only thing that makes any man a "bear" is his own self-image or the image that others see in him. The bear events, cruises, and barbecues that seem to be springing up all over the country are directly a result of that image, not a result of any objective reality. Besides, how would one ever qualify or quantify a "bear"? Exactly how many whiskers are needed to make a beard? (Possible answer: as many times as this topic flames up on the Bears Mailing List before the moderators shut it down.) Bearness is one of the widest categories imaginable, and every man involved is inventing his own version moment by moment, guided purely by his own subjectivity.

When I realized that bears were simply fuzzy gay men who wanted to be seen as desirable, it stripped away even more of my preconceptions. For example, I had always thought that the junior high gym shower was traumatic because it had been embarrassing to reveal my hairless prepubescent body. If only puberty had hit earlier and more lavishly, I imagined, I'd have been spared that humiliation. I was very surprised to learn that many men had felt humiliated at that young age by their own hairy, overgrown bodies. They now tentatively embrace their new "bear" status, barely able to believe that they can be objects of desire, shyly grinning and blushing when they receive compliments. It's adorable to see.

So where does that leave the nonbearish admirer of bears, who doesn't seem to fit into a popular category himself? Actually, he is no worse off than, say, the heterosexual man who bears scant resemblance to his partners. The best-kept secret in all of our mythical Bearland is that bearishness turns out to be not all that big of an issue with bears themselves. One might get the idea from reading personal ads that "bear seeks bear" is the only configuration possible; in reality, though, men tend to be downright bored with features they already possess. Even those few furry critters who insist they are interested only in other furry critters have been known to make exceptions at times. Bears' tastes range as widely as one might imagine. I've known bears who were crazy about slim, smooth, barely legal boys. Other tastes I've encountered included "Asians," "Professional types," "Marines," and "Arabian men with smoldering eyes." Possibly the one that intrigued me most was the woofy leather bear whose life's love was a drag queen. It's clear that there are pairings even more unique out there somewhere.

I'm still struck by how timing played a part in my personal discoveries. There simply wasn't any way that a closeted, clueless guy in the Ozarks in 1990 was going to find out about bear cultural happenings on the coasts, unless he had a personal computer, a modem, access to the Internet, and anonymity. I certainly wasn't the first person to "come out" in cyberspace, but I was an early example of the trend that will be written into the history books as one of the defining forces of the 1990s. Also, as timing would have it, there was someone else in cyberspace going through their own personal discovery, and after realizing we had a few things in common, we agreed to meet for lunch when I visited old friends in the Boston area.

Eight years later, Chris is still sharing his life with me. Is he a bear? I think so. He is fuzzy enough for the part, though he loves to trim his hair and beard radically and often. He is definitely not the bear of fantasy, the gruff-voiced, blue-collar worker in flannel and boots from all the magazine fiction. He works in radio production and has a degree in theater; he plays piano, and chooses selections from his massive collection of show scores. He likes cooking and flower gardening, too. Mostly, though, he makes me feel special, appreciated, and loved. We rarely go to bear bars or events, since few are close to the Ozarks. For now, it's enough to know that someone else is taking care of bear culture in some big urban center somewhere where we might visit someday. I'm still getting all the bear hugs I need.

I have not made a new entry in my spiral notebooks in years; real life has eclipsed my desire to spin an elaborate, unlikely fantasy. Yet every once in a while I think about Joe Thomas in *BEAR* 12, and wonder if his reality ended up being anywhere close to our fantasies. Maybe at this very minute, he is taking off the leather and boots, putting on his comfortable fuzzy slippers, and baking up some chocolate chip cookies . . . or whatever strikes his fancy. I only hope for his sake that he's doing all this with someone who loves him. After all, since we're the ones writing this story, every bear—and admirer—deserves to live happily ever after.

Chapter 7

# A Puerto Rican Bear in the USA

Ali Lopez

I was in search of my own identity in my life and in the gay community as a later bloomer. Confusion and fear were a big part of my life as a young gay man. I became involved in the community in the late 1980s in Baltimore, dancing to the beat of the music of the time, losing myself under the neon lights. But inside, something was not right. I never felt at home. As a "mulatto," or an American of African/Hispanic/Native descent, it was hard to find a place to call home. I discovered "beardom" in 1990 when I was given my first issue of *BEAR*. From that moment on, nothing was the same.

I began to frequent the bars where bears were most likely to be. The Gallery was the only leather/levi club at the time in Charm City, a place that my friends would not go because the type of clientele it served. To my friends, leather people were perverts and no "respectable" gay man would be caught dead near one. I had to judge for myself. I had to find out if what my friends said was true. The bar was small in comparison to the Hippo and other dance bars in the city. It was divided into three sections—the main bar and two small bars and a small dance floor where leather-clad men danced to the beat of Madonna's "Vogue." The disco lights sliced through the heavy cigarette smoke as people greeted each other in carefree fashion. My fears dissipated right there and then. I had found myself.

That night I met Rodger Ream, the quintessential bear. We talked for a long time and became friends. A week later he introduced me

---

This chapter is dedicated to Bob Remington and Rodger Ream, Tim, The Centaurs M.C., Washington, DC, and in memory of Bill Altavogue.

to his lover, Bob Remington, and from there a family was born. Bob and Rodger became my mentors in the bear and leather communities. They introduced me to the Chesapeake Bay Bears and I became a member. In general, I was welcomed in the club, but some people didn't feel the same way; my friends from the dance club began to fall away—they didn't want to mix with "that type of people." To them I was not "me" anymore, I was part of "them." Our friendship ended soon after.

But the most painful moment came when a man that I was attracted to said to me, "Sorry, I don't go out with niggers." I was crushed. Most of my adult life I had faced racism, but never this close to home. I left the club in anger that night and a million things raced through my head. And then it became clear to me—prejudice is born of ignorance, and that by hiding my head in the sand it was not going to go away. From that moment on I became more involved with the club functions; not just as a bystander. I began to enter bear contests, not for personal glory but for representation. Being a minority in the gay community, I believed that there was a need for representation. So, I took it upon myself to be that representation in the bear community as well as the leather community. By becoming more involved, we enrich ourselves as well as the community we are a part of. To be recognized as part of it we must become visible, in the events as well as in publications.

Years later, my resolve is still the same. Progress has come slowly, but magazines such as *Bulk Male* feature biracial couples and multicultural models as well as artwork from artists like Grizz (featured, for example in 5:4, page 34), and now for the first time *American Grizzly* 3 features a biracial couple in "Hard Drive" by Vince Macoy. With this small beginning maybe some of the other publications will follow, or maybe not. But what it comes down to is that as members of the bear community it is up to us to make a mark in the bear movement. We have a responsibility to ourselves to help change come about, and that can only happen by taking part in what is out there. We need to encourage magazines to feature models, stories, and artwork that mirrors the multicultural community that we are.

As gay men we are outcasts of society; all fighting to be recognized as a part of the "mainstream," but at the same time we turn around and discriminate against or label one another. To be able to be accepted we need to accept ourselves first, to accept that we all are in this together, and to remember that in the words of Janet Jackson "in complete darkness we're all the same, it is only our wisdom and knowledge that separates us; don't let the dark deceive you."

My identity as a bear grows from the discovery of myself as a gay man. I'm what I call a "late bloomer," a gay man that finds his sexual identity in his mid- to late twenties. But looking back on my life, I see I was always attracted to large, bearded, hairy men. I just didn't know it at the time. Even my choice of toys while growing up were signs of the type of men I like, toys such as the bearded G.I. Joe with the Kung-Fu grip by Hasbro, and Big Jim and Big Josh by Mattel. Most of the characters that I created for my own comic books as a teen were barrel-chested, hairy men. As I became aware of being gay, I felt that there was something missing. I felt out of place, looking for something I couldn't put my finger on.

When I came across my first issue of *BEAR* my eyes were opened at last. I found the answers to the questions that I didn't know how to ask, but I was extremely frustrated not having friends to help me through those rites of passage. I see myself as a Puerto Rican Black Bear, physically as well as mentally. For years many people have argued over which qualities make a bear a bear, and unfortunately this has created a heated debate that has alienated some people. This argument will probably go on for some time to come, but, in my opinion, being a bear is about more than physical appearance. There are a lot of hairy people out there who shave and remove their hair permanently because the gay media image of beauty is the young, tanned, smooth-skinned blond. Being a bear is more than just an attitude; it is a way of life. It's about the freedom to be yourself, as well as social and sexual inclusiveness; in short, we are not afraid to be ourselves—it's about friendship. It's about family.

### *FAMILY BACKGROUND*

My father was a sergeant major in the U.S. Army, my mother a homemaker and Voodoo queen (no kidding), and I was the youngest of three brothers, born in Fort Carson, Colorado, during a snowstorm, on February 24, 1964. With the Vietnam conflict heating up, my father sent the family back to our permanent home in my parents' childhood home of Dorado, Puerto Rico, a small town on the north coast of the island. Famous for its beautiful sandy beaches and having been voted the cleanest town in Puerto Rico for the last thirty years in a row, it is a town with a lot of history.

Growing up had its ups and downs, especially being the youngest of the three boys. My parents were very protective and I was too independent for my own good. My dad was a very strict disciplinarian, with a very short temper, and had a hard time showing emotion. He had no sense of humor. My mother is a woman ahead of her time, in many ways a strong woman, in a very traditional Hispanic society, capable of standing toe-to-toe in an argument with my dad—and winning every time (even when *he* was right!), a funny lady who always has something to say and who became very popular with my brothers' friends as well as mine. She loves music and dancing and introduced all of us to all kinds of music, from *Danza* (Puerto Rican Dance) to rock and roll.

My brothers were seven and three years older than I and spent their time playing with kids their own age. There were no kids my age in our neighborhood, so I spent my time with older people. My mom's parents lived right across the street and every day I used to go and listen to my grandfather, the grandson of Jacinto Lopez Martinez, the founder of the town, tell stories about the hurricanes and when the Americans liberated Puerto Rico from Spanish rule. Most of all, I remember the coffee—Granddad would pick, roast, and grind his own coffee. He made the best *café con leche* in the world, and like my mom, he had a wonderful sense of humor. Grandma was the religious center of the family. Believe me when I tell you, if she hadn't married my grandfather she would have given Mother Teresa a run for her money. She also had one of the most impressive orchid collections in the town and a variety of animals that I gladly took care of.

My family was very involved in the Catholic Church and I became an altar boy. There I met Padre Guillermo, the man who became more of a father to me than my own father, my first true friend and the only person that actually allowed me to be a child. He helped me focus and change my energy in a positive way.

As a child, I was hyperactive and overly curious, with a love for science, especially biology and chemistry. Unfortunately, I also became a firebug, one of the reasons my parents wouldn't let me out of their sight. My older brothers wouldn't allow me to play baseball with them since I was too young to play with their friends and I was the "chubby little brother." So, on my tenth birthday, I asked my parents for a football—"if I couldn't play their game, I was gonna play mine." So football was introduced to Dorado. No one knew the rules, so we made our own. Soon everyone was playing on Sundays and, to my brothers' surprise, I became the player everyone wanted on their team. Despite being the "little chubby kid" I could run as fast and sometimes faster than some of the older kids, and was strong enough to stop any of them. And, boy, did it feel good!

Back at home, things were not so good. His twenty-eight years in military service, lots of it in wartime, took its toll on Dad and he began to take his anger out on us. He became physically abusive, especially to my older brother. There were times when we would get beaten and not know why. My mom would try to help the best she knew how but he wouldn't stop. My brother left home at sixteen, and I began to hate my dad.

Church, school, and working with my animals became my way out. I looked for other ways to spend less time at home, so I lied about my age to get a newspaper route. Completely naive about sex, I didn't understand the changes going on inside of me, especially why I was getting hard-ons while watching wrestling (things that make you go *hmmmm* . . .). Sex crash-landed on my lap on my eleventh birthday when the nymphomaniac wife of one of my customers began to molest me. I didn't know it at the time, but my sexual identity was taken away from me. The molestation went on until I was sixteen. Because of the physical abuse and the molestation, I began to withdraw from everyone. The anger was released on the football field as well as on the volleyball court. The pressure was overwhelming, but I couldn't tell anyone, especially Padre Guillermo. I was afraid of losing his approval. On March 10, 1976, I felt him slip away as he died from a heart attack.

I escaped to the ocean, where I befriended a pod of dolphins. They became my release, until I met Maria (no *West Side Story* cracks, please), my high school sweetheart. I was in love, we were soul mates, and a three-year love affair began. Alas, she died in a car accident in 1994.

After graduating ahead of my class at sixteen, I began to attend the University of Puerto Rico in Rio Piedras. Out of the blue, the faculty decided to go on a strike that would last seven months. Looking for a way to get away from my family, I decided to join the U.S. Army. On the day that I was due to ship out something happened that changed the way that I saw my father. As I was saying my good-byes, my dad hugged me and for the first time since I've known him, he said, "I love you, son." And with tears in his eyes we said good-bye.

It was quite a culture shock for a seventeen-year-old from a small town in Puerto Rico, but basic training was (to me) like an amusement park, but on a large scale. Like a kid with a new toy, I dove right in, earning the nickname "Superboy." I became an expert in every weapon the army had to offer. I became the ultimate soldier, a sergeant by nineteen, and ranked as one of the top explosive experts in the nation. My job was my only escape, and then I became friends with a new sergeant in my unit. Michael and I hit it off right away and we used to spend a lot of time together off duty. Michael was a stocky, good-looking man, thirty-eight years old, brown hair, light brown eyes, five feet eight with a moderately hairy body and an inviting butt.

We would watch porno movies in my room, since I had a large collection of (straight) tapes—everyone in the barracks would drop by from time to time to watch or borrow them. One night, while we watched Ron Jeremy plowing his ten-inch rod up a blonde bimbo's ass, Michael placed his hand on top of mine. I froze. I just didn't know what to do, but one thing that I did notice was the way that he looked at me and the raging hard-on that was screaming to get out. Nothing happened that night, but after he left I must have jacked off all night long. As our friendship progressed, he became bolder and more suggestive, but I was too naive and scared of the feelings inside of me. It all ended when he became the subject of an investigation and was dishonorably discharged.

It happened so quickly that we never got a chance to say goodbye. But the seed was planted. I began to question my sexuality. I had begun to grow as a gay man. After six and a half years in the

Army, it was time to face who I was. But there was just one problem—I didn't know anything about being gay. Fear of being discovered forced me to be secretive. So I made the decision to leave the Army; in October 1987, I became a civilian. Dealing with my Catholic and Hispanic upbringing was the hardest part. In all my life I had never thought of myself as gay. The image that always came to mind when thinking about homosexuality was men acting like little girls, wearing makeup and dresses and exchanging recipes while discussing interior decorating.

On October 31, 1989, I finally gathered up enough courage to go to my first gay bar, the Hippo, the largest dance bar in Baltimore. I chose Halloween for many reasons. The biggest reason was that wearing a costume I could walk around without being recognized. Also it gave me the ability to blend in. I arrived at about 11:00 p.m. that night, dressed as a zombie. I entered the well-decorated club to see a multitude of people jumping and howling everywhere, the most outrageous costumes and wigs that I had ever seen in my life. A drag queen by the name of Beula was performing on the dance floor to music from *The Little Mermaid*. People stuffed her padded chest with dollar bills as she lip-synced, horribly, to "Dose Unfortunate Souls." The night was wild. The music tried to drown out the noise from the club (without much success). In the meantime, I looked on in amusement as people complimented me on my "zombie look."

The music was blaring as the lights flickered in a surreal dance like a scene from Michael Jackson's *Thriller*, with werewolves, drag queens, historical figures, and creatures beyond belief. I lost myself in the dance—finally, I had confronted my fears. There were people from every walk of life, most of them young, and a few of them were not in costume. One of them was Kenny, a young black man who loved dancing as much as I did. That night we became friends. That night I walked away from the Hippo with a new understanding of myself, a new friend, and $50 richer since I won second place in the costume contest. I began to go out every weekend where my newfound "friends" were, but I was still very uptight. It was very hard for me to let go of my religious and cultural upbringing. As time went on, I began to feel more comfortable with myself, but deep inside something was still missing. The bear was about to break out of captivity.

## *BREAKING OUT OF CAPTIVITY*

In the late spring of 1990 everything changed. My car was in the shop being fixed and my friend was out of town, so I went out to dance at the Hippo. While teaching some people the steps to a new dance, the "Electric Slide," I noticed a new face in the crowd of onlookers. He introduced himself, said his name was Dave. "Could you teach me that step, please?" "Sure, come on," I replied. Dave was about five feet six with the build of a fireplug; his red hair and beard accentuated his pale white skin, his green eyes as well as his smile glowed under the black light, his voice was warm and inviting. After dancing for awhile, we moved away from the dance floor to talk. He was from West Virginia, in his midthirties, and was in town for a Charlie Daniels Band concert at Pier 6.

He was also in the process of divorcing his wife. As we traded life stories he was surprised to hear that I had never been with a man before. "As a matter of fact, I never kissed a man before." As he got closer to me, he looked into my eyes and gave me my first kiss. The room spun around us for what seemed like hours. I was shaking like a leaf as he said, "You are a hot bear, or what?—You don't know what a bear is? You ever get *BEAR* Magazine? You really are a virgin!" He took me by the hand and led me to his car where he gave me a copy of the magazine. My eyes opened wide as I thumbed through the pages, and my heart raced from the experience. In his car his fingers began to explore my chest as he commented on the bulge in my jeans. Dave started the car and looked me in the eye, then looked into his cassette holder and pulled a tape out and placed it into the tape player as he said, "This song is for you."

The song was "Breakaway" from the *Another Place, Another Time* album by Donna Summer. The song filled the air as we kissed and fondled each other. "Let's take you home," he said, and we drove off to my place, a modest little apartment in the suburbs of Baltimore. My roommates were gone and so we had the place all to ourselves. As we closed the door behind us, he gently pushed me against the door and we began to undress each other. Dave's body, now naked, was covered in a light coat of red fur as fine as corn silk. His belly was as solid as the rest of his body and you could bounce a quarter on his butt. The hair of his crotch, sporting a beautiful hard-on, was as silky as his head. Things happened naturally. Before we began, we opted for safe sex. We fucked and sucked all night and on into the morning. I lost my virginity that night but I gained much more—my sexual identity, my "beardom," and a sense of who I really was, a hairy gay man who loved other hairy gay men. I never saw Dave after that but I thank him every day for the night that has defined the rest of my gay life, for making me feel wanted, for explaining what versatile was all about, and for one of the hottest nights of my life.

Once I read the magazine I began to search for the "bear watering holes." I found the Gallery, where I met my "Leather Bear Grandparents." They helped me to understand myself and encouraged my individuality. The bear community became my home and in it I found a family that grew with time. As the Chesapeake Bay Bears found a home in the newly opened Baltimore Eagle, so did I. Soon after that I became more involved in the community, entering contests to represent, not myself, but a small part of the community that had not had representation until then. Through this representation and the support of my closest friends, I became the first Black Bear to enter many contests around the United States, including Bear Pride in Chicago, Bear Bust in Orlando, and Bear Rendezvous in 1995 and 1996. In July of 1995 I had the honor of being selected Chesapeake Bay Bears Muscle Bear in the Bears of Summer Contest, becoming the first Black Bear to win a bear contest in the United States: I have come into my own.

After spending six and a half years as an explosives expert, teaching soldiers and CIA agents how to blow up people, this really became a conflict for me in my last two years in the Army. Unfortunately, my fears were realized years later when the Oklahoma City bombing occurred. I turned my back on my military training and opened a small limo company with my best friend from the Army. Unfortunately, the small company couldn't compete with the larger companies and the recession created by President Read-My-Lips Bush forced us to go under. I decided to go back to one of the loves of my life, working with animals. I got a job working in the largest aquarium store in the Baltimore/Washington area. While working there I got overtime work with the Baltimore National Aquarium in the captive reproduction program with a variety of animals. Then, eight and a half years later, I became a curator for a new restaurant concept that included large parrots and a large aquarium system. After opening a store in Virginia, I was moved to open the Costa Mesa (California) store.

I had begun to draw as a small kid back in Puerto Rico. It all started with a Superman comic book. I became fascinated by the artwork in that thin little book, so I tried to emulate the art that I loved so much. I tried to talk my parents into sending me to an art school, but they were afraid that I would be distracted from my school work. "There will be time for it later," they said, but later never came. Against my parents' wishes I kept drawing. At age eleven I began to create my own super heroes, and started to write short stories to support the characters. Influenced by artists like Tom Lile, George Perez, and Jim Lee, I began to develop my own style. Being my own worst critic, I would only show my art to my closest friends. All that changed one night at the Gallery, when a conversation with Bob, Rodger, and some other friends turned to art. Bruce, a hot-looking daddy bear, was looking for an artist to do an erotic drawing in pencil as a present for a friend. Bob suggested that I give it a try. This was my first time doing erotic art and from that moment on I was hooked. My artwork began to change, but I still kept it to myself. Looking at the artwork of artists like Turtle, Grizz, Tony, Frich, Bill Ward, and Domino in *BEAR* encouraged me to show my stuff, but I didn't know how to begin.

Bill, a friend from the Chesapeake Bay Bears, volunteered to take some of my work to the offices of *BEAR* magazine. Since he was going to Bear Expo '94, he could drop by and show my art. Bill never got a chance to meet with the powers that be at the magazine, and he made a decision that changed the way I look at my artwork. Without my knowledge, Bill entered my artwork in the Bear Expo art contest and, to my suprise, I was chosen Best of Show. Unfortunately, that victory didn't gain me any notice at any of the existing magazines. I was still an unknown to a lot of people, but in the spring of 1995, I was given my first break by Bob Miller and his short-lived magazine *DaddyBear*. The magazine gave me the opportunity to show a small portion of what I could do. After the magazine went under, I kept trying to get work from other magazines—with little success—doing a few pieces for magazines like *Bulk Male* (5:6) and one page in *BEAR* 36. The doors kept slamming as I kept on looking for work. As a last resort I decided to put on paper an idea that I had been kicking around for years—and "Grizzly Fantasies" was born. Originally called "Bear Stories," it gave me the opportunity to create erotic short stories without written dialogue and allow the reader to create his own fantasy from the pictures. It also allowed me to represent a multicultural cast. After trying to get published by different magazines, I was finally given a chance by *American Bear* owner Tim Martin to feature my art in his new magazine, *American Grizzly*. He allowed me great flexibility in the creative process. Right now I am in the process of working with *Bulk Male* on the prototype for a bimonthly strip for the magazine.

Since the beginning of time, art has helped define and distinguish cultures from one another. Bear art has set us apart from the rest of gay media, getting away from the "tan, smooth-skinned surfers" and the V-shaped bodies of Tom of Finland. Bear art has helped to define bears' attitude and lifestyle, and what they find attractive. My art has evolved side-by-side with my self-discovery, becoming an intimate way of self-expression where my feelings, fantasies, sexuality, and attitudes come out to play. It also allows me to help the community by donating the art for fund-raising events. As a strong supporter of safe sex, I feature safe sex practices in my art as much as I can. The bear and leather communities, as well as an overactive imagination, have been big influences in my art. In the present age safe sex is a very serious issue for me and I take every opportunity I can to feature condoms in my art. I believe that as an artist I have a responsibility to the community to encourage the use of condoms. I also try to feature social issues of today, such as gay marriage, hate crimes, and discrimination. In the beginning I would only represent my own views and the kind of men that I found interesting, but it soon became a way to communicate feelings, ideas, sexual fantasies, and to interpret the fantasies of others. Art has created an "alternate universe" that allows me to create, expanding the bear movement through time and space—from the days of the caveman, to our present safe-sex era, and to our distant future.

Most of my art has been heavily influenced by ancient history, fantasy, Greek mythology, and high-tech science fiction. For years, Hollywood, as well as the mainstream gay media, has portrayed heroes like Hercules, Conan, and Tarzan as clean-shaven bodybuilders. Before the modern obsession for clean-shaven faces and smooth-toned bodies, beards were a sign of wisdom and pride. Girth was the embodiment of power and might. Robust bodies were the "in" thing back in the Renaissance, and the "full body" look was glorified for centuries—and far be it from me to argue with history! Traveling back in time through my art allows me to give the bear movement a sense of history. It also lets me explore the animal side of sexuality without compromising my views on safe sex in the process. Science fiction is one of my favorite subjects and will always have a special place in my heart, allowing me to create new worlds where fear and discrimination no longer exist; worlds where bears are the only ray of hope in the darkness, creating our own mythology, our own heroes, and our own identity—to prove once and for all that being a bear is more than just an attitude, it is a lifestyle.

Art became my escape from a world that I was too afraid to face. Drawing opened up a door to my innermost fantasies, allowing me to be as "bad" as I want to be; exploring fetishes like outdoor sex, uncut cocks, one-on-one and group sex, 69, oral sex, anal sex, tight butts, leather wear, blue-collar men, versatile cubs, bears, daddy bears, and long foreskins became easy to express as I became more comfortable with my sexuality.

I try to express my versatility in my art not just in the sexual arena but in the type of men that I find attractive, where size, height, age, and cultural background don't make a difference. I like to convey a sense of primal lust whenever I'm doing my fantasy art. Jungle-primitive and outdoor scenes let me expose the animal aspect of bears. No tenderness, no consequences, just raw animal lust, the scent of musk of man smell or a hot hairy man . . . WOOF!

Ancient cultures worshipped the phallus as a sign of power and fertility and protection from evil. Now in modern times many men still worship the "natural" man. Uncut men hold a special spot in my heart (and other places too—woof!). The sight of a foreskin makes my juices flow. Recently there has been a big movement against circumcision, and foreskin restoration techniques are becoming popular among gays and straights alike. I see it as my duty to be able to present the natural man in all his glory.

Now that my art is beginning to be seen by the public, I've been allowed to do more when working for magazines, letting me "push the envelope." With *American Grizzly*, for example, I'm given the ability to create any fantasy environment, but I find true-to-life situations can be very sensual, as, for example, in an upcoming strip for *American Grizzly* that I have titled "The Anniversary," which shows a couple celebrating their twenty-fifth anniversary with a fuck fest in a secluded cabin in the woods. This strip is dedicated to the long-term couples of the community, who are ignored by most magazines but will always have a special place in my heart (especially if they like to play with others—woof!). Group sex has always been a big turn-on for many of us, opening many possibilities from threesomes to group sex. It has the potential for satisfying many fantasies at the same time—voyeurism, anal, and oral sex—the possibilities for sexual gratification are endless. This also gets back to the roots of beardom, the Bearhug play parties. Just imagine yourself in a room with Michael McDonald, Big Bad Vader, Al from *Home Improvement*, and all the strongest men in the Strongest Man competitions, and watch the fur fly!

The future is one of my favorite playgrounds, giving me free reign to be creative (can you say "god complex"!), where you can make your own rules. It helps me explore the human condition in an indirect manner and allows me to use the duality of the human spirit. It also allows for new sexual scenarios where the only limits are my imagination. It's a chance for bears to create their own folklore where the future can be claimed as our own, a stream of dreams where ideas can flourish and bloom.

The bear movement continues to grow, becoming not just a local fad, but a movement that has gone global and a movement that has proven that bears are here to stay. As beardom continues to expand, unfortunately, sometimes it gets away from the fundamental principles of inclusiveness that made the bear community what it is today. As the controversy over who is and who is not a bear heats up, what suffers is the bear movement as a whole. What sets bears apart from other gay groups is the sense of family, the "come as you are" feeling that many clubs are so good at expressing, making members and visitors feel welcome. Unfortunately, some clubs have become cliquish toward people who don't fit their standard of what a bear is. This has become very apparent when Girth and Mirth members have been discriminated against because of their size, or where black bears have been made to feel unwanted at some bear club events. As the argument rages on, the bear community loses—the true power of beardom is the brotherhood that we share. Our unity is our strength.

Multicultural representation is something that many of us would like to see in magazines and videos. Over the years, it has been very apparent that there is a lack of minorities in most of them. So far the only one daring enough to feature biracial couples and artwork featuring multicultural couples is *Bulk Male*. In the years that I have been reading bear-oriented fiction I have only found one story that featured a multicultural cast. Will there be more black or Asian bears on the cover of a magazine? Will there be a spread of two men of different racial backgrounds fucking each others' brains out in a video or a magazine? Will there ever be bear videos featuring a group scene with some Asian and black bears in the group? Only time will tell. Magazines are not completely responsible for the lack of multicultural bears—magazines have a hard time finding minority bears to pose for them. We need to expose ourselves (no pun intended) if we want to be seen and recognized in the bear community.

Beardom has created a positive change within the gay community in general, as bear clubs continue to grow in this country and around the world. The fundamental message of social and sexual inclusiveness continues to flourish. Bear activities keep popping up and, with them, new members keep joining the "family," a family that expands across the rainbow spectrum of the gay community and beyond. Beardom has also become a strong supporter of the community by becoming active in fund-raising, sometimes more successfully than the gay mainstream. And as we continue to grow, the bear community is becoming more diversified—what many thought of as a fad or a subculture that would disappear in time has proven to be a lasting and welcome change to the community, creating an impact that is not just social but economic as well. Beardom has become an icon that has touched many of us in different ways. Speaking for myself, my life has been enriched greatly by beardom, giving me a sense of purpose, a family that I can count on, and a cause that I can believe in.

# Chapter 8

# One Black Bear Speaks

## Jason R. Clark

The other night I was standing in the bar with another black bear and his friend, inquiring about a certain Northeastern bear club. I asked him how many black bears had joined and he told me there were three other black members. Three is actually a very good number but that's *three* mind you, out of 200 members.

African-American bears or black bears (which I choose to use because it has a nice ring to it and there *are* actually black bears) are alive and well in the bear community. We love big hairy men just as much as the next bear but our club participation may be lacking for many reasons.

Speaking from my experience as a black bear, just being a black gay male has obstacles. Homosexuality in the black community is still not generally understood—exceptions being that distant aunt, uncle, cousin, or that one particular kid down the street that jumped double dutch really well. Being gay is unacceptable.

So once you have overcome this first hurdle you now must become comfortable with the fact that you like your men big, hairy, and possibly (maybe even for a large majority) white. It has been my observation (not generalization) that many of the gay black males I have met are either extremely effeminate or are rarely able to reveal their sexuality, hiding behind a pseudo bisexual facade. Such men usually claim silly things like: "I'm not gay, I just like having my dick sucked" or "I don't care who it is, I just like to fuck." Or they just remain closeted.

Coming to grips with the fact that the majority of men that I'd be meeting would be white was a sudden realization. It all boils down to personal preference. When first coming out I had trouble understanding why one of my friends would only date black men while another only dated white men. Caught in the middle, I would claim I loved all men, and that to exclude any was wrong.

Today, I still love all men—it's just that all of the men I'm attracted to have some of the same characteristics. Just as some prefer blondes to brunettes, thin to hefty, Spanish, black, white, or even blue, each person's attraction is his or her own. No explanation necessary. Although some I've heard about are complete turn-ons! For some the attraction is to contrast or to the complete opposite, some to myth, or to forbidden fruit. It works for me. In fact, I feel it's an extra turn-on when someone tells me they have never slept with a black man before. Then I feel obligated to make sure they never have to think twice about doing it again. I think the bear community is a little more welcoming of the fact that we all like what we like. As my dad would say, "Whatever floats your boat." Whether you like your man black, Asian, or Hispanic, he's still a bear in the whole sense of the word.

The complications of being a black bear/black gay male extend far beyond family and communal issues, and include gaining a personal understanding of mainstream society's and the gay community's struggle with classification. Early bar experiences had me wondering why I wasn't exactly connecting with the people I was meeting. A million things were running through my mind. Was I not thin enough? Not buff enough? Not trendy enough? Or was it because I was black? To be self-concious of these "flaws" was strange since I didn't even look for these traits in others.

And then, one day, I walked into a particular bar and discovered a group of woofy men who called themselves bears. And I'm thinking to myself, there are a lot of men out there who I find attractive and they even have a name. The rest is history. So I've found my place to belong. Weighing all options, questions, and confusion, I'd say being a bear makes me happy. But there were even problems in beardom. Awhile back there was a lot of nonsense going on about what exactly was a bear. Subcategories like otter, grizzly, and walrus were being created. Even though we all basically like the same thing, some found it necessary to complicate matters, excluding a number a people because of weight, hairiness, and age.

My definition of a bear is my own—a term not coined by me but which recognizes my own tastes and preferences for beards, mustaches, and hairy bodies. Body hair for me screams masculinity, and there's nothing hotter than a man whose chest hair peeks out above the neckline of his shirt. Body size is optional, the hair being more important. But for me being a bear is also about attitude. It's possible for someone to look like a bear but to not fit the (attitude) profile. So, if someone chooses to grow a mustache or beard, he isn't automatically locked into this category. What's sometimes missing is an attitude that includes enjoying cold beer and having a good time; wearing jeans, boots, and T-shirts; firm grips and pats on the back; not being afraid to say what you want and be yourself; cuddling, grrrrs and woofs—big hugs and friendship.

That's what being a bear means to me, a black bear—an insight that should be familiar to any other bear you speak to. And *that* is the point of this whole thing.

*P.S. I wrote the following letter to Chris Wittke, author of* BEAR *magazine's "The Wittke Wire."*

> I must give great thanks for the creation of the bear subculture, acknowledgment of its existence, and to *BEAR* magazine for the way it's helped me grow as a person. No, this isn't the hokey part where I claim I felt one-hundred-percent better about myself after viewing the pages of *BEAR*. Instead, it's where I no longer feel guilty about adoring certain hirsute thespians in television and film or the insightful articles. Don't get me wrong; I enjoy the pictures also. But I thank *BEAR* for being an outlet for bear expression. As I mentioned, being a bear is more than a look, but also an attitude and manner—a subculture so misinterpreted by the gay community that it sometimes clouds itself. I think knowing exactly what we want is a main factor of beardom, and that this non-fickle nature has led me to meet many wonderful people over the years. Pointing out problems that riddle clubs and organizations, we run into issues that reach far beyond the original goal of brotherhood and fraternity but to examples of personal, social, and human ugliness that should never surface. They make me angry, but I can overlook these shortcomings for an allowance

of some kind of unity primarily seen at bear gatherings, where one can step back and decipher out of the woofs and growls a utopia others can take notes from.

Thank you, *BEAR*, not for single-handedly performing this function, but for allowing it to enter so many homes.

## Chapter 9

# An Asian Bear in Minnesota

## Dave Gan

I must admit that Minneapolis was a bit of a culture shock when my job brought me here from San Francisco three years ago. Used to a diverse nightlife in The City, I felt as though people went hurriedly home to their families immediately after work, and the entire city shut down. Having been an active member of the San Francisco bear community, I'm no stranger to bears, so I naturally sought out the local bear group to see if I could make a few new friends to jumpstart my social life.

I remember stumbling upon a gay bar called the Town House in St. Paul one night, quite by accident. The building was rather nondescript, like much of St. Paul, and I would have missed it completely if I hadn't noticed all these cars parked out front resplendent with rainbow stickers. Wholesome is probably not an appropriate description, but I remember being pleasantly surprised at how friendly everyone in the bar was. There were the usual oddballs, of course, but people seemed nice and genuine. I found out that there were two main bear groups active in the Twin Cities of Minneapolis and St. Paul, the Minnesota Bears and the North Country Bears, which have since merged into one club. There is also a sizable—no pun intended—Girth and Mirth group, and there is a substantial overlap in the membership of the various groups.

The North Country Bears, the pioneering bear group in Minnesota, bills itself as "an association of gay and bi men who like the look, feel, and company of bear guys from cubs to otters to great gray grizzlies!" The group organizes regular activities twice a month. The Bear Bar Nights in the cooler months are pretty well-attended, often even with some bears driving in from the neighboring states. Bear Bar Nights can be a great way to meet other bears, albeit being a somewhat shotgun approach.

I recall having a lot of fun at various other gatherings such as barbecues, game nights, and pool parties. A bunch of bears tubing down the Cannon River is also quite an experience. Tubing is usually followed by a buffet at a casino in the area, dispelling any doubt that bears love food. Underbear Parties are apparently wildly popular here. I guess bear hugs, the ritual gesture of greeting among bears, often inspire more intimate interaction. Fill a big house with bears, remove clothing, add drinks and munchies, and the effect is greatly enhanced.

One of the highlights of the North Country Bears calendar is the annual Summer Bear Camp in St. Croix State Park over the Fourth of July weekend. The Bears organize bike, canoe, and hiking trips at the wooded, secluded camp on the picturesque St. Croix River. I leave it up to your imagination what goes on in the bunkhouses, but I really enjoyed watching the Bears play volleyball, and relaxing on the beach. This affordable event has been growing in popularity and offers a refreshing alternative to the large-scale events in the vicinity like Bear Pride in Chicago over the Memorial Day weekend.

While the local bear community does not seem very apparent to the casual observer, in some ways the sense of bear community is stronger here in Minneapolis than in cities with much more visible bear populations. Apart from the monthly North Country Bears' activities, bears here like to organize little groups to enjoy coffee or a game of cards. Rain, shine, sleet, or snow, these groups unfailingly meet every week. This is very much a part of the culture here, and many of the bears are native to the area and have known each other for quite some time. In fact, many bear events here take place in private homes. It does take some effort and courage for a bear that's new to the area to seek out these gatherings. For bear admirers who may not be bears themselves, this can be a bit intimidating.

This particular nature of the Minneapolis bear community seems to beg the question: "What must I do to belong?" I'm used to the bear community in San Francisco, which seemed to revolve around a few well-known bear hangouts. Practically everyone is from "somewhere else" and bears would come and go, but the bears had a home, and everyone was welcome all the time. This kind of acceptance, one of the tenets of the original bear movement, seems harder to come by in a gay community made up of small close-knit groups.

It's not that the gay community here is not friendly. On the contrary, Minnesotans are some of the nicest people one could ever meet. You may have heard the term "Minnesota Nice." As far as I can tell, it means Minnesotans are always nice, polite, and cheerful, but at the same time emotionally distant. I thought I noticed this behavior at first, but I've since discovered that "Minnesota Nice" is just another urban myth. Or maybe I've been here long enough to become immune to the phenomenon.

What it is like to be a bear in Minneapolis of course depends on personal expectation and the amount of effort invested. I, for example, do not find hanging out at a bar or at a party with a group of strangers twice a month very satisfying. I prefer having something in common and spending time together with a bunch of really good bear friends. A group of us once actually pretended to be bakers from Beyerly's (a local grocery chain) and crashed a bakery convention. We made out like bandits with all kinds of goodies that day. Even the real Beyerly's people never noticed the deception despite having a "no facial hair" requirement in their company. These are the unique experiences I will remember about bear life here long after I've forgotten everything else.

One particular incident was especially amusing. A good bear buddy of mine here was convinced that there was a "Secret Bear Language of the Skyways." For those of you who have not visited Minneapolis before, the Skyway is a vast system of sealed overpasses interconnecting most of the buildings downtown. The Skyway allows one to get from point A to point B without having to go outdoors, an excellent idea when it's minus seventy degrees outside. The lunchtime crowds offer very entertaining bear watching, especially in winter when a great many guys sport full beards. One day, my buddy noticed that bears passing him in the Skyway would slowly lick their mustaches. Convinced that there was some sexual meaning to this behavior, he started responding with the same gesture. Having tried it, I can't vouch for this Secret Bear Language having any kind of effect other than mostly eliciting strange stares from the bears. But I must admit that I had great fun with this exercise, and I will always fondly cherish the memory.

For a city of its size, Minneapolis has far more than its fair share of festivals and parades. Perhaps it is because everyone wants to party as much as they can before winter sets in and everyone disappears for the next six months. I have noticed that bears here are not separatist, and do not just show up at the Gay, Lesbian, Bisexual, and Transgender Parade, which, by the way, is somewhat tame compared to the ones in cities like San Francisco or Washington, DC. Bears here also show up in full force at events that are not exclusively gay. Apparently the Aquatennial Celebration (the ten best days of summer!) is the place to be seen since I run into more bear friends there than anywhere else. The various block parties in the cities are wonderful venues for bear watching as well.

If you like bear watching or the wildly amusing game of "Guess If the Bear Is Gay or Straight?" you can't miss the Minnesota State Fair, another Midwest institution. If you go, be sure to try my personal favorite State Fair dish: pork chop on a stick. Strong Scandinavian, Germanic, and Celtic features are quite apparent in the crowds, which is always pleasing to bear admirers. I think the Midwest is truly the bear-lover's paradise, for it seems like most of the men here have that rugged, even husky bearish build. Facial hair is also popular here, and it seems like everyone has one of those trendy mustache/goatee combos nowadays. Woof!

I must confess that I wish there were more Asian men (or Asian bears for that matter) in the bear community in Minneapolis. Not because I'm particularly attracted to them, but because diversity is a good thing. It is as though bears and Asians were two different worlds and never the twain shall meet. Often being the only Asian man in a group, I sometimes get the feeling that the bears pass me over like the mystery meat at a Chinese buffet. Other Asian bears or bear lovers may have experienced that feeling. The only person around here that has ever said to me, "Dave, you're such a big ol' bear!" was a straight co-worker of mine who's never heard of the bear movement. It makes me wonder what the bear community stands for?

Then I remember that this is, after all, America's heartland, and people here are not easily impressed by anything. In spite of the trendiness of organized bear activity everywhere, I have realized that here in Minneapolis, a great many bears tend to eschew the so-called bear groups and involve themselves in other social outlets. The numerous charity groups, the lively music scene, the emerging high-tech circles, and, yes, even the grocery store are venues where one can really see that the bear community in Minneapolis is alive and well. Ultimately I find that it only takes a few good bear friends, the ones that embody and exemplify the true spirit of beardom, to nurture and affirm one's bearhood. I have to say, if the last year or two are any indication, I'm in very good company.

# Chapter 10

# The Ephebe Is Dead— Long Live the Bear

## David Greig

Sometimes, if you're lucky, a small crack can appear in what you've assumed was an unalterable reality. If the timing is right, you can squeeze through that crack and find yourself in a new and astonishing place. I recently squeezed through such a crack. I have been able to quit the gay male body chorus and now I'm whistling a brand new tune.

I woke up one day no longer young. No longer beautiful. No longer anything like the acceptable, manufactured image of gay male desire. I am older, fatter, grayer, balder, hairier. Destined, I thought, to follow a legion of fellow aging fags into the bitter and dichotomous syndrome of young and hot or old and troll. Aging has been the enemy of gay men for decades.

I decided one day to face the enemy and confront aging head on. I was quite shocked to discover some remarkable new possibilities. When I embraced my changing body as evolution and not as decay —when I stopped fighting it—I became more erotically alive than I'd been for ages. I've found the most incredible healing in the formerly untapped (or at best merely fetishistic) sexual power of the aging, changing male body. And I don't think I'm the only one who has discovered this. Even though it has degenerated into yet another rigid gay body cult marketing tool, the bear phenomenon was, for a brief moment, a beacon of gay men's body liberation.

To be a bear meant to reject gay image strictures and celebrate the reality of real men's bodies. Not the Greek statue man-boy muscle archetype—the ephebe—but the thick-necked, hairy-forearmed, wide-bellied, raw-whiskered, grinning and leering older guy. Not boys or youths or models or women-like males, but men who are men, with all their testosterone-produced flaws.

Men who no longer strive to remain perpetual sons but who become their own fathers. Men who discover the power of their own natural masculinity, an innate (usually latent) masculinity that is neither cruising mask nor social role nor leather butch-drag costume. A masculinity that celebrates the physical welcoming of men's primal, messy, essential, penis-bearing stag beast selves. Neanderthal bodies with the playfulness of little boys in an all-male erotic sandbox.

When gay men embrace their own innate masculinity, they stop being boys playing with boys and become men playing with men. Grown men. Men who have grown up. Having sex as a grown man with other grown men has never been hotter or better or more satisfying. The erotic transformation of body-loathing, age-fearing, mirror-dwelling boy/queen into a friendly Cro-Magnon, a smiling, hairy-assed, scrotum-scratching, beard-rasping, man-to-man lust buddy is the site of ancient, fundamental, and benevolent male erotic power.

When gay men accept their own aging bodies and learn to lust after the changing bodies of the men around them, they grow up. When gay men cast off their manufactured youth fetish and celebrate essential, healthy, and whole masculine aging (manliness in all its imperfect manifestations), they discover new sexual possibilities, new ways of imaging and creating themselves, a whole new world where gay liberation becomes a limitless journey and not a restricted destination.

The ephebe is dead—long live the bear.

## Chapter 11

# Parlaying Playmates into Lasting Friendships

John R. Yoakam

> It would appear that anyone can now don a flannel shirt and jeans, grow a beard and, hey, presto—bear! What is somehow lacking, however, is any radical appraisal of what it means to be a gay man and how we relate to one another.... Rather than focusing on ever more restrictive modes of behavior it is perhaps time to stand back and reappraise what being a man is, accepting ourselves and our masculinity in its widest form, accepting our need to love and be loved, our need to be affectionate with other men, to enjoy their company, and to be wrapped up in the support, comfort, and love of our fellow man. Literally. (McCann, 1997, p. 259)

In January 1993, Shawn Smith called together the first gathering of the North Country Bears. Sixty furry, burly men packed into the back bar of the Town House, a country western gay bar in St. Paul, Minnesota. For two years the North Country Bears hosted well-attended bar nights, initiated an annual Bear Camp at a state park, and sponsored popular "underbear" parties (Bears in Boxers) in private homes (along with other activities such as picnics and bowling).

Group activities and a quarterly newsletter were planned by a group of friends, with no formal leadership or membership, dues, or incorporation. The North Country Bears described itself as "the Northland's first bear fraternity . . . as an association of gay and bi men who like the look, feel, and company of bear guys from cubs to otters to great gray grizzlies! . . . We're an easygoing group with no dues, frills, or fancy stuff. Just regular monthly events and good times, a place to meet, make friends, and plan with the kind of men you like to be around."

Two years later, in January 1995, Clark Bufkin, publisher of a Twin Cities gay newsmagazine, had a different idea for a bear club. He was looking for more structure and commitment. Clark initiated the Minnesota Bears, or MNBears, as a "social fraternal organization of hirsute men and their admirers . . . whose purpose will be to promote social interaction, communication within the community, while raising money for worthy causes." Clark drew up bylaws, incorporated the club, and found thirty subscribers who paid $50 each for the first year's membership. To promote club events, Clark used his newsmagazine with full-page ads for fund-raising events in gay bars, which featured bear videos, door prizes, loud music, and unlimited tap beer and food for a modest admission. Two hundred attendees at these events became the core mailing list for the club, although the dues-paying membership never rose beyond forty.

Clark left the Twin Cities for San Francisco six months later. A new board was elected. I became the president (and was reelected a year later). MNBears scheduled bar nights and other social activities (musicales, cooking demonstrations, campouts, potluck suppers, etc.) which did not conflict with the North Country Bears events. Bears and friends attended activities of both clubs, though the North Country Bears attracted more men to their bar nights.

After two years, with declining attendance and revenues, the MNBears board and membership decided to merge with North Country Bears, turning over the bylaws, incorporation, and remaining treasury to the NCB. We concluded that we had organized creative events, which were well publicized, accessible, and fun. However, there just weren't enough potental members in the Twin Cities and surrounding area to support two bear groups. With one club charging only pay-as-you-go entrance fees to bar nights, there was little incentive for bears to pay membership dues to another club.

North Country Bears continued to organize activities and appoint officers, but dropped membership fees. The mailing list became the membership. Bar night attendance increased. The Bear Camp expanded to include fall and winter weekend runs as well as the summer event, which drew over 100 participants, many from outside the region. Underbear parties were scheduled for summer and winter as well as autumn and spring.

I stepped back from the club, occasionally attending a bar night, to reassess what being part of a bear group meant to me. I met many bears before, during, and after the two years that MNBears existed. After attending Bear Camp in the summer of 1997, my partner and I began to consider whether or not bear events were meeting our needs to establish lasting friendships.

We began to explore other venues for connecting with gay and lesbian people: church, folk dancing, an international travel network. None of these activities expanded our sexual opportunities, but they did enlarge our circle of friends. Lesbian friends especially reciprocated with dinner invitations, birthday parties, and theater excursions. They were fascinated with the opportunities for sex that gay and bi men had with the underbear parties, as there was no equivalent in the lesbian community. Some of my lesbian friends participated in a network of women called "Out to Brunch." The activities for these groups (there were three: Over 50s; Over 40s; and one for all ages) were initiated by members who posted these events and contact information in a newsletter. Newsletter recipients paid for its cost. There were no dues, no officers. The network existed for almost twenty years. Some events were open to men. I was also intrigued with the connections that lesbians maintained with each other over the years. "My best friend is my ex-lover," was more than a cliché for many women, who did not drop their partners once the romance had worn off the relationship and the two separated.

I searched the literature on gay and lesbian friendships and found one study (Nardi and Drury, S., 1994). From a survey of 161 gay men and 122 lesbians, mostly in their thirties and forties, white, educated, and middle-class, the authors discovered the following characteristics:

1. Both women and men placed a high value on friendships.
2. Men tended to define intimate friendships in terms of shared activities, where women tended to focus on shared feelings and values.

3. Gay men and lesbians appeared to be equally disclosing, equally "instrumental" (e.g., "competing at sports or play"), and equally "expressive" (e.g., "talking about personal problems or relationships") in their friendships.
4. Lesbians reported that they were more bothered by major conflicts with a best friend than gay males were, and that they resolved those conflicts with a best friend differently from gay males. When major conflicts arose, gay males were less likely than lesbians to express their emotions, but were as likely as lesbians to talk about it or ignore it.
5. Gay males were more likely to have had sex with casual and close friends, but not best friends. Lesbians, however, were more likely to say that their best friend was once their lover and significantly more likely than gay men to describe their best friend as their current lover.

Apropos to this research, I do believe that the bears I have known through the Minnesota clubs and other bear gatherings I've attended (Bear Pride and the Fiesta des los Osos) are interested in friendship as well as sex. The continuity of these friendships often depends on attending these events. The emotional depth of these relationships (i.e., the capacity to disclose to others) was difficult to assess, given the casual social nature of bear activities. I do recall a campfire one summer when a dozen bears told stories of remarkable sexual encounters in their lives. Rarely have I heard gay men express such romantic detail. There was no one-upmanship, but an open desire to share meaningful experiences rarely expressed. One man told of being picked up in a limousine on a beach in Hawaii. Another described a romantic dinner he prepared for his new sweetheart.

As a bear club president, I was frequently the mediator of conflict. Personality clashes contributed to officers' abandoning their posts. I received support from the events coordinator, who became the cheerleader for the club. He often telephoned me after an event to ask my opinion of how the activity went or to thank me for my help. He named me "fearless leader." I'm not sure how "fearless" I was; but for two years I was persistent in promoting club activities, calling members, writing press releases, and organizing a "bear presence" at Pride festivals.

At the beginning of my tenure as president, one of the board members advised that the officers act as benevolent dictators, planning the events for the club, taking praise, deflecting criticism, avoiding too much "process." We did hold membership meetings three times a year to solicit input. I found it hard to move members or attendees to initiate events, although with a little badgering and encouragement, shy bears, who were more frequently followers than leaders, did host picnics and potlucks in their homes. To facilitate getting to know each other at MNBear club events, officers introduced themselves and other members to newcomers. We wore name tags. The bimonthly newsletter, *The Growler*, listed the officers, a voice mail number to leave messages, and an e-mail address. Club activities were designed to be interactive and featured the talents of members for musical performance, cooking, and games. A "pajama party" began with a safer-sex seminar. An erotic massage workshop was taught by an experienced masseur. The club held fund-raisers and donated money and teddy bears to three AIDS-related charities. A contingent of the MNBears marched in the Pride parade carrying a banner stitched by my partner's mother, who watched the procession from the sidelines.

When I introduced myself and the club to newcomers at bar nights, I observed how quiet the bears who came were. I discovered that bear events, for some, were their only opportunities to socialize with other gay men. For others these events were connecting points for casual conversations with friends and acquaintances, for sex partners, or for budding relationships. Many had not found a place for themselves in the gay community. Some were married. Others had few friends or primary relationships. Many of the bears worked in solitary jobs, often computer related. They became more animated when they spoke of gigabytes or memory to each other.

Some bears found refuge in the bear clubs after having experienced rejection because of their sexual orientation or their body type. Many bears expressed relief that they could "be themselves" in a bear group while they felt out of place in a gay bar setting that wasn't a club event. Age sometimes was a positive attribute. The "great graying grizzlies" were prized by some as "daddies." The age span of the group extended from early twenties to sixties. Some bears were entering the workforce while others were newly retired. Relationships developed between men with a fifteen- to twenty-year age difference.

My partner and I met several men at local and national bear gatherings with whom we first connected as playmates. While the sex we had was fun, we were also looking for continuing friendships. Some of our acquaintances disappeared after a couple of encounters. With others we grew to become friends because we mutually worked to develop deeper relationships. Some of the things we did to foster these friendships were as follows:

1. We communicated frequently by e-mail.
2. We shared interests beyond bears and sex, which included music, travel, politics, and art.
3. We visited each other when we could. During these visits we became familiar with each other's homes and friends. After we had driven a long distance, one of our friends treated us to a hot tub party, where we met some of his frisky friends.
4. When our bear friends developed new relationships, they introduced their boyfriends to us, thus expanding all of our social networks. We also encouraged two of our friends who were architects and chorus members from different cities to meet each other. They did, in a city other than their hometowns!
5. We worked through conflicts.
6. We listened to each other's frustrations with jobs, boyfriends, families, and offered help when appropriate.

We noticed that other bears organized impromptu dinner parties and excursions with their friends apart from the club events. It took some effort and organization. One member of the club was noted for his "entourage." He was a pied piper of bears and cubs, with a natural ability to pull people together for fun events: trying new restaurants, enjoying amusement parks. He and his "entourage" also attended larger bear events together, using each other as points of contact in order not to get lost in the crowd. A year after my tenure as president, I realized that it was possible to develop continuing, reciprocal friendships with other men.

Can bears parlay playmates or even casual acquaintance, into lasting friendships? To answer this question requires looking at the basis on which bear groups are organized. Shawn Smith described bears as "fetishists," men who are sexually attracted to other men because of their hairiness and body type. Was physical appearance the only common denominator that drew bears and their admirers together?

A subscriber to the Bears Mailing List was seeking to find another bear who was an architect as a lover. He was advised by another subscriber to seek out architects, among whom he might find a gay man who was a bear rather than trying to find an architect among bears. In other words, if one is looking to find common ground for an intimate relationship, it would be better to seek a mate or a friend where others share interests that transcend physical appearance.

I believe that any "radical appraisal of what it means to be a gay man and how we relate to one another" must also look at how we care for one another. At the beginning of the AIDS epidemic, I signed up to be a buddy for a young man who was living with AIDS. I participated in a support group with other buddies. I experienced in that group a profound capacity for caring, not only for the HIV-infected, but for one another. We were not afraid to express our fears and frustrations to one another. We called one another between meetings for support and comfort. I felt strongly that I was doing what gay men needed to be doing at the time, namely, responding to human need in crisis.

Obviously being a bear with other bears and their admirers is not the same thing as being a buddy with other buddies to persons living with AIDS. Nevertheless, I hope that we have learned a few lessons from the epidemic which carry over into bears' social networks: that we do not have to fear sex, but that our natural physical attractions can also survive and thrive when we show respect, sensitivity, and caring for one another. I believe that men of whatever sexual orientation or body type can learn to nurture and maintain friendships. What is necessary to parlay playmates into lasting friendships is a willingness to initiate and to reciprocate. The building of friendships involves communication (listening and talking), and the exercise of mutual love and respect. Bear clubs can facilitate friendships by offering a variety of activities that encourage conversation and interaction. When we are able to do this, I believe we will have learned that "love is more than sex" . . . that it is "the creation and maintenance of relationships of significance" (Dowsett, 1987).

## REFERENCES

Dowsett, G. (1987). "Queer Fears and Gay Examples." *New Internationalist*. 175: 10-12.
McCann, T. (1997). "Atlantic Crossing: The Development of the Eurobear." In *The Bear Book*. Ed., Les Wright. Binghamton, NY: Harrington Park Press, pp. 251-259.
Nardi, P. and Drury, S. (1994). "Friendship in the Lives of Gay Men and Lesbians." *Journal of Social and Personal Relationships*. 11: 185-199.

*PART III:
MORE BEAR SPACES*

Chapter 12

# Theorizing Bearspace

Alex G. Papadopoulos

The opening of Chuck Close's retrospective exhibit of portraiture at Chicago's Museum of Contemporary Art in June 1998 brought memories of bodies in art from a time when I was still fingering indecisively the inner latch of my closet. For me, Close's portraits of himself, friends, and others explored the tension between the self as a sharply-focused singularity trapped in the regularities of modernity, and the self as mosaic of action, will, tone, emotion, and subjectivity, as well as persuasion, indoctrination, disciplining, and structuring. These visual and emotional tensions become manifest through displacement: upon the observer's approach, the huge portraits surrender their near-photographic realism to pixelization. A Cartesian-like grid of thumbprint-sized ovals of grays or color—sometimes flat, sometimes swirling—dissolve the initial impression of "naturalness." The body revealed, in this case, is the body elementally dismantled and abstracted.

## *BEAR BODIES IN SPACE*

The older memory the Close exhibit elicited involves another exhibit, some five years ago. Held in a vacant warehouse in Chicago's Bucktown neighborhood, it showed student work from the School of the Art Institute of Chicago. The pieces in question were photographs of hirsute male bodies and body parts in close-up. They appeared grand and endless, composed—in my eyes—to resemble land forms, hairiness taking the place of reedy savanna vegetation.

Continuing the suspension of disbelief, one could collapse these bodyscapes to the scale of the medical slide resting across the business end of a microscope. Skin blemishes are, then, transformed into mitochondria, hairs into chromosomes. Masculinity is again depicted, elastically stretched, questioned, and queered.

At the time, body as landscape and place was as much a revelation to me as a venue of artistic expression, as was my own surprise and gladness for the apparent celebration of the body "natural." Only in subsequent years, after joining the middle-class gay project myself as a post-latent bear, did I recognize these art pieces as subversive for bringing into critical center-focus maleness and masculinity, through the objectifying of body parts and the image manipulation of their exteriority. Although the artist may not have been queer and the intended image-space different from that of my own interpretation, she or he signaled to me about the existence of unlimited symbolic spaces next to tangible ones where gender, sexual orientation, and body morphing intertwine anywhere between the microscale of the body part and the macro-one of the global community.

My intention here is to explore the spatiality of the bear phenomenon, of bears themselves, and of the bear collective, if one can indeed be discerned. Such an exploration begs some basic questions about the connections between the historical and social construction of space by gay men who describe themselves as bears and the spaces that the broader community of gay men (and to a lesser extent lesbian women) inhabit. Likewise, one needs to consider the connection to an even less explored domain of spatiality—that of people of size—or even more daringly to ask whether bearspace may transcend gender. Moreover, instead of simply identifying these spaces and their putative qualities, it is perhaps more important to explore the manner in which they may be transmuted as bears approach their adolescence as a sociosexual culture of consumption with strong roots in the American middle-class project, and their demise as a subversive movement that sought to redefine the image and practice of desire among some gay men.

For now, bearspace straddles the local-global nexus by the grace of information technologies, capital, and civil liberty. Its ephemeral fixing in localities through bear pride and social events, its fleeting fixing in linear cruise spaces, and the permanent marking of the microspace of the body with bear tattoos and piercings are the manifestations of a new interiority of desire that constitutes a reevaluation of the unconventional body. Symbolic and imaginary spaces have emerged in bear erotica to complement the tangible ones. In both contexts bearspace negotiates cleavages of race, ethnicity, age, class, and role—or the purported rejection of them—in actual or invented sexed or sexual settings.

The definition of "bear," then, is critical to the discerning of bearspace. This volume, much like the original *Bear Book*, attempts to give an answer to the question less by imposing a fixed imagination about bears than by allowing the multiple voices of bears to draw their own definitions, either formal or informal. For the purpose of this discussion, I speak of bears as gay men who differentiate themselves from the so-called clone culture by celebrating their bodies (often large and hirsute) through new open social and sexual rites, and by defining desire in terms of new aesthetic standards. I make the claim that bears and by implication bearspace are defined by, and contained within, the U.S. middle-class gay project that Stonewall brought forth now more than a quarter century ago, in spite of the fact that bears, as a physical type, may be found in all countries. The U.S.-centricity of beardom brings to mind Frank Browning's unsettling question of whether gays are an American invention.[1] An answer in the affirmative would have long-ranging implications for both how we construct an image of the self as profoundly rooted, causally linked, and unswervingly directed toward a particular sexual stance, and how well we wage the campaign for gay rights as the campaign of a "natural" community. If bears, like other gay men, are an American invention, how does that alter our situatedness in queer space?

## *BEARSPACE AND THEORY*

When we think of space and place we often think of maps and the set of graphical conventions that allow us to take control over three-dimensionality. Maps occupy a rather banal place in our imagination as foldable pieces of paper useful only for reducing alien territory to a handful of reference variables. Perhaps we can also think of a map as a selective projection of the willful as well as the unconscious. After all, what is not included on a map is often as important as what is. Authorship of the map, then, is a key criterion for understanding the map and how it was constructed: maps of neighborhoods by children are vastly different from maps that adults would draw, and not just in terms of their sophistication. Likewise, late-eighteenth-century maps of the non-European world by Europeans differed greatly from the maps that Ch'ing Dynasty administrators commissioned. These tangible maps were closely tied with European modernity, the rise of capitalism, which necessitated the accurate measuring of land and resources, and the military-"civilizational" project that gave us the familiar world of sovereign territorial states, "best practices" capitalism, Brazilian soap operas, and the Internet.

Yet there are other maps that are more elusive as they are defined by their subjectivity. A tourist guide of Chicago may precisely place gay and lesbian sites on maps that, on an initial reading, may appear very thorough. In this case, gay spaces are coded as fixed points of consumption. What conventional mapping cannot deal with easily is the dynamic coding and recoding of traditionally heterosexed spaces, such as hotels, beaches, streets and alleys, homes and shops and so on as ephemerally gay, lesbian, or specifically queer. An extreme example may be helpful here. The Paraportiani quarter in Mykonos Town, an erstwhile gay mecca of the Mediterranean, is focused visually around a stunning complex of whitewashed chapels that once stood within the walls of the Venetian castle that protected the town, and now overlook a fabulously wild seascape. During the daylight hours, Paraportiani is heterosexed by hundreds of tourists who consume the traditional landscape of the churches, themselves sentinels of the Orthodox Church's unbending heterosexism. After dusk, Paraportiani is queered by dozens of men—Greeks and foreigners—who use the labyrinthine structure of the quarter for their cruising and encounters. The complex of churches by the waterfront is recoded as gay space for a few hours, having its aspect and substance radically altered by the bodies and erotic projects of gay men. A less exotic and more succinct example may also help: BearPride '98, as an exemplar of all similar regional events, queered Chicago's downtown Marriott all the way to the miniature spaces of its elevators. Bear habitation, cruising, and the temporary usage of that conventionally heterosexed businessperson's environment for the purposes of erotic display, seduction, and sex, turned the Marriott into a bearspace for a period of five days.

Our mission, then, is to develop a vocabulary that will make it possible to understand how bears sex and queer the spaces that they inhabit. If we accept that Mykonian gay men queer a traditional, Christian Orthodox townscape with their bodies and actions, then, perhaps, bears may also queer space in their own peculiar way, since their bodies are peculiar, their philosophies of camaraderie and sex are (supposed to be) peculiar, and the manner they pursue the construction of their identity as bears through travel and the Internet is peculiar, at least as far as mainstream gay culture in the United States is concerned.

Steve Pile and Nigel Thrift show that our casual usage of notions such as the body, the self, the person, identity, and the subject are, in fact, "solid triangulation points with which it is possible to map 'the subject' into the social landscape."[2] One way of situating the subject socially, they continue, is by gleaning the relation of the subject to the notions of agency and structure. On one hand, the actions of individuals and their determinations are the result of internal workings and imaginings that contribute to the molding of the social landscape. On the other hand, social norms, a disciplining state, markets, and so on prescribe the actions of individuals. The challenge, of course, is to marry the two in a meaningful theorem that would allow us to understand the body, the self, and the rest. Thrift conceptualized them in terms of both structures and agency: "human agency must be seen for what it is, a continuous flow of conduct through time and space constantly interpolating social structure."[3] The process of queering space as bearspace, then, is an amalgam of the expression and reflection of the inner being and the imagined projects of the man-bear, and the social and cultural contexts that prescribe limits or filters for those personal projects.

Again, BearPride events come to mind. The fetishization of the large, hairy, male body and its imaginings by other men become the motivation for the periodic tracking of paths to cities such as Chicago, San Francisco, Boston, and St. Louis, where bear clubs hold conventions, prides (pride marches), and fests. Who goes and what happens there, not just sexually but also socially, is very much contingent on the intersections of class, race, age, ethnic background, physical aspect, role, and disposition, or, in other words, frames of conduct, reference, and being that are set in place by the U.S. collective.[4] In spite of what many of us wished would linger—the openness and cross-class camaraderie on which the movement was founded—bear events are very much middle-class sociosexual projects since they require that aspiring participants meet certain financial criteria. Full participation comes at a cost. Participants are often tagged by organizers for easier event management. Organizers plan entertaining diversions that are meant to help participants interact. Much of that centers on the ability to consume; hence the middle-class coding of such events. Very little of the money raised finds its way to gay and HIV/AIDS-related charities. There is a danger here. The progression to a commodified stance for the bear movement supports what Aaron Betsky wrote about the broader gay community in the United States: "[W]e are all becoming part of a consumer society in which there is a premium on interchangeable, malleable data, icons, and symbols. As operators of symbolic knowledge, we are increasingly post-middle class, post-individual, post-body. . . . There is only room for plugging in and jacking in, interacting and play-acting."[5] The subversion, the novelty, the queerness, and the liberation quotient that bear events, 'zines, and Internet-based interaction embodied in the early days of the movement are in danger of giving way to fixed consumables that create another gay mainstream which parallels that of clone culture.

Another way of looking at bear spatiality is in terms of discourses. In that context, Pile and Thrift note that the body, for example, becomes a notion that can bear a multitude of definitions on the basis of the social or historical context, the identity of the observer-interpreter, or the power vortices in which it is trapped. Elspeth Probyn draws a clearer picture:

> Unlike the chickens that are presumably sexed one way or the other, once and for all, the gendered self is constantly reproduced within the changing mutations of difference. While its sex is known, the ways in which it is constantly regendered are never fixed or stable. One way of imaging this self is to think

of it as a combination of acetate transparencies: layers and layers of lines and directions that are figured together and in depth, only then to be rearranged.[6]

In this sense, the self, the body, the identity act as both mirrors of the social structure they embody and mediators of the peculiar interiority of the self through speech, texts, images, gestures, artifacts, and the creation of ephemeral spaces where these regenderings may take place.

Les Wright looks at bear culture and gatherings discursively and with great sensitivity to the positive outcomes that their openness to discursive weavings of shape and size, age and race, ability, and sexual interests has brought to the gay community. Contrarily, Beth Kelly and Kate Kane question Wright's claim that the bears' "sociosexual adhesiveness has its roots in a Whitmanesque democratic appreciation of the common man [in which] working class white gay men are discovering that they have more, sometimes much more, in common with one another and with working-class black or Latino gay men than they do with gay men of any color."[7] Their reading of bear 'zines, such as *BEAR, American Bear,* and *Daddy Bear* revealed an image world of largely white and rarely identifiably ethnic men. They say that "[d]espite the textual claims that in bear culture, racial and socioeconomic boundaries are routinely crossed . . . African American men, or men of any color (besides white), are depicted or described only in the personals—and here as in the editorial copy, whiteness predominates."[8]

The tension between these two positions is important to our understanding of the spaces that bears construct for themselves, and their viability. The key question becomes whether bears are indeed a community and would, therefore, construct and have been constructing social—in their case, also sexual—space like other communities, or whether they are not a community (maybe not anymore), and thus their spaces would be unlike those that, for example, Latinos, Greek Americans, the broader queer community, or the aged may construct. Exploring the emergence of the bear phenomenon as a reaction to the sociosexual absolutism of clone culture, Wright noted its novelty and importance by asserting that bears have been creating "a new spiritual home, a social and sexual community."[9] By implication, ephemeral or permanent couplings between bears, unique or periodic group gatherings, and cyberspatial interaction and voyeurism obtain the luster, if not the substance, of a new sexual politics of liberation. Drawing on Wright's argument, we could assert that bearspaces of seduction, sexual relations, companionship, partnership, group organizing, and activism are not just sexed spaces but also political ones, where community is formed. Less easy to pinpoint, perhaps, but equally intriguing is the notion of bearspace as spiritual home, given the semiotic connection of "home" with heterosexed spaces of the traditional nuclear family. Whereas queer spaces in our collective imagination include either public (cruise) spaces and patently nonheterosexed private ones, like the gentrified warehouse qua loft space, they rarely include the locus of the nuclear family, comedic commentary in films like *La Cage aux Folles* notwithstanding. If I read Wright correctly, he suggests that bears evoke, or at least romanticize, the physical and psychological safety and sustaining character that the putative notion of "home" evokes. Kelly's and Kane's admonition about the "whiteness" of bear magazines stands in near-contrast. Although only self-admittedly bemused observers of bears, they present a serious counterargument to that of Wright.

So, what of theorizing bearspace? Can our spaces be subsumed within the sense of queer space? Aaron Betsky provides us with a seductive definition of the latter:

> Queer space is not one place: it is an act of appropriating the modern world for the continual act of self-construction. It is obscene and artificial by its very nature. It creates its own beauty. It allows us to be alive in a world of technology. There we can continually search within ourselves as we mirror ourselves in the world for that self that has a body, a desire, a life. Queer space queers reality to produce a space to live.

If identity is signaled by and through the rendering of the body, then the placing, spatial ordering, juxtaposition of bodies, and, according to Betsky, the act of appropriating the modern world would create self-presentational spaces: bearspaces that are defined by the butch/swish microscale of the gesture and stance, by the mesoscale of cruising activities in bars, bathhouses, and convention hotels, and by the subjective exteriorizing of bear desire in personal Web pages at the global scale. Next to these measurable, tangible spaces we see imagined spaces of wilderness and log cabins, Western ranches, truck stops, far-off planets, and construction sites where bear sexual fantasies are consummated. Both the tangible, albeit subjective ones, that make up the sociosexual reality of bears in the United States, and the sociosexual fantasy world constitute the spaces we inhabit as bears.

## *BEARSPACE EXPOSED*

I will not linger further on the urban bear in the city since Wright's work on the collective sociosexual rites of bears in San Francisco is, again, key here. I will also let other voices in this volume speak about identity, sense of place, and desire in bear erotica. Kelly and Kane have already honed a promising conceptual frame for looking at bear 'zines from the psychoanalytic and discursive analytic angles. I want to zero in on what I believe has been critical in diffusing spatially the sense of bear identity, the bear body as an alternative vessel of desire and fulfillment, and the existence of a bear collective that allows us to carve out safe spaces to live our lives. Below I will explore the connection between globalization, self-presentation, and identity politics as a means of discussing bearspace-making activities on the Internet.

## *SKEPSIS/BEARS AND GLOBALIZATION*

Bearspace straddles the local-global nexus. The digital wellspring of beardom, www.skepsis.com/bears, has germinated organized information about bears since 1994, while the Internet was swiftly becoming a currency of American male middle-class life. Pages describing what a bear may be, how bears may be classified, what bear or bear-friendly organizations and bars (mesoscale bearspaces?) may be available in your locality continue to nurture awareness. Hundreds of accessible personal pages of bears provide a grand spectrum of self-presentational bearspaces in word and image, usually clumsily, sometimes skillfully, with a view to inform, to continue a personal or dyadic—for couples—coming-out project, to pursue an activist agenda, to celebrate the body, to impress you, to entice you, to seduce you, to draw you. Keeping with the fundamental admonition of beardom—that of openness, friendliness, and sincerity—these personal pages exhibit the full names of the subscribers. The semantics of this public display of identity are significant: they gesture that this is a community of equals, not only to each other, but to the entire digital community. Foremost, it is a daring extension of being "out and proud," since often these pages reveal all, from the names of pets and anecdotes about grandparents, to the most intimate sexual rituals.

In essence, the denizens—as opposed to the visitors—of skepsis are behaving in a deep-rooted American way. Their display celebrates the self and has a strong redemptive and sometimes missionary quality. The courage to reveal the most intimate information about the self is rooted into a conviction that American society is truly protective of liberty and the body, despite the slowness of the civil rights ratchet in the United States. Judging from the activist displays in home pages of bears—in this case much like the home pages of other gay men—freedom of speech and freedom of information are foremost in the minds of those involved. These displays (at a minimum, free-speech ribbons in blue) contribute to political discourse by allowing the observer to glean the wide topography of support, by providing venues for activism, and by making claims of connection between liberty, broadly defined, to liberty of the body—an area of the law that has been largely neglected, if not avoided.

Is the bear phenomenon, then, intimately American, beyond its hearth in the United States? Is its intellectual and activist connection with American society a vital element of its successful diffusion and sustaining? What happens to the "bear principle" once it is embraced by a Briton, or a Belgian? Perhaps more important, how is it transmuted when grafted to the sociosexual identity of a Chinese, a Saudi Arabian, or a Kazak gay man? If the former group of Europeans would find the communitarian principles, the identity politics, and the civil libertarian activism familiar and comfortable facets of beardom, how would members of the latter groups? In their countries, freedom of speech and information and gay rights are questionable if extant at all. It is perhaps not surprising that the vast majority of the personal pages listed with skepsis/bears are of Americans.[10] The balance is made up of pages by Canadian, Australian, British, French, Dutch, Belgian, German, Italian, and Spanish bears. All the polities represented by these bears have strong democratic and civil libertarian traditions, sometimes specific to gay rights.

Broader data collected by skepsis/bears on the frequency and origin of visitors, or "hits," since its inception in 1994, reveal a telling pattern of geographical diffusion of consumption of information about bears, if not the diffusion of the phenomenon itself (Figure 12.1). A closer look at this temporal and spatial diffusion process suggests a certain geopolitics of bear desire: the hypothesis that it is more likely for persons from capitalist, market-driven economies with democratic institutions to access skepsis *earlier* than persons from noncapitalist and/or low-income countries with authoritarian or totalitarian regimes in power holds with a moderate but statistically significant degree of confidence.[11] There appears to be a very strong correlation between the function of capitalist markets, high per capita gross national product and vanguard placement on the Internet and in skepsis/bears. A less strong, though still statistically significant, correlation exists between the presence of democracy and access to the focal bear database. For instance, hits during 1994 originated from North America, all the member states of the European Union, Poland (a candidate member of the EU), Australia, New Zealand, South Africa, Japan, Israel, Kuwait, and all the so-called Asian Tigers (Hong Kong, Singapore, Taiwan, and South Korea). At the other end, only in 1998 did skepsis/bears receive any hits from Iran, Yemen, Saudi Arabia, Vietnam, Cambodia, Papua New Guinea, Ghana, and Mozambique.

The balance of states that remain unrepresented in the database include some of the most politically repressive and economically needy ones: thirty-four of Africa's forty-eight states have not had access. Cuba, North Korea, Iraq, Syria, Burma, Haiti, Bangladesh, Central Asian Turkmenistan, Tajikistan, Kyrgyzstan, and Afghanistan, Mongolia, Laos, and the monarchies of South Asia, Nepal, Bhutan, and Sikkim are also outside the circuit. A further hypothesis that could have been usefully probed, had the public domain

FIGURE 12.1

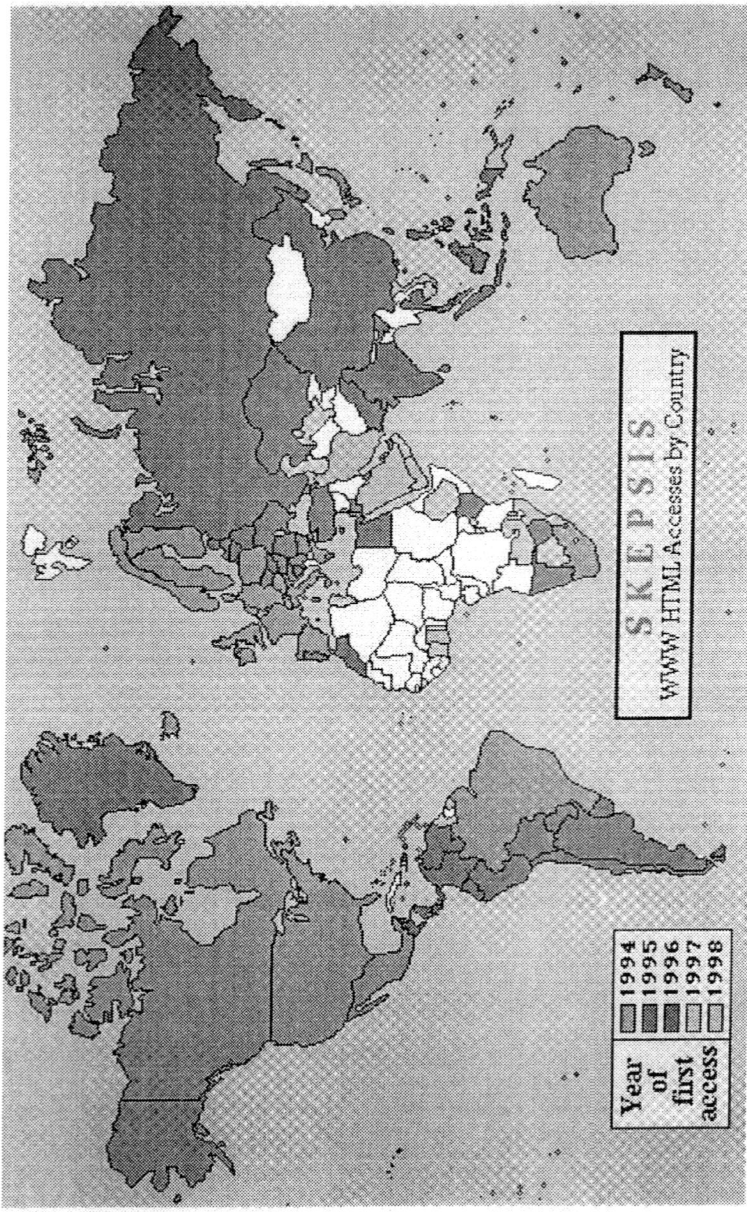
SKEPSIS
WWW HTML Accesses by Country
Year of first access
1994
1995
1996
1997
1998

information allowed it, would have queried the frequency of hits per country per year as a corollary of per capita gross national product and regime type. As the data stand now, states are represented equally regardless of the number of hits that originated in their territory. What is more important for us to understand, though, is that this impressive veneer of internationalization does not necessarily reflect a world of American, or Western world, bears. More appropriately and cautiously, we should count the hits as discursive utterances from around the world about the *American* bodies of bears. Instead of a choropleth map where all states appear equal to the degree that they have digitally accessed "bear central," there should have been a map of flows or vectors into the set of coordinates where that nexus is situated.

It should, thus, not have been surprising to the skepsis/bears staffer and correspondent who recently completed an around-the-world educational tour that the aesthetic of the bear body abounds worldwide but bear identity, as we understand it in the West, does not. Skepsis/bears and the multitude of other bear-related Web sites may reflect the desire and need of bears to queer cyberspace, and create a public forum and digital spaces for meeting, conferring, and engaging in seduction. The bear project, though, is intimately middle class, has grown to be capitalist market-driven, and stands as a counterpoint, or at least a permutation, of the broader Western queer project. I would claim that skepsis.com/bears constitutes a symbolic "homeland" with its own identity, its citizens, its customs and rituals, as well as its own sense of "alterity." That alterity, though, is crafted like a binary: it contains the predictable "Other" of straight society, next to the exclusionary "Other" of mainstream gay men. It is an alterity that is full of external sanction, and alarmingly, perhaps, increasing internal division.

## *BEARSPACES OF SUBJECTIVITY AND FANTASY*

The better personal web pages in skepsis and other bear-relevant sites may be thought of as worlds of artifice, or at least subjectivity. I note this with admiration, not derision. How genial it is to appear "naturalized" as "bear," "otter," or "wolf" by grafting the aesthetics of the outdoors to a quotidian existence of consumption and modernity, with the mediation of the ultimate in artifice—digital technology! The pages are not unlike the sensual spaces that the fictional sophistiqué Jean Des Esseintes in Joris-Karl Huysmans's *À Rebours* (Against nature) created and inhabited: "Already he had begun dreaming a refined Thebaid, a desert hermitage equipped with all modern conveniences, a snugly heated ark on dry land in which he might take refuge from the incessant deluge of human stupidity. . . ."[12] His "oases of sensuous luxury," as Aaron Betsky analyses them—much like the bear pages, I would add—placed "the body at play, as the intermediary between pleasure and consciousness, the converter of one into the other."[13] The bear pages are themselves as sexed and sensual as the imagination of the html author can muster, much like the boudoir of an eighteenth-century courtesan may have been. They are arks of security and control where the self can be mirrored either accurately or whimsically, oscillate between the two, or combine them in endless permutations. They are iconic interiors that use pastiches of images, symbols, text, connectedness with some collective ("favorite links") that amount to a topology of desire and sociosexual status. Their ephemerality, their perpetual "under construction" status, their desire to subvert order (mainstream gay taste, Calvin Klein aesthetics, the alignment of class and desire), their vulnerability to technological havoc underscore the sense of artifice and reinvention that would be characteristic of a group that is building its own symbols, imaginations, and history.[14]

## NOTES

1. Frank Browning, *A Queer Geography: Journeys Toward a Sexual Self* (New York: Noonday Press, 1998), pp. 1-7.

2. Steve Pile and Nigel Thrift, eds., *Mapping the Subject: Geographies of Cultural Transformation* (London: Routledge, 1995), p. 2.

3. Nigel Thrift, "On the Determination of Social Action in Space and Time," *Environment and Planning D: Society and Space* 1: 1 (1983), p. 31.

4. For the best discussion on the subject see Les K. Wright, "The Sociology of the Urban Bear," *Classic BEAR* (1996), pp. 53-55.

5. Aaron Betsky, *Queer Space: Architecture and Same-Sex Desire* (New York: William Morrow and Company, Inc., 1997), p. 14.

6. Elspeth Probyn, *Sexing the Self: Gendered Positions in Cultural Studies* (London: Routledge, 1993), p. 1.

7. Wright, "Sociology of the Urban Bear," p. 54.

8. Elizabeth A. Kelly and Kate Kane, "In Goldilocks' Footsteps: Exploring the Discursive Construction of Gay Masculinity in Bear Magazines," in Sara Miles and Eric Rofes, eds., *Opposite Sex: Gay Men on Lesbians, Lesbians on Gay Men* (New York: New York University Press, 1998), pp. 91-92.

9. Wright, "Sociology of the Urban Bear," p. 53.

10. I use the term American inaccurately but in accordance with common usage in the United States to mean citizen of the United States.

11. Also noticeable is a certain periodicity of frequency within the calendar year. Near-constant levels of access during most of the year give way to reduced numbers of hits during the summer, every summer.

12. Joris-Karl Huysmans, *Against Nature,* trans. Robert Baldick (New York: Penguin Books, 1959 [1884]), p. 25.

13. Betsky, *Queer Space,* p. 76.

14. While these descriptors generally describe the new sense of self-presentation that Western society has been developing since the popularizing of the Internet, I think they are particularly appropriate as descriptors of the spaces of resistance created by bears.

Chapter 13

# Paws Between Two Worlds: Bears and the Leather Community

Robert B. Marks Ridinger

In recent decades, gay and lesbian research subjects have moved from the occasional anthropological study of the society of a neighborhood bar or speculation on the psychological underpinnings of sexual preference to an explosion of diverse topics in literature and the social sciences, among which the question of tracing the history of self-identified segments of the gay male community has become prominent. While this has until recently taken the forms of establishing focused collections along the lines of the Leather Archives and Museum in Chicago and publication of anthologies such as *The Bear Book* (Wright, 1997), less attention has been given to the ways in which these individual factions have influenced each other in their evolution. The definition of "bear" as a recognized and acceptable social identity has made possible new lines of historical inquiry, among them the relationships (of whatever nature) of ursine individuals to the development of other gay male subcultures. This chapter explores the long interaction of bear and leather identities.

The primary question in such a study as this is, of course, a variation on the old riddle of the chicken and the egg—"Which came first, the leatherman or the bear?"—to which the best answer is "both." Each is so closely woven with the other in the history of American alternative cultures that attempting to consider them in isolation quickly becomes an impossible intellectual exercise. To understand the complex interplay of these two populations, the clearest perspective may be gained by a chronological approach to the appearance of men with beards and plentiful body hair within the gay male community in general.

Although the uses of leather in sexual situations had long been present in the private repertoires of individual Americans of all sexual orientations, it was only in the years immediately following World War II that a distinct public leather subculture began to crystallize in the United States. Rooted in several military traditions, among them accepted codes of rules and discipline, "the earliest set of habits that jelled by the mid-to-late 1950s in the men's leather community" (Baldwin, 1993, p. 107) laid the foundations of the contemporary leather world and its structure. Out of these formative years came both the norms of leathersex social and ritual behaviors that would later become known as the "Old Guard" standard, and a new subcultural organization born of the interaction of gay men who enjoyed and desired a freedom to live and love in a personally satisfying manner with the symbol of ultimate freedom and rebellion during the 1950s—the motorcycle. Paradoxically, the highly conservative mass-produced culture of postwar America symbolized the successful resistance of the democratic way of life to authoritarian rule, while at the same time crafting and enforcing a set of stereotypes of its own and manufacturing for the mass market a vehicle that promised easy escape from its confines. Very swiftly, an entire biker culture began to take shape across the country, complete with unique jargon and distinctive styles of public clothing, and centered on both weekend trips and rallies, where skill in control and abilities were shown off in competition.

Although such huge assemblies as the current annual gathering of Harley-Davidson riders at Sturgis, North Dakota, still lay in the future, the number of machines sold made the cycle a recognized part of the roadscape. The best-known (and most distorted) example of the stereotyped biker group were gangs such as the Hell's Angels, whose uninhibited rowdiness, sexuality, and destructive behavior quickly eclipsed all other sorts of motorcycle organizations in the public eye. Photographs of the Angels and similar packs illustrate many facets of their rebellion against mainstream culture, nowhere more visible than in the long flowing beards and shoulder-length hair of the male riders. By 1955, the bikers had achieved the ultimate in mass media saturation, becoming the topic of a popular song. Its lines (recorded by The Cheers and Vaughn Monroe, among others) describe them as wearing "black denim trousers and motorcycle boots and a black leather jacket with an eagle on the back." Within the explosion of cycle popularity, gay men who rode began to find each other and weave together their own unique culture, incorporating elements from mainstream society and adapting them to their needs. Their preference for the denim jeans and leather jackets, vests, chaps, and boots worn by many cyclists as practical protection against windburn set them sharply apart from homosexual culture of the day, with its unathletic emphasis on bar life and aesthetics. As Guy Baldwin notes, "the bike clubs and the bars where they hung out became the magnets of their day which attracted those gay men who were interested in the masculine end of the gay spectrum . . . the leather men defined the masculine extreme of that time" (Baldwin, 1993, p. 110). As their appearance was the same, bikers who were gay could easily mingle with their heterosexual fellows. Both shared leather, motorcycles, and painful memories of a war (Rubin, 1994, p. 108).

One of the best means of following the path of the bear through the leather world is by means of photographs presented to the public through several books which appeared between 1984 and 1998. The first of these, Geoff Mains' *Urban Aboriginals,* has only a few illustrations, one of them being two spectacularly bearded muscular men kissing passionately. Another source may be found in the 1991 anthology *Leatherfolk* (Thompson, 1991) (including a picture of Mains, who had died by that time), plus illustrations of bearded men wearing an array of leather clothing from jockstraps to full-body leather suits, indicating a diversification in the intensity of presentation of beards within the leather community by the beginning of the 1990s, accompanying the gradual erosion of the hairless buffed clone look popular during the 1980s in many leather periodicals such as *Drummer* and in videos such as *Born to Raise Hell* (although the latter does include the muscleman being dominated by a pair of hairy police officers). This shift in visual imagery from absolute power to a diversity of expression can also be seen as mirroring the development of the bear movement, which was occurring at the same time. The widely read book *The Joy of Gay Sex* (Silverstein and White, 1977) also contains line drawings as illustrations, some of which feature a well-pelted man engaged in various sexual activities, as well as an article, "Hair," which records the attitudes toward fur held at the time of its publication.

With the emergence of the bear phenomenon in the late 1980s also came the question of affiliation—where did the leathermen who now recognized themselves as bears as well fit this extra dimension of social identity? Traditional hostility from the mainstream gay male community to men who were overweight, bearded, or hairy was certainly one of the driving forces behind the swift proliferation of clubs devoted to the creation and maintenance of "bearspace"—a situation that set up internal collisions with the several-decades-old network of leather/levi clubs, whose basic focus was SM. The confusion is clearly illustrated in Ivo Dominguez' 1997 collection of essays, *Beneath the Skins,* which poses among its questions "Are the Bear clubs part of the Leather community if they have backpatch clubs?" (Dominguez, 1997, p. 43), noting also that these new bear social phenomena have further muddied the waters by "some . . . leaning toward the Backpatch mode and others toward organizational models more common in the vanilla Queer community" (p. 92). Sensitivity rooted in an awareness of the newborn status of the label "bear" generated a perception in some quarters that bearded men were not welcome in the leather community, or that one was obligated to choose a single social category/role within the gay community, rather than rejoicing in the possession of multiple possibilities for self-fulfillment.

In part, this may be due to the commitment to and involvement with leather characteristic of many men, rooted in the public affirmation of personal sexual identity. Leather versus ursine orthodoxies added fuel to an ongoing discussion as to what, precisely, was a bear and whether, if you were one, you could also be anything else. An excellent example of this collision is found in the 1998 retrospective photo collection *Classic BEAR,* which notes that in 1987, the cover man for *BEAR 3* "was the first *BEAR* model to mix the leather bear image that continues to thrill some readers, and piss off others, to this day" (*Classic BEAR,* 1998, p. 44). The periodical presented intermittent leather imagery from its foundation until the appointment of senior leatherman Joseph Bean as editor in 1994, after which leather themes became a more common part of the visual landscape presented to its readers. It is noteworthy that, in Philip Locke's (1997) study of the appearance of bear images in gay media and the rise of a purely ursine body of publications, none of the magazines serving the leather community, such as *The Leather Journal, Drummer,* or *International Leatherman,* are included.

The interwoven images of bear and leather are most clearly understood as a deft creation of two alternative definitions of masculinity by the gay male community which complement each other within a context of both history and myth. As the bear culture continues to grow and develop, men who fit both categories will find it increasingly easy to have a paw in each world and be valued for doing so.

## BIBLIOGRAPHY

Baldwin, Guy. "Old Guard: Its Origins, Traditions, Mystique and Rules" in *Ties That Bind: The SM/Leather/Fetish Erotic Style: Issue, Commentaries and Advice.* Los Angeles: Daedalus Publishing Company, 1993 (107-115).

Bean, Joseph. *Leathersex.* San Francisco: Daedalus, 1994.

*Classic BEAR* (1996), Brush Creek Media (special publication, subsequently published on an annual basis).

"Cycle Song." *Newsweek* v. 46 (October 10, 1955): 114.

Dominguez, Ivo. *Beneath the Skins: The New Spirit and Politics of the Kink Community.* Los Angeles: Daedalus Publishing Company, 1997.

Lavigne, Yves. *Hell's Angels: Taking Care of Business.* Toronto: Deneau and Wayne, 1987.

Locke, Philip. "Male Images in the Gay Mass Media and Bear-Oriented Magazines: Analysis and Contrast" in *The Bear Book,* ed. Les K. Wright. Binghamton, NY: Harrington Park Press, 1997 (103-140).

Mains, Geoffrey. *Urban Aboriginals: A Celebration of Leather Sexuality.* San Francisco: Gay Sunshine Press, 1984.

Murray, William. "Hell's Angels." *Saturday Evening Post* 238 (November 20, 1965): 32-39.

Rubin, Gayle S. *Valley of the Kings: Leathemen in San Francisco, 1960-1990.* PhD Dissertation, University of Michigan, 1994.

Silverstein, Dr. Charles and Edmund White. *The Joy of Gay Sex.* New York: Crown Publishers, 1977.

Thompson, Hunter S. *Hell's Angels: A Strange and Terrible Saga.* New York: Ballantine Books, 1995.

Thompson, Mark, ed. *Leatherfolk: Radical Sex, People Politics and Practice,* Boston: Alyson Publications, 1991.

Wright, Les, ed. *The Bear Book: Readings in the History and Evolution of a Gay Male Subculture.* Binghamton, NY: Harrington Park Press, 1997.

Wright, Les. "A Concise History of Self-Identifying Bears" in *The Bear Book.* Binghamton, NY: Harrington Park Press, 1997 (21-39).

## Chapter 14

# Gen-X Bears International

### John-Paul Patrick Kucera

How does one introduce a concept, or an idea? I have always believed that the most successful method of introduction or explanation is best accompanied with results. Gen-X Bears International is a result of the labor and dedication of several individuals, beginning with the e-mail digest and the subsequent foundation of the organization by Randy Stern in August 1995. Gen-X Bears International is an organization that has produced results, not only as landmarks for bear youth through its continued growth and success in the community, but more so through its ability to have touched and improved lives since its conceptualization in California.

By mid-1999, the organization had grown to over twenty-five active chapters across the United States and Canada and is spreading overseas to Europe and Asia. Our constitution was drafted in November 1997, and our organization logo was created in the spring of 1998. The Gen-X Bears e-mail digest continues its distribution with now over 600 recipients by 1998; however, the actual organization membership is near 1,000. A main Web page at www.genxbears.org acts as the center for chapter Web pages in addition to providing a face and route to membership registration in the organization. Regional gatherings, such as the recent East Coast Gathering (ECG) in Boston, now occur annually in order to bring together members of several chapters and expand the atmosphere of bear brotherhood. Informational packets are becoming available to chapters and members concerning STD Education/Prevention, alcohol awareness, and many other issues. Our organization's name is now registered with the government, and we are currently seeking federal nonprofit organization status. You may even notice someone wearing a Gen-X Bears T-shirt, hat, or some such item at a bear gathering these days.

The actual concept behind these results is simple: we exist to provide a safe and social atmosphere for bears and cubs from all over to meet, greet, provide support for each other, and make new friends. We believe that in order to provide the best possible support network in a group, you need to surround yourself with a wide variety of supporting voices. These many voices are there to help comfort, strengthen, and add a unique social flair to the purpose of aiding bear youth in the community. Gen-X Bears International provides opportunities for the youth in the bear community to become more self-aware, to create self-respect, and in turn, to obtain mutual respect for the rest of the gay community.

Another key element in how we operate is that Gen-X Bears does not allow its chapters to hold events in settings where younger members would be prohibited from the event. Since bars exclude members under twenty-one, neither meetings nor events can be held in these settings. As I have said, we strive to create environments for meetings, trips, events, etc., that are both comfortable and safe for members to meet and socialize. Situations that could jeopardize a member's safety and stability are carefully avoided in order to try and transition newcomers not only into the Bear world, but into the gay community as well.

An unfortunate misconception, or myth, with regard to Gen-X Bears International is that because we are called "Gen-X" Bears membership is limited to those between ages eighteen and thirty-five. This is incorrect. Though the target audience of our group is bear youth, our overall membership includes a wide range of ages. In fact, in addition to age, Gen-X Bears International has always believed in a nondiscriminatory stance on race, religion, national origin, physical or mental ability, physical stature, sex, sexual orientation, sexual identification, or any other classification that can act as a precedent to divide people. We are a very caring and inclusive group with a specific purpose as stated in our constitution:

1. To provide support for, promote self-affirmation of, and work for the general welfare of communities of younger bears and

their admirers, as well as the global Gay, Lesbian, Bisexual, and Transgendered communities.
2. To provide social opportunities for its members in an inclusive, safe, and comfortable environment. Through this action we shall promote equality, and build bridges of respect and understanding within the global community, while striving to break down traditional barriers which have divided the GLBT and Heterosexual communities from and among themselves.
3. To be an advocate voice in the GLBT community. Gen-X Bears will support global change towards protection of and provide support towards GLBT youth. Gen-X Bears shall also organize, promote, and support educational programs and materials that highlight issues faced by GLBT youth.
4. To help promote, through the culmination of these purposes, the elimination of homophobia and heterosexism, as well as the related issues of discrimination and oppression on a global level.

Gen-X Bears International consists of a council that acts as a steering committee for the entire organization. The job of the council is to coordinate the desires of the membership into action, to help the organization grow, and to maintain and preserve the constitution and purpose of the organization. The council currently consists of a moderator, treasurer, membership director, chapter development director, Webmaster, and council members-at-large. Each chapter has a coordinator that is responsible for the growth and steering of its local membership. The council works closely with, and is responsible for, fulfilling the needs and requests of the coordinators as well as the membership.

My life has been inspired and improved through working to preserve and increase the status of Gen-X Bears International. My undergraduate years back at MIT, in addition to the book-worming, were filled with my life as a fraternity member. I enjoyed the experience in taking various roles of responsibility and leadership, but there was never anything that gave me a door into the bear world. I was too young for the bars and had to confine my exploration to the Internet, talking to the few folks that I could. When I graduated in

1996, I went directly to The Pennsylvania State University, feeling like I had missed something during my four years in college.

I eventually learned about Gen-X Bears International from friends who took me to an event in Washington, DC, in the spring of 1997. It was at this time that I began to learn of the purpose and structure of the organization. Since that time, however, the structure has grown more defined without losing the benefits that the organization as a whole can offer individual members, thus fulfilling its purpose. In the months following my introduction to the organization, I decided to add some spice to my graduate career at Penn State by serving as a coordinator and starting a chapter centered in State College. This was an adventure that I struck out upon in conjunction with beginning to feel comfortable with my sexuality and it began to fill me with a sense of achievement that had been missing until then.

That fall, I felt like trying to do more, and was set to the task of chapter development director on the council by the council moderator at the time, Scott Schumacher. My job was to update, organize, and encourage the growth of new chapters of Gen-X Bears International. My experience and energy from founding the Keystone chapter in central Pennsylvania was put to the test on the international level. My desire to further improve the organization has resulted in my current position as the first elected council moderator. In addition to increasing the amount of work I gave myself, several changes have been effected in my life because of my involvement with Gen-X Bears.

This is the part where I say something like, "Hooked on Gen-X Bears worked for me!" The great thing is that it's a wholeheartedly true statement. I am now much more secure in who I am, in my sexuality, and especially in my bearhood. The many bridges built, decisions made, debates, and steps forward and backward have all taught me how to interact, think, and persevere not only for my own sake, but for the sake of Gen-X Bears International and, more so, for the friends I have within the organization and for all of its members. Since my involvement, there have been many times when I have been able to turn to a friend for help and found more than one ready to listen to my problems, joys, and frustrations.

My dedication and efforts toward the organization have provided me with an opportunity to improve not only my life, but the life of others. I can only say that it has been worth all of the time I have spent in this cause. It is also my sincerest hope that others out there may have the chance to accomplish similar successes as I have in my own personal journey with Gen-X Bears International.

# Introduction To the Image Gallery

Given the limitations of space and technical issues, I have strived to provide a range of images which relate both directly to authors and circumstances discussed elsewhere in this volume as well as give a sample of the range of styles, subject matter, geographical and cultural sources, and type of bears—in fantasy and reality.

Some of the images here have appeared in "Bear Icons " (the New York City exhibition in 1999) or in "Bear Icons II" (the Boston-area exhibition in 2000). Some images come from the Bear History Project archives. The majority of color images were not considered for inclusion here because of the dramatic distortion created by conversion to black and white. Production of a complete exhibition catalog and historical document of the bear icons, as well as other visual projects I am working on, are simply beyond the purview of The BBII, and will be treated in satisfactory length in other media at a future time.

Of particular interest, from my perspective, is the process of self-exclusion which is evidenced in what images have been made available to me for The Bear Book II as well as for the Bear Icons exhibition and collection. Having not the slightest idea what images might be a part of the BI collection, numerous individuals have refused to contribute artwork or even to attend either of the BI exhibitions, having objections to anyone establishing any categorized bear "icons." To the best of my discernment, such reservations seem to be based on false assumptions that my project (or the perhaps misleading choice of words—"icons") is about glorifying what I denigrated in The Bear Book as "glamour bears." The reality is that I have sought to include as wide a range of actual and fantasized images as possible—much in contradistinction of mass-media generated images that sell magazines—to create as comprehensive and encyclopedic a catalog of a composite archetype of gay bears in all the individual peculiarities of many sensibilities.

Closely related to the anti-icon self-disqualifiers are at least two distinct, self-selected factions of artists, both of whom have decided bear icons must be about pornography and, therefore, in a classic case of self-fulfilling prophecy, declined my invitation to be included on grounds that they do now wish to have their art or their names associated with "pornography." By default and by the obvious erotophobia within the bear community, the ensuing catalog of images is unrepresentatively distorted by the self-selected absence of some wonderful artists and art work. The two groups I averred to above would include several cartoon artists (whose published works, ironically, often appear inserted amongst clusters of sex ads in various gay publications) and some "high-concept," professional artists of aesthetic and technical accomplishment who prefer that their art not be associated with any particular (i.e., gay male) sexual orientation. To be fair, I must report the inclusion of several superb works of art (oil paintings in particular) in Bear Icons II; it was my decision to not include examples of these works due to the technical shortcomings of the printing processes available for producing the book you hold in your hand.

Finally, there has emerged a fascinating picture of the "bears of color" problematic. First, the vast majority of bear images portrayed are of Caucasian men, of a wide range of ethnic heritage. In other words, few artists have chosen to create or express a bear aesthetic for non-Caucasian men. I have in my own possession and I have considered numerous photographic portraits of bears of color; however, in very nearly every case, the model portrayed has refused to have his image appear. More than one such bear of color has argued that he is not "out" in his home town or to his family, and does not wish to appear in any publication which may be purchased in his hometown. I am particularly saddened by having to forego an entire portfolio of bears of color portraiture by Lynn Ludwig for this reason. Second, if you note the "small print" of the included artists, you will find that many of them are themselves bears of color, but who eroticize Caucasian men. As of this writing, there is a growing African-American separatist movement for black gay men to disaffiliate themselves with what is seen as a predominantly urban, white, middle-class, and racist consumer movement. This puts pressure on bears of color to not be publicly associated with their Caucasian peers or to be publicly self-defined as "gay" (the category itself being understood as an antiblack racist social construction).

Third, and the least well-represented in the portfolio in hand, is the global phenomenon of creating and eroticizing a gay male bear archetype. Some of the biggest proponents (and producers of interesting bear artwork) are to be found in Japan, Malaysia, China, and other non-Caucasian cultures. Evidence of U.S.-American GWM cultural imperialism and hegemony? Only time will tell.

The reality is that, while small in relative numbers, self-identifying bears of every ethnic or racial background are active in the bear community, and there is a small but burgeoning bear sensibility among some lesbian and female-to-male transsexual self-identifying bears. By the year 2000, it turns out, there are fourteen-year-old boys coming out of the closet, not as "gay," but directly and definitely as "bear."

Bear Icons/Boston Publicity. Used courtesy of the Bear History Project collection.

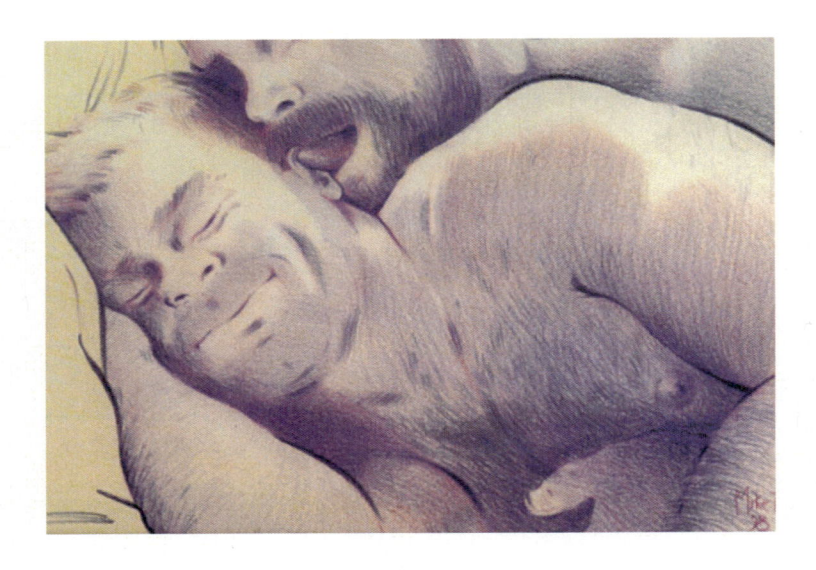

"Bed Bears" by Mike Thorn. Reprinted with permission.

Title Holders: Scott and Steve. Photo by Les Wright.

Les Wright and T J Norris. Photo by Ken delPo. Used courtesy of the Bear History Project collection.

The Bear-A-Tones. Photo by Kent Taylor. Reprinted with permission.

"Self-Portrait" by Ali Lopez. Reprinted with permission.

"Grizzly" by Ali Lopez. Reprinted with permission.

Joseph Palmer. Photo by Les Wright. Used courtesy of the Bear History Project collection.

"Circumcised Moor Devil." From *Satan in the Groin: Male Exhibitionist Carvings on Medieval Churches* by Anthony Weir. Reprinted with permission.

"Winter" by Dmitrij Zinovjev. Reprinted with permission. Used courtesy of the Bear History Project collection.

Jack Radcliffe. Photo by Lynn Ludwig. Reprinted with permission.

"E. H. With Billboard" by T J Norris. Reprinted with permission.

"G. D. With Beamer—Boston, 1999." Photo by T J Norris. Reprinted with permission.

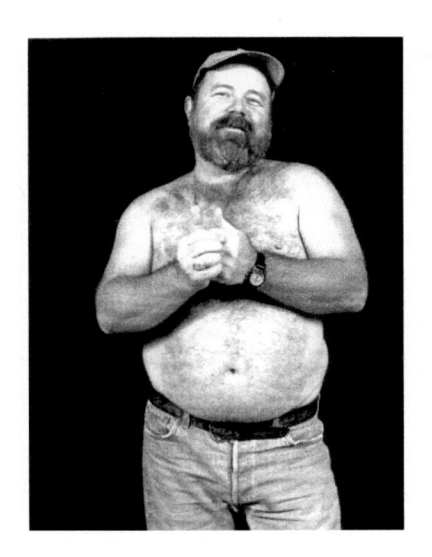

Jim Parton. Photo by John Rand. Reprinted with permission.

"Bertbear." Photo by Bertbear. Reprinted with permission.

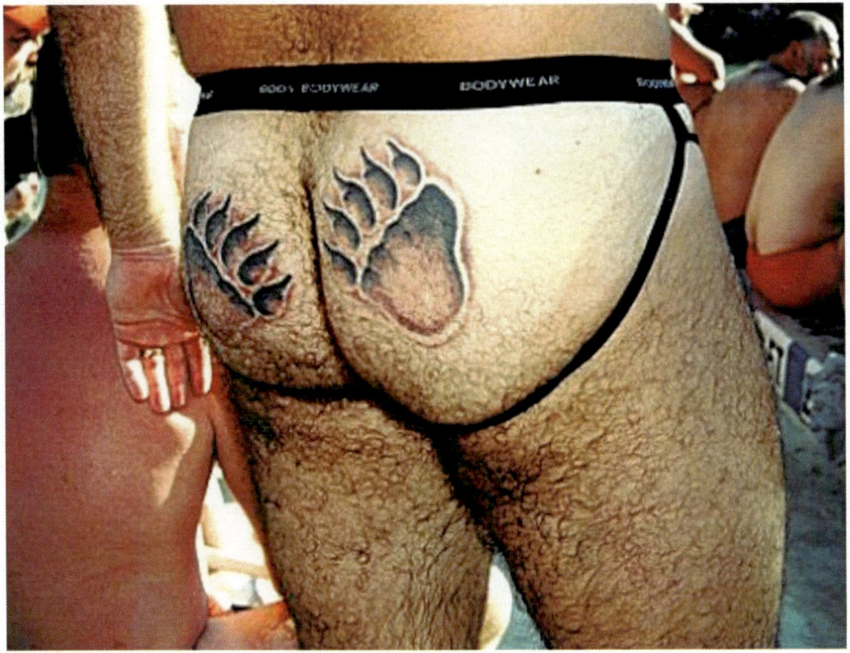

Bear Paws Tattoos. Photo by Lynn Ludwig. Reprinted with permission.

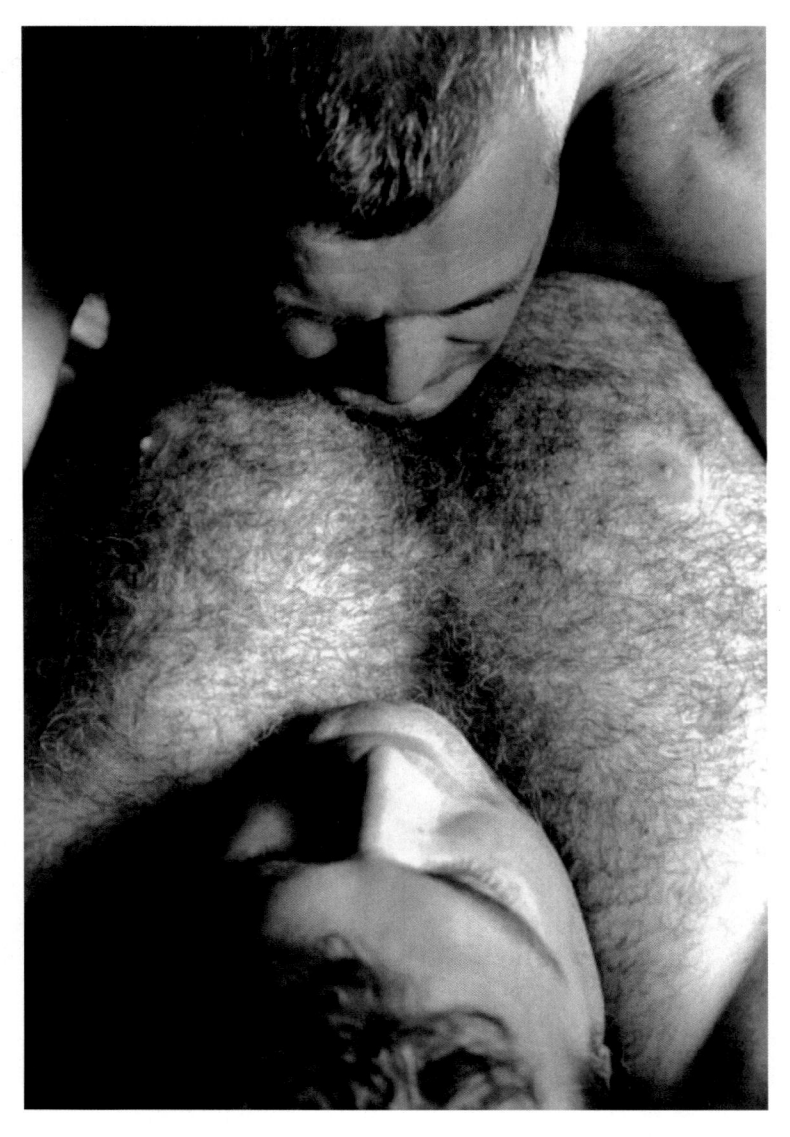

"Untitled" by Paul Roberts. Reprinted with permission.

"Slave Cub" by Christopher Taylor, from the collection of T J Norris. Reprinted with permission.

"The Pride Stripped Bear by Their Bachelor" by David Greig. Reprinted with permission.

"Damianbat (detail)," 1999 by T J Norris. Reprinted with permission.

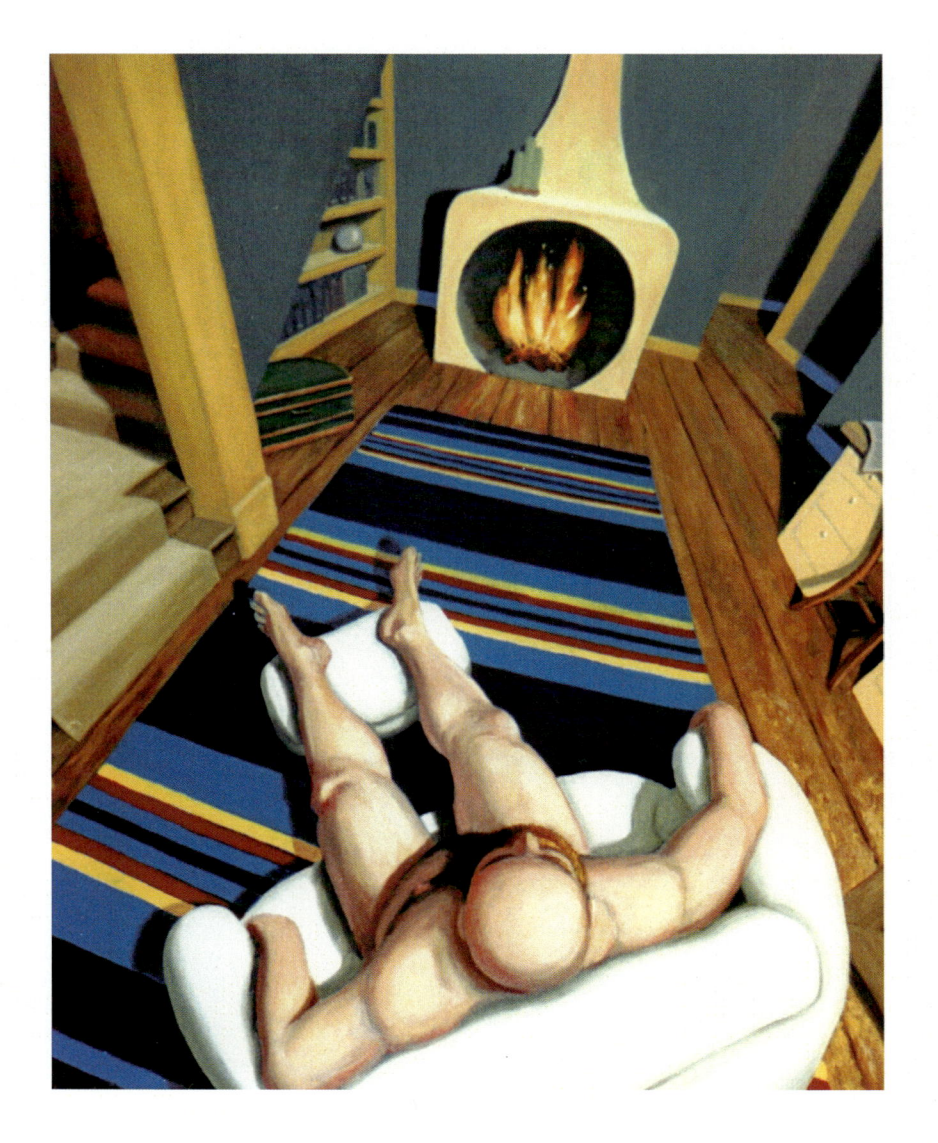

"Reverie" by Richard Ferrugio. Reprinted with permission.

"Larry Mass" (self-portrait). Used courtesy of the Bear History Project collection.

"Polyandrous Leatherbearsex Family Self-Portrait." Photo by Chris Taylor. Reprinted with permission.

"Untitled" by Bob Maidel. Reprinted with permission.

"Joe Bear" Photo by Bertbear. Reprinted with permission.

Chapter 15

# The Bear-A-Tones:
# An Interview with David Salinas

**LKW:** For the record, this is February 15, 1998. We're at IBR 1998 in San Francisco and I'm speaking with David Salinas of Bear-A-Tones. Could you tell us, just very quickly, about what basically the group is and how long it's been in existence?

**DS:** Well, this past January 18, actually, we completed a year of being together, so we've already had our one-year anniversary. Basically the Bear-A-Tones (the Bear-A-Tones of San Francisco and I'll explain why the "SF" is added in a little bit), it's four guys, bears, we're all big, hunky, and hairy and we sing really well together. That's basically us—four guys. It was kind of—I left a retail management job, I was about to get my own store. I was working for Warner Brothers. and I was about to get promoted to get my own store and kinda reality just hit me, and I said, you know, you're not meant to be doing this—you need to be doing what gives you goose bumps and in my mind, what gives you goose bumps is your passion. And for me it's singing. So I basically kinda left with the blessing of my managers and stuff and put an ad in the *B.A.R. (Bay Area Reporter)* and *Frontiers Newsmagazine* for auditions and I had, like, over fifty guys audition for me.

**LKW:** Wow!

**DS:** Yeah! So it was really neat, it was a great turnout. But I knew that I had to have some sort of foundation to it—I knew that it had to have some sort of—people auditioning had to realize that this was not just like a weekend thing for me, because I left a full-time job to do this. When they came to audition they had to read, like, a

*175*

mission statement or vision thing if you will, basically laying out what my vision of the group was, where I saw it going, and basically just telling them how serious it was for me. And I had, like, five or six guys leave without auditioning! So I think it served its purpose. And that way, their time and my time wasn't wasted. In the end, three guys were picked that are phenomenal, very talented—talented individually. They can command the stage by themselves and at the same time we complement each other. We get along. My thing is, it's not about ego up there. We're all good, that's fine. It's about coming together and creating music. That's my thing. So when we're up there it's not about ego. From the get-go they could shine on their own or together.

**LKW:** The group, all four of you, are involved in doing this as a full-time job now?

**DS:** Well, no. Actually, for me, it's become a full-time thing! No, they work, they all have full-time jobs and stuff like that. But it's a serious commitment on their part. We have rehearsals every week and I do have a musical director, who I was very fortunate to get because he was the artistic director for the Gay and Lesbian Chorus of San Francisco for eleven years. I just happened to be referred to him and he's now our musical director. He's incredible. But we have rehearsals every week and the commitment is there. The main thing, you know, is that they have full-time jobs and I work around their schedules, entirely—in terms of scheduling performances and of course scheduling rehearsals—it's all worked around their schedules. But, like, for me it's become a full-time thing. Because in the process of forming the group I've sacrificed a lot and I said, well, you know, this has to mean something. It has to be more than just a thing you do for extra part-time income, so I looked into the process of becoming a nonprofit so now we have a fiscal agent. We're under the QCC, which is the Center for Gay, Lesbian, Bisexual, Transgender Art and Culture. They're our fiscal agent and while we're under their sponsorship, we can start the process of becoming a nonprofit organization, so that the Bear-A-Tones of San Francisco will always exist. The four members, we'll move on to do other things, but there'll always be four guys—four bear-identified guys, who sing really well, and along with providing quality entertainment for the bear community, as well as the gay and lesbian community, of San Francisco, they will have a strong sense of community service. And it's kind of evolved to that, because we've been doing a lot of benefit work since we've started singing.

**LKW:** Where do you perform, what kinds of events, how far geographically do you travel?

**DS:** Well, right now, the farthest we've probably gone to date has been Hayward, you know—at the Turf Club. We got booked in Tahoe this coming Labor Day weekend for the Girth and Mirth convention, so that's pretty exciting. We're going to spend the weekend there. But in terms of the type of events we've sung in, we've sung at the Ritz-Carlton. That was our first benefit for Visiting Nurses Hospice, so it was really exciting to have our first gig at the Ritz-Carlton. We've sung at the Coconut Groove, which is pretty infamous here in the City, for a second-year anniversary for QTV. My hope when I started—I knew that I had to get some sort of gimmick and Bearage [a cappella gay men's choir], yes, they did give me the idea but they didn't go the step further, that I could see a group going. So when I formed the group I knew we had to establish some sort of niche in the community and for me, because I identify with going to the Lone Star and being a bear and all that stuff, the Bear-A-Tones came up. But in our performances we've kind of expanded to QTV, Visiting Nurses Hospice. So that's a whole—that encompasses the straight community as well because a lot of people come to those events. So we've been really fortunate and I guess I've really been pushing the name and sending out press releases—the *San Francisco Examiner* covered us—that's really exciting—and that's national, so that's part of our press kit. It's media mention. So it's really become a positive thing in my life, because I know I'm—I guess I'm fulfilling whatever I need to do in this world. I'm doing what really gets my goat and any stress I have is my stress. It's not somebody else's stress. I'm really happy doing it. And I'm fortunate to work with really talented singers who are committed.

**LKW:** You mentioned it was "Bear-A-Tones San Francisco"—does that mean there are other people using the name?

**DS:** Well, when I formed the group I immediately got an attorney. I have an entertainment lawyer who has, from the very beginning, looked at all the paperwork, who's looked at everything, and we talked about copyrighting the name. We did copyright the logo or the name within a logo, so we have a logo that's copyrighted, but, in exploring actually having a copyright on the name, we found out that there was a Bear-A-Tones group in Seattle! But they'd been using the name since 1986. So because of the period of time that they've been using the name, they have the name, basically. But they're not—from what I understand, the Bear-A-Tones in Seattle are just part of the Gala festival that's a [gay a capella] thing that happens every year. They're not the scale that we're at. So my attorney says, you might want to consider something to separate your group from them. The "SF" in the logo looks like the musical sign, *sf,* so the musical sign kinda goes along. So it's Bear-A-Tones San Francisco. But no one ever remembers that!

**LKW:** So what was your musical preparation for becoming involved? Did you study music? Have you trained?

**DS:** I've been singing since the sixth grade. My sister graduated in 1969 from high school; I remember singing as a kid with the radio with her—but just choir all my life. In college, I didn't leave singing—it always was a part of me. After I graduated from the University of Texas (I'm from Texas originally), the last year the musical [unintelligible] came to audition in Austin, and I auditioned and I made it in. That was my ticket to New York, so I moved to New York for three and a half years. I went to AMDA [American Musical and Dramatic Academy] and stuff so I got some training—musical and theater training there but that was only a year and then I started working full time just to pay my rent there. I did a cabaret show there in the Village. It's just been very hands-on. In terms of the group, because I've developed a press kit that gets sent out, well, and just being a retail manager and doing the whole visual thing, I know presentation is really everything in anything you do. And just to be taken seriously as well, you've got something that looks professional, that's there, that's quality. People are going to take notice and that really helps in and around the city—the press kits that I've sent out—because they know that it's a serious venture, that this is not just, "oh well, they'll die in two weeks" or whatever. They know it's a serious venture because of the work that's been put into it. And the fact that we're becoming a nonprofit. That's really exciting.

**LKW:** I'm a little bit curious—can you tell me a little bit about the cabaret show you were doing in New York?

**DS:** After I left AMDA I decided I didn't want to do the whole musical theater thing; I didn't want to live out of a suitcase—I just wanted to sing. So I got myself a musical director, looked him up in the *Backstage* or whatever. I worked with him, put some music together. There's a cabaret club in the Village called The 88s and I heard that they booked people—you went in, scheduled an audition, and you did, like, a small set, and if they liked you, they booked you. And so I did—I worked out a small set with my musical director and was booked Mondays in April. I had a show every Monday night at ten o'clock in April. And I named the cabaret the "First Step," because it was the very first thing I had ever done. Let me tell you, it's a growing experience because you're there, you're so vulnerable on stage, and it's YOU, it's just you. And Mondays at ten o'clock who's going to come? The second Monday in April there were maybe, what, five—six people in the audience. You really grow a lot. I was happy I did it, but it kills you—because when I sing, when I'm up on stage it's a very personal part of me. I become somebody else—I channel somebody else and I'm just up there and so that side's very open and very vulnerable—so after I finish singing I'm exhausted. I just want to leave!

**LKW:** What kinds of songs does the group sing? Is there a bear sensibility in them?

**DS:** Recently I wanted the group to kind of go with this sixties and seventies rock, stuff that you don't hear on the radio anymore. And at the Lone Star, that's what they usually play, so I thought that would be a good thing to start with. And we have that sort of music on there, but with the different personalities of the guys that have come in, they bring in their own stuff, so we don't limit ourselves to singing—we don't limit ourselves at all. All I ask is if it can be arranged in four voices. [If it can,] then let's do it! We sing everything—Broadway show tunes, ballads, jazz, everything, basically.

And we do switch words, you know. One song that comes to mind is "Dream Girls"—we've changed it to "Dream Bears"—and it worked out. When the opportunity comes to change words here and there and gender-bend we certainly do, just to cater to the audiences. And definitely, we want to keep it bear-identified. Like one song we want to do is "These Boots Were Made for Walking"—"These Boots Were Made for Licking." Things like that, you know! What we do is we establish "musical menus." We have a certain set of songs that we would sing at the Eagle. Now that certain set of songs wouldn't be appropriate at the Ritz-Carlton, so we have "musical menus" for different things that we do. So, certainly, if we're singing at the Eagle or the Lone Star, we're going to sing the "raunchy" stuff—stuff the guys want to hear!

One exciting thing that happened is we were booked in December for a show at Jose's Cabaret and Juice Joint and that was exciting simply for the fact that it's very hard to get booked there, and they asked us—they approached us after seeing us at the Castro Street Fair. So we were booked there for three nights, and as a joke, we were trying to come up with a name for the show and somebody just said, "Oh, just shut up and sing!," and, well, that became the name—it was called "Just Shut Up and Sing!" It was in December so it was a holiday show, like the second half, but we kind of figured that this would be a great fund-raiser for the year. So what we're going to start doing next year is that, "Just Shut Up and Sing!" is going to be produced again and it's going to be produced every year, but it's going to benefit a major Bay Area charity. We're hoping that "Just Shut Up and Sing! II" will benefit LYRIC [Lavender Youth Recreation and Information Center], and I don't know when it's going to be or what theater. I'm kind of hunting around for a theater but that's going to be our major production every year, so all our work will be toward that. And it's very scary because I'm making decisions, because I'm the founding member and stuff like that—I find myself kind of planting seeds and making decisions and stuff like that and a lot of times I don't know if they're always the right ones, but I figure I'm on the right path. Someone told me that [about] my aura, that I was on the right path, I was doing what I was supposed to be doing, so I just kind of followed my gut. It just really scares me sometimes! I go with the blessings of the guys and we certainly decide. It's not just me making the decisions; we have business meetings every month. The guys are cued into everything that we do. All the correspondence that I send out for the group, they'll get copies of that. I didn't want it to be just a "me" thing when I started it because things like that fail in other organizations. It was going to be a joint effort—they voice their opinions. If they don't want to do something, we won't do it. It's by majority rule, so it's not just me running the show. It's a joint effort. And the music part is done by the musical director. You know, I don't claim to know the ins and outs about music—because I don't. That's why I hired a musical director. Pat—he runs the show when it comes to rehearsals. He gets on them if they don't know their music or haven't learned their parts or whatever. And he makes the suggestions of what we should sing. That's not me, and I didn't want it to be me because it shouldn't be me. I run the business end, I guess, right now. Eventually, I just want to learn my music and sing! As we grow, hopefully there will be somebody who will take care of the business stuff, and I won't have to do that anymore. Right now it's been a learning experience to do all that. I'm bringing out talents I didn't know I had!

**LKW:** Is there a bear philosophy for the group?

**DS:** Well, the one thing that has come up consistently is that in every performance that we do, I get a testimonial from whoever hired us, and that's part of our press kit. It's just comments and stuff like that that I've put into quotations. And one thing that everybody has consistently said, and primarily what Albert Oliver of the Bears of San Francisco has said, is that we're promoting the bear image and culture in a very positive way. Because there's four guys that are out there singing, and they're obvious bears and we're doing a lot of community service. So I think there's a philosophy there or a goal, that's what I want it to be. Following the example of the Bears of San Francisco, because they're such a phenomenal group and they raise so much money in the different things that they've done and that's a real positive thing here in the City. People see big, hairy guys and they're intimidated. Bears of San Francisco, an organization like that, they're raising all this money for great causes—following by example, that's what I want the Bear-A-Tones to do. I want us to kind of use our talent and time. I guess music heals and—do it like that, do it in a quality way. I guess that's the philosophy, just to be always conscious of our audiences, always be respectful of our audiences, and know that we're representing the bear community of San Francisco. It has to be quality. It has to be top-notch. It has to be professional.

**LKW:** What do you feel that the Bear-A-Tones symbolize as a positive image of the bear community? What kind of qualities do you think that includes? What is the image? How would you describe that?

**DS:** What I always tell the guys, before we go up to perform anywhere, is to have fun. To have fun up there. The whole purpose of a singer/performer—if you are able to communicate in your singing whatever feeling you're emoting—even if it's just [to] one person out in the audience—then you've done your job. As [for] the Bear-A-Tones, I think if we're able to do that as a unit, as a group, and be representing a certain part of the gay community, then that's pretty cool. I don't think I even answered the question, but I think just going out there, having fun, and being comfortable with ourselves on stage—being that we're big and stuff like that, because a lot of people aren't—maybe we're serving as some sort of example for people that have a problem with their weight or whatever. Up there on stage, we're very comfortable in the way we interact together and perform because of our experience, the individual experience that each one of us has. You know, each one of us has a very solid performance background. But bringing that together with four, well, three big guys and one guy who is not actually too big!—he's a smaller one. Bringing that together in a performance—I think that's in itself something that's positive that people can see. They're not tripping that they're overweight or whatever, and they're proud to be big. They're not tripping that they have to look a certain way if we're performing. That's gone with the past. I used to think that performers were like the Disney types, clean-shaven, perfect Barbies and Kens that you see performing at Disney World. A lot of times that's what you see on Broadway, like the leading man and the leading lady—well, that's not the case anymore. A big guy can command the stage as much as the ingenue. So I think that's a positive thing, a different spectrum. A different side of performing.

**LKW:** And when are you performing next?

**DS:** There was a misprint in the *B.A.R.* They said we'll sing tonight actually, at the Gift Center, but we're not. I guess the next gig is probably the Labor Day gig in Tahoe. But I think we'll be doing stuff before that. But right now the focus for the group is trying to find a theater for "Just Shut Up and Sing!" Something also important to know about the "Just Shut Up and Sing!" thing—it's not going to be just us singing. We're going to have guest performers and stuff like that. We're hoping to get Val Diamond this year for "Just Shut Up and Sing!" She's the premier diva of "Beach Blanket Babylon" here in the City and she does so much for the community. She has a phenomenal voice—she just makes you cry. I'm hoping to get her as celebrity guest star for "Just Shut Up and Sing! II." And that will be the case every year—every year there'll be a celebrity guest star and every year a major Bay Area charity—I want it to be a real big thing in the City. It's a growing process. Step by step.

**LKW:** Congratulations and . . .

**DS:** It's exciting and, like I said, you've got to do your passion—whatever gives you goose bumps, that's your passion. Because you can't fake goose bumps.

**LKW:** Well, thank you very much!

**DS:** Sure!

## Chapter 16

# East Coast Bear Hugz

## Tim Goecke

East Coast Bear Hugz started with Alan. He traveled frequently for work and had been to some of the earliest Bear Hugs parties out in San Francisco. Let me back up a little here. At the time, around late 1988, the Baltimore social/bar scene was probably the same as elsewhere in the country—that is, unless you were a skinny little disco bunny, there was no place to go. There were a couple of dance palaces catering to the young and beautiful along with the occasional, but always embarrassing, chicken hawk trying to prove he still had it. And there were several neighborhood bars with a little more of a mix (if you consider alcoholics *and* substance abusers just the right party mix). What had been a sort-of leather bar was in a neighborhood fast becoming too scary for even the nastiest of leathermen. All of the above were, while quite fun in their own way, still not very welcoming to the full-figured crowd. And we've always considered this to be very odd, considering the preponderance of large and lovely drag queens in this town. Baltimore is, after all, the birthplace of Divine as well as the Miss Gay Universe AT LARGE Pageant, where contestants must be 250 pounds or more to qualify. But I digress.

This was around the time that people first started recovering from the shock wave of the AIDS crisis. While people had finally figured out that casual sex could be safe and sane, there was nowhere to go about doing it outside of one's own home. The one backroom bar in town had been closed a long time before. The parks and other meeting places for casual sex had been pretty much cleaned out by a publicly homophobic (never married, never dated, still lived with

Mom, Norse gods for bodyguards, you know the type) mayor whenever he needed to show he was all man. The bathroom at one of the aforementioned dives, while welcoming, could only hold three at a time. What's a girl to do?

There was a small group in town, that, using discreetly worded ads in the local gay papers, had started an informal jack-off club meeting once a month at one of the member's homes. When Alan started East Coast Bear Hugz, the parties were in conjunction with them. Invitation was by word of mouth, and a posting on the local gay BBS (I got invited through some cheap trick that I never saw again). The idea wasn't specifically to throw a sex party. Alan simply wanted to have a party where big furry guys could go and have a good time meeting other big furry guys. And maybe get laid.

The party had twenty to thirty men there, almost all what we would now call of the bearish type. The most striking thing to me was the range of ages present. At the bars you get used to everyone being of a fairly tight median age, and you certainly don't see anyone with undyed gray hair. Here were guys around my age (thirty-four at the time) and older, many with beards, little paunches, and not a hair transplant or dye job in sight. I thought I'd died and gone to heaven. And the fur, oh, my God!

The party turned out to be great fun, and the sex that was hoped for was accomplished in splendid form by some in the kitchen and pantry. While making the more sedate party guests' access to the bar a bit difficult, the show (especially the part in the sink with the little rinsing hose) was indeed enjoyed by all.

Alan, his husband at the time, and I wound up going over to my place afterward. I was living in the warehouse then, with about 6,500 suare feet of space (plentiful and cheap industrial space being one of the few advantages of life here in Crab City). The first thing out of Alan's mouth was, "We're having the next party here, aren't we, Timmy?" Now, I'd only met Alan for the first time that night, but after we used up the husband and he passed out on the couch, Alan and I started planning the next party. "Hmmm, let's see. . . . The bar can go over there. . . . Oh, and don't block off the wood shop for anyone with a Bob Vila thing going. Do you think those pipes will hold the sling?"

Simultaneously, a small bear community of sorts began to form. Before the arrival of *BEAR* magazine at the local bookstore, the biggest thing helping this along was the opening of the Baltimore Eagle. From the beginning, the Eagle here has not been like the Eagle in most other cities. The attitude is way more relaxed, so much so that those in full leather or rubber regalia are more likely to be met with a "What's her problem?" than anything else. The crowd in the first year or so was a goofy collection of artists, computer geeks, blue-collar types, and others that simply didn't fit in any of the other bars. One of the bar backs used to mix tapes of gothic, techno, country, and ABBA. The guys behind the bars were decidedly not big butch leather beer slingers, and looked the other way or joined in when things started getting a bit steamy in the darker corners. It was in this atmosphere that bears connected, with some self-identifying as bears and actively discussing the idea of a bear community.

The first East Coast Bear Hugz party at the warehouse was three or four months later and probably drew about eighty to a hundred people. Invites were sent using names and addresses gathered from the first parties, and were also handed out at the Eagle to particularly woofy guys. We found ourselves having to explain over and over that "doors close at ten" didn't mean the party was over, but that the sex part of the party was really starting then, and we didn't want to bother with the damn door anymore. We decided to charge for this one to cover our costs, part of which was paying off the heteros, who subleased space from me, to go away for the weekend. At ten we did close the doors and the party really began.

After this first party at the warehouse, things sort of began to snowball. We threw one pretty much quarterly after that, with each one drawing bigger and bigger crowds, still mostly by word-of-mouth invitations. Thanks to the Internet, we started getting bears in from as far away as West Virginia and Boston. We were mentioned several times in the local gay papers' gossip columns (mostly along the lines of "and we hear there was another one of those nasty warehouse sling parties again. Just what do you have to do to get invited to one of these things?"). One time, the Sunday after one of the bigger parties, I went to the Eagle for happy hour and got bitched at by all the bartenders because we were cutting into their tips. "Look, why don't you warn us next time and we'll just close up and come to the damn party ourselves!"

We never planned any real "theme parties" in advance, but the parties started to be remembered by particular occurrences. Like the one where a bunch of guys broke off from the main event, got into the freight elevator, stopped it between floors, and had their own little soirée (rumor has it that there's a video available, but I've never seen it). I only learned about this the Monday after, when I ran into the building super, who asked what the hell went on over the weekend because he just had to clean out a bunch of used rubbers and lube bottles from the thing. We made sure to bolt the back door shut after that little incident. And there was the Thanksgiving party where Ali Lopez wanted to throw a big dinner party for fifty or so of his most intimate friends. Since he lived in a miniscule apartment, and since most of his pals were at all the parties anyway, we put the two together at the warehouse. There was another party advertised as two slings, no waiting. One time we put out moist towelette packets just as a joke, since we had always put out lube and rubbers and paper towels for our guests, and damn if those dizzy queens didn't use up half of them.

As I said, things began to snowball out of control. We had to begin worrying about security, paying my tenants more to disappear, and other tenants in the building wondering what was going on with all these big guys wandering around. Alan and I couldn't go anywhere without getting bugged about when's the next party, when's the next party, when's the next party? It gets a bit embarrassing when you're trying to be all suave and sophisticated and pick up some hunky little furball and there's this guy that you don't know coming up to you blathering on about what a swell time he had at the bottom of the pig pile at your last party and when's the next party? Jesus, give me a break!

We had never started this to make money or become the party kings of Baltimore. We broke even at best most of the time. The idea at the start was simply to have a party where big furry guys could go and have a good time meeting other big furry guys. And maybe get laid. This was becoming the problem: Alan and I were so busy at the parties that we never had time to have any fun at them. Once we realized that neither of us had even gotten so much as a cheap feel at the last couple of parties, we said, forget this, it's too much work. We threw one more party, primarily as a birthday party for my ex. It was his fortieth, so I promised him forty cocks all lined up as his present. Now, *that* we should have made a video of.

After that we closed up shop. Some from the core group had gone on to become the beginnings of the Chesapeake Bay Bears. Neither Alan nor I got much involved with the club. We figured we had already done our job. We'd thrown a lot of good parties, and a lot of bears had met and connected through them. All of us found a way to be sex positive and safe about it. Most important, we all found a way to be comfortable as ourselves. A community had been created.

# Chapter 17

# The Bears Mailing List, Part 2: Interview with Henry Mensch

## Transcribed by Dale Wehrle

**LKW:** This is February 15, 1998. We're at International Bear Rendezvous in San Francisco, California, at the Ramada Plaza Hotel, and this interview is with Henry Mensch, who, perhaps for the record, could state his name, who you are, where you come from, and all that stuff.

**HM:** My name is Henry Mensch. I grew up in New York. After many years of living in the Northeast I ended up in the Boston area working for MIT. I've been in California now seven years. I came here from Boston.

**LKW:** Okay. If you came here seven years ago that would be . . .

**HM:** 1991.

**LKW:** 1991.

**HM:** It's that "math" thing. Came here April '91. It'll be seven years this coming April. I guess I'm here because of my work with the Bear's Digest.

**LKW**: Right. Primarily, anyway, yes. I'm curious—were you involved with bear phenomenon before you moved to San Francisco?

**HM:** Well, Steve Dyer and I—Steve Dyer, who created the Bear's Digest—we used to work together at MIT. So I was aware of it from at least that point on.

**LKW:** Oh, okay.

*191*

**HM:** Of course, at that early stage, there wasn't a lot going on except for the Bear Hug parties out here, as far as I knew—but I wasn't actively tracking it. While I was on the list I wasn't tracking it too carefully. At that point in time I had taken a leave of absence from work—I lived abroad for a while . . . and my life had other priorities at that point so I wasn't really tracking it too carefully.

**LKW:** Well, and then the other track—what has your involvement been with computers and the Internet that got you involved with the BML?

**HM:** Well, my work at MIT was in a project called Project Athena, which is well-known in those circles that understand educational computing very well. Our primary work was to create large networks of computers, like thousands of desktop computers that could communicate with each other seamlessly, without the users having to know arcane bits of stuff. I'd worked with computers years before that as a student and part-time employee in different places around the country. That was my first professional work with computing, really—and I'd been on the Internet and ARPANET and the USENET before that, BITNET since 1980, I guess—1981. So I've been on the various online and e-mail networks for about eighteen years now, seventeen years.

**LKW:** Are your professional activities continuing in a similar vein since coming out here?

**HM:** I work for the Oracle Corporation. I've been there for four years now. My work is generally classed as systems manager/systems administration. Right now, I build *very* large systems for Oracle—systems with terabytes of disk space and gigabytes of memory, for use in our build process. So I've always been involved in computing at that sort of level. When I was at MIT I was doing technical writing. I was doing quality assurance kinds of work, that sort of thing. And "software evangelism"—going to people and telling them why they wanted to use our stuff and why they wanted to adopt our software systems as standards for the product they sell to the public.

**LKW:** So, how did you become involved with the BML?

**HM:** I'm forgetting what year it was at this point—I have to calculate back a bit—that October when Steve had taken the list on hiatus after six years of running it. I guess his life had gotten very busy and people on the list had been—it had just gotten too much. And I remember when that happened, I remember a few months later—December or so, Roger Klorese had decided to pick it up on Queernet. I offered my hand at that point to be of any help since I had run lists before—I was one of the founders of the Men's Issues mailing list on the Internet many years before—in the mid-eighties. Roger had agreed to host it on Queernet as a free-form list and not as a digest and it became clear after about a month that really wasn't going to work very well, so we returned to the digest format at that time. I did it then for about two and a half years.

**LKW:** And you and Roger worked together?

**HM:** Initially we did. Roger hosts many lists on Queernet, so the reason why he took the list on the conditions that he did was that he didn't have to give it much day-to-day maintenance. So when I came on board I was there to give it the day-to-day maintenance that it was going to need. So he ended up providing all the hosting. Since he had many years of experience operating these lists in the gay community, I had him as a resource to fall back on. He would pick up the actual list operation while I was out of town for work or whatever. And that happened a few times.

**LKW:** Could you tell us a little about what Queernet actually is and does?

**HM:** Queernet operates out of Roger Klorese's home. It is a small collection of computer systems that originally only hosted mailing lists and now also hosts a small number of Internet connections for individuals and Web pages for projects for the queer community—not just for gay men, but for people with HIV, women, for chubbies, for all kinds of folks. Transgendered folks have lists there. There are right now more than one hundred mailing lists on Queernet. He puts activists online by giving them accounts and dial-up access. All the day-to-day work is done by Roger on a volunteer basis—outside of his having a life and having a full-time job at a start-up company that actually requires a lot of his time. All the funding comes out of his pocket or donations from individuals.

Just to give a picture of the class of hardware that Queernet runs on, up until a few years ago, Queernet operated on a computer that was like the desktop system you might have at home—a 486 with some extra memory and disk on it. Now it is a larger system—it's a Pentium system. We're not talking about a very big machine room full of equipment here—we're talking about a very modest setup, that Roger manages very effectively, to the community's advantage.

**LKW:** How was it that you came to decide to leave moderating the BML? How did that come about and then where to go from there?

**HM:** Well, that was due to circumstances changing in my life. I decided to return to school to finish my bachelor's degree. There was not going to be a lot of time for me to do my job, and have a life, and go to school, and do the Bear's Digest work. I could very easily come home from work and spend a few hours working on digest issues. From the time that I picked it up from Steve until the time I left it, our membership grew two-and-a-half-fold, from about, I guess, nearly a thousand people to almost three thousand people. The number fluctuates—people go on vacation, so I say two-and-a-half-fold. Right now it's been near three thousand for the past year or so.

**LKW:** On average, how much time per week would you spend working on it?

**HM:** I guess it easily could be twenty hours a week. Since we ran a moderated digest, I actually had to read all of the stuff before it got sent out. Sending out two and three digests a day some days, that meant previewing as many as one hundred messages. Sorting out ones that weren't appropriate, sorting out spam. A lot of work was done by the list management software that Roger uses, something called Majordomo that can separate out obvious spam and things of that sort, and messages from people who weren't members and that sort of thing. But messages which were outside of the published guidelines—you had to read for that class of thing. You had to read for whether this is something people are going to be interested in. Because the list grew so large, the idea of what people would be interested in really varied quite a lot. You're never going to make anyone very happy—any choice that I made that something was irrelevant was going to make somebody cranky. That didn't bother me much but I made sure that it got done.

**LKW:** What kinds of things did you notice that people talked about a lot, recurring topics, redundant topics?

**HM:** The funny thing about that is that over the ten years—the Bear's Digest is now nearly ten years old—the same topics kept coming up over and over again. People always feud about whether or not monogamy is the right thing or the right answer for them—it's to the point that I've put a lot of that in the background. I've learned to skip over it when I see it in the digest now as a reader—you hit spacebar and skip over the business you're not very interested in. People are very passionate about a handful of topics like monogamy—whether it's the thing for everyone or just for you, and people are passionate about their faith—and that was actually one of the things that brought the digest back into moderation. There was a big flame war that was going on that was related to religion. For that short period when it was running as an unmoderated list when Roger took it over, messages were being sent to it and being forwarded pretty immediately so people were encouraged to reply immediately and it became a really big sort of flame war.

**LKW:** And people were responding to . . . ?

**HM:** And people were responding in time and the volume would just grow and grow and grow and it was all heat and no light. So we shut the list down for a day or two just to get everyone set to a safer level—and then we brought it back on moderation. Moderation unfortunately took away some of the immediacy of things—because we were moderated we didn't get the opportunity to send messages out individually which some people would have preferred. But it meant that the service might stay around for a few more years . . .

**LKW:** In the time that you've either been reading or actively constructing the list have you noticed any kind of clear evolution, and particular directions that things have gone?

**HM:** Oh, sure. In the very early days when Steve created the digest there was more of a sense of community, which you get with a small group of people who have shared goals. With three thousand people from around the world, from multiple walks of life and all different backgrounds and all different ideas of the bear experience, the idea of community is basically shot to hell. People don't have that singleness of goal, they don't have the same experience in life or in the nebulous bear community. The digest has become a lot more to a lot more people. Initially it connected together a bunch of folks who were really in community somehow, whether they lived here in San Francisco or they came out here to join that community, like Steve did when he was coming out to the Bear Hug parties and that sort of thing. Right now there are people who join it because it's their only outlet to the gay world—they are living in heterosexual marriages or they're living in very rural places. For many of these people the Bear's Digest is their only outlet into the gay man's life, and it's another place where it makes sense for them to stick around. In ten years there have not been other forums that addressed their needs. The Bear's Digest has always been open to any subscriber, male or female, straight or gay—as long as you are well-behaved and follow the guidelines. That's served us well, I think.

**LKW:** Have you made personal contacts, not necessarily in a sexual sense, but have you made friends or connected with people that have personal interests in common through the list?

**HM:** Absolutely. I think one of the attractive parts of the list is that you end up meeting up with people—from around the world—who share common interests. Even before I operated the list, I was a regular contributor. I have a very distinctive writing style—people remember that. I write concisely, and I don't have a tolerance for bullshit. Folks remember that. That is probably the single best feature of the Bear's Digest. It gives people a forum where they can speak a bit and get known enough and get people interested in them without having to feel very exposed and vulnerable like you might be in a bar. Rejection over e-mail is nothing like being rejected in person in a bar somewhere. It also has the potential to be a lot more friendly and a lot less sexually charged—and that fosters more friendship. On the other hand, I've eschewed a lot of attention as "that person who ran that mailing list." I don't attend the online parties. I just don't do that sort of thing.

**LKW:** Could you describe how the BML fits in with your involvement in the bear community, or what kind of role you play there?

**HM:** I'm not sure I understand. It's certainly as valid and as useful a part as anything else I do.

**LKW:** I think I'm asking in the sense of—I used to be a very avid philatelist and at one point I ended up working for two years as a stamp dealer, and after doing it for a living it just destroyed my desire, took the fun out of it for years and years afterward.

**HM:** Well, I have no professional interest in this stuff certainly. Being a coin collector myself I understand that very well. Taking that sort of interest because you find the artwork on your coin or stamp attractive and then turning it into a business, I can very easily see it taking the wind out of those sails. This is not a professional interest for me certainly. I go to some of these events because I have friends from all over the country who come to them and it's easier to go to one and see some of them than to schlep all over the country. Although I do love to travel, time just isn't there.

**LKW:** How do you see the Internet as it has created or altered community in the gay communities, whether it is specifically the bear community or the gay community in general, and what kinds of social changes do you see this whole Internet phenomenon having caused in the nearly twenty years you've been involved in it?

**HM:** The Internet is certainly enabling but it's still very stratifying. You still have to have a nontrivial bit of resources to get an e-mail address, use a computer, have a modem and a telephone line in your home to do this stuff. Sure, in some places you can do it in your public library, but it simply isn't the same—you don't have the privacy. You may not have the ability to subscribe to lists like the digest where the sexual discussion is pretty frank. And you certainly don't have the resources to pursue individuals or sexually oriented Web sites in those places. So it's very stratified but it is enabling. Resources like Queernet and various freenets across the world at this point do a good job of putting people in touch. It is, to a large degree, becoming yet another common means of keeping people in contact—it's not quite as common as having a phone number but it's almost. No matter where your e-mail address is, whether it's in France, or in New Zealand, or California, it all works the same.

**LKW:** Certainly a lot cheaper and a lot faster.

**HM:** You don't get per-distance charges and the service is generally pretty quick. As an aside to some of this, my just-recent ex, with whom I still live and am good friends, I met over the Internet. He was a student at the University of Texas and for a year I commuted back and forth. To say that the Internet was certainly enabling there would be an understatement. We made the phone calls and all that, but the first six months of our association was spent getting to know each other outside the potential sexual tension of meeting in person or over the phone—by using e-mail, by using IRC—and occasional phone calls, too. It's definitely a very different environment.

**LKW:** Did you find when you met your soon-to-be partner in person that he turned out to be very different from . . .?

**HM:** Not at all. During those first few months—that certainly could be true on the Internet. No one knows if you're a dog or whoever you say you are. There's certainly room for caution there. But I've been using the Internet long enough to know how to get what I needed to be sure that I was getting into the right thing.

**LKW:** I guess part of what I'm wondering about and asking you to comment about is that there's this effort to demonize the Internet—that this is where child molesters lurk, and personal ads where people say one thing and it's actually something else. At least a lot of what's out in the general media is trying to make it sound like it's a bad and dangerous thing.

**HM:** I think that that needs to be placed in context. It's like any big city. Most big cities are very safe. In most big cities there are situations where you can be unsafe. You need to be wary and you need to act accordingly. There is lots of hysteria over it because it is perceived in exactly the way you've described. People perceive it as a place where dubious folks hang out and lure people in. And I'm sure that happens—I've no doubt that it happens. I know many adult men who have gotten involved with other adult men on the Internet only to find out that when they meet up, things were not as they were told. That doesn't mean the Internet is a bad place—it means it's like everywhere else in life. It's a place where you need to be careful.

**LKW:** What I'm thinking of, for example, is someone advertises in an ad. They say they're forty years old and you meet them and they're sixty-five. There's nothing wrong with being sixty-five, but why in the world would somebody do that—misrepresent themselves to such an extreme if they were intending to actually follow through?

**HM:** Well, I can't speak to that. I'm not a good liar. I'm certain that what some people do is that they do that with the idea that they never expect to meet these people in real life, and so they build a character, like you would build a character for a play. They pump it into IRC, they pump it into the mailing lists, and they exchange e-mail with people and make this character. The fellow at the other end gets attracted to the character. It never occurs to the person playing the character that it may become something that he may have to deal with and reveal himself for what he is.

**LKW:** But the vast majority of people on the Internet communicate as themselves pretty much . . .

**HM:** No, you can't tell. There's a certain connection. It's very easy to lie on the Internet—it feels very impersonal. You write these words on your screen, you push them off and that's that. On the telephone you actually hear a live person. It's probably, for many people, harder to lie about that. When confronted with someone that you know is living and breathing and talking on the other end, it's probably harder to bullshit them. Of course in person it's even more difficult. It's not impossible, but it's certainly doable. Physical attributes can't be lied about but other attributes probably could be. People who describe themselves as professionally well-off suddenly become waiters who are living hand-to-mouth. Not a bad thing—it tells you where their insecurities lie, but that's the way they project sometimes.

**LKW:** How do you see the Internet changing the way people interact—are there any cultural changes you can definitely say have happened over the last twenty years?

**HM:** Well, I know that more people are definitely more open to it. And events like this where people do come from geographically diverse places—you meet somebody, you want to keep in touch, and the first thing they ask is, "Do you have an e-mail address? Do you have a Web page? How can I follow your life?" That certainly happens. There are currently teleconferencing technologies which aren't very good—things like CUSeeMe that are primary bandwidth-constrained so they're not very useful. Those will almost certainly come into greater use as more bandwidth becomes available and the picture doesn't become "CU/See Nothing." Right now, because most people have 28.8 modems when they are using CU-SeeMe, they have this camera on top of their computer and it takes a photograph of them and then they move and then the whole picture pixelates into nothing for about three minutes, while the computer is sending the new picture out. As the speeds available to people become faster and with less latency, and as the quality of those images become better, people will use that to communicate, but I can't say for sure that things we do now we'll stop doing. I can't image that things like IBR would stop happening. For all the technology in the world, people still need to meet, and talk, and touch, and whatever. And grope . . .

**LKW:** The big bugaboo in academe right now is that all faculty is going to be replaced by CD-ROM. It's a big fear. People are going to communicate in virtual reality and we'll all be out of jobs.

**HM:** Well, I can speak to that because I'm in a distance learning program myself. I am a student at the Rochester Institute of Technology and that's in New York. I live in California. I don't go there—they have winter there.

**LKW:** Rochester is a horrible place to be stuck, weatherwise!

**HM:** Right, and I don't have to go there, ever. Not even to graduate. The work is conducted over the phone. There's videotape, over the Internet with our online conferencing system. There are still faculty who operate every course, not TAs but real faculty. They're kept small, so we have the materials we need handy but we still have that weekly/daily interaction with instructors and people who have "been there and done that." That's not going to go away. Reducing life to CD-ROM is all well and good but you still have to have people to make that useful for you. Like the people who make the books useful for you, to transfer the information into knowledge and experience.

**LKW:** Any final thoughts on the BML or anything that's happened there that you've observed?

**HM:** Not especially. I'm very grateful that I was able to hornswoggle Steve and Bob Thurman to pick it up. I brought them on six months before I left. I did not bring them on at the time with the idea that I was going to leave, but it worked out that way. They are both doing a marvelous job under very difficult circumstances—it's still getting larger and larger even though we offer, in some respect, fewer services than Steve offered—we don't offer the picture archive for instance, partly because it was very difficult to maintain. It was eating up all his resources and people were misbehaving a bit. Partly because with the advent of things like the Web, as those technologies move into people's hands there's less of a need for a central repository of pictures of people doing things—you can go to a Web page and see it all for yourself. Even though we do few of the things that Steve had done . . . they do a very good job. They do a few things differently than I did and that's their prerogative. I was very focused on keeping the content insofar as there is no other place on the Net where we can have these kinds of discussions in a sane, reasonable way. So things like gay politics, I didn't do too much for, even though I'm an activist myself. There are plenty of places on the Internet where you can read that stuff. There are Web pages and newsgroups and mailing lists and not just one, but many.

**LKW:** Thank you very much!

# PART IV:
# BEAR CLUB SCENE

## Chapter 18

# A Bear's Autobiography

## Jim Parton

Over the past five years of my life, I have become a bear. It took awhile for this evolution to occur, as bears were just appearing and becoming defined as a group when I came out, and I took my cues from Bears LA as I began to formulate the idea for Bears Ventura with some local friends. I had stumbled upon them by accident, attending one of their "busts" in Los Angeles at the Faultline Bar.

In reflecting upon what I have just written, I see that I have totally avoided referring to my sexuality, or to the purpose of this short autobiography. I am a bear: I am a short, stocky, very hairy, hugging, friendly type of gay man. That would be what the majority of the gay community would say that a bear is. A few years ago, that term had much less meaning than it does today, and certainly less acceptance or understanding in our community.

I've tired of trying to define a bear or answer that constant question of "What is a bear?", but I'm always hopeful that the bear community may adapt my general attitude toward this wonderful addition to the diversity of the gay community, and that my own particular philosophy will become ingrained, or at least adapted, into the community as it grows.

In 1996, I became determined to enter the 1997 Mr. Southern California Bear contest hosted by Bears LA in Los Angeles. I wanted to get some exposure for our fledgling club, Bears Ventura. I, along with some of my friends, had decided to see if a club would make it in our own area.

On the night of the contest, I felt "old." Many of the thirteen or so contestants were much younger, in better shape physically, and certainly more handsome. But I had committed, and wanted Bears Ventura to be represented, so I resolved to carry it through, even as I wondered if I belonged in the group.

I had come to California in 1977, directly after graduation from Oklahoma State University, and in that same year I had married a co-worker from Sequoia National Park where I had worked in college. At that time, I had no idea *why* I had the feelings I had about being gay, as I had no basis of reference for *being* gay. Growing up in small-town Oklahoma, I had no gay reference point in my life. All the gay men I could identify were the strange and socially "tweaked," and they were whispered about or laughed at openly, and made fun of. This was not going to be me.

I had some experiences with other men in college, but was totally unprepared to consider that any of these had been valid relationships, but rather something that should never be spoken of again, and had best be forgotten. This had worked after being molested repeatedly by some older men in our church when I was younger, and those experiences had also convinced me that any consideration of male sexuality had best be ignored. The leap from "pedophile" to "gay" was unclear to me then, and scary as hell. Couple all these feelings with a horrific upbringing in a "HELL and BRIMSTONE" religion, an unforgiving and relentless god standing ready to torture me for eternity for these thoughts and sins, and a family already wondering *why* I wasn't married at twenty-one, and you can see why I found myself considering the next logical step of getting married.

After seven years of marriage, realizing that we were never going to be able to have children, we completed our family with three wonderful children from Korea. After years of "test-tube" heroics, miscarriages, and other problems, these wonderful children came into my life through international adoption. My older daughter first, then my son, then my younger daughter arrived at LAX [Los Angeles International Airport], and immediately completed my soul and heart. But even this could not quiet the unrest I felt in my life. Three children, wonderful in-laws, a good job teaching, and a wife that seemed to complete the picture, and I had become totally exhausted from getting up each morning and wondering *who* I was going to be, and how I was possibly going to accomplish it.

Over the fifteen years I was married, I had met other gay dads, but it was certainly nothing we could be open about, discuss, or even be remotely proud of. We were all still married, and although we had things in common, we had no allegiance to one another, and thus the friendships never cemented. There was no sense of permanence or family. Although at the time I considered these friendships of great importance, they were a sorry crutch to help me try and make sense of a life that was only half lived.

As my marriage was ending, and I had begun living on my own for the first time, adjusting to being away from my children a great deal, I met someone who touched my soul. From the first time I had spoken with Rick, I knew he was important to me. He answered something in me that, to overuse a cliché, "completed" me, and although I didn't understand it well, I had begun to heal into a person, living openly and honestly for the first time, without constant compromise and hurt.

So, now here I stood in Los Angeles, at a totally gay event, among a group of men, a few of my friends among them, a part of the bear movement that had become my new social circle. The bears had offered me acceptance when my entire group of straight and married friends, with few exceptions, completely dismissed me from their lives and thoughts, unless those thoughts included dark and brooding fears about *who* might be connected with my "web of deceit" during my years of marriage.

A group of blue-collar men, a group who did not fit the media hype of the sculpted, shaved, young, hair-styled gay man in tights, had offered me a safe and accepting atmosphere where it was not only okay to be short, stocky, and hairy, but it was considered part of the bear image! My circle of friends in Bears Ventura had grown so quickly, it was hard to imagine how scared and lonely I had been during the previous few years when I had been separating, divorcing, and agonizing over my shattered life and my children.

Rick, my lover, had been reluctant to see me get so involved, but he had come along to the contest for support. Rick had been out for years, and had, I think, tired of the scene. He was wary of groups, as well as this "new" one, the bears. I was there, waiting for the contest to begin, a bit nervous, but used to speaking to groups from my teaching experiences. I was used to chaos, but nothing had prepared me to stand among my peers in my "bear wear," and have my wildest fantasy read to the crowd! But, in the spirit of fun, and promoting my local club, I wanted to be there.

As the contest progressed, my friends were tremendously supportive with applause and shouts of encouragement, and I seemed to sense the crowd's acceptance, but *no one* was more surprised than I was when I was announced the winner! I was astounded, and honestly had to consider whether I was being mocked or honored. I'll also never forget my feeling of absolute horror when, as my best bud Robert Dollwet was taking me to a wonderful party afterward, I realized that this now meant I had to represent Southern California in the Mr. International Bear contest a short month away! This international gathering hosted by Bears of San Francisco was a major fund-raiser in the gay community, and each year had grown in size and importance.

I now began to seriously consider what I believed to be true about the bears, and how I fit into the picture. My own philosophy is that bear is not a body type, as some put it so simply. It is a way of viewing others, and our relationship to them. The bears that I know that are true to the bear way of thinking care less about how a person looks, and more about how the person lives his friendships with others. Acceptance and, more important, *tolerance* is what sets the bears apart.

It seems to me that as gay men, we have been so critically judged by others in straight society, and so harshly, that we can't set that aside, but rather sometimes *adapt* that way of thinking into our "gay persona." We all are familiar with the cutting razor edge of gay wit and observation, and I have seen many bitter gay men apply that to almost everyone, equally and without hesitation. This is the element I find most difficult to deal with in the gay community, and what I treasure about the bears so much is its absence. The bears, largely, leave this pettiness out of their activities, and, aside from the occasional infighting normal to any group, tend to live and let live as their clubs and groups evolve. Those who thrive on the misery and misfortune of others, and who find their humor at others' expense, tend to get bored with the bears and move on to other entertainment.

That month between contests, I spent a *lot* of time considering how a gay *dad* had gotten onto this platform representing a bear group. I had determined not to hide out in my life any longer, and this contest in front of about a thousand guys in San Francisco would certainly cement that resolve. After reassuring my lover that I would not stand a chance in the larger Mr. International Bear contest, I prepared a few words about my bear way of thinking, gathered my outfits for the different parts of the contest, endured the relentless friendly jibes from my friends, and steeled myself for San Francisco! A large part of the contest there is the oral interview with the judges, and I felt I was now ready to share my way of thinking with them.

The weekend of fund-raising, raffle ticket sales, and meeting new people along with the other contestants became a scheduling blur. Rick spent much of his time alone or with our friends, as I was consumed with the details of the contest. I was determined to see it through, intimidating as the venue of the huge San Francisco Gift Center was. As in Los Angeles, I drew the *last* number for the contest, and had to wait all day after rehearsal to do the interview.

The night of the contest was overwhelming in so many ways. I had spent most of the day with Bill Adams, Mr. San Francisco Bear 1997, as he had drawn the number before mine. He was such a wonderful person, and the absolute epitome of a bear, that I ceased to worry about the contest, and focused on cheering on the hometown bear, as he was to me a clear choice, and well deserved this title. Knowing that the BOSF [Bears of San Francisco] would raise over twenty thousand dollars that weekend for charity, and now relaxing a bit seeing such a clear choice, I began to enjoy having at least represented our club. I was enjoying being a part of this process and raising money for the gay community.

As the contest progressed, and even though my faithful friends from all over my area were giving me great support, once again I was absolutely amazed to be announced the winner after the other titles had been given. I couldn't believe that I had been given the honor to represent our wonderful group as Mr. International Bear 1997. During that year, as BOSF and my local club helped me to attend some wonderful national events in Chicago, Orlando, Sacramento, San Francisco, and Los Angeles, I hope I was able to share my own brand of beardom with my friends from all over. I tried to impart my own philosophy that I hope has guided my local club.

"Friends are important. Value the friendship, and forgive the small transgressions." My own "southern Oklahoma" way of saying that is, "You have to forgive a certain amount of warts on anyone."

My own local club will soon celebrate five years of wonderful growth and popularity. We have gone from a core group of about twenty or so to over two hundred members, and we have raised much money for local and state charities. Bears such as Ken Lankard, Robert Dollwet, Durk Hubel, and others from our original core remain on the board working year after year to see our group succeed. We have tried hard to remain true to our friendship philosophy, providing a social outlet of accepting, tolerant, comfortable gay men, of all types and descriptions.

I can't imagine the harshness of my life without having been a part of the bears, and what they have given to me. We all have lovers, friends, and family, but including the social group of bears in this formula has given me such gifts. I will always be trying to find new ways to keep the group active, true to their origins, and fun. I hope your experiences with the bears will be as wonderful and rewarding.

## Chapter 19

# Bear Contests

### Les Wright

Today beauty is a consensus opinion, staged, choreographed, and disseminated in mass media. Its contemporary manifestations run from the Miss America and Miss Universe pageants to children's contests, bodybuilders' competitions, bathing beauties from the pages of *Sports Illustrated* to the *High Gear* catalog, the Mr. Drummer contest, and hundreds, if not thousands, of gay porno movies.

The beauty contest, a keystone of Western culture, descends from the Judgment of Paris, a test in which Paris was asked to choose among three women. Paris, of course, was considered the most handsome mortal man. For that reason, he was asked to resolve an argument which arose at a wedding party when Eris (Strife) threw out a golden apple marked "For the Fairest." Three goddesses laid claim to the title and each of them offered Paris a bribe if he would choose her—Hera offered him greatness; Athena, success in war; and Aphrodite, to procure for him the most beautiful woman in the world. Naturally, Paris opted for the last offer, being himself the hottest man alive. Consequently, this obliged Aphrodite to help him abduct the most beautiful woman in the world. Yes, that's right, Helen of Troy. We all know what that led to, don't we?

The American gay community has traditionally taken three approaches to ideal beauty—enshrining the boyish appeal of the young, smooth-skinned, gym-toned "dumb blonde" surfer; elevating the hypervirile, mature, often equally gym-toned, leather-clad,

---

*Note:* Earlier versions of this essay appeared in the *NEB Newsletter* (June 1994) and *American Bear* 5 (February 1995).

sometimes hairy-chested, dominant daddy type; and outrageously camping every and any ideal under the sun. In the late 1970s and 1980s, the annual Castro Street Dog Show became a popular community event in San Francisco. People's pets were judged in a camp parody of the beauty contest—every winner was guaranteed to be a dog!

The emergence of Mr. Bear contests have tended to straddle the fence between two sides—parodying traditional gay ideals of beauty while striving to establish a new, legitimate bear ideal. The International Mr. Bear contest, a component of the San Francisco-based International Bear Rendezvous (begun at the IBR's predecessor, Bear Expo), evolved in its first three years from poking fun somewhat self-consciously at traditional gay values to striving in an increasingly serious manner to project an image of a self-confident bear ideal, a new icon assuming its place among the archetypes of male beauty.

From the beginning, there has been an emphasis on personal warmth, a compassionate nature, civic-mindedness in the gay community, and spiritual playfulness. Title holders John Caldera (IMB '92) and Steve Heyl (IMB '93) worked hard during their "reign," and remain genuinely and deeply committed to the bear community. Yet, in the progression of title holders and the proliferation of Mr. Bear-type contests in recent years, I see a strong tendency toward consolidating the bear image away from the fairly chunky type to the more mesomorphic stockiness celebrated in the pages of the more recent issues of *BEAR* and *American Bear* magazine—and always with a full beard.

While my personal predilection in defining a bear emphasizes intangible qualities ("A bear is a gay man who is as comfortable with being gay as he is being a man and who has a good heart"), I confess to an overriding fetish for male body hair and full beards. (To the sentiment "you can never be too rich or too thin" I always add "or too hairy.") And, as we all know, sexual attraction knows no political correctness. That said, let us consider the traditional markers of bears—beards, bellies, and body hair, for there has been no end to this discussion (thank goodness!). When does a bear cross the line into "chubby" territory; when does a well-sculpted bear become a "twinkie" with body hair or a musclebear, and when does a taste for leather or S&M tendencies eject a bear from our midst and into the realm of the leatherfolk? Can a clean-shaven man be a bear? Are "otters," "wolves," "hamsters," or "badgers" really bears or not? When is a potbelly merely a sign of quaffing habits?

So I was a little nervous and very much surprised when the New England Bears invited me to be a judge for the Mr. New England Bear contest last August [i.e., 1994]. The criteria were thoroughly professional. NEB Mike Bibeault, a former competitive skater, provided us with the ice skaters' guidelines. Imagination, sense of humor, stage presence, community involvement, elements of combining civic-mindedness and affability ("real-people-ness") were at the heart of the matter. At the same time I was conscious of those self-defining physical qualities which in Boston are different from what I knew in San Francisco—our New England bears, as a whole, were younger (only one contestant was over forty) and less Rubenesque than their San Francisco counterparts. It was a difficult decision, for all the finalists were worthy to hold the title.

What do we all want as bears? A bear was noted for his desire and ability to draw in and recognize as his own kind, short and tall, young and old, fat and thin, hairy and hairless, all genuine men being themselves. The one thing we had in common was having overcome the self-limiting belief that we had to conform to media images of gay male beauty, images that either we did not fit, and never would, or which were of no sexual interest to us. As we choose our icons, men who embody our ideal images of ourselves and who become simplified images circulated in mass media, harbingers to the world at large of our presence, self-image, and ideals, may we appreciate the fact that we are—whether phenomenon, movement, or community—something new under the sun.

\* \* \*

In the five years since I wrote the preceding piece, much has changed in my values, perceptions, and understandings, and even more has changed in the bear community. These reflections are recorded in the introduction to this book. But I would like to conclude here with the observations that (1) bear contests often serve as much to create or deepen a sense of community among bears regionally as to select title holders; (2) the range of ideal bear types continues to expand beyond the awareness of any particular individual or group, which I have been exploring and documenting in the Bear Icons exhibition; and (3) a gay bear's idea of a bear is substantially more complex than the stocky lumberjack image which has been co-opted by and continues to proliferate in mainstream mass media (advertising, television shows, and films). Bear icons now have a life of their own, and the fact that mainstream media has "discovered" us—or at least certain images of us—is a sign of the remarkable growth of beardom over the past fifteen years.

Chapter 20

# A Short History of Bear Clubs in Iowa: The Bear Paws of Iowa and The Ursine Group

Larry Toothman

It was an extraordinarily hot June day in 1997 when my huscub and I met Bill Palmer from The Haworth Press while he was visiting Iowa City. It was a pleasant surprise when he handed me a copy of Les Wright's *The Bear Book,* which listed my name in the index, and made a short mention of the Bear Paws of Iowa in the chapter titled "A Concise History of Self-Identifying Bears." A short time later, Dr. Wright informed me that he was about to start work on a second book about bears and wondered if I would be interested in submitting a short piece about the Bear Paws. I jumped at the idea but thought that rather than just tell the tale of the Bear Paws, it would be better to include The Ursine Group too, since the origins and development of both organizations are intertwined.

While working on this project, I was able to uncover several old issues of *The Bear Facts,* the newsletter for the Bear Paws. I decided that rather than just describe the history of the Bear Paws, I would instead use sections of the old newsletters to tell the story from the perspective of the participants while it was unfolding in front of them.

The Bear Paws started out as a way for like-minded men to find each other, and to have fun—to have barbecues, parties, watch Star Trek, you name it. The Ursine Group (TUG) was founded later with the same goals in mind, but with a more informal structure so that the goals of the group would not be obscured by the mechanics of the group.

Les Wright wrote in *The Bear Book,* in the chapter titled "A Concise History of Self-Identifying Bears," that the Bear Paws was founded in 1989.[1] However, the following piece of text is from Volume 1, Number 1, of *The Bear Facts,* the newsletter I published for two years for the Bear Paws starting in November 1990.

## *FIRST MEETING*

On Saturday, November 3, around 3 p.m. it started. Several of us had been working for months trying to build contacts, develop ideas, and most important—*hunt bears!* It all seemed to come into focus on that Saturday. We were not sure what to expect, or even if anyone would care to show up!

Finally, the men started arriving one at a time. Soon we were a group of fourteen. I was very happy with the response to our mailings and numerous phone calls. I do apologize to anyone who fell through the cracks and was not informed about the first meeting in time to travel, but from this point forward, we will make every effort to keep you informed on a timely basis.

Being a club that was just starting out, we were faced with some necessary business which we easily accomplished. We circulated copies of the proposed bylaws and *Robert's Rules of Order* for everyone's inspection and comments (the adjustments and voting on these documents will take place during the December meeting). The official name of the club was chosen: The Iowa Bear Paws (IBP).

We announced a temporary board of directors and officers to act until the December elections. The temporary officers are: Larry T., President; Dave A., Vice President; Darren P., Secretary; Dean B., Treasurer; Bill L., Road Captain. Dues were set at $5.00 per month, and we decided *not* to collect dues until the December meeting. Donations, however, were accepted to help defray the cost of membership fees to the Mid-America Conference of [motocycle] clubs, and the costs of sponsoring the Saturday After-Hours Cocktail Party during the Castaways [motorcycle] run in Milwaukee.

A committee was formed to design our club colors, and Dave A. produced a temporary set of traveling colors which we used in Milwaukee for the Parade of Colors and our cocktail party during the run. We set a time and location for our next meeting and then ended the official meeting and started our social gathering where videos of bears, runs, and club events were displayed, and much food and drink were consumed. (A few patches of fur were rubbed and more than one beard was nuzzled!) All in all, it was a very successful meeting and we hope a beginning of an organization that we can be proud of.[2]

Yes, we were all proud of our club, and even today, ten years later, through all of the hurt feelings surrounding the split that formed The Ursine Group, we are still proud of what was started on that Saturday afternoon. But how did it get started?

Even though the club was officially started in 1990, events were happening in 1989 that eventually led to the club's formation. The following are some of the events that led up to forming the Bear Paws:

| November 1989 | Went to San Francisco for a birthday present from my lover at the time, Ed Luisi, in Chicago. While I was there I met Alan Hurst, whom I had been corresponding with on HTG BBS for several months. It turned out that Alan was an "ex" of Les [Cooyman] who was the sysop of Bears Lair BBS. At this time I started getting the idea of forming something—maybe not a club, but at least an event where bears from all over the country could gather and have some fun. |
| --- | --- |
| February 1990 | Black Frost Run, Minneapolis. I met Fran Frisch, the beartoonist. While discussing the subject of bears with Mr. Frisch, I started commenting on how great it would be if there were a series of bear clubs which could host events similar to the one we were both attending, hosted by the Black Guard MC. |
|  | Mardi Gras—I stayed with Gary D'Aurora, who hosted several bears that week. While sharing Gary's hot tub with the other bears, I talked about how much fun it would be to have a bear event, attracting bears from all over. |

| | |
|---|---|
| Spring 1990 | I was the Road Captain for the Blue Max CC in St. Louis, and I believe that all of the membership knew how "bear crazy" I had become. I had even started talking about forming a bear club. This suggestion was greeted with several reactions, including "A bear club? Who would join? You would never be able to get enough members to keep it going." |
| June 1990 | I moved to Iowa City, Iowa, to be with my new lover, Darren Pierrot. While I loved him and loved Iowa City, I was very disappointed with the lack of available social life for an adult gay male. (Iowa City had only one gay bar, named the 620. Being a college town, it was what members of our group later described as a "twinkie collegiate" bar where everyone there was either under twenty-five years old, or desperately trying to look like they were under twenty-five.) There seemed to be a large gay population in Iowa City, but it seemed impossible to find adult gay bears and cubs out and about. So we did what we could: We started answering ads from *BEAR* magazine, including the one placed by Dave Annis in Des Moines, Iowa. |
| July 1990 | We started corresponding on a regular basis with Dave Annis and I started bouncing the idea of a bear club off of Dave and Darren. |
| August 1990 | I decided to get the ball rolling. With Darren's help with creating the graphics, I designed a flyer and a letter promoting the idea of forming a bear club. Now that we had something to say, where would we say it and to whom? I asked Dave and Darren if they could give me a list of names and addresses of men that they thought would be receptive to the idea of helping form a club. I then gathered every address I could find listed in a *Damron's Guide* for any lesbigay business, bar, or bookstore listed for the state of Iowa. We sent out a letter and a group of flyers to each of the businesses informing them of our intent to form a new club and asked for their assistance by placing the flyers in a prominent spot for distribution. We then sent a letter and a flyer to each of the men from the lists supplied by Darren and Dave. From that point on I continued sending letters every few weeks to everyone on the list. Eventually those letters grew into the newsletter for the club. |

| | |
|---|---|
| September 1990 | Darren and I attended the annual run put on by the Corn Haulers, a Levi/Leather club based in Des Moines, Iowa. I spent Saturday afternoon driving around with Dave, looking for little teddy bear pins. I could find the little bears, but not as pins, so we went to a local hobby supply store where I bought bears, pins, and glue and spent the rest of the afternoon creating what became the first "friendship pins" for our prospective club. Later, at the main banquet for the run, I stood up and announced our intention of forming a new club, a bear club. |
| October 1990 | Darren and I attended the "Show Me" run put on by my good friends in the Gateway MC in St. Louis. While there we met Bill Laur and Dean Blum, both from Des Moines, and both bears. We enlisted their support and worked on setting up the first informal meeting. |
| November 3, 1990, 3:00 pm | First meeting of the bear club. Selected the name "Iowa Bear Paws." The name was quickly changed during the December meeting to Bear Paws of Iowa. This happened because I used the initials of the club several times in the first edition of *The Bear Facts*, the club's newsletter. And being a recent transplant to the state of Iowa from St. Louis, Missouri, I was unaware of the presence of a series of meat packing plants in the state that was well known by the initials "IBP." (My suggestions for a name for the new club included "Ursus," which many thought was a bit too cerebral, Iowa Bears, and Corn Fed Cubs.) |
| December 1990 | Bylaws were voted in and elections were held for the 1991 board. A photograph was taken of the newly elected board members, a copy of which was sent by Dave to *BEAR* magazine and was later published in issue 16. |
| January 1991 | New executive board sworn in by the then current president of the Corn Haulers, a Levi/Leather club based in Des Moines, Iowa |

Another point that Les Wright makes in his history is that "Bear clubs have generally followed along the lines of their older cousins, the leather motorcycle clubs."[3] Prior to my relocation from St. Louis to Iowa City I had been a member of the Blue Max CC motorcycle club. In fact, for the year leading up to my move, I was serving as road captain. This was really the only club structure that I had known and so consequently it was the model that I drew from when it became time to design the structure for the Bear Paws. Of all of my experiences while attending Levi/Leather and motorcycle club events in the Midwest, the spirit of brotherhood and camaraderie among the other participants always impressed me. I wanted to create an environment that would help bears, cubs, and bear hunters to experience that same sort of brotherhood, or "bearhood."

Once we knew that the formation of the new bear club was inevitable, I contacted an old friend in Blue Max CC for a copy of their bylaws so that I could use it as a boilerplate for the new club. In retrospect, I now wish that I had taken a different path.

The bylaws, as we adapted them, laid the groundwork for two problems which eventually split the group and became the moving force that created The Ursine Group: (1) citing *Robert's Rules of Order* for the meeting protocols, and (2) strict membership controls, which called for all prospective members to attend three meetings as a guest before they could submit their applications for membership, and once their membership was voted upon and accepted by the members they had a three-month "cubship" when they were "trained" for membership by the road captain, followed by another vote before being granted full membership.

Using *Robert's Rules of Order* caused all of our monthly meetings to last for increasingly long periods of time. What started out as a fun process soon became four and a half hours of tedium. In the hands of people who knew how to manipulate the rules, the meetings became a convoluted, confusing mess. It did not take very long for people to start avoiding the monthly meetings, in essence silencing their own opinions in favor of the few who were willing to attend.

This was a source of frustration for both myself and Andy Cummings, who was president of the Bear Paws in its second year. Andy would often joke, "I don't know who this fellow Robert is, or why he had to make so many rules, but I would love to get him out behind the barn just once to show him my appreciation!" Likewise, the formal closed membership procedures became a tool which, in some people's opinion, carried the potential for abuse or manipulation.

Because of this, The Ursine Group was formed around the concept of "less is better." The bylaws for The Ursine Group are "bare bones," and exist only to satisfy the requirements to register the group with the state of Iowa and, of course, the IRS. For all practical purposes, the club works as if the bylaws do not exist. The Ursine Group does not hold elections, positions are held by volunteers, the meetings are very "loose," and an effort is made to keep things simple and to avoid long drawn-out business meetings. The Ursine Group also developed a very open membership policy. Basically, if you filled out the form and paid your money, you were a member.

Dr. Wright also stated, "A formal club membership structure creates automatically an insider/outsider division, even if membership is 'open to all' (usually defined as 'bears and their admirers'). Having a club also invites quibbling over definitions of who is a 'real' bear."[4] Although we did find ourselves caught up in the argument over the definition of a bear from time to time, more often than not we found ourselves fighting for an identity as a club for bears.

## ISSUES AND FEEDBACK RAISED IN ARTICLES *IN* THE BEAR FACTS

From my perspective, the issue raised its head in March 1991, when I was about to put that month's issue of *The Bear Facts* to bed. I had a final copy of the newsletter with me at the March meeting. I showed it to the rest of the board members while we were assembling the agenda for the meeting about to start in the next room. By this time, *The Bear Facts* had grown to six pages in length. The newsletter contained information about the previous meeting, designs for our friendship pins, an article by Andy Cummings about professional wrestlers that he had met, a bit of fun by Alan Hurst in San Mateo titled the "Bear Bill of Rights," a blurb about the Bear Hug parties in San Francisco, an article about computer bulletin boards and how to use them, and upcoming events. All fine, except for one thing—an insert advertising a new magazine that was starting up, titled *Bulk Male*.

It seemed that some of the members were already embarrassed about the association in some people's minds between a bear and a big man and they wanted to distance themselves from the issue. After a bit of debate at that board meeting, I agreed to alter the newsletter and to start including the following disclaimer in that issue and all following issues:

> **Disclaimer:** We recognize that there are as many different "tastes" in men as there are men themselves. For the most part, we the members of the Bear Paws of Iowa are interested in other types of men than what can be found in most mainstream gay publications (i.e., young, blonde, muscular, and hairless). From time to time, you may see enclosures with *The Bear Facts* newsletter for alternative styles of gay publications. By enclosing said materials, we the Bear Paws are not making a statement about our own personal choice or taste. However, we do believe that these publications deserve publicity and distribution to different segments of the gay population.[5]

I had hoped that agreeing to the disclaimer would have solved the problem, but unfortunately it did not stop there. Two months later, in the May 1991 issue of *The Bear Facts*, I published the following article:

## THE BEAR COMMUNITY

There has been more than a little discussion in our group as to what qualities make a bear. Some members were worried that outsiders, not knowing about the bear community would get the wrong impression as to the making of a bear.

I could do what has been done at bars and such over the past few months, and go into a series of "NOT's": NOT a Chubby Club, NOT a Levi/Leather Club, NOT a Sex Club, NOT an S/M Club, NOT the Mommy, etc. But that would mean that we define ourselves by exclusion—a very negative method at best.

I prefer to define our organization by what it INCLUDES. The bear community is not an isolated one. We are made up of many of the other subcommunities in the larger world. Some people define a bear as a large, hairy, bearded, masculine man. However, we find that bears come in all different sizes, shapes, and attitudes. Some people make the dividing line between bears and cubs in terms of Top/Bottom, or Hairy/Smooth, Tall/Short,

Dominant/Submissive. This does NOT matter. What really matters is how you define yourself! If you see yourself as a bear, then a bear you are.

While no one person must fit all of the qualities as a Bear, Cub, or Bear Hunter, we must realize that the bear on your right just might identify himself as a "Leather Bear," while the one on your left might be a "Daddy Bear."

Shown in the diagram are only a few of the subcultures and interests that bears have in common with the rest of the world. This is by no means complete. I could add others, such as computers, mud wrestling, camping, etc. But WHY?

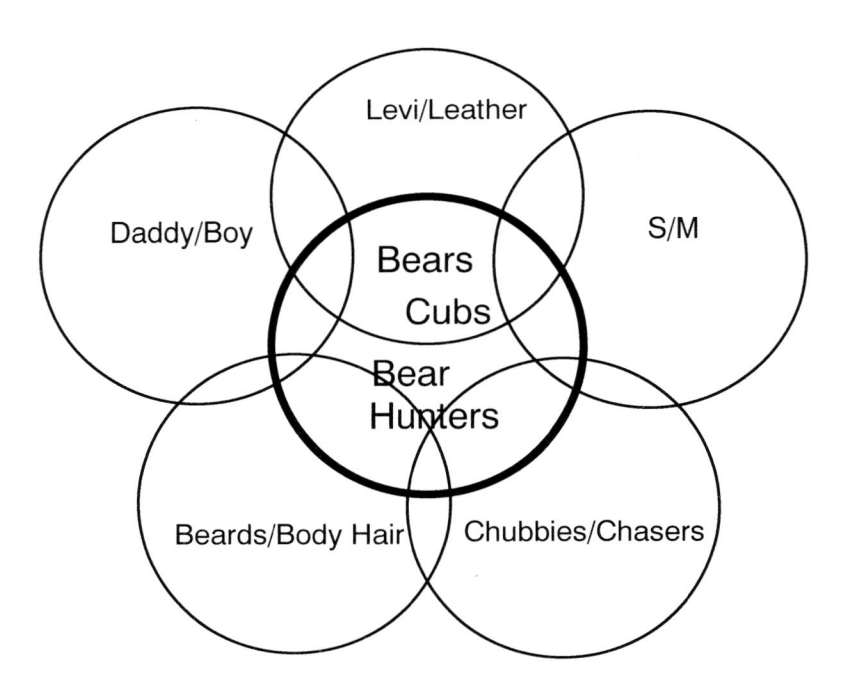

We are bears, cubs, and/or bear hunters. Take it at that. If someone from the "outside" seems confused, try to explain it to them. After all, there are a few people out there that apparently find it impossible to believe that someone may NOT be interested in the "blond-haired, blue-eyed, skinny, hairless, twinkie" or "typical" gay model. Some of us prefer Grizzly Adams and the Big Bossman.[6]

Two months later, in the July 1991 issue, Darren Pierrot wrote:

> It has been brought up that some people outside of our club see us as a chubby chaser organization, and some of our membership seems to be very concerned about this. I would like to remind members who are afraid of being perceived as being part of a fat man's club that this paranoia will only lead to perpetuating body discrimination that a lot of your club brothers already face. So if someone comes up to you and asks why are you part of that fat man's group simply explain that Bear Paws is not a chubby chaser organization, but that we enjoy men of all types.[7]

Later in the same issue, when asked the question, "What do you think defines the term 'bear'?" Darren responded:

> Bears, I feel, are primarily "no bullshit" people who call things as they see them and are not afraid to be who they are, whether that is big, gruff, mean, and ferocious or if that is quiet, gentle, and playful like a cub. I like bears because they are REAL people. Not plastic clones or William Higgins models. I like big bears and small bears, and I am getting kind of tired of the bullshit size debate! It just doesn't matter: a bear is a bear whether that bear weighs 140 pounds or 390 pounds. My entire purpose for being involved in the Bear Paws is to make people aware that we ("gay men") are not all attracted to the same people. So fuck the labels that people try to pin on us: we are what we are![8]

Andy Cummings, a founding member of the Bear Paws who became the president of the Bear Paws for 1992, wrote in his bio, which was published in August 1991:

### What Do You Think Defines the Term "Bear"?

What is a bear? That age old question? To be honest, I do not know. I used to think that to be a bear you had to be big, hairy, and bearded. But after being in Bear Paws, I have met all types of bears. Short ones, skinny ones, and big ones. And the list goes on and on. Some people think that it is the attitude that makes one a bear. Yes, that has something to do with it. But with me, when I look at someone, I can tell that they are a bear. Do not ask me how, I just know.

*What Do You Think About the Bear Paws Being Labeled As a "Fat Club"?*

I think that it is BS (BEAR SHIT!). Because we have big members, and small members, and every size in between. If someone looked at us, they might think that we are also a leather club. But we are NOT a leather club. I think that we are two things: (1) we are GAY men and (2) we are bears and we are PROUD of who and what we are. And THAT IS THAT. [9]

Seven months later, while Andy was serving as president of the Bear Paws, I published the following editorial he wrote for the March 1992 issue of *The Bear Facts:*

### WAKE UP!
By Andy Cummings

Wake up and smell the Bears. If you have read this newsletter for any length of time you know me very well. You know that I do not climb on a soapbox and yell for action. But I feel that I need to get a few things off my chest.

Over the past year I have heard many people say what the Bear Paws are not. We are not a leather club, we are not a big man's club, and on and on. To be very honest, I am sick of telling people what we are not. When someone asks what the Bear Paws are, the answer should be a very simple one. **We are bears!**

Yes, the Bear Paws have members who are into leather. We have members that are big men. We even have members that are into sweaters and discos. I for one think this is great to have a large diverse group of taste in our club. This is an asset to our club, not a problem. If you have a problem with leather, get to know someone who is into leather, then if you still have a problem, **get over it!** The same goes for big men. Get to know them and then get over it! This also goes for anyone that does not fit your idea of what a bear is. Get to know that person, then get over it.

Finally, I would ask the members if they know what it means to be a Bear Paw, or to belong to any other Bear club? If not let me tell you.

The bear clubs that have started up in the last two years are breaking new ground. We are on the cutting edge of Bearness and we are giving men that never fit the gay clone a place to call home. A place where they are welcomed with bear hugs and open arms. A place where they do not have to lose weight or shave their beards to fit in.

Do you remember how good you felt when you found a place that you fit in? I do! I knew that I was gay years and years before I came out because I did not fit the gay clone that I thought you had to be to be gay, and there was no way in hell that I would become something that I was not. Because I was a Bear and I was a bear long before any magazine called their models bears.

When the Bear movement came along it was the first time that I found a place to call my own. I had found my home in the gay community. I found a place that I fit in!

What I am trying to say is, be proud that you are a bear. Be proud when you hear of a new Bear club forming. Because you helped with all of this just by saying one day that "I am a Bear." [10]

Unfortunately, it was this very issue that created the split in the membership of the Bear Paws that ultimately caused the birth of The Ursine Group. Not long after Andy's editorial was published, both he and his lover, Jerry Kruse, left the Bear Paws, followed shortly by myself and my "huscub," Frank Bolick.

## THE CREATION OF THE URSINE GROUP

While I was feeling burned out from my experience with the Bear Paws and just wanted to stay away from any club activity for a while, Andy and Jerry started creating The Ursine Group (TUG). Bylaws for TUG were kept simple. In fact, I believe that the second or third item in the original set created by Andy and Jerry stated that there would be no more bylaws, and *Robert's Rules of Order* was expressly excluded from that original set, as they are today from the current TUG bylaws.

While the set of bylaws that Andy and Jerry wrote for TUG were intended to be a joke, it clearly expressed both their and our own frustration over the problems we had all experienced over the past two and a half years of monthly Bear Paws meetings. Not much was done with TUG during the first few months of its existence. No real meetings were held since at that time Andy and Jerry were its entire membership, with Frank and myself involved only on the periphery. About a year after Frank and I left the Bear Paws, Andy contacted us to see if we wanted to take over the operations of TUG since he did not have the time to really work on building TUG into a larger organization.

Frank and I started reestablishing contacts with men that we knew from the time that we were involved in the Bear Paws. We had a quick meeting consisting of ourselves, Carl Fongheiser, and Paul Harper to start the ball rolling. We set up a very loose organizational structure, avoided elections, and we set our priorities on having fun and not business meetings. Where the Bear Paws had a single monthly meeting, TUG met every other Saturday, with maybe fifteen minutes or so dedicated to actual business and the rest of the time spent socializing, going out to dinner, going to movies, renting videos, or just hanging out together.

### *TUG's Goals and Overall Message*

While the structures of the two clubs differed, so did the overall goals. TUG started to deal more with men's self-images, and ways of helping men overcome bad self-images and bad body images. The following is the text from a brochure distributed by TUG.

## What Is a Bear?

A bear is usually defined as a large, hairy, masculine man. Prime examples are Grizzly Adams and Al on *Home Improvement*. But you could also count Sebastian Cabot and Santa Claus as types of bears as well. Being a bear also involves a natural form of masculinity and a certain ease in regard to accepting one's own sexual orientation. The bear culture, as started in the mid-1980s, was started as a way of fighting back against stereotyped ideas of what the mainstream gay media was trying to present as the one and only body type, or standard of beauty. The pressure from the mainstream gay media has caused just as much damage and wasted effort as the type of drivel foisted upon women by such things as "The Waif Look."

## Brainwashed!

We have people who are brainwashed into thinking that they are ugly because they do not fit the standard set by gay media. We have people who are brainwashed into thinking they are sick because they are attracted to people who do not fit the standard set by gay media.

## A Positive Image

There is a bear gay subculture/movement that has been going on since the mid-1980s. It developed out of a need of a positive identity in the face of a flood of "gay icons" from all over mainstream gay media. These icons were all young, muscular, clean. At the same time this "mainstream gay media" seemed to vilify and reject as "trolls" anyone over the age of twenty-five, or people who were fat or did not fit into what the gay media marketed as "acceptable" types.

## A Second Closet!

For some of these men they had to come out of a second closet, a closet that was built out of peer pressure. More often than not, these men were afraid to tell their friends that their sexual preferences were not alike, but that they liked men who their friends might call "trolls," "geeks," or "fatso."

So the prejudice was in two directions:

- The "types" that did not fit in or were vilified by mainstream gay media, and
- The men who like them. Both are still facing an uphill battle, but some things are changing.

*The Ursine Group*

We are a group of fun-loving bears who hope that you will join us. We are trying to build a positive image of the Bear community here in Iowa, as well as nationally and worldwide. We also try to enable Bears to meet other Bears in an environment that does not center on the bar scene. We are planning monthly events. These events will include potluck meals, picnics, camp outs, historical events, amusement park tours, etc.

Individual members can host events, as well as the group itself. That is not to say that one person is responsible for the ENTIRE event, for others will be available to help. In this way, we hope to encourage each and every member to promote their idea of a positive Bear community as they see it.

*TUG Is a Bear Club. Am I a Bear?*

Part of being a bear is about being accepting and enjoying diversity! Bears and cubs come in all shapes, sizes, furry, smooth, bearded or even clean-shaven! There are even men who are not bears but who like bears and are called Bear Hunters. So the main binding factor for the entire group is either to be a bear or cub, or to be someone who likes and enjoys the company of bears and cubs. All of the above are welcome in The Ursine Group.[11]

TUG held its first event in July 1995, in a format that has become somewhat of a staple for the group, an "UnderBear" party. The success of that party helped to spread the word of TUG's existence. Since both Frank and myself along with many TUG members are computer professionals, creating a set of Web pages seemed only natural. The original set of Web pages were very similar to the ones that exist now. There is a section that features photographs and biographies of TUG members, and a section that features photographs and reviews of club-sponsored events. We noticed that the number of visitors to TUG's Web pages increased dramatically after the UnderBear photographs made their appearance on those pages. The combination of TUG's open membership policy and the popularity of TUG's Web site has resulted in a membership that covers several states, and several countries as well!

The two organizations differ in how they went about publicizing themselves. For the Bear Paws, it was their newsletter *The Bear Facts*. During 1991 and 1992 *The Bear Facts* averaged ten to twelve pages per month, and was mailed out to over 275 locations every month including addresses in Canada, Mexico, the United Kingdom, Belgium, France, Algeria, and Malaysia. One major boost to the Bear Paws' visibility happened when *BEAR* magazine published a photo of our first elected board as well as a note about the club in issue 16. "I recently read a copy of your newsletter. Nice little piece of work. I was amazed at the range of topics covered—everything from BBSs to wrestling and photos of members. I wish you boys nothing but the best."[12] After that issue of *BEAR* magazine hit the stands our mailbox started to explode with letters and cards from bears all over the world. We started getting letters from men who congratulated us for forming the Bear Paws and inquiries on how to either join the Bear Paws or suggestions on how to start a club of their own. I tried to answer as many of the letters as possible, either directly or through the newsletter. Several of the men who wrote to us started up bear clubs of their own. In looking back at how things have grown over the years, I am very pleased to see that while more than a few succumbed to internal problems and disbanded, quite a few still exist today and seem to be going strong.

I believe that TUG's presence on the Internet allows access for a large number of rural gay and bisexual men who otherwise may not normally have come in contact with a club such as TUG. Many gay and bisexual men are out there, living on farms or in small rural towns, who for one reason or another feel uncomfortable seeking out and entering a gay bar or even a gay adult bookstore. Yet many of these men have a computer, modem, and access to the Internet.

I consider the Bear Paws to represent the older type of club, while TUG seems to follow a newer trend in clubs. The Bear Paws had an older type of structure, had a "home bar," hosted numerous bar and alcohol-related events, and required that members be at least twenty-one years old. TUG has a free-form structure, does not have a "home bar," actively tries to create non-bar-related activities, avoids alcohol-related events such as "Bear Blasts," and has a minimum age requirement of eighteen.

I have not intended this to be a complete history of either the Bear Paws or The Ursine Group. My intention was to show some of the forces that helped create and form both organizations. I have had a wonderful time over the past nine years while being involved in both the Bear Paws and The Ursine Group. I have also enjoyed watching other bear clubs and organizations spring up all over the globe. My wish is that all of the organizations and their members can keep in mind why they exist, not let the mechanisms of their organizations overshadow their origins and goals, and that they take care not to replace one form of looks-ism with another.

## NOTES

1. Les Wright, A Concise History of Self-Identifying Bears. *The Bear Book*, Binghamton, NY: Harrington Park Press, 1997, pp. 21-39.
2. Larry Toothman, *The Bear Facts:* Newsletter for The Bear Paws of Iowa, Volume 1, Number 1.
3. Les Wright, A Concise History of Self-Identifying Bears, p. 34.
4. Ibid.
5. *The Bear Facts:* Newsletter for The Bear Paws of Iowa, Volume 2, Number 3.
6. Larry Toothman, The Bear Community. *The Bear Facts*: Newsletter for the Bear Paws of Iowa, Volume 2, Number 5.
7. Darren Pierrot, Cubby's Corner. *The Bear Facts:* Newsletter for The Bear Paws of Iowa, Volume 2, Number 7.
8. Darren Pierrot, Bear Paw Bio. *The Bear Facts:* Newsletter for the Bear Paws of Iowa, Volume 2, Number 7.
9. Andy Cummings, Bear Paw Bio. *The Bear Facts:* Newsletter for the Bear Paws of Iowa, Volume 2, Number 8.
10. Andy Cummings, Wake Up! *The Bear Facts:* Newsletter for the Bear Paws of Iowa, Volume 3, Number 3.
11. The Ursine Group, promotional pamphlet.
12. Letter to the editor (probably Killer), *BEAR* Magazine, Issue 16 (1991), p. 5.

Chapter 21

# Houston Area Bears

## Mitch Froehlich

May 1994. I'm on a plane from Chicago to Houston. I'm returning from BIG & BEAR (the forerunner of BearPride) in Chicago over Memorial Day weekend. This has been an eye-opening weekend. The thought keeps crossing my mind—why doesn't Houston have a bear group? Houston is the fourth most populous city in the United States, so why don't we have a bear group? I haven't a clue how to go about starting one, but I really want to do something.

I would like to take credit for starting Houston Area Bears, but I can't. That distinction lies with other people, but I can say I helped. During that summer of 1994, I had a date with a man I met through *BEAR* magazine. While we were talking, he mentioned that friends of his were working on setting up a bear club. They had a couple of meetings and soon would be going public. I couldn't believe my ears—finally someone with interests like mine had decided to do what I had been wishing. I made him promise to keep me informed, because I wanted to be there when they called for members. The summer wore on. I didn't hear anything. I checked in with him, but all he had to report was that they had not agreed on everything yet. A small group was still meeting to try to organize things "soon!"

In August, I had a chance meeting on the street with an acquaintance. We exchanged a few words. As we parted, Bill said he had asked a group of people through a local BBS (a computer bulletin board) to meet to see about forming a bear club. I was welcome to

---

This chapter is lovingly dedicated to our members that we have lost: Doug Lake, John Mata (a.k.a. Anita Mann), and Lyle Barrett.

join them. So Bill receives the credit for getting the ball rolling. It seems he, too, had heard about a group forming. He had some messages from them through the BBS but no real promise of when they would be ready. He was impatient and decided to ask a group to get together to just start meeting.

So begins the history of the Houston Area Bears, né Gulf Coast Bears. In early September 1994, we met at a coffeehouse. There were maybe twelve to fifteen of us, all drawn by a common interest. Some of those attending were from the other bear group that had been trying to form. The opinion from them was they had gotten bogged down in organizing tasks and that it seemed not to be coming together. The meeting was loosely organized and loosely run, a characteristic that we were to continue. Someone suggested that they had a draft of bylaws from the other organization, but the group thought that we were not yet ready for anything so structured. A consensus thought that we were a social organization, designed to hold social events for the benefit and enjoyment of our members. Houston had a number of service groups in the gay and lesbian community, so another was not necessary. We had a volunteer take some meeting notes and gather names so we could have a phone list. Then a name; we had to have a name if we were to be a group. An easy solution presented itself. A member of the other bear group said that they had picked Gulf Coast Bears. Since they were not active and we were going to be active, we could use that. The members accepted the new name, so Gulf Coast Bears went live.

The October and November meetings were times to bring other people into the fold, an opportunity to discuss what we wanted to do and what we could do. A group of members had been out to a local gay bar together one night and had a lot of fun. They suggested that we have an organized group night at a bar. It would be a way to socialize among ourselves and to be more visible. It could be a way to attract new members. Some people did not feel comfortable about going to a bar. We agreed that we would have one meeting per month at a bar and plan other activities outside the bars. We settled on a location and time. We would meet on the Saturday evening before our meetings, which were on Sunday afternoon. Saturday night out at the bar we would socialize and Sunday afternoon we would meet to do business and dish about the night before.

We started to plan ahead. Christmas was coming and a party was suggested. Someone volunteered his home. People volunteered to organize and set up a potluck. Other future activities were tied to upcoming holidays and events: a Superbowl party in January, a Valentine's Day party in February. We seemed to be off and running.

In January the rumbling began. Members noticed that a few people seemed to attend meetings and direct the focus of the group but then did not participate in the work or didn't follow through on commitments. The lack of an official structure and responsible individuals let the focus of the group drift. It allowed anyone to start something but did not require them to be responsible to the group. There was a growing need for some type of organization. Our membership was growing. Contacting every individual in just a few minutes was no longer possible for one person. It was now a lengthy contact list of ninety-plus people who wanted to know what was happening and many who expected to have a voice in decision making. Plans for the Valentine party were progressing. To accomplish them, individual members were spending personal funds to do the work with a vague expectation that donations from other members would cover their costs. Definitely, we needed organization.

The March meeting was the turning point. The normal agenda disappeared as we raised the topic of becoming more organized. We quickly formed into two camps. Both groups thought that some operational guidelines were now necessary. One group proposed a model based upon the Heart of Texas Bears, Austin; a list of bylaws that consisted of only five items. The other group proposed using the bylaws that had been under development by the other bear group. After much discussion by everyone, the vote of those attending was to adopt the minimalist bylaws from Austin. "Less is more" was definitely the feeling. We reviewed the bylaws to see if any changes needed to be made. A member objected to the wording of the bylaw which originally read "membership is open to any gay male." He thought that the restrictive language was not in keeping with the bear philosophy. A proposal to change it to "any male" was made. People then questioned why we would limit it to just men. The discussion of men versus men and women was spirited and lengthy. However, the final result was that membership was open to any individual. With the meeting already exceeding our normal time, the decision was made to move ahead to elect officers and defer other items until next month. The new bylaws specified the governing of the group by three members. There were no titles or positions, just three officers—the Triad.

Bill, our original organizer, stood up and proposed three names as possible officers: Bill, Jimmie, and Mitch. All three accepted. Three other people came forward and expressed interest in being officers. So we had six candidates for three positions. Each candidate introduced himself to the group and said a few words. Paper was passed around and members were instructed to vote for any three. They needed to remember that the three had to work together. When the results came back, the three people proposed by Bill had been elected. We thought we had accomplished quite a lot and could wrap up the rest at the next meeting.

After this meeting, Bill received a post through the BBS. It represented some members who, after the whirlwind of the last meeting, thought that something had gone wrong. Bill shared the post with the officers. Apparently, a few members who came to us from the unformed bear group thought that this was their group. They maintained that it had the same name and that people from that group were present in this group. They thought that the election of officers and adoption of bylaws was out of order. Their group's bylaws were actually in effect since they read "Gulf Coast Bears" and that the bylaws specified who was eligible to be officers and could vote. Only they had voting privileges and they wished to have the activities of the last meeting declared void and themselves placed as the officers.

We were dumbfounded. This made no sense to us. We were not that other group. Most people at our meetings were not from that group and had no interest in it. They were there for the activities that we were doing. The officers scheduled a meeting to discuss this letter with its writers. They insisted that they had the bylaws for Gulf Coast Bears. They had the right to the name Gulf Coast Bears and they were the only recognized members of Gulf Coast Bears. They had chosen officers among themselves and wished to present the bylaws and officers at the next meeting. We presented the history of our group. We showed that Bill had called people together independently of any work that the other group had done. If people in this group had also done work on their group, that was coincidental. We had used the name because one of their people had offered us "Gulf Coast Bears" as an unused name. We may have taken the same name but we felt strongly we had not taken the group attached to the name. When discussion proved fruitless in providing a resolution that satisfied both sides, the Triad simply informed these individuals that at the next meeting, the group would formally adopt a new name. The approved bylaws and officers would continue under that new name. This would break all possible connections to their group, Gulf Coast Bears. They were free to continue to participate with us as members but we would change or rescind nothing.

The April meeting was set up to finish our "household" activities so that we could move ahead with the real purpose, social activities and fun. The Triad explained to those present that the name Gulf Coast Bears was no longer available to the group. To avoid problems, the officers thought it best to find a new name that would belong to the club itself. We asked for suggestions and accepted Houston Area Bears. We officially registered the name the next day. Seven months after we first formed in September, we now had a real name, bylaws, officers, dues, and a newsletter. This explains, to outsiders, why we celebrate our anniversary in September but don't elect officers until March.

The Triad continued to meet. We looked at everything we did as precedent-setting, trying to make decisions that would seem logical to future officers yet allow flexibility for change. We had no model to work from, and no leader. We all felt very free but also confused. We spoke openly with one another about how we thought the club should be organized to develop a consensus among us. Then we took that "Triad vision" and moved it into concrete tasks. We individually took ownership of tasks according to what we saw as our personal strengths. I took administrative tasks, since I handled administrative duties at my job. Bill took on social events as he loved to throw a party and had done a lot of organizing for our past events. Jimmie did membership and logistics. Other duties were taken up in the same way. We saw a lot of possibilities in this structure. Things did not have to be done only by the president or the secretary. We found that if our personal lives got hectic, we could ask for help from the other Triad members. We were able to accommodate multiple events, even if held at the same time, by each attending one. So an officer was present at all events. However, this would only work if all three had good communication and were committed to working as a team, not just for themselves.

In 1995 we embarked on new projects. We commissioned a logo and had our first set of T-shirts made. We started our tradition of monthly dine-outs at local restaurants. With our first anniversary party in September 1995, we celebrated the fact that we were still here. Not only still here, but accelerating and growing. Our second year saw us continue with activities that were popular with our members. But we continued to try to find new things that would appeal to more people. Many people think of bear clubs as sex clubs. Houston Area Bears had already taken a position that we did not want to be viewed as a sex club. We do not officially sponsor sex parties, Bear Hugs, etc., but we are certainly glad to allow our members to organize such events and promote them within the club. It does seem odd, however, that while we don't sponsor sex parties, we have had some very successful parties at Club Houston (formerly part of the Club Bath chain in the 1970s and 1980s). The manager and the staff there have been very friendly to hosting a Bear's Afternoon during the summer when we would gather around the pool to sunbathe, swim, play water volleyball and, of course, eat and drink. If a member wishes to explore the inside of the club, that is certainly an option but not a requirement for a good time. The official party is outside on the deck.

One of our biggest traditions got a start in 1995—our trip to New Orleans for Southern Decadence. Some very enterprising members set up this trip. Instead of just finding motel space, they made arrangements to rent an entire guest house in the French Quarter (or almost the entire house). We have gone back every year since then, to the same guest house. People have begun to recognize Chez Houston Area Bears during Decadence. We even have splendid videos to show what a wonderful time we all had (for those who can't or don't want to remember).

We moved from affiliated group to member group within the "Let Us Entertain You" (L.U.E.Y.) organization, which puts on a post–Mardi Gras weekend party that draws 500-plus people from across the country and the world. We felt proud to be accepted into the group and thought that it was recognition of Houston Area Bears as a legitimate part of the gay and lesbian community. We were proud to promote L.U.E.Y. among the bears in this country. It was like having a big bear event without committing as many resources to it. Our official status in L.U.E.Y. got us participation in the entertainment portion of the weekend. Our "Three Wishes" skit has earned us the reputation of being very sick and twisted, which we strive to uphold each year during L.U.E.Y.

After L.U.E.Y. came time for our elections, our first attempt to pass the torch. I was the only officer to decide to run for a second year. I was returned to office along with Jeff and John in March 1996. The second slate of officers went on to continue traditional things such as L.U.E.Y., Southern Decadence, etc., but we set up our own continuing activities. We started to "guest bartend" at our home bar. This meant that on an evening or afternoon arranged by the bar, our members would bartend. The bar would promote the event, we would encourage people to come out to see us, and we would get to keep all the tips our members earned. One of our members, John, a.k.a. Anita Mann, started a monthly Bear Contest at the same bar. While the Bears did not sponsor the contest, we were supportive of it, and many members attended or even participated. As a member of L.U.E.Y., we contributed to fund-raising for them, which most often consisted of a skit or number in a variety-type show. We found that we had quite a few members who did not balk at putting on a dress, wig, and makeup for a good cause and a good laugh.

Our membership increased. At the time we organized and started collecting dues, our contact list dropped from 110-plus to about sixty, but we were back up to 100 dues-paying members by 1995-1996. We even had members in three other states. We made our presence known by officially attending BearPride, Dallas Bear Round Up, and International Bear Rendezvous. We participated in Houston's Gay and Lesbian Pride Parade and rally.

This new Triad had its hurdles to overcome. The biggest of these occurred when one of the Triad decided to relocate to Chicago to join his new partner. The Triad's plan was for John to continue as an officer by participating in work by conference calls and trips back to Houston. That idea did not seem acceptable to many members.

They thought that an officer needed to be present, that John needed to resign. This led to a discussion of what was going to be an acceptable commitment for an officer. Many members lived an hour or more away from Houston. Would these members not be eligible to be officers? Does being an officer require attendance at all club meetings and functions? If not all, then how many missed events are too many? We did not set exact numbers or miles, but the membership indicated that an officer had to live within a reasonable distance of Houston so that attendance at weeknight events was possible. Officers should attend as many meetings and events as their work and personal schedules allowed. If schedules routinely precluded their attendance at a majority of these events, the individual needed to reconsider becoming or staying an officer. The membership requested that John withdraw from the Triad and allow a special election to fill the vacant position. At the next month's meeting we held elections and a second Jeff was elected to fill the vacant slot.

Our next general election in March 1997 replaced two Triad members and kept one. The original Jeff ran a second time; we other two officers did not. Jeff was joined by Lyle and Stanley as the Triad. As I had always handled the administrative activities, this was our first time transferring these duties. The transition was more difficult than we had thought. Practical matters such as transferring the member database or the financial accounts proved naggingly problematic, so members felt the rough transition. Soon life seemed back to normal and events continued.

Other groups did guest bartending at the same bar where we did. One group, National Leather Association: Houston, began to bartend for us at our monthly socials. We got to know their members well. NLA:H had formed close ties with Houston Area Bears since our beginning. They supported us as we grew, and we had members in common. One night one of the guest bartenders was Tiffany, a female member of NLA:H. She was always noticed at any event by her big smile, wicked sense of humor, and unbounded friendliness. Tiffany decided since she was bartending for the Bears, she wanted to fit in. So, she stuffed pillows down her backside and across her stomach to give her "girth." She wore a low-cut top to display "chest hair" she had painted on with mascara. She had brought along some burgers to chow down on with us. She had gone all-out to fit in. We could not stop laughing at her costume, her antics, and her running commentary on bears and us! At the next monthly meeting, we proposed an honorary membership in recognition of her valiant efforts to join us. We definitely wanted her to join. Tiffany became our first female member and we have enjoyed her company.

Earlier in the year, one of our members, John, ran for and was elected Empress of the Royal, Sovereign, and Imperial Court of the Single Star, as Anita Mann, Empress XIII. Anita proudly bestowed recognition on Houston Area Bears and on several individual members. Houston Area Bears was proud to support Anita during her reign by participating in the many fund-raising events that she held. During her reign, Anita became seriously ill. She recently passed away. After her reign, the court thanked the bears officially for their support of Anita and the assistance the club and many very special members provided to her during her illness. Her crown is proudly displayed in our trophy case.

The Triad also suffered a loss. Just months before their term of office expired, Lyle suddenly became seriously ill. He required immediate hospitalization. Within weeks, after a short rally, he passed away unexpectedly. The club was devastated. Very few of our members have passed away. It was even more of a shock when an officer died. Due to Lyle's illness, some club affairs were disordered or disrupted. The remaining Triad quickly stepped in to manage day-to-day activities. Several members offered their help and we moved forward to our new elections. This was a difficult time. With Lyle's passing so fresh in members' minds, we had to look ahead to find new leadership. Jeff had served two terms and wished to step down to a more normal level of involvement. Stanley requested the same. When nominations were completed, all those running would be new to the Triad. We would not have an experienced officer in the Triad to provide continuity. We all knew this could happen, given the structure of the office, but it had not yet actually occurred. We elected John, Joe, and Steve as the new Triad in March 1998. The two retiring Triad members and other former officers volunteered their help to establish a transition and help the new officers get off to a running start.

A totally new Triad also brought a new perspective. They gladly accepted all the advice and information from the volunteers but also, early on, established that they wished to do things in what they considered the best way regardless of whether it was the same or different than in the past. They started immediately to work on the bank account, membership lists, and to clarify and finish our tax status, a project Lyle had begun for the club. They made sure that our trip to Southern Decadence went on. Lyle had just started work on it and they brought in a former Triad officer, Bill, who had helped organize a prior year's trip. They accepted input from the many new members we had. They established themselves as not bound to tradition by allowing an unusual fourth anniversary party. The anniversary committee had proposed something different that year and they supported the idea. They recommended that the committee present it, as designed, to the membership, who voted to go with it.

I have tried to present a history of our organization that shows everything, warts and all. So many times other members of other clubs may become frustrated by what they see around them. Newsletters and press releases from organizations do not show you the debate and discussions that have occurred. I wanted to highlight our unique points and then show that every group has its problems. Problems are solved by coming together and discussing. Groups and individuals change over time. What was fun two years ago is now not of interest to people. The challenge for a group is to meet that changing need. The officers should present changes to members in a way that helps them understand the need for change. Then we can move on and grow.

This is a history from the standpoint of a member who was there from the beginning to the present day. If my memory or notes have been incorrect, I apologize.

## Chapter 22

# The Bears Come to Rochester

## John O. Noble

Rochester, New York, has always had a great mix of people. Founded in the early years of the nineteenth century, it was one of the first great frontier cities in the expanding United States after the War of 1812. It was the early flour-milling capital of the country, producing grain for the growing East Coast cities and for export through the Erie Canal to the Port of New York City. The canal brought pioneer settlers with new ideas, fostering a tradition of tolerance and social reform in the region, soon called the "Burnt Over District" because of the growth of new religious and social ideas. Rochester was home to the Suffragist and Abolitionist movements of Susan B. Anthony and Frederick Douglass, respectively. Later in the nineteenth century it was the home of great technological innovations, creating new levels of employment for all comers and more social reform. The Progressive Era Social Gospel Movement got its start here in the 1890s. Radical political reform also grew here and Emma Goldman, as one of its early and most visible leaders, talked about economic and social justice and sexual freedom to her fellow Rochesterians.

This tradition of diverse employment, from immigrant laborers to technical innovators and skilled craftsmen, continued into the twentieth century and by mid-century Rochester was called "Smug Town, USA" in national publications—it was socially and politically conservative, yet tolerant of reform-minded people and ideas. Rochester, according to oral tradition in the gay community, had "gay bars" with same-sex dancing, not hidden on side streets without front windows, in the 1950s, long before major East Coast cities. Prominent political leaders who were gay were often seen in such establishments, according to older men in the community. High levels of employment in this community allowed both single women and single men to hold good-paying jobs and not have to compete with married "family" men for scarce jobs.

In 1970, soon after the Stonewall Rebellion, a gay liberationist group was founded at the University of Rochester, open to both community and academic members. This group started publishing the *Empty Closet,* the oldest continuously published gay newspaper in New York State, and one of the oldest in the United States. The Gay Alliance of the Genesee Valley, which runs the local Gay Community Center, celebrated its twenty-fifth anniversary in 1998.

With this brief background, a picture of a tolerant metropolitan community of about a million people, with an old central city of about a quarter of a million, emerges. Over seventy lesbian and gay organizations existed by the mid-1990s, but there was still no group for bears or their admirers. About five years ago, using as a communications medium the local gay BBS, Multicom IV, a number of gay men interested in the bear movement started to discuss the possibilities of a bear club in Rochester. In December 1995 a group of gay men met at the Gay Community Center and organized the Empire Bears.

Fewer than ten men were at that first meeting and several are still involved and active with the club. During 1996 several critical issues emerged which helped define the club. More men attended each monthly meeting at the Community Center, and many joined. One of the themes of the new club was that it would be inclusive, and not an exclusive club with a predetermined definition of "beardom." That is not to say that there were not many heated discussions on such matters as goals and objectives as the club attempted to work through the development of a set of operating bylaws.

Several competing concepts of bear clubs emerged during the six-month organizational period. Should the club be a top-down managed organization with a board of directors given total control once elected, or should the officers propose and the members decide the policies and programs of the club at regular meetings?

Policies for age and gender requirements for membership and a bar-centered versus a community center-based organization were subjects that the membership struggled with in those early months. During those times we had wonderful potluck dinners and other social events. Men who thought that there was no one else in the gay community who looked like them or had similar interests learned that there was a whole new aspect of the gay community for them to explore.

The bear movement can draw upon the best of several other elements in the gay community. The men in the Empire Bears have come to this club with a full range of these experiences. Currently, the Empire Bears have members who were active in other bear clubs before they moved to Rochester; several men come out of the leather tradition. Some men look to the Girth and Mirth club style for inspiration. (Oh, but do we all love to eat! We are bears!) Some men thought we would be a singular source of sexual playtime. Some men have found partners, but those who were looking for a sex club were probably disappointed for the most part. We, like all gay men, have the full range of sexual interests and desires not necessarily met in a social club environment. A strong leather element is present in the club. Many couples and single men are active in a full range of club programs. Many of the younger men are into fantasy gaming, toy and card collecting—this environment has allowed them to meet other gay men with similar interests.

Soon after forming, the Empire Bears were asked to take over a function of the local cyber-bear group that had sponsored an informal bar night at a local gay bar, which has a western/leather theme. This was an opportunity for the new club to introduce itself to more gay men and deal with the fact that some of our members wanted to socialize in a bar environment. The club had decided that social events were going to be nonalcoholic, for both practical and policy reasons. The Community Center facility was both a nonsmoking and nonalcoholic space; and some of our members were active in the twelve-step recovery movement.

Much to the surprise of many of the members, men from other parts of Western New York State and many local African-American men soon began attending meetings and social functions. It soon became clear that the club was meeting social needs that were never discussed or planned for in the formation of the club. Men who have come out of the political/AIDS activist communities have also found a warm welcoming group of men to socialize with. Over the last three years the Empire Bears has averaged fifty members; most recently the age range has been twenty-three to seventy-three. Each age cohort is well represented.

I would call 1997 the period of stabilization for the club. The bylaws and club governance issues were basically settled, we are now incorporated by New York State, the first team of elected officers was installed, and a quarterly newsletter and social calendar were developed. Club administrative procedures were established and formal record-keeping policies instituted.

Camping and out-of-town trips became fixtures on the calendar. Generally, a third to a half of the membership participates in these functions. Monthly potluck dinners and Sunday brunches have been great icebreakers for potential members. Weekly movie nights were established and continue to be very popular.

Each summer, besides regular Bear Weekends at Hillside Campgrounds in Pennsylvania, the club rents a campground for a club-members-only weekend. This networking event has helped bring the club members together in a very relaxing atmosphere.

The following year, 1998, saw stability and steady growth. Most members of the club renewed their membership but a few men developed new interests, some moved away, and a few did not rejoin because of the personality conflicts usual in many organizations. Several new activities were instituted, including a boxer shorts party and sleepover at the home of two members. This event, scheduled in late winter after the long season of bear hibernation, encouraged many members to make the trek to the Southern Tier region of New York State. This event was followed by a hearty breakfast at a local maple sugar restaurant. Having enjoyed this weekend so much, ten members later traveled to Montreal to join the Montreal Bears in a traditional French-Canadian Sugar Shack Party. Attendance at sporting events has grown into a popular club activity—many are not sure if the reason is the sport or the men in attendance.

Active debate and three ballots were necessary to select a new club logo, conceived and designed by club members, before a decision was reached in 1998. Our local bar nights floundered for part of the year—after many extended discussions, the concept has been reworked and our "Foraging" events now have a theme, usually a charitable cause. Participation has drawn support from members, nonmembers, and the local leather club—for example, when we did a food basket collection for AIDS organizations in our area.

The Empire Bears continue to meet and hold many functions at the local Gay Community Center. This standard location has helped develop continuity and participation in the larger gay community and a nonthreatening place for first-time attendees.

The elections in the fall of 1998 marked the third year of the election process as outlined in the club bylaws. It was an active year of participation, by members both running and voting, with two out of three offices up for election contested and nearly a 70 percent voter response to mailed ballots.

As the Empire Bears prepared to celebrate our third anniversary in January 1999 with a weekend of activities, the club seemed to be entering a new level of participation and planned activities. Following two very successful Toronto weekends in 1998 and with the friendships developed, dates were set for 1999 Toronto weekends at the Toolbox, Toronto's bear bar.

The Empire Bears has grown from a small group of men seeking a network for friendship and group activities into a solid member of the lesbian and gay community in Rochester. The club looks forward to many more years of solid growth as a local source of information and support for gay men who are bears or bear admirers.

Chapter 23

# A Short History of the Brisbears

Peter Sharman

Brisbears was formed in October 1993 out of a deep need for a masculine group to participate in the gay community of Brisbane. Many groups were around at the time, but none catered to the hirsute "ordinary" man. Smooth men and drag queens dominated the clubs and bars and the only hope most bears had in Brisbane was the local beats (public toilets) or truck stops—which could be quite dangerous, not only for the risk of bashings but, if caught by police, being publicly "outed."

Brisbears held its first meeting which saw the attendance of forty men, enough to secure the use of a private bar, one night a month, for our exclusive use. An introductory newsletter was distributed and the third Saturday of each month was designated Brisbears official social night. The club's motto is "Brisbears: For Men Who Like Hairy Men." Our first meeting in our new bar saw sixty men come out of the woodwork, and with the gathering being hailed a success, Brisbears was on its way.

Now, four years on, Brisbears is an incorporated club. It is recognized by the state of Queensland and boasts over 150 paid members. Our social nights regularly have over 200 hairy men attend. We have certainly become an extremely well-known group within Brisbane's gay community, and indeed the rest of the bear community all around Australia, but our management committee is determined to steer clear of the internal politics that plague many other clubs. Our policy is easygoing, providing a kind of safe haven for masculine men who have only recently come out and are unsure of what the bear world holds. We also believe that there are enough gay groups in the political arena of their community without yet another entering it. This is not to say that the club has segregated itself from the mainstream gay community, as Brisbears often lends support to other gay groups and activities. Brisbears has never had and will never have restrictions to membership on the basis of race, religion, color, size, economic status, or whether a guy is into leather, uniforms, or just plain fur—all are welcome. Brisbears maintains only one real restriction, which is that the club is for men only. For one night a month, men can come to our club and enjoy a men-only space.

Throughout the four years since its inception, the club has strived to be a club for its members. There is a nonprofit policy, and with this, Brisbears members receive benefits on a regular basis. Membership dues are given back by way of subsidized events, parties, dinners (this list goes on), and all are available to members. But the courtesy doesn't end with the members of the club. As a lot more gay men are traveling the globe these days, either physically or via the Internet, Brisbears is more than happy to welcome visitors into the fold. As a club which is becoming well known around the world, it is our responsibility (along with clubs both in Australia and overseas) to keep the bear phenomenon alive and growing. Being a bear is not just about being a hairy man, although this is a major factor of course; an attitude is attached. We must not alienate those who admire bear men simply because they themselves lack the bear "image," but embrace their interest and receive them as brothers.

It is important to both Brisbears and the other bear clubs in Australia to be a single driving force, by keeping in close contact with each other, while at the same time retaining a firm hold on our own individual identities. The bear movement has come a long way in the past few years and to see it stray from the path would seem like a crime to all who have followed. On a global scale, Brisbears may be a small part of this movement, but as it grows from strength to strength it will always be at the very least a part of that movement.

# PART V:
# MORE BEARS ABROAD

# Chapter 24

# A Bear Voice from Turkey

## Mehmet Ali Sahin

I'm Mehmet Ali "Mali" Sahin. I was born, brought up, and live in Ankara, the capital of Turkey. In 1986, I started to study mechanical engineering at a university in another city. In my second year I decided that I did not want to be an engineer, so I returned to Ankara and attended Hacettepe University, Faculty of Arts. I studied ceramics, and graduated in 1993. As I write this, I'm working on an MFA degree and plan to have it by the end of 1998.

I love ceramics, but I have always been more interested in graphics. I have been using computers to create graphics since 1985. In 1994, I was recommended to TUBITAK's (Turkish Government's Scientific and Technical Research Institute) Multimedia Laboratory by a friend and I became a professional graphic designer. I worked in the process of making many products including TV commercials, various information systems, even an educational arcade adventure game. In 1996, the laboratory closed and all employees joined the crew of a newly created company which produces educational CD-ROM products. Since then I have been working at this company as a professional graphic artist and designer.

I am the youngest of five children. Father was not a good man; Mother was very busy with taking care of the housework and her other children. After moving to a new house in a new district when I was just a little kid, I had problems adapting myself to the new place. I had no friends, so I can simply say that I grew up alone. When I was growing up, no one in the family told me about sex. When I started to learn about sex on my own, I fantasized about big hairy men having sex with women. Later I decided that I wasn't really interested in women and the big hairy men became my whole fantasy. I was thirteen when I figured out that I was attracted to guys. Figuring out that I was an *ibne* (a Turkish slang word, which is very close to "faggot" in English) was not easy. I was alone, no friends, and no family members around to help. I was fighting with myself. The thought of being a "faggot" was unbearable. What would my family and the other people around me think? They would be hurt, that was for sure. This caused me to isolate myself from the people around me. I concentrated on books and school. I was a good student, a smart boy, but when it came to socializing, I was nothing, a zero. Later I gave up fighting with myself, completely came out, and accepted myself as being gay. I gave up worrying about what anyone else would think or do when they learned about the real me. That wouldn't kill me nor anybody else. This "coming out" cost me three years and turned me into an antisocial individual.

My first partner, who was a fifty-year-old daddy bear type when we met, helped me to break down the walls around me, and I managed to socialize a little. After our relationship ended, the walls went back up again.

There have never been many people around me whom I could call "friends," and my relationship with my family has never been close. Therefore, I had never felt that I had to come out to anybody, until I met my second long-term partner. I was in love; he was the most important person in my life. One week after we became involved, he moved into the ground floor of the building where I live. Every day, every night we were together. Every night, I went to him after dinner and got back home to sleep after midnight. My family knew him as a good friend of mine. I came out to my only friend when he told me that I was spending more time with my new friend than with him. I told my friend that this new guy was my lover, not just a friend. He said, "I already know that. It does not make any difference to me, as long as you don't get any ideas about me. I want you to promise that you will try to be straight." I could be anything, I could do anything, as long as I had no ideas about him. And that "promise." He never understood that being gay is not a choice.

I have been gay since the day I was born. I've never even been a bisexual, and he wanted a promise from me to be something I could never be. I guess this is a common sentiment of straight people because later, when I came out to another friend of mine, he told me exactly the same thing. They think you can't be happy if you're not straight. Another thing they said along these lines when I came out is that I don't look "gay."

In Turkey, the common image of a gay male, or, in their word, an *ibne,* is a "feminine, hairless, beautiful boy who looks and acts like a woman." Tops never counted as *ibne;* they are just men looking for a different pleasure and named with different words, such as *oglanci* (boy admirer) and *kulanpara* (masculine top male). This goes back to the days of the Ottoman Empire. And while modern Turkey is not directly descended from the Ottoman Empire—in fact the War of Independence was started *against* the Ottomans—the culture of the Ottomans deeply affected the culture of Turkey.

During the Ottoman period, sex between males (generally men with boys) was very common. The reputation of *hamams* (baths) comes from this era. *Tellaks* (young boys who help in bathing men) also served as male prostitutes. A book called *Dellakname-i Dilkusa* (A record of the *tellaks*) in the Ottoman archives describes the most famous *tellaks* of Istanbul and their personal success serving their customers, including prices and details.

In Ottoman literature, which is also called "Divan Literature," [a rare western treatment of this material can be found in the German author Goethe's *West-East Divan, LKW*] there are many poems written by male poets about or for their male lovers. Most of these poems are about the beauty of their boys and in some the poet complains about his boy's beard starting to grow and reducing his beauty. But there are some poems in which an older male lover's masculinity, body hair, and body size are praised. These poems are written in ancient Turkish, called Ottoman, and while very hard to understand, are typically included in literature books for high school students.

There was no censure from the authorities against poets for writing such poems. Some Ottoman sultans were poets, too and wrote homoerotic poems. Sex with boys was not legally forbidden and even the sultans engaged in it. There was a palace in Bursa for boys who served the men in the Ottoman army. (This is why some heterosexuals call gays *Bursali.*) In those days, when the army was at war, away from home for months, sometimes years—and as it was not possible to bring women to the front—these boys were used for sex. These men engaged in sex with women too; sex with boys was just something pleasant for them, but they believed they really needed women.

With the adoption of Western culture by the nineteenth century, this tolerance for homosexuality disappeared. The source of these reforms were the French, from whom not only governmental and social systems, but philosophical ideas as well, were adopted. The rejection of male-to-male sex within the Christian Church of that era influenced Ottoman society, and these relationships came to be looked down upon.

Of course, hundreds of years of tradition didn't just disappear. There is still a *hamam* culture, though not as common as it used to be. Extreme nationalists who are very proud of Ottoman culture deny this side of the Ottomans. After 1923, with the Westernization of Turkey, these traditions were further weakened. But there's still a general acceptance of effeminate male entertainers. For example, Zeki Muren, the most famous Turkish classical singer, has been openly gay since the 1950s, and Bulent Ersoy, transsexual, is very popular and has albums selling in the millions.

Turkey has a macho culture, and this is reflected in attitudes about gayness. Gays were traditionally divided into the active and the passive, but by the beginning of the 1990s a more Westernized gay culture, where no categorization is felt necessary, started to take hold.

After military forces took over the government in 1980, and politics began returning to life, the unofficial Radical Democratic Green Party was established by twelve gay males. They aimed to start an organized gay movement in Turkey. Unfortunately, this party was short lived. Since 1980, the old laws remain valid; the age of consent is eighteen. There are no specific articles on homosexuality in the laws, but rather vague references to public morals and public order. The police have wide powers and have the legal right to take into custody anyone who looks suspicious for interrogation. Some factions in the police force have close relations with radical nationalist extreme right wing groups. Gays have not been allowed to come out and organize openly and the gay movement has mostly gone underground.

By the 1980s, a Westernization (or Americanization) movement started in Turkey, which has also affected gay life. Young male homosexuals aware of Western gay movements started to identify themselves with the English word "gay." An "International Christopher Street Day" was planned to take place in Istanbul in July 1993, but was then banned by local government officials. After this ban, people who worked for the festival founded the largest queer group in Turkey, Lambda Istanbul. A similar attempt to organize a cultural week in September 1995 by Lambda Istanbul was banned on the grounds "of public morals."

At the HABITAT II conference, Lambda attracted the attention of the media, and since then the number of people attending Lambda events has increased. A radio program started by two members of Lambda was the one and only radio program for gays. The aim of the program was to help gays gain confidence and identity. This program was canceled in 1998. The first gay-lesbian magazine in Turkey was *100 percent GL*. It has recently changed its name to *Cins*, which is Lambda's own publication. The first issue was released in 1995. It is published bimonthly and can be found in larger bookstores.

After my first relationship, I had a good gay friend who would later be one of the two people behind the radio program. I stood by and watched their first efforts—keeping my distance because many of the gays that I knew from gay gathering places had rejected and made fun of me simply because I was into big, hairy, middle-aged guys with facial hair. This had hurt me a lot. A few months later I met my second partner. When I made up my mind to be a part of what they were trying to do, my partner wouldn't let me. I was in love and I did what he said. In those days, I did nothing for the gay movement, even when I could have. This is still a burning pain inside of me. The love died slowly, and breaking up after seven years was not easy, but what I saw on a Web page caused me to make up my mind.

Five months after the company I work for moved to its new building, our full-time Internet connection was completed. After work hours and weekends I started to surf the Web. It was June

1997. I was trying keywords on search engines and surfing the results. I was searching for some photographs of hairy chests (I'm very much into male chests) and some nude photos of big men.

I was experiencing a real sense of adventure in those days, and it was really fun. I tried many keywords such as "hairy," "fat," "big," and "chest." The results were disappointing, not because there were no results, but because there were millions! Later I realized that I was using single keywords. I typed two magic words: "hairy chest" and bingo! The URL of the Hairy Chest Page appeared on screen. I surfed the page, and others linked to it, with great excitement. When I first encounterd the word "bear" on the Internet, it was the beginning of August. At first it sounded funny to me and I thought it was just a nickname or something. When I found Resources for Bears, Bear Networks, and Bear Quay on the same day, I figured out that this was more serious than I'd thought. It was very exciting to find that so many people think the same way I do, and like what I like. That day I figured out that "bear" is what I've always been and what I've always wanted.

My entrance into the bear scene was not fast. I was unsure of myself and was shy, and I waited until September 1997 to make my first contact with other bears. I sent e-mails to two bears, and if they hadn't replied, it would have been very hard for me. When I did receive replies from them, I stepped into the bear scene. I saw that identification as a bear is not static, nor does it have exact limits. Everybody has his own definition. There are many types of bears, varying from big to small, hairy to hairless, bearded to clean shaven, depending on the varying taste of guys in the bear scene. If I tried to define a bear, it would be a mix reflecting myself, my own taste in bears, and my bear ideal and my definition would not match, word-for-word, anyone else's.

Right after I learned about the bear phenomenon, I started to search out other Turkish bears on the Internet. I tried visiting bear pages to see if there were any Turkish guys out there. I visited nearly all the Bear Ring pages and those listed in Bear Quay, but there were none. During this search I discovered the BML (Bears Mailing List), subscribed to it, and sent a posting to ask if there were any other Turkish bears. I received many e-mails welcoming me. I made some new friends, but I didn't hear from any Turkish bears. Two months later, I read a posting from another Turkish bear, contacted him, and we became good friends and continued the search together. He also invited me to a local IRC server's gay chat channel and we started to spread the word on the bear phenomenon there. As there are millions of bearish men in Turkey, some other guys started to identify themselves as bears. Later we learned that the first visit to the Bear Resources page from Turkey was in 1995. This info excited us a lot; we started to search for those guys. I am sorry to say that we still couldn't find them, but after I constructed a bear Web page, we met another self-identifying Turkish bear who is more experienced in the bear movement and had been attending bear events for three years—but he was not one of those who had visited Bear Resources. We are still searching for those guys, and we're telling those we meet online or face-to-face about the bear movement.

As of the end of July 1998, there are around ten online guys who know about the bear movement and identify themselves as a part of the bear scene in Turkey (as bears, otters, or cubs). Some of them are: TRBear, Half Bear, bOutcider, KeyaBear, BiBear, HotBear35, and BearLover. And, of course, there are some more bears, who don't have computers and/or an Internet connection.

There are class differences among gay men in Turkey, too. We think that the bear idea will reach every social class. We have plans to spread the bear idea all around Turkey (as all of us are from Istanbul or Ankara, the two largest cities). Lower-class gays usually do not come out of the closet. They marry and try to continue their lives bisexually. Middle-class gays don't usually come out completely. Many live with their family; they usually identify themselves as gay, and some, who have economic power, come out. Most upper-middle-class gays do come out, and either live alone or with their partner. Class difference shows itself at places where gays cruise. Lower- and middle-class gays go to cruising places, parks, and baths, and some upper-middle-class gays do, too. Most of the upper-middle-class gays go to those places only rarely. They usually go to bars or try to organize to find others. Upper-class gays have their own organizations which are completely underground; they don't accept newcomers easily. The visible gay scene consists of middle- and upper-middle-class gays. They have tried to organize to make the gay movement visible.

At first, we targeted upper-middle and middle-class gays who have computers and Internet access. Internet and IRC seemed to be two great tools for us. People are more open in cyberspace, and you can meet those who are shy or can't come out in the real world. We are constructing a Web page for Bears of Turkey, both in Turkish and English (aimed to be a guide to those foreign bears who visit Turkey). In my opinion, the bear phenomenon could reach them and would be accepted easily, but it can't reach lower-class men easily. Maybe when it becomes visible, the bear phenomenon will find many admirers from this class, too.

I'm asked many times by the guys I educate about the bear phenomenon whether I learned about the phenomenon in the United States or in some other country while I was living there. My answer is "no." There are Turkish bears who have lived outside Turkey and learned about the bear phenomenon there, but I have never been outside Turkey. This surprises them, and the next question they ask is why I chose (!) to be a bear. This always starts a long conversation. To me, a gay man does not choose to be a bear; he comes out as a bear. Maybe he doesn't even know that he's a bear but being a bear is in the heart and mind, from the day he figures out his gayness. You can't make somebody a bear nor make him like bears. If he becomes a bear, he was a bear.

I think that this is one of two main reasons for the rapid growth in the number of self-identifying Turkish bears. The other is how Turkish men look. A "bearish look" is natural to Turkish men. They are hairy (not all of them, but most), more than half wear facial hair (the rate is decreasing but still over 60 percent), and there are many big guys. Where the men are bearish, and gay men grow up seeing such men, many become bears or bear admirers naturally.

American (Western) culture has started to be accepted by all classes in Turkey. Turkey's upper class is completely Americanized or Westernized, as is most of the upper middle class. Because it is hard to reach upper-class gays, this Americanization is the main reason for our targeting middle-class men. As modernization has turned into Americanization (or Europeanization), those who want to be modern become Americanized. This will help us a lot in bringing the bear phenomenon within their reach. At first look it may seem like an American notion, but they will find, as we have before them, many aspects of beardom that come from within themselves.

At the beginning of July 1998, we had planned a bear meeting, but as we were so few in number, it was canceled. A next meeting is being planned for around the last week of August or the first week of September. We'll invite some more bearish guys to introduce them to the idea of bears, and when we have enough bears among us, creating bear social space will be easier and we can reach gays of other social classes.

Wish us luck, guys!

Chapter 25

# Falstaff's Legacy: The Bears of Albion

## Howard Watson

In Anglo-Saxon England, before the Normans invaded in 1066, it was regarded as a point of honor to claim descent from a wild animal: Earl Siward, Earl of Northumbria, claimed that his grandmother had been raped by a bear. Such exotic ancestry no longer applies as wild bears became extinct in the British Isles several centuries ago, although the barbaric spectacle of bear-baiting and dancing bears took longer to outlaw. The British have not always been a nation of animal lovers. If one wishes to spot a real bear now it is more than likely to be in a zoo or at a circus. Unlike our American cousins, we no longer have the pleasure of seeing bears roam our forests or northern wastelands. There are very few traces of the existence of wild bears in England, apart from the occasional symbol for a county cricket club or the rather cumbersome headdress, known as bearskins, worn by British guardsman on sentry duty outside Buckingham Palace.

The rise of the modern bear cult, however, has inspired those outside of the United States to look for their own symbols, specific to their nationality, which have bearlike characteristics. For instance, bears in Germany have adopted Saint Nicholas, or Santa Claus, as their patron saint; who, as we all know, displays those bearish qualities we have come to know and love. Familiar to British children, Father Christmas, however, is a recent addition to the traditional English festivities. The English, as opposed to the Scots or the Irish, are often assumed to have no national identity. We have no kilt, bagpipes, or shamrock with which to assert our sense of patriotic pride, although in recent years the flag of Saint George has been much in evidence at soccer matches. Unfortunately, this has gone hand in hand with a rise in hooliganism, especially abroad. Anyway, Saint George was not even an Englishman! If Saint George sends out the wrong signals, how about Shakespeare's loveable rogue, the "bully Hercules" himself, Sir John Falstaff? It is no surprise that this choice comes from the age of the Virgin Queen, the Armada, and Walter Raleigh.

The origins of the word "gay" are distinctly English—Elizabethan English to be precise, along with those other Americanisms such as okay, the fall, and punk. This is one of the last periods when men could openly express their affection for other men. In Shakespeare's day, people of the same sex would send flowers to the one they loved. Women would send violets to another woman. Men would send pansies. For years, effeminate English boys have been called pansies—one of the more lame examples of homophobic language.

Falstaff is the Bard of Stratford's most famous comic character. As real as Peter Pan or Sherlock Holmes, but as with those literary creations of J. M. Barrie and Arthur Conan Doyle, Sir John is no superhero. Holding forth at his favorite watering hole, the Boar's Head Tavern, surrounded by his rascally crew, he indulges his senses with impunity. Unapologetic perhaps, but he is far from bad company. His lust for life and his knavery offset the more robust traits of his personality, which have made him one of the best-loved characters in English literature.

Apart from Hogarth's depiction of Sir John in *Falstaff Examining the Recruits,* visual representations tend to be fairly consistent, especially in the theatre. He is usually played by an actor in his forties, or older. He sports a full beard, a large belly, and is dressed in traditional Elizabethan garb. Verdi created a whole opera around him and Orson Welles delivered one of his best cinematic performances playing the old retainer on the silver screen. Despite being married and having an eye for the ladies, this burly knight of Albion obviously prefers the company of men, especially that of his young friend, Prince Hal, the future Henry V. In Robert Nye's fictional biography, we catch a glimpse of the depth of that special relationship: "I was the fellow with the great belly. And he my dog." So, who is fit to inherit Falstaff's legacy? Who is worthy to follow in his giant footsteps? Wherefore the bears of Albion? Perhaps in another English queen's reign?

No self-respecting man of means shaved in those days at the height of the British Empire. There were many bears, it seems, in Victorian England. If any one individual stands out and fits the Falstaffian bill, it surely has to be that cricketing doctor, W. G. Grace. Although he found fame as one of the greatest batters, he was a perfect all-rounder and dominated the cricket world of his day. To many he is the traditional face of the game, a tall, potbellied man with a beard that would make Billy Gibbons of ZZ Top green with envy. His almost mythical reputation owes as much to his rumbustious behaviour as his aptitude for the sport. He could be given to a spot of gamesmanship, but this roguish side to his nature only endeared him to the sporting public.

Are there more, I hear you ask? How about, instead of a doctor in the field, a doctor in the house? Robertson Justice was a regular feature in British movies for over twenty years. He is best remembered, and loved, for his fulsome portrayal of the irascible Sir Lancelot Spratt in the "Doctor" series of movies. Although Scottish by birth, he spent a lifetime on screen playing no-nonsense Englishmen. His portly demeanour, bluff exterior, and luxuriant beard graced many a film set from the classic comedy, *Whisky Galore!*, (U.S. title: *Tight Little Island*) to *Scott of the Antarctic*, where he did the unthinkable—desperate to play Oates, he actually shaved off his beard!

In the 1950s, when Robertson Justice was gracing the big screen, Jimmy Edwards, the comic actor, was becoming a household name through his outrageous characterisations on radio and television. A former RAF pilot, he embarked on a career as a comic actor after the war. His striking handlebar moustache (a legacy of his flying days), hectoring manner, and earthy humour added up to a comic persona which endeared itself to a postwar audience which was ready to laugh at itself. Starting off at the Windmill Theatre, a notorious proving ground for ex-servicemen who were trying to make their way in show business, he survived and within two years he landed his own radio programme, *Take It from Here*. This featured his first major comic role as Pa Glum, the irascible working-class ne'er-do-well, constantly foiling his son's attempts to bed his sexually frustrated girlfriend, Eth.

Now a regular fixture on the wireless, Edwards also managed to cross over to television, starring in *Whack-O!,* where he played the part of Professor Edwards, the demon headmaster of a single-sex English public boarding school, where he not only terrorised the pupils but the staff as well. Such a hit was the show with the public that 1959's top toy was a game based on the series. An accomplished pilot, he also had a love for drink, fox hunting, and the tuba; although not necessarily in that order. In his twilight years, tabloid allegations regarding his bisexuality led to rather unsavoury headlines, but failed to dent his longtime love affair with his public.

In more recent years, British cinema has featured several worthy successors to Falstaff's mantle. Uncle Monty, the character played to such superb effect by Richard Griffiths in Bruce Robinson's 1986 cult classic, *Withnail and I,* is surely deserving of a mention, although technically speaking not a bear—hey, who cares?! Despite his fruitless efforts to bed the strangely reluctant Marwood, he still manages to endear us—a failed thespian, never to play the Dane, left with nothing but "vintage wine and memories." It is no surprise to discover that the fair, but hefty, Montague Withnail even has his own fan club.

Bears have even infiltrated outer space. Who can forget the wonderfully robust performance of that fine English actor, Brian Blessed, as Vultan, King of the Hawkmen, in the 1980 big-screen adaptation of *Flash Gordon,* directed by the deeply underrated Mike Hodges. As leader of the seriously hirsute Hawkmen, Blessed is a fine inheritor of the Falstaffian tradition, displaying a roguish charm and impish sense of humour.

The most famous bear of Albion, however, has to be Simon Callow's glorious portrayal of the ill-fated Gareth in 1994's hit British comedy *Four Weddings and a Funeral.* In the screenplay, written by Richard Curtis, he is described thusly: He "is about forty-five—overweight, bearded, with rosy cheeks and disposition." Indeed, who can forget Gareth's exclamation, when arriving in the grand hall of the Scottish manor house, for the reception after the third wedding, "O bravo—it's Brigadoon. It's bloody Brigadoon!" Later on, while chatting with an American woman, he confides to her that he can give her Oscar Wilde's fax number!

Gareth's character, however, has slightly more substance than simply providing comic padding to the central, and very heterosexual, romance. At the same Scottish wedding, he instructs the stolidly single among them to find marriage partners, in order that in their dotage they can be proud to say that they had once been adored. Of course, this simple request takes on a different tone entirely.

Gareth's funeral is notable for the oration given by Matthew, played by John Hannah, of Auden's poem, but many have overlooked a scene between Tom, James Fleet's character, and Hugh Grant's Charles: "Surely if that service shows anything, it shows that there is such a thing as a perfect match. If we can't be like Gareth and Matthew, then maybe we should just let it go. Some of us are not going to get married." A gay marriage being exalted as the "perfect match" in a movie that made over $200 million, and no one bats an eyelid.

The coda of this piece, however, is dedicated to the memory of the late David Hutter (1935-1988), the watercolourist. Indeed, what could be more English than this particular artistic medium? Hutter's work is notable for his portrayals of naked, or partially naked, men placed against stark white backgrounds, isolating his subjects. In most gay imagery of the late twentieth century, models are normally chosen for their youth, beauty, and lack of body hair. His *In Praise of Older Men* could not be further from the typical homoerotic pose, or subject. A bearded man in his forties, or maybe fifties, stands with his hands on his hip, looking to his left. He appears to have just risen, as a dressing gown hangs loosely from his shoulders. He is relaxed, uninhibited, and ready for breakfast, while perusing the Sunday newspapers. Using very few props, the artist suggests a context without having to make a great song or dance about it.

My favorite Hutter is *Winter,* which follows the same approach as *In Praise of Older Men,* but has a less reverential tone. The subject of this watercolour is again an older man. A pleasantly plump subject, he stands with his back to the artist, wearing nothing but a woollen scarf, casually draped over his left shoulder, tassels almost touching the back of left knee. His left thumb rests on his left buttock in a playful, although far from effeminate, stance. It is simply one of casual insouciance, as if to say, "C'mon, get on with it!"

## BIBLIOGRAPHY

Bindman, David. (1981). *Hogarth,* Thames & Hudson.
Cooper, Emanuel. (1994). *The Sexual Perspective* (Second Edition), Routledge & Kegan Paul.
Curtis, Richard. (1994). *Four Weddings and a Funeral,* Corgi Books.
Douglas, Adam. (1992). *The Beast Within,* Chapmans.
Hutter, David. (1984). *Nudes and Flowers,* GMP Publishers Ltd.
Low, Robert. (1997). *W.G.,* Richard Cohen Books.
Nye, Robert. (1976). *Falstaff,* Hamish Hamilton Ltd.
Robinson, Bruce. (1989). *Withnail and I,* Bloomsbury Publishing.
Thomas, Keith. (1983) *Man and the Natural World: Changing Attitudes in England from 1500-1800,* Allen Lane.

Chapter 26

# The Rise of the Australian Bear Community Since 1995

Seumas Hyslop

The last major published writing regarding beardom in Australia appeared in *The Bear Book* (Hay, 1997). This article presented a fairly grim view of the bear movement in Australia. It suggested that bear was an identity that had largely outlived its useful life, and one which would not sit well with Australian gay men moving into the new millennium.

That chapter, "Bears in the Land Down Under," was written in mid-1995, just weeks following the closure of the first Sydney-based bear club, Ozbears. At that time, a lot of emotions were being vented over the death of Australia's first bear club. Yet, in hindsight, the death of Ozbears had few repercussions for the survival of the bear community in Australia. In fact, the bear movement in Sydney appeared to have gone to new heights as a direct result of the death of Ozbears. It was unfortunate, then, that an essay on the doom of the bear community in Australia was published in 1997, at a time when the bear community in Australia had never appeared stronger.

Because a great deal has happened since that first chapter was written, and most of its predictions about bears in Australia have since been proven incorrect, this chapter will give an overview of events around Australia since 1995.

## *JUNE 1995: THE DEATH OF OZBEARS*

Sydney was the only city affected by the closure of Ozbears. For many months, even years after the closure, emotions were still running high, with allegations being thrown in all directions over the cause of the death of the club.

Ozbears started in 1990 and in the early days had its own venue, a disused bitumen factory known affectionately as Zetland (in the inner city suburb of the same name). For many reasons (Hay, 1997), Ozbears was rapidly declining by 1994, and was officially closed by the then-president, Bob Hay, in 1995. As has happened with many presidents of bear clubs in the past, Bob wrote a fairly impassioned letter to friends and contacts some time afterward, explaining that he felt "burnt-out" after Ozbears and other bear-related projects, and decided to return to "hibernation" for an indefinite period.

## *AUGUST 1995:*
## *THE BIRTH OF HARBOUR CITY BEARS*

It was not even a month after the close of Ozbears in June 1995 that a number of local bears began work on establishing a new club. A group of about thirty men met on August 30, 1995, in the Stronghold bar, a well-known bear/leather bar in Surry Hills about a kilometre from Oxford Street, to start a new club known as Harbour City Bears. A working committee was established, organising events such as bar nights, sauna nights, movie trips, etc.

The committee of Harbour City Bears was committed to maintain Harbour City Bears as an open club, and accepting people from all walks of life. This stemmed from the alienation of many people, including the leather community, from Ozbears in the past (Hay, 1997). Since its inception, Harbour City Bears has made substantial links between the bear and leather communities, including the motor clubs nationwide, with the leather bears feeling just as much at home in the club as those not interested in leather. It has given the club a unique feeling of inclusiveness that has not gone unnoticed by those who attend their events.

Harbour City Bears has largely taken its direction from its president, David Coburn. A somewhat larger bear himself, and to some degree a workaholic, he has been with the club since its inception, and has played, arguably, the most significant role in the development of the bear club and the bear community in Sydney since 1995. David's charismatic style and open nature encouraged many people to get involved—his talent at "meeting, greeting, and introducing" made many people feel welcome at Harbour City Bears events.

The early days of Harbour City Bears were incredibly successful for a fledgling club. Within months, membership of Harbour City Bears exceeded the membership of Ozbears, even in its heyday, the most successful event being the monthly bar night, with over 100 bears attending regularly. However, within six months, Harbour City Bears had its first major crisis. The Stronghold closed in late 1995 amid rumours of a staff-management dispute. It was a relief to see the bar reopen two weeks later, renamed the Keep. The bar operated for three to four more months, but was then closed down by South Sydney Council due to noncompliance with fire safety regulations. Harbour City Bears spent a number of months in turmoil, there being no identifiable bear/leather bars in Sydney.

One of the most noticeable things about Sydney's gay social scene, in particular the Oxford Street and Newtown "golden miles," is that despite having the second largest organized gay and lesbian population in the world (second only to San Francisco), Sydney still fails to have a broad diversity of bars. Bars in Sydney have traditionally catered to "gym bunnies," "disco bunnies," and "scene queens." When contacted by HCB, many bars seemed reluctant to allow a group of hirsute, often larger men to hold their meetings at their establishments for fear of alienating their traditional crowds. This presented a problem for Harbour City Bears—where to meet? The management of the Stronghold established a new venue, a basement area one block from Oxford Street, and Harbour City Bears moved there, but it was problematic. The venue was too small (it was licensed for only seventy people), and one member described the decor as "caravan-esque."

Just as the popularity of the venue, and thus the regular bar night, was waning, it was fortunate that another bar opened, aiming at the leather market but encouraging a strong bear presence. The Barracks bar opened in the basement area of the Taylor Square Hotel, directly on Oxford Street. Harbour City Bears shifted to the Barracks bar, taking up its regular spot on the first Friday of the month, where it has remained ever since.

The other regular event that Harbour City Bears maintained in the early years was its sauna night, known as "Gorillas in the Mist." Held on the third Friday of the month at a local bear-oriented bathhouse, Kingsteam, the event had a good mix of the social and the sexual. Other events organized over time by Harbour City Bears included beach days, movie trips, tenpin bowling, coffee and cake afternoons, and day winery trips to the Hunter Valley.

### APRIL 1996: THE BIRTH OF VICBEARS (ORIGINALLY MELBOURNE OZBEARS)

Melbourne's early attempt at a bear club in the early 1990s was less than successful, closing within one year. It was not until April 1996 that a man known as "Be(ar)n" resurrected Melbourne Ozbears. Paying all expenses himself, he established a mailing list of approximately seventy bears in Melbourne and ran the club largely on his own.

It was February 1997 that Be(ar)n decided to leave Melbourne Ozbears, and sent out a notice giving the time and date of an "Extraordinary General Meeting." From that meeting, two committee members arose: Shane Byrnes (who was instated as "den convenor," and later president) and Gavin Rainey. The earliest change to the club was the name, VicBears, which has remained with the club until the present. Shane and Gavin set about looking for a regular bar night and a Sunday nonbar event.

Eventually establishing a bar night at The Laird Hotel in Collingwood, they were only given the option of having it on a Monday night. However, as each month passed, the numbers grew until it was the largest community "den night" in Melbourne. Similarly, their regular monthly "Pleasant Sunday Afternoon" events at a local bear- owned café proved hugely successful, and it too has been a feature of the monthly VicBears calendar since its inception.

### FEBRUARY 1997: BEAR ESSENTIALS '97 AND THE SYDNEY GAY AND LESBIAN MARDI GRAS

Harbour City Bears had been working on a number of different projects over time. Most of these were single events (e.g., movie trips, nude beach visits, bar nights), and required little in the way of organisation. However, as the 1997 Sydney Gay and Lesbian Mardi Gras drew nearer, it was becoming apparent that there was a need for an event during the annual Mardi Gras Festival. Initially, the committee of Harbour City Bears was apprehensive about attempting a large-scale bear festival in the tradition of the major American bear gatherings, but the HCB president, David Coburn, insisted, and Bear Essentials '97 was born. Having worked in the event coordination industry, David took Bear Essentials from an unknown just a few months earlier to an Australian bear "household name." Thanks to David's charisma and ability to organise, a five-day bear festival was planned, featuring the Bear Essentials "Bear Bust" (a bar night at the Barracks), "Bears at the Beach" (a nude beach afternoon), the "Teddy Bears' Picnic," "Bears at the Baths" (a somewhat cheeky and comical chicken and champagne event at the local sauna—elegance and sex all in one event!), and the Mardi Gras Parade Entry.

Despite the apprehensiveness of some of the committee, it wasn't until the registrations arrived during February that it was realized how successful the festival would be. One-hundred forty-seven registrations were accepted for BE97, limited mainly by lack of registration kits. Many more turned up at the events, including bears from the United States, the United Kingdom, and Europe (mostly Germany).

While very successful, Bear Essentials '97 did not go completely as planned. The Mr. Bear Essentials competition planned to coincide with the Bear Bust was cancelled at the eleventh hour due to disagreements with the manager of the venue. This caused some anger among some bears, but generally the participants enjoyed themselves immensely. The Parade Event was particularly successful, with the participants of Bear Essentials '97 marching under banners, Bear Pride Flags of various designs, and more than twenty polystyrene bears on poles dressed in various outfits, including flannelette and leather. The leading man of the parade, Ted Gott, managed to be interviewed for the television broadcast. The crowd seemed particularly mesmerized by the polystyrene bears, and a number of them even made their way into the major dance parties that night. Today, those original twenty polystyrene bears are collector's items.

Bear Essentials '97 was a major event that did a great deal for the credibility of bears in Australia, and in particular for Harbour City Bears. With many of the interstate and international visitors deciding to return for Bear EssentialS '98, the future of the event was guaranteed. Membership of the club almost doubled in the months surrounding BE97. Numbers at the regular bar nights grew to the point that they are currently the largest club in Sydney. Suddenly, it seemed everyone was interested in bear clubs in Sydney.

### *MAY 1997: THE MELBOURNE BEAR AND CUB COMPETITION*

Hot on the tail of Bear Essentials '97 came one of the biggest things to happen to VicBears and Melbourne, and indeed bears in Australia in general. The Melbourne Bear and Cub Competition was staged on May 31, 1997, just three months after BE97. Conceived by No Attitude Guys, a partnership run by Paul "Daddy-Paul" Evans and Tex McKenzie, they embraced VicBears as a co-organizing body on the event and promoted the living hell out of it. It was an event that in months went from start-up to a national event. JOY-FM (Melbourne's well-established gay and lesbian radio station) broadcast live from the event, and 400 people crammed The Laird Hotel to capacity for the competition. With superb organisation, it gave VicBears huge exposure as a bear club both in Melbourne and nationally.

The high profile that VicBears enjoyed through the Melbourne Bear and Cub Competition quickly shot VicBears to the forefront of the Melbourne gay scene. Becoming the largest gay social club in Melbourne almost overnight, VicBears found itself being courted by many of the local venues to shift their regular bar night. The Laird itself even offered the club a choice of nights to meet, but the club stuck to its original Mondays.

In the time since the Melbourne Bear and Cub Competition, VicBears has grown from a club run largely on the charisma of Shane Byrnes to a well-organized club with a strong and diverse committee. The club's major weekend run, "Grrrampians '97" (named after the mountain range that they visited) was a huge success, and the range of special events that VicBears run are varied and cater to all tastes.

## MID-1997: BRISBEARS VOTED BEST MALE CLUB IN BRISBANE

The last of the "big three" clubs in Australia is Brisbears, the bear club in Brisbane, Queensland, and the northernmost bear club in Australia. Established in 1993 under the founding president, Andrew Dyason, and a strong committee, Brisbears is the longest running of the "big three" clubs in Australia.

If any club was least affected by the fall of Ozbears in Sydney, it was Brisbears. Perhaps it was Sydney's belief that it is the centre of the gay universe in Australia that led people in Sydney to think that once Ozbears fell, other bear clubs around Australia would naturally follow (Hay, 1997). It is pleasing to note that Brisbears has resoundingly defied this belief, which it has done by remaining focussed on its local community, and avoiding the politics that had dogged bear clubs in the early 1990s (Hay, 1997).

Brisbears' regular monthly event is its bar night on the third Saturday each month at the Sportsman's Hotel, in Spring Hill. Well attended, it is one of the major bar nights in Brisbane. One of the most unique things about the Brisbears bar night is that it operates in a basement bar of the Sportsman's Hotel as a private club, charging a few dollars admission to events. The 200 or so people (many nonmembers) coming to Brisbears bar nights ensure that the club has a regular cash flow, something to which no other club can lay claim. This allows the club to offer a range of events to their members at either no cost or at a substantially subsidized price, including camping trips, brewery tours, and bus trips—again, something no other bear club in Australia can offer its members.

Brisbears' success is based largely on its focus on the local community. It is very fortunate that it has its own private club under the Liquor Licensing Regulations, which gives it leverage within the Brisbane community. It is very much the public face of bears in Brisbane and enjoys a high public profile in Australia and internationally. In mid-1997, Brisbears was voted the "best male club" and their bar nights the "best night out in Brisbane" by a local poll.

Like all the clubs that make up the "big three" in Australia (Brisbears, Harbour City Bears, and VicBears), it seems as though there is nothing that can stop Brisbears—there is a strong core group of members committed to the club, and their monthly events are as successful as ever. Their events have a strong reputation among the other bear clubs in Australia, and their long list of free or subsidized events, impossible for any other club in Australia to match, means tremendous value for any bear considering joining. They have strong links with other bear clubs in Australia, and their committee works tremendously well without the politics often seen in other bear clubs.

With forecasts showing Brisbane and Queensland rapidly growing in population in the new millennium, and the gay and lesbian community in Brisbane having developed dramatically during the 1990s, Brisbears remains at the forefront of bears in Australia.

## LATE 1997: NEW BEAR CLUB IN CANBERRA

While clubs on the eastern seaboard of Australia all seemed to be reaching new heights, one noticeable exception existed—Canberra. The nation's capital, Canberra is a unique town in Australia, and has a gay and lesbian social scene that is often the scorn of many of the other cities. Socially, Canberra is best described as a city of "clusters"—a number of social circles exist within the city, but there is little that seems to unify them, and information is rarely disseminated from one cluster to another. There is a small recognized club circuit (the Meridian Club, a gay and lesbian cooperative that runs a small venue just to the north of the Civic Centre), but it is far from a unifying influence in the community.

Despite what could be regarded as a difficult situation in which to start a club, a group of interested men met in late 1997 to start the nation's sixth bear club, BearsCanberra, and the first ever in the national capital. The committee, headed by president Michael Dooley, vice president Don Harding, and secretary Glen McDonald, has set up a regular monthly event, held at one of the local hotels in Eastern Canberra. With a strong core membership growing, it is expected that things will remain good for the club.

## JANUARY 1998:
## THE SECOND BEAR CLUB IN SYDNEY

Bear identity in Sydney appears to be enjoying a renaissance in recent times. The huge popularity of the Bear Essentials festivals, the success of the Barracks bar and the bear nights there, and the massive exposure of the Melbourne Bear and Cub Competition has led to a new level of excitement regarding bears in the Harbour City. Where it was previously predicted that bears would not survive in Sydney (Hay, 1997), these days bears are acquiring a new level of respectability and exposure. Within the Sydney gay and lesbian community, bears are now seen as a strong and valid subculture rather than a marginal entity.

With this in mind, there has been room for a second bear club in Sydney—named Sydney Bears. Commenced in January 1998, Sydney Bears was not established as competition to Harbour City Bears, but merely to provide a weekend daytime event in Sydney, which takes place at local pubs within the Inner Western suburbs of Sydney. Sydney Bears' intention was to remain informal—as such, the club was not incorporated, and had no formal organising committee. Previously run by Anthony Mercader and now Kerry Bashford, the club attracts some twenty to thirty regulars for a Sunday event each month in a smaller, more casual environment. Harbour City Bears has remained the formal club in Sydney, but Sydney Bears provides further regular events. With two bear clubs in Sydney, the bear community is a winner, with more choice in opportunities to meet other bears than ever before—quite a far cry from the situation in 1995 with the closure of Ozbears.

## FEBRUARY 1998: BEAR ESSENTIALS '98
## AND SYDNEY GAY AND LESBIAN MARDI GRAS
## BECOME THE BIGGEST BEAR FESTIVAL
## IN AUSTRALIA AT THE TIME

Bear Essentials '97 was such a tough act to follow that a small committee (ultimately seven bears, mostly from the Harbour City Bears executive committee) gathered in mid-1997 to start work on

Bear Essentials '98 (February 25 to March 1, 1998). They were aware that Bear Essentials '97 was a major success story at the previous Mardi Gras Festival, and that the Bear Essentials had at least national "brand recognition." The question remained: where to go next? After a lot of ideas, and an arduous whittling down process, the committee decided on the following events: a pool party, a harbour cruise, a sauna night, picnic, the march in the Sydney Gay and Lesbian Mardi Gras Parade, and a recovery event. All events were held in the evening or over the weekend to allow the widest possible audience to attend.

Interest in Bear Essentials '98 was beyond expectations. The international interest was particularly inspiring, with bears from Europe, the United Kingdom, and the United States coming to Sydney for Mardi Gras and interested in attending the Bear Essentials events. By the end of the festival, registrations (limited to 230 due to the Harbour Cruise) had been filled, with casual entry at the events bringing the total number to almost 450.

The pool party, harbour cruise, and sauna night were all regarded as the best they could be, each attracting between 200 and 300 bears. Even the Teddy Bears' Picnic, which was rained out, still managed to gather some forty bears. But by far the most visible and exciting development was the entry in the Sydney Gay and Lesbian Mardi Gras Parade, held on February 28, 1998. In the biggest show of bear solidarity in Australia, some 150 to 200 bears from all of the bear clubs in Australia and many international clubs marched unified in the Bears of Australia parade entry, over *four times* larger than any previous bear entry in the parade. This made the entry one of the largest in the entire parade.

The bear entry was well received by the 700,000-strong crowd, especially when it was described to them by the commentators as a reaction against the "pumped up, young, and gorgeous" set that is seen so commonly on Oxford Street. There were enormous cheers right along the parade route.

Bear Essentials is now a nationally recognized bear event of international standing, and its coincidence with the Sydney Gay and Lesbian Mardi Gras virtually ensures that there will always be a healthy influx of hairy, bearded men who want to spend time with other bears in Sydney. Bear Essentials '99, held in February 1999, was expected to reach the 500 bears mark, and it is expected that it will continue to grow as a national bear institution.

## JUNE 1998: SOUTHERN HIBEARNATION '98 AND THE MR. AUSTRALIAN BEAR AND CUB COMPETITION BECOME THE SECOND FLAGSHIP EVENT FOR THE AUSTRALIAN BEAR COMMUNITY

Following the success of the Melbourne Bear and Cub Competition, No Attitude Guys (under the control of Paul Evans and new NAG organiser Rob Camm) and VicBears began work on the 1998 event. With the support of the Bear Clubs of Australia, they expanded the competition nationally, renaming it the Mr. Australian Bear and Cub Competition.

Drawing contestants and judges from all states in Australia and the Australian Capital Territory, the competition was the first event to encourage national involvement in a bear event. The 1998 Mr. Australian Bear and Cub Competition also provided the centrepiece for a weekend of events called Southern Hibearnation '98, Melbourne's first bear festival, which had over 100 registrations.

A total of eight bears and eight cubs entered, vying for the inaugural title of Mr. Australian Bear and Mr. Australian Cub 1998. The opening party, with the "Drowning Teddy," a specially designed cocktail, kicked off in Collingwood, a suburb in the inner north of Melbourne, drawing some 200 people. With the identity of the judges hidden, the nervous contestants were forced to introduce themselves to everyone.

Prejudging commenced on the afternoon of Saturday, June 27, with the identity of the judges being revealed—Shane Byrnes (VicBears), Kevin Dicker (Brisbears), Kevin Knighton (WOMBATS), Seumas Hyslop (Harbour City Bears), and Don Harding (BearsCanberra). However, the standout event of the weekend was the major competition that night, where just under 500 spectators packed The Laird Hotel to see the bears strut their stuff on stage. The local gay weekly, *Melbourne Star Observer*, covered the event, and it proved to be the largest individual bear event in Australia.

Emceed by Barry "Bazbear" Taylor and Laurie Lane, two well-known local personalities, three rounds of judging (Casual Bear,

Bear Minimum, and Fantasy Bear) commenced. Two hours later, two winners emerged: Mr. Paul Bear (yes, that *is* his legal name) as Mr. Australian Bear 1998, and P. J. Sandland as Mr. Australian Cub 1998.

The weekend ended with a catered barbecue in Yarra Bend Park, complete with Barry Taylor's "Yarra Bend Park Beat Tour," and a Beer Bust at a local Collingwood pub.

VicBears is another Australian club that is going full steam ahead. Their regular events are well attended and their special events have gained a name for themselves. Their strong networking with other clubs has meant that VicBears has become involved with the bear community on a national scale. There is little doubt that VicBears will enter the new millennium stronger than ever before.

## *LATE 1998: COUGAR LEATHER CLUB CATERS TO BEARS IN SOUTH AUSTRALIA*

Adelaide is the capital of the state of South Australia and is the fifth largest city in Australia. However, Adelaide had not had a strong bear presence within the local gay and lesbian community. Ozbears South Australia, while it had been around since the early 1990s, held events some distance from Adelaide, so was hampered by accessibility issues for much of that time.

It was in late 1996 that Garry McCormack and Tony Hemming founded Cougar Leather, a local club designed for the leather community in Adelaide. However, in 1998, seeing the success of the club, many bears became interested in attending, and found themselves strongly encouraged to do so. It has become Australia's most sucessful bear/leather hybrid club. While maintaining its roots deep within the Australian leather community, it has become a club that caters to both communities in South Australia, maintaining links to both leather and bear clubs nationally.

Cougar's mainstay event is the twice-monthly bar night at The Wheatsheaf Hotel, a local pub in the inner west of Adelaide, close to the city center. These events and their "parties" for special occasions attract over 200 bears and leathermen. As a result of the work that the small committee has done, the club was voted Community Group of the Year within the South Australian gay and lesbian community in 1998, and in 1999 was made responsible for organising a leather dance party for Adelaide's annual FEAST gay and lesbian festival.

Cougar Leather has become another success story for bears in Australia, demonstrating that bears do not exist only in the eastern states of Australia.

## *BEARSPERTH (FORMERLY WOMBATS) AND OZBEARS SOUTH AUSTRALIA\**

Both of these clubs have been operating since prior to 1995, and appear to have largely maintained the status quo over the years. Both clubs are among the smaller of the Australian Bear Clubs, and tend to be groups of friends. Nonetheless, BearsPerth (formerly known as WOMBATS) has been particularly innovative over the years, organising trips to local disused gaols, camping trips, barbecues, and trivia nights in addition to their regular meeting in the Den.

## *1999: FURTHER DEVELOPMENTS*

While there were no new clubs or events, bear events consolidated around the country in 1999. The year brought with it some new developments, including the inaugural Australian Bear Calendar, the brainchild of Ken Iversen (then vice president of Harbour City Bears) and Kerry Brown. While it did not include any nudity, it presented a diverse range of bears in many different settings, and was well received by the Australian bear community.

Bear Essentials '99 broke the 500-bear barrier during the festival. For the first time in the annual Sydney Gay and Lesbian Mardi Gras Parade's history, the "Bears of Australia" entry was the largest, with 320 bears from around the nation and the world marching together.

---

*Both WOMBATS and Ozbears South Australia did not return requests for information sent out in the process of research for this chapter. Therefore, the author regrets any potentially missing information in relation to these clubs.

Despite this, the bears' entry and Sydney Leather Pride's entry, as well as many other "flagship" floats in the parade, were not shown on the delayed national television broadcast. A letter campaign was commenced within hours of the broadcast, and within days Sydney Gay and Lesbian Mardi Gras was swamped with e-mails, letters, faxes, and phone calls from individuals and clubs—it is estimated that some 300 letters of protest were sent to Mardi Gras.

Involvement of the local media in the issue helped to heighten the profile of bears within Sydney and beyond. The story of the bears being dropped was reported in the news worldwide. After protracted negotiations, the local bears and Mardi Gras were able to come to an understanding about the role of community groups within the parade, and it is expected that community consultation will improve as a result of the campaign.

The middle of the year brought a quick succession of events. In May 1999 in Chicago, for the first time, an Australian (Melbourne bear Joe Rocca) won the major international bear title, Mr. Bear Pride 1999. June 1999 brought the annual Southern Hibearnation festival and the Mr. Australian Bear and Cub Competition, with VicBears surpassing the 500-bear mark with the event. The winner of the competition, Dale Kruse, attended a major U.S. bear event in early 2000. Of major interest was the development of a bear art exhibition to showcase Australian bear artists, which rivals much of the bear art in the United States.

July 1999 brought two important bear landmarks: BearsCanberra's second annual Christmas in July event at Parliament House, and the spawning of an "associate" club of Brisbears, called "SunCoast Bears." Based at the Sunshine Coast north of Brisbane, and developed by local bear Alan Hubbard, SunCoast Bears will integrate tightly with Brisbears, and offer bears in Queensland even more events.

## THE FUTURE OF BEARS IN AUSTRALIA

Bears, as a personal identity and as a community, have a very bright future in Australia. The number of bear clubs in Australia is at an all-time high, and we now have bear events of national and international significance. Indeed, Australia is fast becoming an important international tourist destination for bears. The development of an annual calendar of bear events, featuring most notably Bear Essentials and Southern Hibearnation, can only help the bear community in Australia promote itself nationally and internationally.

Regardless of what happens, the bear community is stronger and more visible than ever. "Bear" as an identity has changed for the better in Australia. In a short time, bears have gone from being a marginalized group to being a recognized, strong, and valid gay subculture with a high profile and a vibrant social ethic. Bear clubs in Australia are now one of the few environments that transcends age—where twenty-year-old men can happily rub shoulders with forty-year-old and even sixty-year-old men in a relaxed environment. The openness and inclusiveness of the major bear clubs of Australia virtually ensures the continued success of the bear identity in this country, and will continue to make Australia a popular destination for bear and bearhunting tourists the world over.

## *ACKNOWLEDGMENTS*

The author would like to thank the following people for their assistance in preparing this article: Shane Byrnes (founding and current president, VicBears), Andrew Dyason (founding president, Brisbears), David Coburn, (founding president, Harbour City Bears, Sydney), Don Harding (founding vice president) and Glen McDonald (founding secretary, BearsCanberra), Tony Hemming (founding president) and Garry McCormack (founding vice president, Cougar Leather Club), Ted Gott (for general support when I go crazy), and Bob Hay.

## REFERENCE

Hay, B. (1997). "Bears in the Land Down Under" in Wright, L. (ed.) *The Bear Book: Readings in the History and Evolution of a Gay Male Subculture* (pp. 225-238). Binghamton, NY: Harrington Park Press.

# PART VI:
# *BEARS IN MEDIA*

Chapter 27

# You Can Lead a Bear to Culture, but . . . or Bears in Literature and Culture: A Discussion with David Bergman and Michael Bronski

Ron Suresha

**Ron:** Let's start by talking about the *Song of the Loon* pulp sex novel trilogy by Richard Amory. These books (published 1966-1968, and now out of print) were early representations of bear types: frontiersmen, cowboys, and Native Americans who were hairy, bearded, strong, well-hung (of course), sexually available, and primarily concerned (except for minor plot constraints) with male-to-male love. Are the men of the *Loon* series anything like a bear archetype?

**David:** Amory clearly thought he was dealing with an archetype. The *Loon* trilogy is a melding of the cowboy novel of Zane Grey and the classical pastoral romance of Longus, both of which rely more on archetypes than on psychological realism. Gregory Woods, in his new book *A History of Gay Literature*, has a very fine chapter on the homoerotic element of the pastoral romance, and the Native American has always been associated in the Western mind with male-male sex. The Spanish explorers noted with horror how Native Americans engaged so freely in sodomy. So I think both the *Loon* books and bear culture are overdetermined by very strong cultural vectors that have shaped it and brought it into being. The myth that developed was of the natural Native releasing the positive aspects of the white man's homosexuality. This mythic sense of the natural powers the appreciation of the hairy, thicker male bodies of bear culture.

**Ron:** Were the readers of the *Loon* books back in the 1960s anything like the readers of *BEAR* and *American Bear* today?

**Michael:** Before the *Loon* books, in the 1950s and 1960s, there was very little openly gay material available for gay men to read. There were some quite depressing and even homophobic books that even appeared as mainstream novels and then were published as pulps. And they were quite, quite different from the first porn books that appeared in the mid-1960s, which had explicit sexual activity and were not burdened with unhappy endings, but they were *not* real novels. They were jerk-off books. The *Loon* books were openly gay, sexy, and written as novels. The *Loon* books were read by lots of different people—men looking to read about gay relationships, as well as men looking to read about sex. They were a revelation because they were very positive about gay lives and I think that their enormous readership was drawn to that, not to the types of men in the books.

**Ron:** Can we discuss the genre of writing—the gay pastoral—that these books represented, and its relevant symbolism?

**Michael:** You have to place the *Loon* books in the larger context of a tradition of United States writing that presented the West, the wilderness, the forest—the pastoral in a larger sense—as a symbol of the natural, the healthy, and even the morally right. This tradition is the cornerstone of U.S. writing and includes James Fenimore Cooper's *Leather-Stocking Tales,* Melville's *Moby-Dick,* and even Mark Twain's *Huckleberry Finn*. In all of these novels men have to leave civilization and go into the wilderness either to find themselves or to find freedom. In the process they also discovered deep feelings—and love—with other men: Natty Bumppo and Chingachgook, Ishmael and Queequeg, Huck and Jim. The homoerotic strain in all of this literature is completely self-evident. Leslie Fiedler talks about it at length in *Love and Death in the American Novel*. His famous essay on Huckleberry Finn, "Come Back to the Raft Again, Huck Honey," was published in 1949. This is no secret. And certainly the *Loon* books fit right into this—they are, in essence, a continuation and even at times a parody of it.

**Ron:** How does the conspicuous absence of women affect the male characters in these works?

**Michael:** There are two things to keep in mind with this. The first is that, in this tradition, men have to leave civilization because women are preventing them from being full human beings. This situation is predicated on "civilization" being repressive because men can't act out their inner feelings, and "the forest" being good because it is natural—no women present. There is a clear understanding in all the work that women make unreasonable, repressive demands upon men to act better—that is, not to be so sexual—and therefore women are to be avoided.

**David:** I agree with Michael that the absence of women is central to these representations of entering the natural. Of course, this also corresponds to the demographics of the American West, in which the society was dominated by men and women were scarce.

**Michael:** It is interesting to look at how people relate to the books now and how they see that context. And I think that this context has to include an observation of all the aspects—historical, social, sexual—that make up the tradition. Why might bears be attracted to the *Loon* books? Is it just because some of the men have beards? Well, lots of men in the Bible have beards and live in the wilderness. Hell—the Book of Hosea even describes God as a female bear protecting her cubs.

**Ron:** Earlier in the Old Testament actually, in Genesis, the character of Esau, Joseph's hairy older brother, might be considered the first biblical bear. In order to receive their father's blessing, Joseph impersonates Esau by wearing a pelt. Esau is depicted as a very instinctual and sensual man, and a loving brother, who is in essence Joseph's shadow.

**Michael:** But to get back to the *Loon* books: Do bears relate to these books because they are about men getting together away from civilization and being free of social restraints? Some bears may see these restraints now as getting away from repressive aspects of gay male culture—the gym body, the enforced hairlessness of some porn magazines. But it is also important to think about what it means to indulge in the fantasy of men alone to be sexually free in a broader context as well—can men only be free and sexual without women present? What are the conditions and the fantasies that make all-male—even bear—groups special, and what does that mean?

**David:** I think you're falling into the trap of regarding any culture outside of the West as being without constraints, as being without a culture. But the Indians in the *Loon* books have a very elaborate legal and religious system. It just isn't sexually repressive. The *Loon* books and the bear movement are not escapes from culture, but a desire to find a culture that is not repressive of sexual desire and not offended by the realities of the human body, its hairiness, tendency to sag, its mortality.

**Michael:** Good point. It is vital not to essentialize non-Western cultures as "freer." Certainly Edward Said in *Orientalism* has made clear what happens with this process. And certainly nonwhite cultures, in this case Native American cultures, had complex legal, religious, and moral systems. But what I was speaking about was how the white-male-Eurocentric writer and reader construct this fantasy world. In the *Loon* books, the freedom—embedded in the complex legal and religious codes (which are, as far as I can tell, pretty much invented by the author)—is *predicated* on the absence of women, which allows a pervasive homoeroticism.

**Ron:** Turning our attention to more recent times: some consider the bears to be one of the first movements following the onset of AIDS to provide gay men with healthy images of sex. It was a way, in part, for some men to reconnect with images of strength and power and virility, and to some extent longevity—qualities connected with bear body traits: beards, fur, fat, and sexual prowess.

**Michael:** I wonder what you mean by a "movement"—as opposed to a bunch of guys that felt good about how they looked and hung out together and their good feelings about themselves, all of which helped them to have safe sex. That is *great,* but is not a "movement" to feel good about sex. Which is not to say that the bear thing did not come into being and evolve as a response—directly and indirectly—to AIDS.

**Ron:** Perhaps not a "movement" in a political sense, but in the way it created community, art, and identity that tens of thousands of men around the world can relate to.

**Michael:** I would not personally use the phrase "bear movement." I rather see it as a "phenomenon"—a sort of varied, multilevel, mostly grass roots (although increasingly commodified) response to many factors, especially AIDS.

**David:** I think AIDS is an important part of what brought about the bear groups, but I think its origins go back further to a desire in certain gay men to find something especially beautiful and sexy in their own masculinity. I think it is also a response to certain cultural images of gay men that gay men produced of themselves which emphasized (perhaps overemphasized) youth, hairlessness, gym bodies, and wealth.

**Michael:** Of course, that is true. And I think that historically this is an American as opposed to a European image. This is reflected in the *Loon* books and in colonial and postcolonial American literature and we see it today with the bears versus the Calvin Klein look. It is natural versus unnatural or manufactured.

**David:** I was just looking at the Tom Bianchi book of photography, *In Defense of Beauty*—and it represents exactly the problem that the bear movement was supposed to respond to. Bianchi can conceive of only one kind of beauty, and that is a sculptural dehumanized beauty in which people look like they are marble rather than flesh.

**Ron:** Of course bears reacted as outsiders to this dehumanized gay ideal—it was just plain unworkable for bears to live up to that standard. Nor did they feel they ought to.

**Michael:** I think it is interesting to call Bianchi's work a problem—for whom? Not for the men who look like they do—wouldn't they like it? There may be a larger social problem, such as social interests prioritizing and promoting one type of body over another. That has been a feminist critique of the media for years. And certainly the bear thing has been a response to that. Bianchi is not interested in defending "beauty"—which can mean almost anything—except for a special type of socially approved beauty. Of course, Bianchi—and other photographers, such as Bruce Webber, and so on—dehumanize. That is one way to deal with how scary sexuality is. That is why they are not real or true artists—the purpose of their work is to view the world through a limited, narrow lens, not a broader one that shows its complexity.

**Ron:** As you said earlier, Michael, this "enforced hairlessness" would seem to point to some exclusion of bear-type images, as reflected in the types of body images the gay media produces—print, broadcast, photography, advertising, porn.

**Michael:** The reason why there are few bear images in some magazines and books is because they are seen as not popular. You know that the minute Bianchi thought he could sell bears he would; the minute that the fashion world decides that bear is *in,* the images will be there. These images occur in commercial venues—what sells, sells. As for representations of gay men in porn and the gay media: porn sells because it markets images that are perceived to be salable. Richard Locke and lots of late-1970s porn stars were bear-like. The minute bears become marketable, bears will be sold as such.

**David:** Bears are being marketed already, but not as successfully as the buff. However, I think we should be glad that someone isn't marketable and rejoice in that failure.

**Ron:** So, why doesn't it sell?

**David:** Part of it is technical. It's harder to photograph hairy bodies and get the same sort of physical definition. Light does not come off a hairy body in as photogenic a way as it does a smoothly oiled one. Then there are the class issues of thinness—the rich can afford the diets and exercise one needs to stay thin. But I think there is something else. Hair is a deeply psychological symbol of both sexuality and mortality. Remember, Samson loses his power when he gets his locks shorn—and society in its attempt to control power wants to have us all shorn. But body hair especially is part of the abject—part of the dirty, smelly, detachable parts of the self that are associated with being mortal. And today especially, American society in general, and gay culture in particular, is torn by its feelings about its mortality. So along with the Bianchi models who look like marble statues, we also have the anorexic male models who look like they're on speed or heroin—gaunt figures of the nearly dead.

**Ron:** So what happened—what made it possible—in the mid-1980s to make bears become marketable?

**Michael:** Bears became more marketable because of a lot of reasons. First, some men couldn't fit into the youngish, hairless images. Second, AIDS became a reality and somehow that was associated with a gay culture that was too centered on urban life and living—the result was a fantasy flight to the natural and the woods, and the nonurban. Also, there were too many baby boomers who no longer fit a young image. But let's face it: the people marketing *BEAR* and *American Bear* would love to have a larger market. That is what happened to *Drummer:* it was lost in the dust when every other gay porn mag—*Honcho, Mandate,* etc.—began printing SM images.

**David:** AIDS left a vacuum in gay image making that allowed a small window for bears to emerge as a group. Also, the image of thin, willowy models was problematic for gay men because they reminded gay men too much of AIDS. There was a need to see burly, healthy, mature men, with hairy bodies, to confirm the idea that they had survived. Younger men went to the gym and turned their bodies into stone or metal—body armor to protect them—but other gay men saw protection in fur, as we have always done.

**Michael:** What was the vacuum? There were plenty of other magazines. I think it is important to see these as simultaneous occurrences. There are still plenty of willowy bodies and a whole new wave of young man porn—*XY* magazine—that is decidedly *no BEAR* and quite hostile to the idea.

**Ron:** That's true: many gay men are rather perplexed, if not outright hostile, to the whole concept of bears.

**Michael:** I like the idea that we have always seen protection in fur, and it is certainly true for some cultures and time periods. But let's not overgeneralize. The invincible gym body is as much a response to AIDS as the bear body is. If men see themselves at war with a disease, then they want to be fit to fight. This Spartan image is as valid an interpretation as the bear response. And, realistically, not all men can *be* bears—or choose to appreciate the bear look. I think it is great that there are now a multiplicity of looks in the gay world, but the slim, boyish look is in as well—look at Leonardo DiCaprio, and Matt Damon, and Marky Mark—all straight-boy icons for some gay men, and certainly for the mainstream media.

**David:** Michael, I never said the gym body *wasn't* a response to AIDS. In fact, I said just the opposite. But I think during the mid-eighties there was a lot of anxiety about how to regard our bodies and sexuality, and this uncertainty opened a range of possibilities. It has only been in the last few years that I have been receiving, as editor of *Men on Men,* stories that are sexually explicit, and that openness has been fiercely attacked by people such as Larry Kramer. Yes, the willowy, drugged-out body has returned with a vengeance. I think it is also part of the glamorization of the AIDS body. In fact, Bianchi was on the cover of the AIDS arts journal *A&U* [May 1998]. So AIDS has produced lots of confusion about how gay men regard their bodies.

**Ron:** And the formation of the bear body helped those types of men achieve a certain clarity about how they view themselves.

**Michael:** I think a real question is how much this media—as alternative as it is and wants to be seen—actually influences how people see themselves as much as Calvin Klein ads and *XY* magazine do. Do all bears really want to be bears? Or is this just another image they have been sold? How much of this influence is natural is as socially constructed as anything else.

**David:** I don't know about you, Michael, but as for me, I'm never going to have the sleek, hairless, long-legged body of the Calvin Klein ads. I have a bear body because of genetics. But bear culture has taught me not to be ashamed of it. And I think that when you have a certain body type, you have trouble imagining yourself ever fitting into a Calvin Klein ad. Certain kinds of gay men for a long time have felt very out of it. "bearness" becomes a way of seeing yourself, a discovery of a way to view yourself, that makes it possible to see your body as desirable and gay at the same time.

**Michael:** Well, actually, I sometimes have a more "bearish" body because I am overly fond of eating junk food and don't get enough physical exercise. I'm not even talking about a "gym body," but simple physical exertion. Genetically I tend to be rather thin. But what I was really talking about was that *all* men can fit into a certain type—bear, gym body, willowy queen—people do have body types.

I was referring to the proliferation of certain media images of how "gay men should look" and how that can make people feel that they want to look that way even if it is an impossibility. Certainly, not all women can look like a Cosmo girl, but many feel that they *should*. The good part is that, if bears now feel that they can resist the temptation to want to look elsewise, we are all better off. But how much better off would we be if we struggled toward a culture in which a person's body was their body and there was no need to conform to *any* type, no matter how varied the choices were!

**Ron:** Let's return to this idea of the split in the psyche of bears between the urban and the wilderness. How does that read into bear media representations?

**Michael:** The flight from the urban happened after Stonewall with the gay commune movement, as well as with a back-to-the-wilds impulse in het communities. A strong aspect of gay culture has always been the decadents and a preoccupation with death and decline. The Bianchi and AIDS stuff plays into that. In a sense, the bears are a rejection of that history. The natural over the unnatural—in drug terms, mushrooms over K and speed. In a sense, urban bears are an oxymoron—they are displaced people creating a subculture in hostile territory. Gay bars are essentially an urban, decadent phenomenon and bears can be in them—meet there—but they're almost antithetical to that impulse to run away from the urban.

**David:** As Michael is pointing out, the bear movement is paradoxical. Anyone really brought up in the wild knows that it isn't half as romantic as bear images try to make it. It is an urban fantasy about what a world in the wild would be like. It goes back to the decadents, as Michael says, which was a very urban and urbane movement: what they prized was the artificiality of the so-called natural. I think that is why so many bears are in love with cyberspace. The bear idyll has always taken place in a cyberspace, which is nostalgia for something that never was.

**Michael:** American culture—gay and straight—has always had a love affair with the fantasy of the naturalness of the wild forest or the unexplored. The American Western movie is a prime example. And the conflict in Westerns is: how to tame the West and keep the fantasy. Bear culture grew up in San Francisco—an extraordinarily urbane place—with enough connection to a history of oddness and the West that it allowed the bear image to grow and become noticed by others. I think we also have to look at the culture of 'zines and that sort of punk counterculture (an antibear one, at that) for helping to create publishing networks that allowed *BEAR* magazine to really work and grow.

**David:** The magazines have been a powerful force in gay life, far more a force than for straights. I've often said that the queerest thing about gay people is that they read, and Americans as a rule don't read at all.

**Michael:** My friend Will Leber has always claimed that if gay people were on TV and in movies we would not have any gay literature or publishing because it exists only to fill a media void. Gay people are like all Americans—they only read because they have to.

**David:** But Michael was making another very important point. And that is that bear culture is an especially American expression (although I can imagine Australians with a similar background having something like a bear culture). The West of the imagination relies on two opposing forces: the need to conquer nature, and the desire to be absorbed by an alien culture in which one can find oneself. I don't think there will ever be an International Mr. Bear.

**Michael:** My boyfriend Drew lived in Korea for two years and found men there who identified as bears based on the magazines and media.

**Ron:** There are bear clubs throughout Western Europe. Australians translate it into Marsupial bears or Wombats. There's even a bear club in Japan. And actually, there is an International Mr. Bear contest, although it primarily features only winners from contests of U.S. clubs.

**David:** I forget about the hegemony of American culture. Even gay culture is part of the imperialistic spread of America.

**Michael:** I don't find it surprising to hear that there is an International Mr. Bear because gay culture around the world has historically come from U.S. culture. Is this a good thing or a bad thing? Well,

I think that the more we market looks and trends and fashions as being *the* way to look—be it disco, hairless gym bodies, or bears—we have to do some deep thinking and questioning about what is going on. It is all a manifestation of people not wanting to be themselves. There is always the impulse to eroticize the Other, so that an Asian man might want to eroticize what is essentially a Western bear look—but to *be* that look? That seems odd to me.

**Ron:** Despite many positive archetypal images of the bear mammal—such as the one in the Bible that Michael mentioned, or in the Hindu epic the *Ramayana,* or in Native American lore—contemporary American culture views the creature as negative and fearsome—as the dictionary puts it, a bear is a surly, uncouth, or shambling person. To me this sounds very much like the biker types among whom the bear thing first emerged—but I doubt it is how most self-identified urban bears now see themselves, or would care to see themselves represented.

**Michael:** Are bears outlaws—or simply refugees from an urban culture they don't feel comfortable in? What does it mean to be an outlaw? It seems to me that bears may be fashion outlaws because they don't—adamantly refuse to—conform to certain media-produced body types. But real outlaws? Not really. Not socially, or even politically, that makes any sort of difference in the material world. And that is fine, but let's not confuse our terms here.

**Ron:** How do you feel personally when gay men type you as a bear?

**David:** Ironically, I don't even consider myself a bear. I don't feel bad when people think of me as a bear. But I'm not comfortable with the instant sort of brotherhood that some people think being a bear automatically gives you. I find that rather disturbing. It's a false intimacy. But America is the land of false intimacy, so I'm not surprised. I'm just taken a little aback by someone thinking that I was a person who belonged anywhere. I'm not used to that sense of belonging.

**Michael:** People can think of me any way they like. I am more interested if they will go to bed with me. Not always the case. It is that false intimacy that David mentioned.

**David:** In any case, I've never gone to bear club meetings, or to get-togethers with bears. I've always disliked the clubby kind of mentality that is also so much of American culture. Bear clubs sometimes strike me as Elks clubs for homosexuals.

**Michael:** America is a country of joiners—from Rotary and Junior League to Girth and Mirth to gay bowling leagues. Why do we think gay people should be different from the rest of the country? People want to be accepted—but that is very tricky. What does acceptance mean? I am far more eager to be accepted because of my wit, or intelligence, or ability to get a job done, than by my build, or whiteness, or even my gayness. I generally don't want to be accepted for the most, in some ways, superficial aspects—or more important, for certain physical aspects, like whiteness, over which I have no control. I am glad to be accepted as a bear—although I don't identify as such—because that does not set me apart from other people. Being accepted for being white—at least in how our culture is now—is actually predicated on nonwhite people being *not* accepted. Which is repugnant.

**Ron:** Shouldn't bear types have their own spaces, where they can socialize with other similarly socially identified folks?

**David:** Bears should have their place as everyone else should be able to claim a space of his own.

**Michael:** People can create any space they want. It's not a bad thing. I just think that a bear space is no different—in theory or concept—from other spaces that Americans create to be with people whom they view to be like them. What is the necessity for a separate space for bears? What can happen there that cannot happen in a non-bear-exclusive space? A bear space seems to be a social space and I think it is interesting to keep thinking about what is going on behind the urge for it.

**Ron:** Bear spaces often become collegial "group gropes" where anybody (thus the egalitarian slant) can participate. But often this is behavior the same men wouldn't think of doing elsewhere.

**David:** I don't know how things are in Boston, but in Baltimore where I live, it is clear that I'm not wanted in some of the bars, especially the dance bars. People want to claim a space when they are excluded or made to feel unwanted in other spaces. I don't think there is any mystery to the desire for feeling wanted, for feeling that you belong.

**Ron:** True—if you've ever been the only bearded man cruising in a bar full of clean-shaven guys and "clones," you know by experience that particular kind of exclusion, which I call *smoothism*.

**Michael:** I am bothered about this idea of claiming space. Is this like restricted country clubs? The very notion that people might want to be with their own kind has, well, a troubled history. There are several things going on here, though, about the nature of difference and the responses to it. Let's say that one does not feel welcomed in a public space—like the dance bars David mentioned. Sure, in that case you may want to go to—or create—a space (a bear bar) in which you would feel comfortable. That is a reaction to a form of social ostracism. But is the identity of "bear" simply a reaction to what is experienced as an oppressive gay male culture, or is it something unique in and of itself? This is not a new question. African-American culture has evolved and flourished in resistance to—and been suppressed and harmed by—a dominant culture of white racism. The same is true of gay culture. I don't really see "bear culture" as that sort of entity or construction, but it is a question if the bear identity is proactive, or simply reactive. I suspect that the bear image started out as a reflexive revolt against beauty norms (among other things) but has evolved into a stabilized identity and image that wants to be accepted as mainstream. This, of course, is a contradiction that one sees in the gay movement as well. Are gay people in some way profoundly different, or are we just like everyone else?

**Ron:** This brings up an interesting aspect of bear representation: how so many of them try to pass as straight, working-class Joes (or Harrys, perhaps) yet in reality are just furry technoqueers.

**David:** My answer is that for the most part we are invisible to straight people. I think most gay people are still seen by the straight world in the old stereotypes. When I mention bears to straights who are pretty "cool," they don't even know what I'm talking about.

**Michael:** But do you think that bears are at all visible as *gay* to straight people? They just look like older men. There is nothing *gay* about the look to those who don't know.

**Ron:** What impact have the bears had on queer culture at large?

**Michael:** I don't think there is a great deal of impact by bears on gay culture. I think that what we call gay culture is actually an enormous set of overlapping subcultures that have little impact on one another. I do think that the *importance* of bears and bear culture is that it shows that gay culture is growing and becoming more and more interesting with age. And that is great—it is a sign of maturity.

**David:** I think with some of my students that they are often more comfortable with a greater range of what it means to be gay, and seem to have a less stereotyped notion of what they have to live up to. That might be a response to bear culture, but I have never heard them speak of it. They seem to be very oblivious to the idea. In fact the only gay person under thirty that has ever mentioned bear culture to me is my niece and her girlfriend, who think of themselves as lady bears.

**Michael:** I also think that gay male culture has an enormous capacity to reinvent and self-invent. There is a chapter in *The Pleasure Principle*, my new book, that charts how the gay male body changed how straight men viewed their own bodies. I think that the capacity to invent the bear has shown straight culture—just as the clone and the daddy and other gay types did—that men can be any number of things. And more importantly that that image can be sexy.

**David:** Gay men are always showing straight men how to look at themselves. Look at James Dean and any number of gay movie stars who came to represent American maleness.

**Ron:** And that's the impact that bears had—they made visible to the larger gay culture a far greater range of images, and thereby broke through the contemporary gay male beauty code.

**Michael:** I think that gay men and gay sensibility have usually paved the way for how Americans think about a whole range of body types and images. But this is always complicated. The reality is that the Marlboro Man—as an image, and I suspect as a model—came out of certain gay types of the 1960s and 1970s. He can also be seen as an early proto-bear. But that would not have had the impact it did if it were not connected to a major advertising campaign put together by the cigarette industry. The image may have started out gay, but its effect was through a mainstream venue. The same with James Dean—his was a gay image, but developed through the Hollywood studio system. I think that at this point in history—as with all social trends that are media-influenced—what causes what is the most interesting question.

**Ron:** You mean, which came first: the chicken or the bear? (Sorry, couldn't resist that.) No—you mean, did the individuals who were bears create the magazine that created the movement, or some other way around?

**Michael:** As David said earlier, bears did not come out of nowhere. And bears have been commercialized from the beginning. There would be no "movement" without the magazines.

**Ron:** But you stated earlier, Michael, that the bear 'zines do not comprise a movement by themselves. You don't think that the bear bulletin board groups along with the bear bars and the Bear Hug groups helped the bear culture to spread far and fast?

**Michael:** Sure, the bulletin boards did, but the magazines started it. And kept it going with products and videos, and on and on. It became marketing, like everything else in U.S. culture.

**Ron:** How do you feel about the emerging under-forty bear groups calling themselves Gen-X bears?

**Michael:** Gen-X bears are another spinoff, another market.

**David:** It is very important that they are not locked off by age groups. One of the most marvelous parts of the *Loon* books was their celebration of intergenerational sex. What I think is very harmful in contemporary gay society is the separation of age groups. Gay bars are now much more age differentiated than they were when I was coming out. Too much of American society is about finding a niche for yourself, a small place where you can feel safe, a gated community. Gay life follows that path too, and one would hope that bear culture, which had resisted this, would not fall under the spell of having different age groups.

**Ron:** As David touched on earlier, there's been some discussion on the topic of women as bears—primarily lesbians, I believe—who self-identify as lady bears or mama bears, relating to other perceived qualities of bears, such as nurturance and protection of loved ones.

**Michael:** I wonder how many. This seems totally idiosyncratic with little resonance for most women.

**David:** I'm in no position to speak about "most women," but I do sense greater visibility of women who are crossing gender lines, queering the boundaries of maleness, and my impression is that "bearness" might have a particular appeal for such women. I would welcome it. The presence of women in bear groups might be helpful, but I think it would be resisted by the men. But these women are strong, and they are likely to outlast the resistance of the men.

**Michael:** Bear groups seem to be based on sexual cruising and flirting. Why would women help the group?

**Ron:** Besides, there's resistance to nonbear types within bear groups.

**David:** Because they might break down the cliquishness and insularity of bear clubs. Besides, when there have been women at bars at the same time as bears are gathering, I haven't noticed any diminution of the cruising, or even of sex. My impression is that the women who go to such bars (and admittedly the number is small) are ones that, rather than discourage cruising between men, enjoy the greater sexual freedom they find there.

**Michael:** This brings up the question: what do bears really have in common except an attraction to one another and the desire to be in a group of like-minded-bodied people? Which is not a necessarily bad thing—but what do they have in common?

**Ron:** Perhaps they share the same class, or at least the same class values—or the illusion of shared-class values?

**Michael:** Do you mean class as in economic class? I find that hard to believe. And if you are implying that class value—and I am not sure that means in the context of the U.S. and its history and economy—are things like not dressing or acting middle class, that strikes me as, well, superficial, and sort of insulting to working-class men who *have* to dress that way because they don't have enough money to dress up. I still wonder what bears have in common except a body type. Which, again, is a fine thing to have in common. But it seems bear clubs are like restricted country clubs: No thin people need apply?

**Ron:** But bears don't necessarily have a common body type. Although I'm trim, I've never felt out of place in a bear space—at least, not because of my body type. Certainly I've never gone to a bear event or a bear space and felt, oh, I'm not fat enough or hairy enough. In contrast with predominant media images and dance-bar attitudes, you will find people in the bear groups who are thin, and clean-shaven, and smooth-bodied—just not usually with *all* of those characteristics.

**David:** We must distinguish between bear groups as they are, and how they might be. I would like to see bears as a force of resistance against the fashion industry, the style industry, and other types of classist ways of separating people. It would be nice to find in the gay world a group whose aim was inclusion, between and among genders. I think that would be the attraction for women to join bear groups, and it might be a source of attraction for men.

**Michael:** Sorry to be cynical, but good luck. If we have seen anything it has been a desire for bears to become fashionable. What else does *BEAR* magazine promote?

**David:** I hardly think that anyone would call *BEAR* magazine fashionable, although it could be said to celebrate a certain style. It doesn't have the circulation of *OUT* or *The Advocate*, which are clearly small mass-market journals.

**Michael:** Of course, *BEAR* magazine is not *fashionable* in the sense that Calvin Klein is *fashionable* but it is trying to celebrate, promote, and market a *style* and a *look*. It exists—and presumably makes money—by *selling* that look. If Calvin Klein or Ralph Lauren started a "bear line" next season—not an impossible thought in an age when the economics of the industry cause fashions to change so quickly—bears would be *in*.

**Ron:** There's been some mobilization around AIDS, but otherwise bears are hardly political creatures.

**Michael:** I do think that there is a patina of anticlass bias in bear culture but this is actually a fantasy of working-class life. It's an idealization that implies that the working class is more masculine and natural than those of greater influence and wealth and looks. But this is a fantasy and one that is at totally at odds with real people's real lives.

**Ron:** Unfortunately, bear clubs tend to further stratify their members into inner circles—the A-bears—and the rest of the group. Bear contests idealize pretty-boy bears—sometimes called Glamour Bears over the rest of the unfortunate plain-Jane bears. It's the same old looks-ism all over again.

**Michael:** My point exactly. Bear culture, like all socially constructed cultures based on certain identifiable attributes, becomes hierarchical.

**David:** Yes, bears are becoming more and more like everyone else. They are the sweater queens of the nineties, but instead of wearing their angora over their bodies, the fur is applied directly to the skin.

**Ron:** Very good. Final comments?

**Michael:** I am glad that—in this increasingly mandated world of sexual and body conformity—bears have created a new and approved way for gay men to look. The point, it seems to me, is to create endless ways for people to look and to make sure that, no matter how someone looks, they are not ostracized, ignored, or discriminated against.

**David:** Bear life, like gay life in general, is part of American culture, not separate from it. And it has the same limitations and problems as American culture. Insofar as bears have become exclusive and hierarchical, it is because American culture is. Bear culture denies this because America denies its classist base. I think Michael and I are in virtual agreement.

**Ron:** Great. Thank you both very much.

# Chapter 28

# Laid Bear: Masculinity with All the Trappings

Thomas McCann

> He had coal black hair, thinning just a little in front, and just a touch of grey on the sides. His beard . . . was as thick as carpet and black as a crow . . . this stud was fur-covered from head to foot.
>
> In the Clouds, *BEAR* 31

Blessed with a fertile imagination, like many other bear-identified gay men, I can read the above quote and, with my mind's eye, conjure up a vivid picture. Such written images are designed to arouse. And arouse they do. Pushing the collective button, guiding our fantasies, and leading us into a world where every man is hairy, willing, and able. Yet how much of my own experience of bear culture do I bring to that "picture" and how much is being created for me—fed to me?

Gay men do not exist within a vacuum. Each one of us has been influenced to varying degrees by the images around us, and specifically by the specialist gay press. In the case of bears, the proliferation of these images, both visual and written, has intensified over the last few years with the steady growth of bear-oriented books and magazines. Where once bears had to content themselves with Chris Nelson's *The Bear Cult* and *BEAR* magazine, they can now choose between a variety of other magazines catering both to "mainstream" bears (e.g., *American Bear, American Grizzly, German Bear, G.R.U.F., Southern Cumfort*) or more special-interest bears (e.g., *Daddy Bear*), and even bear 'zines. In addition, there are the images of bears as presented in other books and magazines, which, while not specifically aimed at a bear readership, still manage to appeal in terms of both their visuals and text (e.g., *Handjobs, Daddy*).

All of these publications have a clear idea of the type of men they wish to present. An aspiring porn writer must first examine closely the kind of stories printed in his magazine of choice. In addition, they will often be constrained by the writer's guidelines provided by the prospective employer (i.e., the magazine editor), which list many (if not all) of the standard requirements necessary to make the manuscript acceptable: X + Y + Z = bear porn, for example. Finally, the manuscript must then be filtered through the editor's own subjective selection process. Imaginative scenarios are not the priority—the formula will always take precedent. The iconography is defined, and as Wright (1997) has pointed out, the gay mass media sells consumable, standardized images of "real" bears. Indeed, "the promulgation of idealizing bears in the gay mass media . . . is the single most powerful force in the current construction of bears. The explicit, often intense, and ubiquitous sexual imagery of the gay media and advertising has undoubtedly had tremendous influence in shaping many gay men's sexuality" (Wright, 1997, p. 9).

The primary intention of this chapter is to examine the types of images presented to us in bear erotica—the stories contained within the various mainstream bear publications—in order to determine and discuss what exactly a bear is, in erotic terms. Can bears be erotically defined as a group apart from, say, the types of men described in *Men* or *Drummer?* Are bears intrinsically interested in different forms of sex or erotic play than other gay men, or are we broadly similar to other gay men? To do this, I have analyzed a sizable number of erotic stories from a variety of gay publications. Examination of the results of this study will, I hope, provide some further clues to what it is to be a bear.

## *METHODOLOGY*

In trying to define the type of man represented in bear erotica, it was necessary to examine a broad range of magazines. These included *BEAR*, *American Bear,* and *Daddy Bear,* abbreviated in this chapter as B, AB, and DB respectively. All of the stories in each chosen issue were analyzed on the premise that a wide selection of tastes would be catered to in each issue of the magazine, if not necessarily in each story. Analysis of the resulting data was used to define what bear erotica is. This was then compared with other genres of gay erotica, most notably, those from the gay mainstream (e.g., *Advocate Men, Indulge*) and from Leather/SM publications (e.g., *Drummer, Mach*) in order to determine the similarities and differences which may exist between the various genres of erotica within the gay male market, both in terms of mainstream representation and also by comparison with another niche group.

## *BEAR EROTICA*

A total of twenty-two stories, derived from bear-oriented publications, were analyzed for this study. These are representative of the bear erotica currently available. The term "bear" is used widely in the various stories, and the context in which it is used varies from the cuddly and comfortable: "the big Teddy bear came over" (The Summer of 1980 Chronicles, AB1/4); "breaks into a big teddy bear smile" (Fuzz, AB1/2); "Randell gave me a big bear hug" (The Three Bears and Me, AB1/4), to the nondescriptive, but understood: "He waved at the bear on the porch" (14 Days in July, AB1/2); "He was one of the most handsome bears I'd ever seen" (bearwood, AB1/3), or where the term is contextualized, in terms of other physical attributes: "'You fuckin' hot bear,' he whispered, rubbing my short hair and beard" (The Exhibit, AB2/2) to situations where the term is sexualized, or used in such a context as to make it very much part of the erotic charge: "you big fuckin' bear, how I'd like to ride you for a few hours and take care of that fat dick of yours" (14 Days in July, AB1/2).

In these various ways, the use of the word helps to strengthen the reader's identification with the participants of the story. The term is really only used in bear erotica, and did not feature as a descriptive term in the other genres of erotica analyzed.

### Number of Participants

Of the twenty-two stories analyzed, seventeen (77 percent) had just two participants, while the remaining five (23 percent) had two or more characters.

### Physical Appearance

Analysis of physical appearance can be classified into four major categories. Fifty-four characters were featured in total. Some of these were not described (usually the protagonist), but for the remainder certain features were of primary importance, given that they were almost universally mentioned (see Table 28.1). These will be discussed in order of their relative importance. It should be noted that all of the characters described were white.

### Facial Hair

This is, perhaps, the prime characteristic ascribed to bears, and it is clearly reflected in the character descriptions. Of the thirty-seven (68.5 percent) characters whose facial hair, or the lack of, is alluded to, a full twenty-eight (51.9 percent) had beards. A further seven (13 percent) had other forms of facial hair (e.g., goatees) while one (1.8 percent) had a moustache and only one (1.8 percent) was clean shaven. Facial hair is eroticized extensively in the majority of the stories and clearly is a significant attribute. This ranges from the descriptive, where the presence of facial hair denotes attractiveness: "He's just your type—a bear—dark hair and a nice, full beard. He's wearing a flannel shirt unbuttoned. . . . You can see thick fur from his neck to mid tummy" (Fuzz, AB1/2); ". . . my new nervous habit was playing with my beard—a common quirk among my bear buddies" (Trembler, AB1/3), to comments on the mutual attraction of having a beard: "We took turns nibbling and nuzzling our way through each other's beards" (Helping Hand, B31); "We chewed each other's beards and licked the sweat from our faces" (Reach the Peak, B20), to the more sensual, where facial hair is eroticized as part of sexual activity: "We licked his balls from either side. We slathered our tongues up . . . the shaft until we felt a hot bead

TABLE 28.1. Bearish Physical Attributes

| Magazine | Facial Hair | | | | | Body Hair | | | | Body Shape | | |
|---|---|---|---|---|---|---|---|---|---|---|---|---|
| | % Described | Beard | Goatee | Moustache | Other | % Described | Hairy | Smooth | | % Described | Stocky/Musc. | Thin |
| Bear | 68.5 | 51.9 | 13 | 1.8 | 1.8 | 64.8 | 63 | 1.8 | | 42.6 | 39 | 3.6 |
| Mainstream | 5.5 | 0 | 0 | 3.6 | 1.9 | 38.9 | 25.9 | 13 | | 51.9 | 48.2 | 3.7 |
| SM | 20 | 6 | 4 | 8 | 2 | 24 | 20 | 4 | | 58 | 58 | 0 |

*309*

running down our beards." (The Summer of 1980 Chronicles, AB1/4); "I moved down his chest, pausing long enough to scratch my brick-colored beard over his nipples" (Poleclimber, B30); "I rubbed his meat back and forth across my face and beard. . . . Its earthy smell excited my passion" (The Exhibit, AB2/2).

All of this culminates, of course, in more direct sexualization/ fetishization of facial hair, in which ejaculation and facial hair are directly linked: "I'm gonna nail you right in your fuckin' beard with my jizz" (Helping Hand, B31); ". . . he moaned with satisfaction as I fucked his black fur-framed mouth" (The Exhibit, AB2/2); "the first surge sent a rope of cum onto his beard. . . . Globs of my semen dripped from his beard onto his chest" (Reach the Peak, B20).

*Body Hair*

This is clearly a significant bear feature. Of the thirty-five (64.8 percent) characters described as hirsute, thirty-four (63 percent) were described as having hair on their bodies, with just one (1.8 percent) described as hairless. Body hair is frequently described as being attractive, or desirable: "furry chest of death" (Fuzz, AB1/2). It may also be described in terms of tactile pleasure: "He ran his hand up Paul's back to feel the silky hair that continued up Paul's back up to his neck" (Paul's Opening Night, B27); "My fingers gripped and clung to the hair on his back" (Santa's Sackful, B46). Or body hair may be sexualized, as with beards, to combine ejaculation and fetishization: "I pulled out of his hot butt, pulled off the rubber and strung my cum all over his hairy chest" (The Summer of 1980 Chronicles, AB1/4).

*Body Shape*

This is not such a defining characteristic, although still clearly an important one. Of the twenty-three (42.6 percent) characters whose body shape was described, twenty-one (39 percent) were described as being stocky (not fat) or muscular. Two characters (3.6 percent) were described as being thin.

## Additional Features

Under this heading are included greying hair or baldness. These features were included in just five characters, where five were grey and one was, in addition, balding.

Not surprisingly, the primary defining feature of bears in erotica is their hairiness. When described, the typical bear almost always has facial and/or body hair. The men described have stocky to muscular bodies and are definitely not fat. They may, in a few cases, be greying or balding.

## Tenderness

A number of practices may be associated with tenderness both leading into, and as part of, the sex scene itself. These traits conform to the conventions of typical bear behavior—affectionate and demonstrative—and are indicative of some form of gentleness and male bonding: "The bear cop falls asleep in your arms . . . your hand resting on his hairy belly, your face nuzzled against his furry back" (Fuzz, AB1/2). Kissing is described in twenty (90.9 percent) of the stories, while hugging and body licking are described in eleven (50 percent) and twelve (54.5 percent), respectively (see Table 28.2).

## Sexual Practices

### Sucking

This is by far the most common sexual practice described in bear erotica, with all the stories having it as a central feature of the action (see Table 28.3). A total of forty acts were described and of these, nineteen (47.5 percent) described the protagonist as sucking some

TABLE 28.2. Percentage of Genres of Erotica Containing the Following Tactile Actions

|  | Kiss | Hug | Lick |
|---|---|---|---|
| Bear | 90.9 | 50 | 54.5 |
| Mainstream | 66.7 | 28.6 | 42.9 |
| SM | 40 | 0 | 5 |

TABLE 28.3. Percentage of Genres of Erotica Containing the Following Sex Acts

|  | Suck | Fuck | Tits | Finger | Mast. | Rim | Frottage |
|---|---|---|---|---|---|---|---|
| Bear | 100 | 86.3 | 86.3 | 63.6 | 54.5 | 50 | 27.2 |
| Mainstream | 86.4 | 63.6 | 61.9 | 66.7 | 47.6 | 54.2 | 19 |
| SM | 75 | 45 | 50 | 35 | 0 | 30 | 0 |

other character. In seventeen (42.5 percent) the protagonist gets sucked. More than half of the situations described involved mutual sucking: ". . . he moaned with satisfaction as I fucked his black fur-framed mouth" (The Exhibit, AB2/2).

*Fucking*

This closely follows oral sex as being the most common sexual practice described, with fucking scenes present in nineteen (86.3 percent) of the stories. From the twenty-seven acts described, the protagonist takes the active role in fourteen (52 percent) and the passive role in eleven (48 percent). Interestingly, there were no descriptions of the protagonist fucking and getting fucked in the same story: "Fuck me, you goddam Daddy Bear" (Bearwood, AB1/3).

*Tit Play*

This is a particularly common sex practice, being described in nineteen cases (86.3 percent): ". . . reached around front to hunt for the pink nipples almost lost in his chest hair" (Paul's Opening Night, B27).

*Finger Fucking*

This is also a popular sexual activity, being described in fourteen cases (63.6 percent).

*Masturbation*

This is slightly less common, being mentioned in just twelve cases (54.5 percent).

## Rimming

This is described in eleven cases (50 percent): ". . . then I dove in, bathing every crevice with spittle. His hair matted into dark wads and spikes, becoming plastered to his fleshy purple sphincter as I drove my tongue ever deeper" (Santa's Sackful, B46).

## Frottage/Body Rubbing

This is described in six cases (27.2 percent).

## **Physical Attributes**

Under this heading are listed various physical attributes which may contribute to either the erotic charge of the story or of a particular character. None of these attributes featured significantly, the most common being the eroticization of body odor or sweat (mentioned in five stories [22.7 percent]), in either a general way, e.g., ". . . his fur was moist and smelled of a day's worth of fresh, manly sweat" (Helping Hand, B31) or more specifically, when armpits were also eroticized (one, or 4.5 percent), e.g., ". . . giving me a good view of the forest of dense hair in his armpits, and a whiff of the musky maleness that emanated from them" (In the Clouds, B31); "I remember breathing deep every time he went by . . . the faint, but oniony aroma from the man's armpits and chest . . . there was even a whiff of that special and wholly erotic masculine tang that can only be found in the crotch sweat of a horny man" (West Texas Riggers, B29).

Smegma, or cock cheese, was mentioned in three stories (13.5 percent), and would appear to be a fairly specialist interest, e.g., "I pulled back the thick foreskin, revealing his mild, cheesy surprise and lovingly licked and cleaned every speck with my tongue" (Lost Dad, DB3/2); ". . . savouring the salt-and-meat taste of dicksweat and dickmusk and dicklube" (Field Work, B20).

## **SM Practices**

In keeping with the style of bear erotica, these practices, where described or alluded to, are in all cases at the "soft" end of SM, i.e., mild bondage, ass slapping, etc (see Table 28.4).

TABLE 28.4. Percentage of Genres of Erotica Containing the Following SM Practices

|  | Piss | Body Mod. (P/T) | Pain | Leather | Shave | Toys | Bondage | M/S | Boots |
|---|---|---|---|---|---|---|---|---|---|
| Bear | 31.8 | 18 (9/9) | 4.5 | 4.5 | 4.5 | 4.5 | 0 | 0 | 0 |
| Mainstream | 23.8 | 14.3 (9.5/4.8) | 4.8 | 0 | 4.8 | 9.8 | 0 | 0 | 0 |
| SM | 45 | 35 (20/15) | 70 | 35 | 15 | 10 | 25 | 30 | 30 |

*Piss*

This was by far the most popular practice, either actual golden showers or simply by using piss as an erotic device (i.e., mentioning that characters had to piss, or had just done so, or two characters watching each other piss). Seven (31.8 percent) of the stories featured this: "His cock dangled above Jahme's head. He spread his legs wide so his cock lowered into Jahme's mouth. . . . It came slowly at first, musk and salt, then faster than Jahme could swallow. It exploded out of his nose, out of his mouth, around the massive cockhead. The Chief pulled out with a pop, piss streaming into Jahme's open mouth, splashing onto his red pelt, matting it. Jahme lapped up as much as he could . . ." (Bear Island, B46).

*Body Modification*

Two (9 percent) featured piercing, while a further two (9 percent) mentioned tattoos: ". . . a small tattoo of a bear just next to the base of his dick" (14 Days in July, AB1/2).

*Physical Pain*

Only one story (4.5 percent) involved pain of any description (mild beating with a riding crop), while another featured some ass slapping.

*Leather*

Leather is only featured in one story (4.5 percent), where one of the participants is a judge in a leather bear competition. The character in this story also wears chaps: "Everywhere I looked there were hot leather bears, their chest hair matted and damp . . ." (Oh Daddy, AB2/2).

## Body Shaving

This is mentioned in only one story (4.5 percent), where one of the characters has shaved balls.

## Sex Toys

Surprisingly, given the frequency of their depiction in visual erotica, and the large market for them, sex toys are featured in only one story (4.5 percent).

## Location

The place where sexual activity occurred was not always described. In most cases, it was at the house of one of the participants, but it also occurred in a variety of non-gay-identified locations, for example, outdoors, on a plane, in an art gallery, office, bookstore, or, in one particularly memorable instance, Santa's cave. In only three of the stories could the locations be described as "gay," i.e., gay bar, gay resort, and cruising rest stop.

## Occupation

Interestingly, of all of the occupations mentioned (twenty-eight) relatively few could be termed "blue-collar," e.g., oil-rig workers (two), and construction workers (three). A further three were police officers, while the rest ranged from academics and craftsmen to white-collar professionals.

## MAINSTREAM GAY EROTICA

Twenty-two stories were analyzed from a range of magazines including *Advocate Men* and *Men*. Thirteen (59 percent) of the stories featured two characters while nine (41 percent) featured more than two characters. Fifty-four characters were mentioned in total.

### *Facial Hair*

Three characters (5.5 percent) were described: two (3.6 percent) had a moustache, and one (1.9 percent) was clean shaven (see Table 28.1).

### *Body Hair*

Twenty-one characters (38.9 percent) were described, fourteen (25.9 percent) of which were hairy (though usually not excessively) and seven (13 percent) smooth. One character was mentioned with slightly receding hair. Body or facial hair was never eroticized.

### *Body Shape*

Twenty-eight (51.9 percent) were described in total: twenty-six (48.2 percent) were muscular or stocky and two (3.7 percent) were thin. Standard erotica contained the highest proportion of nonwhite participants, including Latinos, Native Americans, and African Americans.

### *Tenderness*

Kissing was a major practice, featured in fourteen stories (66.7 percent). Licking (nine, or 42.9 percent), and, to a lesser extent, hugging (six, or 28.6 percent) was also featured (see Table 28.2).

### *Sexual Practices*

Sucking was the most common sexual practice, featured in nineteen (86.4 percent) of the stories (see Table 28.3). Thirty acts were described in total: in eighteen (60 percent) the protagonist was active, while in twelve (40 percent) he was passive. Nine cases involved mutual sucking. Fucking featured in fourteen of the stories (63.6 percent). A total of nineteen acts were described: in eleven

(57.5 percent) the protagonist was active and in eight (42.1 percent) passive. Of other sexual practices mentioned, the most common were: tit play (thirteen, or 61.9 percent), finger fucking (fourteen, or 66.7 percent), rimming (eleven, or 52.4 percent), masturbation (ten, or 47.6 percent), and frottage (fourteen, or 19 percent).

## *Physical Attributes*

Sweat was commonly featured (eleven, or 52.4 percent), with armpits more specifically mentioned in two (9.5 percent) stories.

## *SM Practices*

Pissing was the most common practice, mentioned in five stories (23.8 percent). Other practices were much less common, including piercing (two, or 9.5 percent), tattoos (one, or 4.8 percent), physical pain (one, or 4.8 percent), shaving (one, or 4.8 percent), enemas (one, or 4.8 percent), and sex toys (two, or 9.5 percent) (see Table 28.4).

## *Location*

Settings varied and included army camps, apartments, condo swimming pools, a doctor's office, garden center, home, truck, hotels, office, elevator. The only "gay" space mentioned was the back alley of a gay bar.

## *Occupation*

Occupations varied, but fell mainly within the realm of traditional gay fantasy—soldier, marine, doctor, writer, businessman, gardener, physical therapist, etc. Interestingly, a number of the characters were mentioned as being "straight" or "straight-identified," or "closeted," suggesting that this is of some importance to readers of mainstream erotica.

## *LEATHER/SM EROTICA*

Twenty stories were analyzed from a range of magazines including *Drummer, Mach, International Leatherman,* and *Powerplay.*

Ten (50 percent) of the stories featured two characters with the other ten (50 percent) featuring more than two characters, including one with a robot. Fifty characters were mentioned in total.

### *Facial Hair*

Ten (20 percent) characters were described; four (8 percent) had a moustache, three (6 percent) were bearded, two (4 percent) had goatees, and one (2 percent) was clean shaven (see Table 28.1).

### *Body Hair*

This was described for twelve characters (24 percent); ten (20 percent) were hairy and two (4 percent) were smooth. Two characters were mentioned who were greying. Body or facial hair was rarely eroticized.

### *Body Shape*

Twenty-nine (58 percent) were described and all were muscular or stocky. The sample contained one nonwhite participant (Latino).

### *Tenderness*

Kissing featured in eight stories (40 percent). Licking featured just once (5 percent) and hugging not at all (see Table 28.2).

### *Sexual Practices*

Sucking was the most common sexual practice, featured in fifteen (75 percent) of the stories (see Table 28.3). Twenty acts were described in total: in thirteen (65 percent) the protagonist was active, while in seven (35 percent) he was passive. One situation described mutual sucking, while another involved biting more than sucking. Fucking featured in nine (45 percent) of the stories. A total of fourteen acts were described: in six (42.9 percent) the protagonist was active and in seven (50 percent) passive. One case (7 percent) involved a sandwich. Of other sexual practices mentioned, the most common were: tit play (ten, or 50 percent), finger fucking (seven, or 35 percent) and rimming (six, or 30 percent).

*Physical Attributes*

Sweat was commonly featured (four, or 20 percent).

*SM Practices*

As anticipated, this was the predominant feature of this form of erotica (see Table 28.4). Pain (fourteen, or 70 percent), of some form, was the predominant feature. This varied from the relatively mild (similar to that described in bear or standard erotica, e.g., mild ass slapping) through to burning, electrocution, rape, and death. Piss was the most common feature, mentioned in nine stories (45 percent). Other features included piercing (four, or 20 percent) although these included stories of actually being pierced, instead of just having piercings, tattoos (three, or 15 percent), smoking (three, or 15 percent), leather (seven, or 35 percent), shaving (three, or 15 percent), enemas (two, or 10 percent) and sex toys (two, or 10 percent), bondage (five, or 25 percent), master/servant (six, or 30 percent), and boot licking (six, or 30 percent). Minor interests included shit, eating dog food, drinking piss, scarification, and toe cheese.

*Location*

Settings varied and included army camps, apartments, and a summer camp. The only "gay" spaces mentioned were a sex club and a rest room.

*Occupation*

These varied, but were rarely described. Typical examples include a miner, cop, soldiers, and prisoners.

## *DISCUSSION*

There were two messages after gay liberation, the first that it was okay to get fucked, and the second that you didn't have to go after straight trade. Also as the Stonewall generation were getting older the men in the magazines were a little older, butcher, hairier, bigger (Michael Bronski in Rowe, 1995). Ongoing debates within the bear community often focus on what the distinguishing characteristics of bears are. While facial and body hair are frequently identified as being the sine qua non of being a bear, there are others who would choose bear "qualities" (e.g., tenderness, being in touch with one's feelings) over the visual aspects. These debates have led to the subdivision of the original term "bear" to now include otters, wolves, behrs, and a host of other, more specific bear categories, including the Girth and Mirth bear, the hippie bear [the muscle bear, *LKW*], or the glamour bear. Leather bears are another distinct group, providing a crossover between bears and the leather/SM communities.

These subtleties and differences, however, were not at all evident from the descriptions in the analyzed stories (apart, perhaps, from some examples of hippie and leather bears). Instead, the featured bears mostly conformed to given stereotypes, similar to those outlined by Silverstein and Picano (1992). According to them, the bear look is

> all-natural, rural, even woodsy . . . Full beards are common, as are bushy moustaches. Bears are stay at home wild men who enjoy football, trout fishing, carpentry, plumbing, and electrical repair work. They're just regular guys—only they're gay. The clothing . . . [includes] wool workshirts . . . wide belts with big buckles holding up torn-leg shorts or standard denims. Bears wear heavy hiking boots, with Pendleton shirt jackets. Bears are definitely hairy. . . . Their bodies are strong and masculine. They've got weight and are proud . . . to show it. . . . Everything about bears is several hands bigger than usual. (p. 130)

This narrow definition, however, concentrates just on how bears look (outdoorsy) and their interests (blue collar). It merely reinforces the stereotype. Life is far more complex. What of all the urban, middle-class, white-collar bears we all know and love— teachers, bankers, computer programmers? Are these men just bear wannabes? What does this definition really offer our community—"You might wear the uniform but you're not a real bear"?

According to Wright (1997), being a bear may signify an image, but it can also indicate an attitude (or lack of one), an icon of desirability, or a refusal to submit to categorization. Clearly, therefore, the term "bear" carries with it a multitude of meanings, and each self-identifying bear will have his own idea of what it means to him to be a bear. Bear erotica, however, does not allow for complicated multiple meanings and instead provides us with a composite, i.e., what the generic bear is and does.

As previously mentioned, facial and/or body hair is often used as a primary indicator of whether someone is, or is not, a bear. Both of these features score very highly when compared to erotica from other sources (Table 28.1). In short, bears are hairy. They have beards (either full or goatee) and, in the majority of cases, body hair, too. Hair is erotic and seen to be so. Bears are also stocky or muscular, to a lesser extent, perhaps, than in other forms of erotica (Table 28.1), but it is still an important feature. This would appear to contradict the notion that bears are heavyset or overweight. The evidence suggests that bears themselves do not want to read about erotic encounters with, or between, heavier men. Magazines and clubs exist where body weight, in and of itself, is eroticized (e.g., *Big Ad*, *Girth & Mirth*). However, mainstream bear erotica steers clear of this area almost completely. [*Big Ad*, *Bulk*, and similar magazines cater to heavyset bear fantasy and readership. *LKW*]

The stories contained within bear-oriented magazines do not stand alone. They are printed alongside photographic images of bear "pinups." A previous study on bears concluded that the visual images presented in bear media were quite different from those in, say, *Advocate Men* (Locke, 1997). The current analysis of written erotica confirms this notion that the men eroticized are visually distinctive from other forms of erotica. I would, however, go further to also suggest that the sexual acts featured in bear-oriented magazines differ from those described elsewhere (see Tables 28.1-28.4).

Wright (1997) suggests that bears are engaged with hegemonic masculinity, and thus, they can be contradictory (masculine and nurturing) in terms of their gender identity. The masculine aspects of bears are clearly demonstrated by their physical descriptions, which emphasize secondary physical characteristics (e.g., body hair). The more nurturing aspect of bears is expressed by how the characters described value tenderness in other men. Aspects of physical contact which may be indicative of this (e.g., kissing, licking, hugging) featured much more strongly in bear erotica than in any other (Table 28.2). This would suggest that bears themselves want to read stories in which these activities occur, since these activities are important for bears.

In terms of the sexual acts performed in bear erotica, we differ significantly from other groups (Table 28.3). Bears are portrayed as enjoying sucking, fucking, and tit play more than any other form of activity, and more than in other genres of erotica. With regard to fingering, rimming, masturbation, and frottage, bears are the same as mainstream erotica. This would suggest, perhaps, that bears are basically conservative (vanilla) in their sexual habits, but enthusiastically so!

Previously, Dyer (1985) had suggested that in gay erotica

> the narrative is never organised around the desire to be fucked, but around the desire to ejaculate (whether or not following on from anal intercourse). Thus although at the level of public representation, gay men may be thought of as deviant and disruptive of masculine norms because we assert the pleasures of being fucked and the eroticism of the anus, in our pornography this takes a back seat. (p. 27)

Waugh (1995) suggests that this may not be completely the case, and this is confirmed, to a certain extent, by the current findings.

In bear erotica the protagonist both fucks (52 percent) and gets fucked (48 percent). These figures are broadly similar to those derived from mainstream erotica (57.5 percent and 42.1 percent respectively) and SM (42.9 percent and 50 percent respectively). Furthermore, the predominance of finger fucking and rimming as sexual activities (Table 28.3) would suggest that eroticization of the anus is a significant feature. That these figures appear to contradict Dyer's assertion may have more to do with the fact that his work dates from the early 1980s, whereas the current work is based on work published more than fifteen years later, a period of significant change in attitudes to sex in general, and specifically to gay sex.

The final area of analysis revealed that in terms of SM practices, bear and mainstream erotica were very similar in that these practices were not a significant feature of either (Table 28.4). This would suggest that groups, such as leather bears, will continue to remain on the margins of both groups, although they would, perhaps, find more in common with the leather/SM community, where, at least in terms of sexual practices, they are united.

While much of the previous discussion was concerned with the progressive aspects of gay erotica, there are also negative aspects. Erotica, as a genre, is fundamentally conservative. For example, Waugh (1995) suggested that in gay erotica, there is a taboo on descriptions or depictions of male-female sex, effeminacy, age, obesity, and drag. In other words, aspects of sexuality with which many gay men feel uncomfortable or unsure of. This mainstreaming of gay sexuality was confirmed by the current study, in which none of these were featured.

Of perhaps even greater significance was the fact that in bear erotica all of the characters described were white. The gay community is not exclusively white, as anyone at a bear function in the United States can testify, and this needs to be more accurately reflected in the magazines. Locke (1997), in his study of bear images in the magazines, noted that although the men featured were mostly white, there were exceptions. This has not yet filtered through to the written word, and is something that requires change.

A final but important point is that bear-oriented magazines are part of the larger sex industry, and that for all of their apparent altruism and attempts to produce a Brotherhood of Bears (via club pages, or the featuring of bear events, or contact advertising), they are ultimately about profit. Should we, therefore, be surprised to find that these magazines offer a homogenized, or idealized, image of a bear—one designed to have the broadest commercial appeal? These magazines have built on and developed what was initially a grass roots initiative, although this has since been repackaged for a wider consumption. Bear images are now sold to an ever-increasing circle of admirers (as evidenced by Catalina producing videos aimed at the bear market).

The images now being purveyed will have a major influence on the self-image of new generations of bears. We are not alone in having to confront this issue. Michael Bronski, quoted in Rowe (1995), noted how every month in *Mandate* a variety of gay stereotypes were featured, including "cowboys, leather guys, butch men . . . (and how) John Preston would talk about how this meant that people all over America would have something to model themselves on . . . (but I felt that it was) taking away people's imaginations and giving them a package . . . that they had to live up to" (p. 59). This dichotomy, where we are presented with something which is both liberating but at the same time restricting was previously noted by Waugh (1995). He suggested that gay erotica functions as a progressive, educative, or ideological (consciousness-raising) force, working against self-oppression, the closet, and isolation. At the same time, however, it is also a potentially regressive force, since it valorizes sexism, looks-ism, sizeism, racism, and ageism.

The duality of erotica, being both progressive and regressive at the same time, allows us to blur the edges between the images and messages with which we are presented, and what these are showing or saying to us. Our understanding of whether the image is us or we are the image becomes more difficult to unravel. Thus, we internalize the mixed messages with which we are presented—on one hand reveling in our liberation and liberalism while at the same time binding ourselves ever deeper into a construct which is not of our making. It is all a little like Dr. Frankenstein making his monster. At some point we need to step back and ask ourselves whether what has been created really is in our image, or is it something that lives and breathes all on its own?

## BIBLIOGRAPHY

Dyer, R. 1985. Male Gay Porn: Coming to Terms. *Jump Cut* 30: 25-29. Reprinted as Coming to Terms: Gay Pornography. In: *Only Entertainment* (Richard Dyer, Ed.). Routledge: New York (1992).

Locke, P. 1997. Male Images in the Gay Mass Media and Bear-Oriented Magazines: Analysis and Contrast. In: *The Bear Book: Readings in the History and Evolution of a Gay Male Subculture* (L. Wright, Ed.). Harrington Park Press, Binghamton, NY, pp. 103-140.

Rowe, M. 1995. *Writing Below the Belt: Conversations with Erotic Authors.* Masquerade Books: New York.

Silverstein, C. and Picano, F. 1992. *The New Joy of Gay Sex.* Harper Collins: New York.

Waugh, T. 1995. Men's Pornography: Gay vs Straight. In: *Out in Culture: Gay, Lesbian and Queer Essays on Popular Culture* (C.K. Creekmur and A. Doty, Eds). Cassell: London, pp. 307-327.

Wright, L. 1997. Theoretical bears. In: *The Bear Book: Readings in the History and Evolution of a Gay Male Subculture* (L. Wright, Ed.). Harrington Park Press: Binghamton, NY, pp. 1-17.

The following magazines were used as part of this survey:

*Advocate Men* (1/94, 9/94, 11/96, 1/97, 3/97, 3/98)
*American Bear* (1/1, 1/2, 1/3, 1/4, 1/5, 1/6, 2/2)
*BEAR* (16, 17, 20, 27, 29, 30, 31, 46)
*Daddy Bear* (3/2)
*Drummer* (197)
*Honcho* (17/10)
*International Leatherman* (9, 12)
*Mach* (38)
*Men* (10/97)
*Powerplay* (2/5, 16)
*Tough Customers* (8)

Chapter 29

# In Goldilocks's Footsteps: Exploring the Discursive Construction of Gay Masculinity in Bear Magazines

Elizabeth A. Kelly
Kate Kane

*El hombre es como el oso: mientras más feo más hermoso*[1]

Colombian saying

### WE COME UPON THIS PROJECT

Maybe it begins like the fairy tale in which once upon a time Goldilocks finds herself an uninvited guest at the home of the three bears. Or maybe it begins over coffee in a Chicago cybercafé when a friend of Beth's describes *Opposite Sex* and mentions that the editors are looking for a lesbian take on "bears"—a category of gay male sexuality that Beth's never heard of and is astonished to hear described. Within minutes, she is watching him pull various bear publications off the porn rack at the back of the lesbian and gay bookstore. Images of large, hairy, preponderantly white, male bodies—mostly naked, some playing with penises (their own or other men's) materialize before her eyes.

At first glance, these images are both fascinating and repulsive. Beth has always thought that the tyranny of slenderness was even

Reprinted with permission from *Opposite Sex: Gay Men on Lesbians, Lesbians on Gay Men,* Sara Miles and Eric Rofes, eds., © New York University Press, 1998.

more inscribed in gay male culture than in the normative "femininity" of compulsory heterosexuality to which she was thoroughly and oppressively socialized as a young girl and adolescent in the 1950s and 1960s and that she has spent most of her adult life resisting. It fascinates her to see bulky bodies idealized objects of gay male desire instead of the slender, buff Adonis types she would have expected. The depictions also repel: she finds problematic the naked male bodies, however hairy/smooth or heavy/slender, even when only seen in photographs and not in the flesh.[2] Later that evening, after the first flush of scholarly enthusiasm has worn off, Beth realizes she doesn't want to write this article alone. On the one hand, she wonders whether there might be connections between the bears and the "alternative public spheres" and "intentional communities" she has written about elsewhere.[3] But, on the other hand, she worries about the complications of being a lone, uninvited guest setting off to explore the bears. So she calls on Kate, a colleague who teaches the graduate course "Representations of the Body" and is not squeamish about naked men.

Kate's theoretical interests focus on bodies, boundaries, and categories. She has a friend who is a self-identified bear. An assignment to analyze gay bodies honored, valued, and desired their for largeness has great appeal to her. She immediately begins to explore the genre by quizzing her male colleagues at a lesbian and gay faculty potluck. She learns that the bear is not only a phenotype that deviates from the slender, smooth, altogether buff ideal of straight advertising and gay porn. Most of the colleagues she questions are "regular-guy" types, but all of them know of bears, and her queries evoke an assortment of definitions and responses. The gym queen recoils in horror: "Fat, hairy slobs!" Most of the men acknowledge an acquaintance with the type but disavow any personal connections to bear culture. A postlatent bear nods, "Ah, you mean the sociocultural minority of large, hairy men." There is consensus that a bear is defined by size ("a certain fleshiness") and hirsutism but less agreement on other factors such as height and age.

We learn that bears emerged as a gay male subculture in the early 1980s with a variety of forms of cultural expression, including bear bars, "clean and sober" social clubs, party weekends, conventions, and camping trips. A range of publications from porn magazines to compilations of personal ads, all focusing on bear culture in general or specific aspects of it, are available. Magazines such as *BEAR* and *American Bear* feature photo spreads of large men—most of whom are tattooed, bearded, and/or noticeably hairy—along with fiction, feature articles, and an impressive array of personal ads, often accompanied by photographs. Other publications cater to even more specialized interests. *Daddybear* focuses on intergenerational sexual relations between "daddy bears" and "bear cubs"; *Heavy Duty*, as the name implies, caters to those who desire large men; and *CR (Chiron Rising Magazine)* bills itself as offering "maturity with class" and features lots of gray- or white-haired men, intergenerational couples, and, unlike any of the others, ads for Sun Belt real estate firms and investment counselors. Although the age, hair, decorations, and size of the male bodies featured in these publications vary widely, the men depicted in the photographs and line drawings are almost exclusively white.

Kate's passion for names leads her to investigate the terminology used by gay men to mark their objects of desire. These are not unproblematic categories: a man who likes Asian men is a "rice queen"; one who admires Latinos is known variously as a "taco," "bean," "salsa," or "chili" queen; one who likes Caucasians is a "mayonnaise queen." In bell hooks's terms, this might be considered "eating the Others."[4] Kate muses about what to call a man who lusts after large hairy men—a "ranger" or a "honey queen?" Could one refer to a short bear as a "Boo-Boo?"[5] Kate's bear friend advises her to keep her silly pop-culture metaphors to herself. But Kate will not give up on one point: the bear is an interesting category in part because it designates a desiring subject and not only the object of lust.

A month goes by. Meanwhile, a package of bear magazines has arrived from San Francisco. On a warm midsummer afternoon, we meet. Kate has insisted that Beth not open the package unless both of us can be present. We decide to tape-record our reactions and conversation, in hopes that the discussion can serve as a point of reference for future analysis. The plain brown wrapper is removed with great ceremony. Nervous laughter and some fascinated perusal of images and texts ensue. At times, more than a little confusion reigns:

> **Kate:** I'm noticing that not all the penises in these pictures are erect.
> **Beth:** That rather escaped me—
> **Kate:** I think they're NOT—
> **Beth:** Well, is this erect? (pointing to an image) You know, it's been so long since I've seen one that I don't think I'd know an erect penis if I fell over one.
> **Kate:** I don't think it is [erect].
> **Beth:** Well, who could we call?

Eventually a few vague glimmers of thematization and analysis begin to emerge:

> **Kate:** I wasn't sure if there was anything to this beyond the shopping-mall theory of attraction; you were thinking that there might be something resistant going on.
> **Beth:** It seems to me that there might be a reading of this literature that draws on themes of resisting the commodification of the body and the commodification of sex. One thing that strikes me is that these are real people—these aren't gorgeous models.
> **Kate:** Yes, I do think we might be able to say something about these being grassroots-organized expressions of desire. This isn't unique to beardom; it's found in many marginalized sexual groups.
> **Beth:** Still, why would you want to hang your penis through a macramé hammock? Never having had a penis, this is hard for me to imagine.

Many of the photographs in the magazines we examined depict bodies and settings that are a far cry from the glossy techno-porn with the cold hard edges, huge erect dicks, and unattainable models gazing up and beyond the viewer that we usually associate with gay male iconography. There is a warm, fuzzy, countrified (if not nostalgic) quality to many of the images—hammocks, wagon wheels, flannel shirts, denim, woodsy settings.[6] Care and concern for others suffuse the verbal text accompanying bear iconography. A "Legal Perspectives" column in *BEAR* discussing "Assault, Battery, and Spousal Abuse" came as a surprise. With a few pronouns and referents changed, it could easily have been found in an early edition of

*MS* magazine.[7] In a 1990 column, "Bear Pause: Hug Your Teddy," the ethic of care becomes explicit when the author recalls jerking off to a picture of John Matuszak ("big, furry, friendly, and sexy" image) in his then-wife's copy of *Playgirl* magazine. This memory surfaces in the wake of Matuszak's death from a drug overdose, and the comment is simple: "Bears don't let bears die from drugs. We help each other out, it's not like that. How sad."[8]

It seems clear that a process of "reembodiment" is at work; a new discourse of gender and sexuality emerges from the texts before us. But it also seems to us that although sex and gender are focal points, the iconographies, articles, personal advertisements, trade ads, and fiction in the publications we examined presage the emergence of an alternative public sphere in which the textual configurations of sexuality and sociability are not merely articulated but enacted in ways that may be lending new meaning to the lives of the gay men who participate.

The bear "public sphere" is a fluid admixture of gay social and cultural practices—some established, such as bars, and some newly created or rediscovered, ranging from cybersex and online networking through two-step and country line-dance clubs to clean and sober barbecues, cruises, or day trips to the zoo.[9] A description of "Great Lakes Bear Pride," a Memorial Day weekend gathering of a thousand gay men at a Chicago hotel, includes Ferris wheel rides on Navy Pier and picnicking at a lakefront park, along with notes on the "Mr. Bear Pride" competition, hot sex parties, nipple piercing, and a raffle that netted more than $3,000 to benefit local queer charities.[10] At times, out-front sexuality seems to blend with out-front political rhetoric in bear publications. For example, an interview with Mr. International Bear 1996 includes an exhortation to activism and solidarity:

> The price for segregating ourselves is turning the country over to the Christian Coalition. There are a lot of people out there in "straight" society that choose to hate us simply because of who we love. If we don't come together as a community, the entire gay community, they are going to continue to do the bad stuff to us. . . . People need to get out there and register to vote, volunteer, and make a statement for themselves.[11]

If all this can be taken at face value, then perhaps bear cultural spaces provide a point of entry into the task of reconfiguring the sort of "democratic public spheres" theorized by Jürgen Habermas and others.[12]

It's not just the public sphere with its political possibilities that we notice, however. Beth confesses (with appropriate embarrassment) that she has long been an avid reader of short stories in "women's magazines"—*Good Housekeeping, Ladies' Home Journal,* and the like.[13] She is as struck by the similarities between formula fiction for straight women and the formula fiction found in *BEAR* and *American Bear* as she is by the differences. Whereas phrases such as "Daddy's boy's a good cocksucker" or "There's nothing like the taste of a cigar-smokin' man who's had his dick up your ass" will never appear in the pages of *Good Housekeeping,* romantic denouements on the order of "He folds me into an embrace, a long, strong sweetness. We both are trembling" certainly have.[14]

The personal ads in bear publications sometimes seem reminiscent of aspects of mid-1970s lesbian sexual expression. An 'attractive loving gay man bottom cub . . . seeks attractive masculine sexually aggressive gay white/hispanic/black man. . . . *I am looking for a top man who is gentle enough to cuddle*" (emphasis added). We wonder whether twenty years ago this would have made it to the printed page of most gay male publications. Another example is from a couple of men who are "regular Joes, living in the real world, not gay bars, and pretty much at ease with ourselves, innocent, devilish, honest, twisted, cuddly, kiss-able, hungry, eager to please, and be pleased." Change "Joe" to "Jane" and this could have been placed by many generic lesbian-feminists in 1976, ourselves included.[15]

The rhetoric is not, however, vanilla. Not by a long shot. There is also raunch—lots of body smells and body fluids, from sweat to semen, and everything in between. Some of the language seems straight out of *Home Improvement* or *Coach,* or any television sitcom that makes fun of the hypermasculine space where "manly men" want to belch and head for the woods and drink beer; the "manly man" likes the smell of "manly sweat" and "manly shit" and other "manly" secretions. Yet in contrast to the impenetrable hard body of the model clone "type" of gay masculinity that emerged in the 1970s, the bear's fleshy self is not threatened by penetration, humor, or tenderness.[16]

Moreover, in his very flesh, the bear is grounded in a dual materiality: besides the large present, there are also historical precedents. Many relate the popularity of bears to AIDS and the fear of emaciated bodies as signifying illness. We see a more complex dynamic at work, however. Similar to the way in which AIDS has debilitated and decimated gay male populations in the United States for nearly twenty years, in the mid-nineteenth century, tuberculosis raged in epidemic proportions. It affected both sexes, but young women were particularly vulnerable and often died at twice the rate of men in the same age group. Of one hundred women aged twenty in 1865, more than five would die of tuberculosis before reaching thirty, and nearly ten more would die of it before reaching fifty.[17] Everyone knew someone who suffered from the disease; unlike other epidemic illnesses, it was a constant presence in everyday life. Those who contracted tuberculosis faced—and everybody feared—a lengthy illness and a slow death.[18]

In the mid-nineteenth century, epidemic tuberculosis may morally have been embodied in women who attempted to triumph over fears of infection by affecting its symptoms—the fashionable female body of the day was slender, fragile, and submissive in the extreme.[19] The desire for delicacy was so powerful that simulated illness became stylish. Such unconscious expressions of solidarity with women who contracted the disease have served to somewhat anesthetize its dreaded impact.[20] But as the epidemic continued and hundreds of thousands of women died, an *embodied reaction* set in, and thin bodies became unfashionable. By 1880, popular medical theorists were equating amplitude and health. The large, hearty, buxom female body had become the model of beauty and (heterosexual) desirability, and it was no longer stylish to express solidarity with those who were ill.[21] Although the devastating impact of epidemic tuberculosis did not abate until well into the twentieth century (with the discovery of antibiotics), a voluptuous woman now symbolized, with her flesh, a specific form of denial.

We see parallel forms of denial of AIDS operating in the generously fleshed bear body in which amplitude and health once again cohere. The bear—at least iconographically—embodies comfort, security, and safety, perhaps even evoking the polymorphous perversity of infancy. Susan Bordo's *Unbearable Weight: Feminism, Western Culture, and the Body* begins with a reading of Delmore Schwartz's poem "The Heavy Bear."[22] She suggests as part of an extended discussion that "the bear is above all else a creature of instinct, of primitive need. Ruled by orality, by hunger, blindly 'mouthing' experience, seeking honey and sugar, he is 'in love' but with the most basic, infantile desires: to be soothed by sweet things, to discharge his hunger, to fall exhausted into stupor."[23]

We begin to see the bear publications as a set of what Kate calls "symptomatic texts" from which we can draw out discourses of gay male masculinity, but we are concerned about what conclusions we might reach. We wonder about the question of legitimacy—what grants us the right to say anything authoritative about constructions of gay male masculinity or sexual desire? Perhaps it is possible to look at bears as both challenge and inspiration. We wonder whether we are confronting a new gay male aesthetic in the process of defining itself both with and against the memories/experiences of other gay male aesthetic (for example, "queens," "clones," "swish") by both rejecting and incorporating elements of former styles?[24]

We realize that further investigations are in order. Beth wants more texts; Kate suggests arranging a field trip to "Bear Night" at a local bar, with her bear friend as a guide. We decamp to the local gay bookstore where we behave entirely in character. Kate makes for the gay male porn rack and spends half an hour selecting a pile of possible titles. Beth, meanwhile, wanders through the lesbian theory and mystery sections, trying not to feel embarrassed. We ultimately converge on a sofa in the bookstore's bay window, sorting through the pile of magazines, picking a representative selection. When it comes time to pay, Beth hangs back: "You go ahead and pay, Kate—I just want to check something I was looking at earlier." Her hope is that Kate will explain the unusual nature of our purchases to the young woman at the register. Kate tries to brazen out the moment but nonetheless finds herself explaining our research to the amused clerk. On way out of the store, we laugh ruefully. The Catholic confessional imperatives of childhood retain a powerful hold on both our adult imaginations despite the vast contextual dissonance between the white organdy dresses and veils of our First Holy Communions and this field trip to the porn rack at the queer bookstore.[25]

That evening, in her journal, Beth writes:

> Reading Ruth Behar tonight, I am struck by a realization.[26] Kate, with her insistence on attending to the bears' taxonomy that A. supplied from the Internet and on going with C. to the bear bar next week, is pushing me toward ethnography (with all its limitations). I, of course, am pulling her toward the textual analysis of the political theorist (with its limitations). Thus we seem to become, at least methodologically, more partial, more tentative, perhaps more fluid with regard to our work as this process unfolds.

Both of us deal in theory, but from different disciplinary perspectives; Kate's field is critical film and media studies, subsumed by cultural theory, and Beth's is political theory, with a strong feminist bent. Despite the "failures" of socialist experiments over the past decade, we refuse to relinquish our shared belief in a utopian ideal of a society that would benefit everyone, satisfying human needs and nurturing human creativity despite differences of sex, sexual preference, gender, gender preference, color, culture, age, size, abilities, or class. Our tentativeness about our "right" to undertake this project is thus fueled by the same values that propel its urgency. On one hand, how can we not engage in questions of how identity is signaled by and through the human body, of the role of the physical in acquiring and maintaining gender and sexual identity, and of how human bodies become vehicles for self-presentation when all these are central to the political ideals of empowerment, dignity, and respect we want to encourage? On the other hand, when the identities in question are not—indeed can never be (or become)—our own—how could we?

We realize that we are holding here a number of tenuous strands of history, politics, and culture. Our awareness of a reluctance to play into any presumption that we as women, a couple of fat dykes, can define experiences that are not and can never be our own is too much with us. Reluctantly, we conclude that ethnography is simply beyond us:

> **Kate:** I realized I couldn't face the field trip to the bar—it just sounds too much like a roomful of men.
> **Beth:** Well, wouldn't that be inevitable?
> **Kate:** Yes, but I'd underestimated that aspect of it—
> **Beth:** So pictures are one thing, the flesh quite another?

What we can do in these pages is raise some questions about possible readings and meanings of what we see in these snapshots (literal and metaphorical) of bears and bear culture, with an eye to alliance, not surveillance, border crossing, or invasion.

## CONFIGURING GAY MASCULINITY/DESIRE: THE BARE/BEAR BODY

It may be easier to be gay or lesbian today than it was twenty years ago, but in a society that remains predicated on compulsory heterosexuality, being gay, lesbian, or any of the other "alternatives" does not represent a free or easy choice. Historians have only recently begun to map the configurations and constructions of queer lives and communities.[27] The real stories of what the earthshaking shifts in these configurations and constructions in the latter half of the twentieth century have meant to gay men remain largely untold. From McCarthyism and Mattachine to Stonewall, Gay Liberation, disco, and "Don't Ask, Don't Tell" and with the decimating force of the AIDS pandemic looming for more than fifteen years, homophobic myths promulgated by mainstream media (and at times by the gay media as well) have all too often gone uncontested, along with the tendencies toward erotophobia that have blossomed in straight and gay culture since 1980.

As lesbians aware of the complicated and intertwining strands of individuality, community, culture, sexuality, iconography, and other representational practices that go into the construction of any forms of desire, we can only begin to imagine the difficulties faced by gay men who have had to "grapple with an ever-changing terrain" in the "struggle to erect edifices of hope" in the wake of AIDS.[28] Even though this chapter is not about AIDS, it seems impossible to talk about historical configurations of gay masculinity or sexuality without some acknowledgment of AIDS's differential impact on our communities.[29]

The politics of sexuality is not "just" about community or lifestyle choices, however. It is about desire and the delicate balances of pleasure, danger, and power attached to or flowing from moments of sexual intimacy and/or vulnerability. But we know so little about these things. Speaking of lesbian constructions of "butch/femme" desire, Amber Hollibaugh acutely captures this problem:

> I don't think we know very much about what the erotic engine is that makes us move. . . . The ways that we've constructed our ideas of sexuality are very tiny. It's critical that we be able to say to each other that this is not about style, not about roles as though we put them on because we bought them in a store. It's about loving each other. It's about caring passionately about each other's existence. It's about feeling each other's mouths on each other's bodies. That isn't small. . . . The desire between us is the engine that moves us.[30]

In short, a politics of sexuality is about embodied sex, embodied desire, embodied commitment, and the categories we use to express them. We do not see any good reasons for distinguishing between lesbian and gay male sexualities at this juncture, at which desire and categories such as butch/femme or bear remain abstractions, although we acknowledge that in actual practice, theoretical similarities may not emerge clearly or at all. This does not diminish the conceptual or practical utility of categorical formulations of sexual desire in the least. As Gayle Rubin pointed out:

> Our categories are important. We cannot organize a social life, a political movement, or our individual identities and desires without the fact that categories invariably leak and can never contain all the relevant "existing things" does not render them useless, only limited. Categories like "woman," "butch," "lesbian," or "transsexual" are all imperfect, historical, temporary, and arbitrary. We use them, and they mold us. We use them to construct meaningful lives, and they mold us historically spe-

cific forms of personhood. Instead of fighting for late classifications and impenetrable boundaries, let us strive to maintain a community that understands diversity as a gift, sees anomalies as precious, and treats all basic principles with a hefty dose of skepticism.[31]

The question becomes one of articulating the engines of desire that move bears forward (sexually and/or culturally), of distinguishing some of the categories in which these engines operate. In an article by Les K. Wright entitled "The Sociology of the Urban Bear," we find a helpful set of insights into the representation of bears and their culture.[32] Although Wright admits to seeing bears "through the rose-colored glasses of an avid participant-observer" and his text is highly subjective, its main points are corroborated by other texts and testimonies. Wright asserts "bears have been developing a new spiritual home, a social sexual community that reflects a new simplicity and candor, matter-of-factness about erotic survival in a time when some of the most sexually repressive energy is emanating from the larger gay community."[33] We wonder at the emphasis on "new" in Wright's analysis—does he mean that before bears came on the scene, gay men lacked opportunities for building spiritual homes and creating community? We think it might be more productive to consider ways in which "newer" and older cultural expressions might intersect and, in so doing, raise some interesting questions regarding gendered configurations and expressions of sexual desire.

The embodied representation of the bear, as we have already noted, is burly and hairy and/or full bearded, perhaps balding. This appears to be a conscious rejection of the Castro-clone style of gay masculinity dating from the 1970s. Wright criticizes clone phenomenon as "a middle-class fetishization of working-class masculinity," which, while retaining an emphasis on status and slenderness, had attempted to stake out a middle ground between the extremely effeminate style of "queens" and the hypermasculinity of the "leather scene."[34] The bear sensibility is thus a rejection of a rejection, with multivalent trajectories. In other words, movement between and among multiple aspects of identity and other forms of "border crossing" becomes the order of the day. Bears thus must be conceived as engaged in ongoing sociopolitical struggle in which many—gay men, lesbians, straight people—have been fighting to reclaim the erotic in the face of claims that "Sex = Death," injunctions to "Just Say No," and the similar expressions of erotophobia that have emerged alongside AIDS.

Even though the bear aesthetic may reject the macho ethic of the clone and may represent a significant departure from other configurations of gay male masculinity, it does not necessarily negate what has gone before. Indeed, it may equally well incorporate earlier cultural forms and styles in "both/and" constructions that militate against whole-cloth rejections predicated on "either/or." Thus one might be simultaneously both swishy and bear or camp it up one minute and be a wild man the next, without erasing either experience. Ultimately, as Wright puts it, this means a "kind of reintegration [that might] make for spiritually sounder and emotionally healthier people—a bit more *Roseanne* (John Goodman makes a perfect bear), a bit less *Brideshead Revisited.*"[35]

An interesting variation on one of the major themes in recent feminist theory, the "ethic of care" articulated by Carol Gilligan, Virginia Held, Joan Tronto, and others, is incorporated by bear semiotics.[36] According to Wright, dissatisfaction with the "colored-hanky" semiotics by which a number of gay men had been signaling interest in specific sexual acts led some to replace the hanky with small teddy bears in their back pockets, deemphasizing competitive, performance-based aspects of sex as sport: "Sticking a little teddy bear in your back pocket or shirt pocket was a way of saying 'I'm a human being. I give and receive affection.'"[37] The forging of common emotional bonds came to be presented in "a kind of protective tenderness" toward other men that is based on tolerance that crosses boundaries of class or race and is "attested by the social interaction between bears, the leather community . . . chubby chasers and daddy admirers" as well as those who are "recovering" or "clean and sober." The claim is that "an intense blend of purely physical lust and genuine affection and deeply experienced sense of community informs the bear movement," despite there being "as many scenes as there are people."[38]

Caretaking, tolerance, and affection have not been central to the orthodox masculinity of compulsory heterosexuality, nor do they appear to have figured strongly in the clone cultural expressions that emerged in gay male communities during the 1970s. If anything, the clone ethic appears to have been predicated on a nearly total rejection of all "feminine" behavioral forms, especially those associated with the effeminate stereotypes such as queens, sissies, and swishes. Nurturance was not salient to the discourse (although we suspect that it may have been more evident in practice than it was in rhetoric). It seems far more marked, however, in the rhetorical and iconographic public presentations of bears—clearly in fantasy and perhaps in actual practice.

In fictional accounts, the bear ethic of nurturance is literally embodied. The bear's body is permeable, his boundaries fluid enough to permit the exchange of both semen and affection, further signifying a generous incorporation of marginality in various forms. In "Lost Dad," the narrator befriends an older homeless man, and the two become lovers:

> "Oh Shawn," I found myself saying. "Be my daddy. Hold me in your arms. I want to be a little boy for just a little while" . . . Suddenly Shawn was getting up and sitting on the edge of the tub. In slow motion the water ran off his large, hairy body. I watched, fascinated, as his fat, uncut cock came into view. Beneath it were two massive balls. The water ran off them in a single stream. I wanted to drink that water.[39]

Later, the narrator notices that he has come to orgasm without touching himself, one of the few times he has ever climaxed in that manner. The moment when he realizes this concretizes the bear's capacity for identification with, and nurturance of, the Other. "Soon Shawn was asleep and snoring softly. As I lay there, content, I had a feeling that Shawn had found a home. I didn't know how long he would stay but I hoped it would be for a long time.[40]

The bear's "naturalness" may be expressed through an interest in body secretions. Witness a representative passage from "The Bruin" in which a young employee has sex with his boss:

> Holding onto his belt loops, I lowered my head and took that German sausage into my eager mouth, savoring the taste of his man-meat, inhaling the ripe, musky aroma surrounding it. I

pulled back the thick foreskin, revealing his mild, cheesy surprise, and lovingly licked and cleaned every speck with my tongue. . . . I swallowed every inch of his seasoned manhood.[41]

The earthy sensitivity of the narrator is further evidenced in his description of the boss's bodily aroma: "a combination of sweat and inexpensive Daddy aftershave."[42]

> **Kate:** I'm wondering whether this discourse of nurturance has to be presented through a discourse of sex in order to make it OK for men to participate? Or is it a way of reclaiming the whole body for eroticism and thereby dephallicizing the cock? And besides the nurturance, what about the playfulness? I think that really mitigates my discomfort with the wild man myth's seeming to reproduce old time sexism.
> 
> **Beth:** You know, I can't help going back to the guy in the hammock with his cock sticking out. When I got past thinking "that looks painful," it became funny. It's really funny. And yes, it's very playful.

Unraveling the skeins of one's own desire is no easy task let alone approaching other tangled weaves. We see in the bear a valorization of the ur-butch "wild man" who may not be far removed from Sam Keen's vision of the "fierce gentleman."[43] The wild-man aspect of the gay bear evokes a natural creature, untamed by culture and unfettered by prudish convention. He is "at home" in his body as it is, comfortable with its girth, growths and secretions, unafraid to encounter his primal self. The bear is free in a way that no one else is—not only to satisfy his hunger[44] but also to venture into the dark cave of his "feminine" unconscious. His life cycle represents a symbiosis of conscious/unconscious, rational/emotional. He may appear at one moment as the fierce grizzly, at the next the playful, cuddly teddy (who is also a play*mate*)—and back again. Power, pleasure, and danger hang in his balance.

What or, indeed, whom does the "wild man" represent? The claim is that bear images "play on romanticized fantasies which blend sexual 'freedom' with 'frontier living' with 'independence,' and blur distinctions between frontiersmen—the simple, unfettered lives of trappers, loggers, hunters—and the wild-animal-man object of their desire."[45] Can this be taken at face value? Or is there perhaps something radically subversive of orthodox masculinity at work here, despite all the butch trappings? Might not bears represent the sort of "marginalized men" that Susan Bordo describes as "bearers of the shadow of the phallus, who have been the alchemical agents disturbing the (deceptively) stable elements" of orthodox masculinity in a newly percolating social psyche?[46]

What spaces are available for gay self-representation(s) and forging of collective identities in the mid-1990s? Are the images and rhetoric of bears more consonant with the process of bricolage, in which available signs and practices are manipulated and revalued within historically specific cultural parameters, than with a wholecloth adoption of tropes of orthodox masculinity? How and why are these particular "signs and practices" chosen and embodied? Is there something here about refusals—"just saying no" to being bound by certain standards that regulate and sanitize the body? If you are part of a culture in which many have spent or are spending considerable time in hospitals—you might not be sick, but your friends and lovers are—or if you're frustrated trying to make sense of the often contradictory, sometimes useless, but always clinical rhetoric surrounding "safe sex," wouldn't you want to resist the medicalization of the body? Is there a logic to the appeal of sweaty, smelly, organic, raunchy, wet stuff that makes sex "dirty" again—as it ought to be? And what about the power of desire—in all its seductive, and perhaps profoundly patriarchal, glory?

In bear culture, the locus of desire appears to be fairly consistently articulated in terms of sameness and by the desiring subject. One of the more interesting ways in which this plays out is with the valorization of age in the daddy figure, which may incorporate intergenerational relations between older (or dominant) daddy bears and younger (or submissive) cubs. Daddy-boy roles appear in leather and other gay male subcultures, but in the bear subculture a specific, differentiated meaning is attached. Daddy bears are mature in the sense that they know themselves and their own desires. They are strong, manly, and at the same time unashamed to express their feelings of affection and need. Daddy bears are generous, indulgent, and tactile. As with all things sexual, multivalent meanings and symbols abound. Is a desire for daddy an expression of longing for protection and nurturance or of wishing to draw close to phallic power or some combination of both or something else entirely?

We think it is important to differentiate between the meanings of father and daddy here. Father is often absent, all but aural: the god in the sky whose name cannot be inscribed. He is the ultimate locus of the unknowable, of phallocentric power and authority—a strong, silent type. "Father Bear" in the Goldilocks story gets the big chair, the big bowl, the hard bed (the hard-on?). He clearly wears the phallus in his household. In modern Western societies, the father also signifies the ultimate enforcement of sanctions against effeminate behavior by boys.[47] Alienation and estrangement are what make Father most himself. When Father is most himself, he is "not-Mother." Her boundaries are always already permeable and often entirely dissolved—which may be the real source of both her power and his envy.

Daddy, on the other hand, is a metaphor of companionship, not conquest or competition. Children play with "Daddy." There are the games of catch in the backyard, the pillow fights at bedtime. You can get dirty with Daddy. His love is warm, all-enfolding, unconditional—at a far remove from the severe father who doles out punishment, apparently arbitrarily, yet always for your own good.

Is "Daddy" perhaps always already inscribed as fantasy in some gay male imaginations? Age itself, with all its connotations—girth, wrinkles, gray hair, hair loss—may offer magical properties to the "daddy" phenomenon among bears and other gay male subcultures in which the role appears. For many gay men, the very idea of getting old, or at least living past forty, has taken on new meaning. We both recall conversations with gay male friends around 1980, a time when we all were turning or approaching thirty. Many dykes embraced this. As Beth put it, "Thirty meant you could start not giving a shit as a woman and getting away with it." But for many gay men, it meant you were over the hill, you were never going to get a date. The memory of these discussions is grim because so many of the men who feared thirty never made it to forty.

If daddy is a magical figure, the stuff of fantasy or reality, what does it mean to fuck him or be fucked by him? Is there perhaps a call here to retheorize the oedipal trajectory in which the father is introjected in the total absence of the mother? What role might the mother play *in absentia?* Do the connections to "ethics of care" articulated earlier demand that we search, at least interpretively, for a maternal subtext that might, as Coppélia Kahn puts it, demonstrate "the imprint of mothering on the male psyche, the psychological presence of the mother in men whether or not mothers are represented in the texts they write"?[48] In other words, do all three bears in the fairy tale become one here, mutually introjecting and resisting simultaneously in a perfect postmodernist moment that radically revisions and rewrites a narrative of relational (dephallocentric) authority?

Here we return to the question of categories of desire and the ways in which they may be deployed strategically, subversively, and politically. Although some aspects of reconfigured sexuality, desire, embodiment, and gay masculinity emerge clearly from the bear texts and discourse, others, especially those attached to race and class, are more complicated. Both class and race are discursively addressed in the bear texts, to a degree that is not evident in heterosexual pornography or other commodified forms of heterosexuality. The cultural meanings of this discourse, however, are unclear. Why, we wonder, do bears feel the need to adopt a rhetoric of racial inclusivity when the iconography of the texts before us is so overwhelmingly white? Why is so much emphasis placed on significations of working-class identity? To what political ends are these stylistic forms deployed?

The rhetorical assertion forwarded by bear proponents of inclusivity is simple. Wright, for example, suggests that as opposed to the "middle-class fetishization of working class masculinity" noted earlier as a central component of clone culture, the subcultures of leathersex, bears, and the vast working-class gay population of San Francisco intersect in the assertion of "an openly and genuinely working-class homosexual ethic."[49] Although not all bears belong to the working class, the claim is that their "sociosexual adhesiveness has its roots in a Whitmanesque democratic appreciation of the common man" in which "working-class white gay men are discovering that they have more, sometimes much more, in common with one another and working-class black or Latino gay men than they do with middle-class gay men of any color."[50] Indeed, bear gatherings may strive for a particular ambience of openness, at which "men of all shapes and sizes and ages and races and sexual interests converge with "little or none of the old bath-house tension." A "model type," for example, is described as having "left a recent bear party within twenty minutes, once he realized his buffed appearance didn't draw instant adulation."[51]

Some aspects of the bear discourses of sexuality and gender that we examined do seem to configure a new democratization of gay male sexual relations in the wake of AIDS. The texts emphasize participant observation to a high degree and utilize tropes largely absent from earlier configurations of gay male sexual desire: associations to gritty, working-class experiences (truckers, gimme caps, auto mechanics, flannel shirts, mountain men, etc.) juxtaposed with naked, hairy bodies that would not be deemed "model" in any other context. The images themselves, along with accompanying texts of formula fiction, promote a general sensuality that remains rough, natural, and organic while simultaneously incorporating humor. As Kate observed, these are spaces where "men can look like they're aging, and still have their tits played with."

The publications we studied, even those clearly produced for a mass market, retain a grassroots sensibility more evocative of locally produced, photocopied "zines" than of the slick, glossy pages we have come to associate with gay male porn.[52] But how democratized are the cultural spaces they depict? For one thing, the images presented are, almost without exception, white and only rarely identifiable as "ethnic" in any way. Despite the textual claims that in bear culture, racial and socioeconomic boundaries are routinely crossed, we are skeptical: African-American men, or men of any color (besides white), are depicted or described only in the personals—and here, as in the editorial copy, whiteness predominates. A few ads describe men with disabilities, but no images of physically challenged individuals appeared in the publications we examined.

Although a full exploration of how the complicated relations of race and class shape constructions of gay or straight masculinity is beyond the scope of this chapter, we want to put some cautionary brakes on any facile claims regarding the democratization of bear cultural spaces and productions. The bear public sphere may present an opening for democracy in a particular gay male cultural space, but there is little evidence in the texts we examined to show that bears have made significant strides away from privileging whiteness and/or middle-class masculinity. A rhetoric valorizing inclusivity and working-class experience is certainly present, but we see no movement toward questioning the contradictions between rhetoric and reality in the pages of these texts. Why aren't letters to the editors questioning the whiteness of the images? What is really going on if CPAs don blue jeans and doff gimme caps when they go off to a party weekend on Friday afternoon only to return to a corporate uniform of suits and ties (and collect higher paychecks) come Monday? Given the intensification of class polarization over the past decade, what does it mean when lawyers masquerade as automobile mechanics or assembly-line workers? Where in these texts are the voices of "Other" bears—men marked not by whiteness but by color, ethnicity, disability, and the like?

There may be openings among the bears for new possibilities, new cultural, social, and political configurations of gay male desire, new constructions of gender—and thereby new possibilities for solidarity, alliance, and community among lesbians and gay men. However, we recognize that any conclusive determinations in this regard will have to come out of analyses undertaken by those who are able to participate in, as well as observe, the bear cultural universe. For when all is said and done, we remain, with Goldilocks, uninvited guests among the bears.

## NOTES

1. "A man is like a bear: the uglier, the prettier." Beth's friend Michael Forman recalled this favorite saying of his mother from his childhood in Bogotá, Colombia. When asked to provide its provenance, however, she could not remember when she learned the aphorism or in what context. We thank Forman for sharing this and for providing helpful commentary on early versions of this essay, as did Kevin Cathcart, Frida Furman, Sandra Jackson, Ann Russo, and Jackie Taylor. Thanks are also due to Gene Sampson for his superb clerical support and generous good humor and to Craig Kois for his insights and friendship.

2. Then there's the ick factor. See Chapter 4 in Sara Miles and Eric Rofes, eds., *Opposite Sex: Gay Men on Lesbians, Lesbians on Gay Men* (New York: New York: University Press, 1998)

3. Elizabeth A. Kelly, "Grounds for Criticism: Coffee, Passion, and the Politics of Feminist Discourse," in Lois Lovelace Duke, ed., *Women in Politics:*

*Outsiders or Insiders?* rev. ed. (Upper Saddle River, NJ: Prentice-Hall, 1996), pp. 351-368; see also Elizabeth A. Kelly, *Education, Democracy, and Public Knowledge* (Boulder, CO: Westview Press, 1995).

    4. See bell hooks, "Eating the Other: Desire and Resistance," in bell hooks, *Black Looks: Race and Representation* (Boston: South End Press, 1992), pp. 21-39. For hooks, "eating the Other" describes "the Eurocentric habit of consuming images of exotics (those marked by color, ethnicity, and/or other forms of difference)." In the case of gay men, however, definitions of the desiring subject/desired object, either or both may be Other; thus an Asian man who likes Asian men can call himself a rice queen.

    5. As in the 1960s Hanna-Barbera cartoon series, *Yogi Bear*. Boo-Boo was Yogi's sidekick.

    6. At a number of points we recalled the early Michigan Women's Music Festivals, with dykes going bananas because here, finally, was a safe space where we could take off our T-shirts and get sunburned "down to there."

    7. *BEAR* 38, p. 21.

    8. *Classic BEAR* (special issue) p. 13.

    9. See Nancy Fraser, "Rethinking the Public Sphere: A Contribution to the Critique of Actually Existing Democracy," *Social Text* 25/26 (Winter 1990): 56-80, for a provocative treatment of the concept of alternative public spheres.

    10. Rangercub, "From a Cub's-Eye View," *Heavy Duty Premier,* July-September 1996, pp. 33-35.

    11. David Tilton, "Intercourse with Steve Blanscet, Mr. International Bear 1996," *American Bear* 3, p. 13.

    12. Jürgen Habermas, *The Structural Transformation of the Public Sphere: An Inquiry into a Category of Bourgeois Society,* trans. Thomas Burger with the assistance of Frederick Lawrence (Cambridge, MA: MIT Press, 1989); see also Craig Calhoun, ed., *Habermas and the Public Sphere* (Cambridge, MA: MIT Press, 1985); and David Rasmussen, ed., *Universalism vs. Communitarianism: Contemporary Debates in Ethics* (Cambridge, MA: MIT Press, 1990). For a specifically feminist analysis, see Joan B. Landes, *Women and the Public Sphere in the Age of the French Revolution* (Ithaca, NY: Cornell University Press, 1988).

    13. She suspects that this habit was formed while she was in utero, when her lonely, pregnant mother read aloud from women's magazines in order to hear the sound of a human voice—even if it was her own.

    14. *Classic BEAR,* pp. 15-16, *BEAR,* pp. 36, 38.

    15. As a number of lesbian theorists have argued, we are perhaps more powerfully charged with the erotic than women have traditionally been socialized to admit—or this sort of language reflects. See, for example, Audre Lorde's classic "Uses of the Erotic: The Erotic as Power," in Audre Lorde, *Sister Outsider: Essays and Speeches* (Trumansburg, NY: Crossing Press), pp. 53-59.

    16. See Yvonne Tasker, *Spectacular Bodies: Gender, Genre, and the Action Cinema* (London: Routledge, 1993), for a discussion of the hard body and penetrability.

17. Barbara Ehrenreich and Deirdre English, *For Her Own Good: 150 Years of the Experts' Advice to Women* (Garden City, NY: Doubleday/Anchor, 1979).

18. Lois Banner, *American Beauty* (Chicago: University of Chicago Press, 1983), pp. 51-52.

19. Mary Wollstonecraft, for instance, scathingly criticized women "who have fostered a romantic, unnatural delicacy" for their "docility and . . . spaniel-like affection." Mary Wollstonecraft, *A Vindication of the Rights of Woman* (1792; reprint, Buffalo, NY: Prometheus Books, 1989), pp. 41-43.

20. Banner, *American Beauty*, p. 51.

21. Ibid., pp. 106-107.

22. Delmore Schwartz, "The Heavy Bear," from Delmore Schwartz, *Selected Poems: Summer Knowledge* (New York: New Directions, 1959), quoted in Susan Bordo, *Unbearable Weight: Feminism, Western Culture, and the Body* (Berkeley and Los Angeles: University of California Press, 1993); for Bordo's reading of the poem, see pp. 2-15.

23. Bordo, *Unbearable Weight*, p. 2.

24. For a discussion of recent "lesbian style wars" and the construction of lesbian aesthetics, Arlene Stein, "All Dressed Up But No Place to Go? Style Wars and the New Lesbianism," in Corey K. Creekmur and Alexander Doty, eds., *Out in Culture: Gay, Lesbian, and Queer Essays on Popular Culture* (Durham, NC: Duke University Press, 1995), pp. 476-483.

25. The texts explored in this essay are *AMERICAN BEAR* no. 13, June/July 1996; *BEAR* 38, June 1996; *CR (Chiron Rising Magazine)*, 74, June-July 1996; *Classic BEAR*, February 1996; *DADDY-The Magazine* 28, June 1996; *Daddybear* 3 (n.d.); and *Heavy Duty Premier,* July-September 1996.

26. Behar writes, "With all the discussion of ethnographic writing going on at the moment, so little is said about how each of us comes to the pen and the computer and the authority to speak and author texts . . . authorship is a privilege to which many of us are not born, arrive at, often clumsily, often painfully, often through a process of self-betrayal and denial . . . authorship is a privilege constituted by the gender, sociohistorical background, and class origins, or lately class diasporas, of the anthropologist doing the writing." We suggest that this applies equally well to other "social scientists," indeed to any of us who write about cross-cultural encounters. Ruth Behar, *Translated Woman: Crossing the Border with Esperanza's Story* (Boston: Beacon Press, 1993), p. 338.

27. See, for example, Allan Bérubé, *Coming Out Under Fire* (New York: Free Press, 1990); George Chauncey, *Gay New York: Gender, Urban Culture, and the Making of the Gay Male World 1890-1940* (New York: Basic Books, 1994); John D'Emilio, *Sexual Politics, Sexual Communities: The Making of a Homosexual Minority in the United States, 1940-1970* (Chicago: University of Chicago Press, 1983); Martin Bauml Duberman, Martha Vicinus, and George Chauncy Jr., eds., *Hidden from History: Reclaiming the Gay and Lesbian Past* (New York: New American Library, 1989); Lillian Faderman, *Odd Girls and Twilight Lovers: A History of Lesbian Life in Twentieth Century America* (New York: Columbia University Press, 1991); Elizabeth Lapovsky Kennedy and Madeline D. Davis; *Boots*

*of Leather, Slippers of Gold: The History of a Lesbian Community* (New York: Penguin Books, 1994).

28. Eric Rofes, *Reviving the Tribe: Regenerating Gay Men's Sexuality and Culture in the Ongoing Epidemic* (Binghamton, NY: Harrington Park Press, 1996). Rofes's courageous documentation of how this task has been complicated by the sheer rapidity of changes in gay masculinity, the institutional possibilities of gay sexual experience, and the configuration of gay desire over the past three or four decades is provocative and insightful.

29. For provocative thinking on this, see Judith McDaniel and Judith Mazza, "Safe Sex for Lesbians: What's It All About?" and Amber Hollibaugh, "Transmission, Transmission, Where's the Transmission?" both in Karen Kahn, ed., *Front Line Feminism, 1975-1995: Essays from Sojourner's First 20 Years* (San Francisco: Aunt Lute Books, 1995), pp. 277-280, 281-287; also Katie J. Hogan, "'Victim Feminism' and the Complexities of AIDS" in Nan Bauer Maglin and Donna Perry, eds., *Bad Girls: Women, Sex, and Power in the Nineties* (New Brunswick, NJ: Rutgers University Press, 1996), pp. 68-89.

30. A celebration of butch-femme identities in the lesbian community, a panel discussion held at the New York Lesbian and Gay Community Service Center, December 6, 1990. The panelists included Sue Hyde, Amber Hollibaugh, Deanna Alida, Lisa Winters, Val Taval, Jewelle Gomez, Jill Harris, and Joan Nestle, with Stephanie Grant moderating; in Joan Nestle, ed., *The Persistent Desire: A Femme-Butch Reader* (Boston: Alyson Publications, 1992), pp. 454-463.

31. P. 477 in Gayle Rubin, "Of Catamites and Kings: Reflections on Butch, Gender, and Boundaries," in Joan Nestle, ed., *The Persistent Desire: A Femme-Butch Reader* (Boston: Alyson Publications, 1992), pp. 466-482.

32. Les K. Wright, "The Sociology of the Urban Bear," *Drummer* 140, June 1990, reprinted in *Classic BEAR* (1996): 53-55.

33. Ibid, p. 53.

34. Ibid.

35. Ibid.

36. Carol Gilligan, *In a Different Voice: Psychological Theory and Women's Development* (Cambridge, MA: Harvard University Press, 1982); Virginia Held, *Feminist Morality: Transforming Culture, Society, and Politics* (Chicago, University Press, 1993); and Joan Tronto, *Moral Boundaries: A Political Argument for an Ethic of Care* (New York: Routledge, 1993). Uma Narayan's cogent reminder that "while contemporary care discourse correctly insists on acknowledging human needs and relationships, it needs to worry about who defines these often contested terms" is worth noting here. Uma Narayan, "Colonialism and Its Others: Considerations on Rights and Care Discourses," *Hypatia* 10 (Spring 1995): 133-140, 133.

37. Wright, "Sociology of the Urban Bear," p. 54.

38. Ibid.

39. Nicholas Mann, "Lost Dad," *Daddy Bear* 3, p. 18.

40. Ibid, p. 19. Once again, note the similarity in tone to formula romance in women's magazines.

41. Boomer, "The Bruin," *Daddy Bear* 3, p. 33.

42. Ibid.

43. Sam Keen, *Fire in the Belly: On Being a Man* (New York: Bantam, 1992), p. 112.

44. See the Delmore Schwartz poem cited earlier.

45. Wright, "Sociology of the Urban Bear," p. 53.

46. Bordo, "Reading the Male Body," p. 281.

47. Christine Di Stefano notes that such sanctions are "consistent . . . with the suggestion that modern masculinity resembles a reaction formation rather than an originary model of selfhood. As such, it is unstable and vulnerable, particularly to the 'polluting' influence of feminine elements. A rigid enforcement of masculine norms of behavior suggests a powerful horror at the prospect of mixing or confusing cherished and vulnerable categories." See Christine Di Stefano, *Configurations of Masculinity: A Feminist Perspective on Modern Political Theory* (Ithaca, NY: Cornell University Press, 1991), p. 46.

48. Coppélia Kahn, "Excavating 'those Dim Minoan Regions': Maternal Subtexts in Patriarchal Literature," *Diacritics: A Review of Contemporary Criticism* 12 (Summer 1982): 36.

49. *Classic BEAR,* p. 53.

50. Ibid., p. 54.

51. Ibid., p. 55.

52. See Richard Dyer, "Don't Look Now: The Instabilities of the Male Pinup," in Richard Dyer, *Only Entertainment* (New York: Routledge, 1992), pp. 121-134.

# Appendix

# Early Published Writings on Bears by Les Wright

### *EXPLORING THE "BEAR" PHENOMENA*
### *(SEATTLE GAY NEWS, AUGUST 3, 1990, pp. 20-21)*

Amid the social and sexual interactions I have had over the past two or three years, I have become aware of growing sentiment among a widening range of gay men, one that reflects my social and sexual ideals.

I am powerfully attracted to most of these men. They seem to embody the spirit and the flesh, the passion and the playfulness of what is rapidly emerging as a new movement. While the term "movement" might be considered a bit premature, I would characterize the bear phenomenon at the very least as a shift in consciousness in the burgeoning post-panic sexual thaw. Undoubtedly, I view "gay bears" through the rose-colored glasses of an avid participant observer. But in the social interactions of an ever-growing circle of kindred spirits, bears have been discovering a new spiritual home, a social and sexual community that reflects a new simplicity and candor, a new matter-of-factness about erotic survival in a time when some of the most sexually repressive energy is emanating from the larger gay community.

What follows is based on my own impressions and experiences. In those experiences I have found growing patterns that have arisen spontaneously, and a good many bears, if queried, would undoubtedly be surprised at the comments. What seems to have begun as a straightforward assertion of private desire is rapidly transforming into a whole new sexual aesthetic.

### *What Is a Bear?*

The most obvious symbols of bearness—body hair and beards and burliness, traits traditionally acceptable in leathersex circles—underscore a direct sexual interest in certain physical types. Bears are self-identified as hairy and/or full-bearded, often balding, and they may describe themselves as black, brown, kodiak or polar, grizzly, teddy, or cub. Mustaches qualify as "demi-bear." In 1989 *BEAR* magazine conducted an informal poll, asking whether a full beard, a hirsute body, or a full-figured frame were all necessary to be considered a bear. The response was anything but uniform. Each man chose to determine his own particular fetish (beard, body hair, and/or weight), but most felt that a shared outlook, discovered among kindred spirits, was the most important thing.

Gay bears tend toward the heavy side—husky, heavyset, burly or simply and forthrightly fat. Many clones and non-clones who put on weight early in the epidemic later discovered the pounds no longer came off. Some bears perhaps eroticized body weight from the erroneous assumption that "heavier equals healthier." And some respond in (fat) dyke-like fashion, rejecting (buffed) clone fashion outright.

In the 1970s the Castro clone look became the hallmark of post-Stonewall gay men. Clones were traditionally masculine in appearance, embracing a generically working-class look of jeans and flannel shirt. The clone was in fact a middle-class fetishization of working-class masculinity. At the time it seemed like an exciting alternative, a middle-of-the-road, normalizing social face that placed gay men somewhere between the (still perceived) extremes of drag and chicken queens and the "dangerous hypermasculinity" of the leather scene.

These bear images play on romanticized fantasies which blend (sexual) "freedom" with "frontier living," with "independence," and blurs the distinctions between frontiersmen—the simple, unfettered life of trappers, loggers, hunters—and the wild animal-man object of their desire. Part of the anti-clone, anti-status stance arises from the assertion of a working-class ethic. The subculture of leathersex, bears, and the vast working-class gay population intersect in the assertion of an openly working-class homosexual ethic and a different sort of uncloseted gayness which passes between gay and straight demarcated realms with a great deal more fluidity than the Financial-Genius-by-day-Castro-Clone-by-night schizophrenia.

The origin of bear semiotics is traceable back to 1981 or 1982, just before AIDS erupted into an epidemic. At the time there was a great deal of dissatisfaction expressed over the colored hankies semiotics which reduced gay men to very specific sexual behaviors. A lot of gay men pulled the colored hankies out of their back pockets and stuffed a little teddy bear in instead. The talk on the street then was about lightening things up, making sex playful again, de-emphasizing sex as a competitive performance sport. Sticking a little teddy bear in your back pocket or shirt pocket was a way of saying, "I'm human. I give and receive affection."

One note on race and bears here. While the bear fetish of body hair clearly indicates a preference for hairy types, beardedness or likemindedness serve as acceptable entrees. The type of racism I am anticipating encountering here is in fact a middle-class projection of working-class prejudice. The men I have encountered, whom *I* consider kindred spirits in "bearness," tend to cross racial and socioeconomic lines in complicated ways. What they all have in common is a cohesiveness in their sexual identity. I could set up several grids and cross-reference the hairy types by race, but how do I account for bears who prefer a full beard and a full figure, but who could care less about a hairy chest? What about cross-generational attractions that also cross racial lines? The archetypal bear exists in virtually every culture and totemic correlations exist in many diverse manifestations. The type of "we'll just make do with what we have" philosophical approach I see bears welcoming each other with seems a bona fide working-class value, one idealized, if not parodied, in the world of the TV family *The Waltons*.

### *Bears' Social Cohesion*

A key to the cohesiveness of bears appears to lie in a shared class-based experience of the world. By no means do I assert that all bears are working-class, but rather that socioeconomic adhesiveness has its roots in a Whitmanesque democratic appreciation of the common man. It is my belief that in many ways working-class white gay men are discovering they have more—sometimes much more—in common with each other and with working-class Black or Latino gay men than they do with middle-class gay men of any color.

The common emotional bond for bears has been a kind of protective tenderness toward each other. Tolerance for differences in sexual interests are attested to by the social interaction between bears, the leathersex community, what I will tentatively call the interracial sexual community, chubby chasers and daddy advocates, and the recovering community. (Let me be clear. Bears are not synonymous with leather or SM, although the three overlap in interesting ways.)

### *The Post-Panic Sex Thaw*

"AIDS shutdown" transformed Castro Street from a daily Mardi Gras to a virtual ghost town in a matter of twenty-some months at the start of the

1980s. After several years of shell shock, fear, and ignorance, and/or coming to terms with HIV and adjusting to a siege mentality in the midst of the epidemic, most of us have been able to resume some semblance of daily living. The most important aspect of the bear phenomenon is the reintegration of sex into our lives. This includes the adoption and normalization of "safer sex" practices, achieving a social consensus of maintaining such limits, of overcoming the AIDS-instilled fear that "sex equals death," making some realistic assessments of risk factors, and deciding, on the whole, that sex is still a wonderful thing.

Among the bears I have talked with there is a general sentiment that "unsafe sex" practices, defined as the exchange of certain bodily fluids, is the de facto bottom line, the actual determining factor in deciding whether, when, and how to have sex. Determining individual limits and agreeing on them with sex partners increasingly has become part of bear protocol for negotiating sex, and in virtually every sexual contact, it is assumed that everyone is HIV-infected.

There is another commonly held view that minimal or non-use of mind-altering chemical substances is not only healthier but a prerequisite to having a relationship with each other. Along with the larger gay community, bears have learned that the shift to abstinence, both as a general societal trend and as the result of twelve-stepping one's way to recovery in the 1980s, opens the way to a new, direct communication.

An important part of this new "sexual sobriety" is the "anti-clone" response. I want to say it's a generational thing, that "the Castro clones," whoever they really are, have finally grown up. The Stonewall generation (of which I consider myself a part) is now twenty-some years older, approaching or well into middle age, slowing down, and getting a bit paunchier, a bit mellower. More and more gay men are realizing they are not willing to give up sex just because their bodies no longer approximate the commercialized icons of Porno Gaydom. Perhaps surprising is the realization that older, paunchier gay men are attracted to each other. There are literally more bear-loving bears than ever before, reconnecting sexually with themselves and each other.

### *Blue-Collar Sensibilities*

Other subcultures which intersect in the bear movement are unmistakably blue-collar. For example, the truckers/truck stop fetish, the fantasy and actual occupations of many bears, and the points of contact for bears. This latter is very interesting in that much contact takes place through sex ads, in magazines and contact clubs, like *BEAR, Chiron Rising, Country Exchange, Blue-Collar Buddies,* and several others. Many men seek contact and maintain an underground network among like-minded men, all across rural and urban America. Biker clubs, both of the Hell's Angels (i.e., heterosexual) varieties and the gay MC clubs, are close in ambiance to the old VFW post my grandfather belonged to (where he and others were busted for running an illegal numbers racket), the volunteer fire department my own father fraternized with, or the workingman's club my best friend Ken once took me to in the industrial West Yorkshire city of Bradford, England.

And while the clone look intentionally went for a blue-collar image (I grew up wearing blue jeans and flannel shirts, resenting it as proof positive of my family's working-class status: it meant we were poor), the bear phenomenon seems to be a genuine manifestation of blue-collar sensibility. In reasserting a positive sexuality, many gay men are now also actively asserting who we are in terms of class origins and sensibilities—rather than who we tried to become by coming out or what we aspired to (but could never get the money or profession together to become). In the current Republican age of redistribution of wealth, just making ends meet is a daily struggle for more and more people. A lot of gay men have come to terms not only with AIDS and the biology of aging, but, in large numbers, with a decreased expectation of social and economic advancement.

### *The "Bear Phenomenon" at the Publicly Visible Level*

I have attended "bear play parties" in Berkeley and San Francisco and there is an ambiance I have not encountered elsewhere, at least not where sexual and social spaces are so merged. Men of all shapes and sizes and ages and races and sexual interests converge, as if for a fireman's field day or a family wedding or a gay motorcycle run. The main difference is that everyone is friendly and open to "dalliances" in the garden, on the dance floor, in the sex spaces. And men mingle and engage each other, fully dressed, in social chitchat, sexual undress, play, or leather scenes. Men engage in sex and there is missing that odd tension in the old bathhouse scene.

Another recent phenomenon is *BEAR* magazine, which popularizes and glamorizes the bear image. *BEAR* magazine published its first issue in 1987, growing from a small, locally produced, photocopied pamphlet for aficionados to a(n inter)nationally circulated, glossy-covered magazine. The magazine's subtitle is that "bearness" be understood as "masculinity . . . without the trappings." The magazine engages in the same kind of participant observer dynamic in which I find myself (engaged).

The burgeoning phenomenon of AIDS has left few leather bars in its wake. The big excitement last summer was the opening of a new bear-friendly bar, called the Lone Star Saloon. It was slow to warm up, but once it caught on, became hugely popular—until the October 17 (1989 Loma Prieta) earthquake reduced the place to rubble. It appears that as of early 1990 My Place has become *the* hangout bar for bears on the prowl.

## The Value of Adhesiveness

Bears' socioeconomic networking shifts gay politics in subtle but potentially significant ways. It represents a new democratization of sex, it normalizes gay sexual relations in the Age of AIDS, it asserts a certain matter-of-factness about the role of sex in an individual's social space. It makes a positive statement about the value of the individual, independent of that individual's economic status.

Bears are on a journey, some out of the gay ghetto and back into the world, some of us out of the sexual freeze and back into a resexualized gay society, neither apologetic nor unduly compromising. Much of the strength of the bear movement comes from the experiential realm, of knowing reasonable limits, but also proclaiming that it's time to simply claim some of the social and sexual space the gay movement has been fighting for, in theory if not in practice. While there may be no such thing as a "whole" person in late capitalist societies, this kind of reintegration seems to make for spiritually sounder and emotionally healthier people. A bit more *Roseanne* (John Goodman makes a perfect bear), a bit less *Brideshead Revisited*.

San Francisco is widely noted as a romantic's capital, and the burgeoning bear movement's first blossom undoubtedly owes much to this first flush of rosy freedom. No doubt, the bear movement will get slicked up, commercialized, acquire a more differentiated status ranking system, and become a new source for entrepreneurial profit-taking. But for now, while the rest of the society seems to spin further and further out of control into a hypertechnologized, hypermasculinized dystopia, the bear movement offers a grassroots alternative to survive and flourish in the face of the big social freeze. *Carpe diem.*

Note: This is the full-length version of my first article on bears. Abbreviated versions of it appeared as "The Sociology of the Urban Bear" cover story, *Drummer* 140 (June 1990) 30-32; reprinted in *Classic BEAR* (February 1996) 53-55; and as "Gay Bears on the Prowl," *San Francisco Sentinel*, 18: 32, August 9, 1990: 29ff. I circulated the article to all the major local gay newspapers of the day, and did not receive so much as acknowledgment of receipt of my letter of submission. The only paper to pick it up was the *Seattle Gay Times*, and that thanks primarily to their typesetter, John Roadhouse, who lobbied for its publication and to whom I again express my deepest gratitude.

### IN THE COMPANY OF BEARS: FINDING MY WAY TO THE BEAR HUGS/LEATHER BEARS (BEAR FAX 6, 1990, pp. 10-11)

The Bear Hugs/Leather Bears were my destiny. I just moved back to the Bay Area last summer and learned about the Lone Star Saloon a week before the October '89 quake. My friend John (Musselman) mentioned, almost in passing, a play party he thought I might enjoy. As it turned out, it was the last Berkeley party. The drive to and from that night was a major trek since the Bay Bridge was still out.

But, as I say, I was to find *you*.

I have worked and studied in Berkeley for many years, and I lived in North Berkeley for a year in the late 1980s. But for some very sad tearoom action on campus, I had not been able to connect with any gay men who actually have sex with other men in Berkeley. Being invited by word-of-mouth, meeting in a private home, joining a group that not a lot of people seemed to know anything about, all appealed to my sense of adventure and mystery.

The party was certainly more than I had bargained for, the grizzlies very huggable, the flow of social and sexual energies inspiring. I came for a sleazy good time and left with a new sense of joy and pride. At that first party I found boon companions. Loyal friends, and lots of big, hairy men, all into each other. It was the end of clone tyranny.

The range of sexual possibilities stretched from your basic good karma hug to dalliance in the kitchen, from frisky pawing through clothes to cock-sucking to serious S&M, all under one roof. All the parties I have played at since then have continued and expanded; catering to our smorgasbord of sexual appetites. Both the easygoing tolerance in the pack for diverging tastes and the unembarrassed ease with which all proclivities are pursued seemed a kind of milestone in the continuing evolution of gay sexuality as practiced in the San Francisco Bay Area. There's something for everyone, and all are welcome.

Part of what is most special about the leathersex community has spilled over into bear circles. In postmodern lingo, the BearHugs/Leather Bears' parties represent "bearspace"—leather bears and regular bears in the same place, social and sexual spheres merged together, a sense of solidarity among outsiders (from the clone culture), the availability of all those bearded or hairy men. The invitation list includes bears and their fans from up and down the West Coast, the Midwest and the South, and the Northeast—even New York and New Jersey.

Something is definitely going on here!

What the late Geoff Mains so eloquently stated in *Urban Aboriginals,* that sadomasochism is not "merely" primarily a psychosexual dynamic of ritualized sexual acts, deeply bonding trust, and pain-as-pleasure, applies equally to bearspace.

> Leatherspace is a movement that is both tribal and magical. It is founded in a mythos that speaks clearly of men and who they are and has been formulated by the tribe itself. This mythos is expressed in the way that the tribe interacts socially and finds its real strengths in the transcendent and cathartic scenes shared between small groups of its members. Although these activities are usually sexual and intimate, they are far more than that. These activities have strong social, intellectual and emotional meanings, and common knowledge of both activities and meanings is freely shared within the tribe. To tribesmen, these inner spaces and the activities that take place therein are magical because they can transform their lives. (Mains, 1984, p. 40)

Bears' sociosexual networking shifts gay politics in subtle but potentially significant ways. It represents a re-democratization of sex, it normalizes gay sexual relations in the Age of AIDS, it asserts a certain matter-of-factness about the role of sex in an individual's social space. A clear mind in an alert body is bearish sobriety and it makes a positive statement about the value of the individual, independent of the individual's economic status.

Part of what I find so exciting about joining in the bear gatherings is the eager acceptance I have found of me and of each other. It feels and looks like the working-class ethics I grew up with—each person cherished for being that person and everyone accepted because they are family and belong together. At bear parties I am overwhelmed with the sense that we are family, and get to have sex too. (Does that make us incestuous?)

The difference is this: most gay men do not escape the effects of growing up feeling different. Many of us got to San Francisco and found out we still didn't "measure up" or "fit in"—too heavy, not drop-dead handsome enough, insufficient income, wrong line of work. Bears are real people who accept themselves and others as they are, not how well they can imitate commercial images, how much disposable income they have for expensive gyms, or how much backbiting they can come up with to fill their otherwise empty lives.

An occasional hairy-chested starlet has found their way to one of our parties, having heard the good news, only to leave quickly when (1) they discovered their drop-dead good looks didn't automatically make them the center of attention and/or (2) they realized bears tend to be big and hairy and very friendly, take it or leave it.

Gentlemen, you are the crest of a new wave. Bears are on a journey, some of us out of the gay ghetto and back into the world, some of us out of the sexual freeze and back into a resexualized gay society, neither apologetic nor unduly compromising. Much of our strength as a bear movement comes from experience, from knowing reasonable limits, but also from claiming some of our turf, the social and sexual space the gay movement has been fighting for, in theory if not in practice. [ . . . ]

When I go to a bear party there's a whole lotta shakin' goin' on. I'm catching up with bear friends, running into guys from the "outside world" at their first party, I'm joining the hunt and being true to bear colors—wildly promiscuous, as they say, making a new friend, or just standing back and taking it all in, watching you do the same, with great satisfaction and admiration.

## *SEX AND THE IMMUTABLE LAWS OF RECIPROCITY (HAVING FUN AT BEAR PARTIES, AND MORE)* **(BEAR FAX 7, 1991, p. 10)**

Everyone who comes to a bear play party for the first time notices there's something different about it. The men are friendlier, the atmosphere is casual and comfortable. Not everyone will find everyone else the hottest thing on Planet Earth, and a friendly hug or squeeze does not mean, Do it now! Do it here! Not necessarily, unless you want to.

In other words, we do have some tacit rules of etiquette, whether we're aware of them or not. Occasionally, someone will complain that the group doesn't seem friendly, everyone else knows each other. Maybe the person has dropped by the Lone Star and figures we're all bar buddies. We're not. Not necessarily. And I am one of those people who is easily intimidated when I think everyone else knows each other and I'm the only stranger. Somehow, I imagine, my being unknown is a quality against my favor. I've been playing at bear parties for a while now, and what kept me coming back was that I never felt an outsider among you men.

But if you have gone to a couple of parties, and especially if you hang out at the Lone Star, take the time to say hello and maybe introduce a first-timer to the grizzly on your right and on your left. Y'all might meet someone new yourself, and you can show a first-timer how easy it is to connect.

I find each party is very different, a good half of the guys are there for the first time, or are back for the first time in several months. And yet we maintain the friendly tone. Bears are very much self-defining. We're not primarily or exclusively massively hairy and able to crush normal-sized humans in a hug. We seem to be very friendly, sexually voracious, and whatever our individual tastes, by and large turned on by reciprocity. (Lack of sexual reciprocity is right up there on the list of unwelcome attitude traits. Let's keep it there.)

What makes sex such an intensely spiritual experience for me is this reciprocal dimension. It keeps the sexual energy flowing in a circular pattern, the more I give away, the more I get back, and we each end up filled with something wonderful, and leave the experience enriched. This is what I fear the most when I venture out into other play spaces or take risks with a new sex partner (met on a street corner, through an ad, at other play parties, wherever). The girls from the A-list are primarily interested in trading upward, the proverbial sexual social climbers of Balzac and Updike. Other folks are souvenir hunters, collecting the biggest cocks ever sucked or the most muscles ever flexed. Some are into sex partners as better-than-latex, living, breathing dildos. Has this happened to you?

All that is part of the world of sexual etiquette. Or should be. I suppose it comes down to what do you expect of sex and from your play partners? For me, spiritual enhancement and balance, having abandoned good times, meeting interesting men and making friends, are among my primary intentions. (I also happen to be looking for True Love and the Perfect Husband right now, but that's another story.) [In fact, I did find the bastard, eventually; in the end, it was the most emotionally traumatizing experience I have ever had, but has been an endless font of useful experience for keeping myself grounded in reality.] I think this becomes more crucial when you get into answering sex ads. (You may have bought this issue of *Bear Fax* for the ads.)

Well, when you answer an ad it's important to be clear what your intentions are. At a party it's fairly straightforward, and you can pan between sex space and back again. With an ad, you find that people are looking for a lot of different things. Some guys are direct, even blunt. Others are not sure what they're seeking exactly, or are flying a trial balloon to see what happens. Maybe they're confused or just shy, or running some kind of sexual hustle. It's important to be honest, give your correct statistics and outline your boundaries. Are you looking for a simple one-time trick, are you looking for a guy to date, a fuck buddy, a regular bottom/top partner, are you interviewing for your next husband, or what?!

Some of us have been around the block a few dozen times, and some of us are just venturing out for the first time. Or experimenting with a newly discovered aspect of our sexuality. It helps to be open and considerate. We all went through our first times. Despite rumors to the contrary, we all started out as virgins. And if someone is an inappropriate match, let that go and move on. Just say you don't think it's a good match (this applies at the parties just as well). You don't have to make a person feel badly about himself; this is not an A-list crowd; you don't get triple-extra bonus points for being cruel (unless that's what you mutually desire).

If you have a bad experience, learn from it and move on to the next man. It will be different. And if it isn't, try this rule of thumb: first time is an honest mistake; second time means you're not paying attention; third time means you really dig it, or maybe that you need to get some clarity on what you think you want and what you're getting. If it doesn't feel like a good fit, say so before you're in the restaurant or have his cock in your mouth or your fist up his ass.

### *BEAR SEX AND HERO WORSHIP* (BEAR FAX *8, 1991, p. 10*)

Among the first bears in western history were Achilles and his lover Patroclus. I like to think about these guys a lot. Maybe I've seen too many Steve Reeves movies, but in my mind's eye I see two sweaty, hulking bears with thick, curly beards, broad, deep chests, big furry man-bellies, heaving and rubbing up against each other. I can see the rings in their nipples and the Prince Albert rings that hold their foreskins loose. After a tough day of fighting against the Trojans, Achilles and Patroclus would retire to their tent. (I should point out that the war lasted ten years, Achilles was the greatest warrior-leader on the Greek side, and Patroclus was Achilles' most favorite companion, as the phrase has it—over and above wives, concubines, female slaves or other Greek warriors.)

The Greeks would take breathers from the battle sometimes. All the warriors would get together and build huge pyres to cook a huge banquet, get together in their tents and have a full-blown orgy—kind of like a Bearhug party, with catering. Only this stuff got left out of history books and literature classes: they don't tell you that Achilles, the greatest Greek warrior, loved Patroclus with all his soul, or that to Patroclus, Achilles was the sun, the moon, and all the stars. They don't tell you that Plato's theory of love was anything but "platonic"—according to Plato the only way you get to understanding Love and ultimate Beauty (with a capital "B" just like that), is by starting at the beginning. And the beginning is utter carnal, ravening sexual lust of one man for another. So, while Achilles was contemplating the Beautiful, as it was expressed in the shape of his lover Patroclus, he was also having wild, sweaty, cum-dripping, lip-and-nipple-chewing, hairy-torso-pressed-against-hairy-torso sex with him.

The sad part (and this'll take a bit of explaining) is that Achilles' fellow warrior-leader, Agamemnon, took one of Achilles' slave girls away during a lull in the battle without asking permission. Achilles got mightily pissed off and stalked off to his tent to sulk, taking Patroclus with him. Agamemnon soon began to think better of this and attempted to assuage Achilles' wrath. It seems Agamemnon was losing battles because Achilles' troops were no longer there to help fight the Trojans. Achilles threatened to set sail for home and leave them all in the lurch anyway, just to spite them. Patroclus felt so bad about this that he offered to stay on and fight. He was kind of embarrassed by Achilles' immature behavior. After all, Achilles *was* a Greek hero and Greek heroes are half-human and half-god, with the blood of some Olympian god or goddess coursing through their veins.

Tragedy struck that day. Achilles gave his armor to Patroclus because he was feeling poorly about all this himself by now. Patroclus went out on the battlefield and, of course, everyone thought he was Achilles come back to fight. Anyway, you get the picture: Patroclus gets killed. This pushes Achilles completely over the edge and so he goes out and slays Patroclus' murderer, Hector, the greatest warrior of Troy. By the end of this story you got scores and scores of dead bodies, beautiful, broad-chested, loin-girded men lying in heaps on the parched plains outside the gates of Troy—all deader than a gross of door nails.

So, I say, next time someone steals your slave, don't get even, go to a Bearhug party. Have some raunchy, jizm-spilling, groin-gnashing sex with Patroclus, or someone who looks and fucks like him. Suck your hero off, ball him, fist him, make love till your seed runs dry. Make love, not war.

### *BEARS GO FOR EACH OTHER*
### (**BEAR FAX** *9, 1991, p. 10*)

The fact of the matter is there isn't an ursine sexual aesthetic, or at least there wasn't one until recently. Up until recently there was no particular expression of a homosexual aesthetic for mature men attracted to each other. What we had are two narrow types: the leather master (which requires an interest in leathersex or acquiring one, and the proverbial "leather drag" as plumage to attract sexual partners) and the pedagogical lover (where the sexual attractiveness of the youthful beloved is what is taken into consideration—the youth offers his body in exchange for knowledge and protection; the older mentor is not considered sexually appealing).

Bears' sexual aesthetic is "natural" and working-class in look. We dress like rangers, lumberjacks, truck drivers, ex-military, farmers, etc., that many of us, in fact, are. And many of us have alert and fascinating brains and a deep human need to touch and be touched, to show and receive affection. We neither buy attraction by recreating ourselves in consumer/consumable images (traditionally the world of designer fashion and gym-toned designer bodies) nor by acting out straight male behavior which is hostile to gay men and to women.

Over the last decade there have been a couple of attempts to look at what I am calling ursine sexual aesthetic. Jack Fritscher published a short-lived magazine Called *Man2Man* around 1980, and describes the rise and fall of the magazine and its philosophy of "homomasculinity" in *Some Dance to Remember*. Male poet and father icon of the men's movement Robert Bly has been disseminating his ideas about men's myths in volumes of poetry, in men's workshops, in the famous PBS interview with Bill Moyers. Bly, unfortunately, avoids the gay aspect of his myth-building. With all the name-calling going on these days it is very disturbing to see talk about gay bear sexuality castigated as politically incorrect in the gay community. It is very encouraging that explorations of gay men's emotional and sexual needs are occurring nonetheless.

My own interest is keyed in particular to gay male sexual energy, and how that has been able to express itself at the bear parties. It has been exciting to see us play together and to share friendships and to being two inches away from the consumer mentality so prevalent at the bars and elsewhere in the community. Rather than being prizes or trophies, we are real people to each other, each free to be himself.

Speaking of which, in a 1992 column of *Magnus* (a German cross between the *Advocate* and *Out/Look*), Detlev Meyer comments on the "Teddy Bear Group" in Stuttgart.

> When adult men stick little stuffed animals in the hip pockets, then something is wrong in the gay community [in Germany]. Indeed, it becomes doubtful that there even is such a thing. The fragmentation of gays into 'Rhenish Left-Bank Friends of Children' and 'Lower Pomeranian Rubber Freaks' and other clubs attests dramatically to the fact that we are hiding out in a lot or itle niches, that we are

fearful of squatting on our bar stools in sleepy little corners, holding hands—shuddering for fear of being discovered.

It is no doubt deplorable that the closet continues to oppress, especially in the more rural corners of supposedly enlightened societies. However, anyone who can figure out Meyer's logic, please explain.

### WHAT IS A BEAR? FURTHER REFLECTIONS
### (BEAR FAX *13, 1992, p. 13*)

When I first came upon the Bear Hug parties a few years ago, I was amazed and delighted. It was real hot, it felt right for me, and I was very excited to come across a whole group of like-minded men. At the time, I was not aware of an on-going bear tradition and was really excited to find there was a whole subculture. I was drawn to the (physical) maturity of the BearHug/Leather Bear men—their body hair, their beards, their wide ranges of ages (roughly mid-30s to 60s), and their acceptance of self and others. There was much less emphasis on being "in shape" or having to have a beard or a hairy chest or a specific body weight. The image and feel was easy-going, low-stress, very comfortable.

My own scholarly work brought me to the realization that there is something even more profound afoot among us. (I straddle both the highbrow academic and the from-the-bottom-up grassroots approach of the most valuable work in gay history; my interest is in how gay men define and create "gay community".) What has seeped into my consciousness over the last few years is the realization that bear energy is also all about what Walt Whitman called "camaraderie," "adhesiveness."

Whitman wrote passionately about men loving men, but was horrified when English "homosexualists" saw in Whitman one of their own kind. At that time, the latest scientific theory held that men sexually attracted to other men were psychological freaks—women's souls born in men's bodies. Whitman did not see things that way, and ever since there has been the deep, unresolved reason for many gay men to ask—Are we "really" men? If we are, how can we be homosexual, since homosexuals by definition are not "real" men? Traditionally, this problem has been played out by men identifying either with their feminine side (nelly queens) or their masculine side (leathermen, but often only as a facade, as in, "leather queens who were butch until they opened their mouth").

What strikes me the most about bears is that they, or we, seem to have made peace with this identity problem, on the side of being "quietly masculine." It is not for nought that the San Francisco bear group split up into two smaller groups: Bear Huggers and Leather Bears. And while camp is undoubtedly our cultural birthright, it seems that we are moving toward a new group- and self-identity.

Only recently has a municipality of men's groups begun to look at these things within us seriously. Often such groups have been vaguely homophobic or strangely unconscious about men's sexual energy with other men. Because of the great restrictions on public discourse about social prejudice, it has also been very difficult to carry on any meaningful dialogue, for fear of being branded misogynistic. There certainly has been an anti-woman sentiment in (especially) straight men's dialogue.

But what I intuitively liked the most from the beginning was the sense of being at peace with all this. Bears seem to be "quietly masculine," accepting the nurturing, affectionate, sensitive ("feminine") side of themselves just as much as the "masculine" aspects. I do not know how other self-identified bears feel about this, and I hope you will consider these ideas and be willing to talk to other like-minded men. If you do, then be sure to participate in one of the "What Is a Bear?" workshops that I will be facilitating (how California!) at the Bear Expo in February. See you there!

## REFERENCE

Mains, Geoff. *Urban Aboriginals: A Celebration of Leathersexuality.* San Francisco: Gay Sunshine Press, 1984, p. 40.

# Index

Abolitionist movement, 99, 243
Academy Training Center, *xlvii*
Acceptance. *See* Inclusivity
Achilles, 361-362
Activism. *See* Politics
Adam and Company, *lxi*
Adams, Bill, 209
Adams, Gary (Gary Lockwood), *xxxi*
Adams, Grizzly, 224, 228
Addiction
    to alcohol, 2, 12n2, 32, 185
    health and, 29-31
    less common among bears, 28, 32, 185, 331, 354
    recovery movement, 30, 245, 328, 354
Admirers
    bear chasers, 40, 42-43, 52, 75, 224, 353
    inclusion of, 106-107, 130, 171, 221
    lacking, 68, 228-229
    of otters, 78, 80, 81-83, 88
"The Adventures of Hairy Chess" (Jay), *xxxvii*
Advertising. *See* Media; Personal ads
*The Advocate* magazine, *xlvi*, 2, 16, 71, 303
*Advocate Men* magazine, *lvi*, 307, 315-317, 321
Aesthetics. *See* Body images
African Americans. *See also* Ethnicity
    black bear experiences, 109, 111, 117, 122, 125-127
    in clubs, 110, 122, 245
    in publications, 5, 153, 316, 345
    racism against, 9, 53, 110, 299

Agamemnon, 362
Age. *See also* Daddies; Youth
    acceptance of, 42, 59, 135-136, 141-142, 342, 355
    diversity in, *lvii*, 186, 328, 364
    intergenerational relationships, 61-62, 301, 353, 363
    in media, *xlvii*, 66, 293, 323, 329, 345
    in otter questionnaire, 80, 82, 83
    prejudice and, 9, 66, 126
    sexually transmitted diseases and, 60-61
AIDS
    age and, 61
    beauty images and, *lix*, 35, 333-334
    causes of, *xxvi*, *xlv-xlvi*
    community action and, *xlviii*, 141, 143, 152, 303
    cultural responses to, 17, 293-295, 337, 345, 353-354
    impact of, *lii*, *lvii-lviii*, 11, 32, 41, 352-355
    media and, *xxxv-xxxvii*
    sexuality and, 28, 185, 290-291, 339, 358
Al *(Home Improvement)*, 121, 228
Alan (East Coast Bear Hugz), 185-189
Albert, Steve, 31, 32-33
Alcohol
    addiction to, 2, 12n2, 32, 185
    clubs and, 169, 185, 245, 328
    health and, 22
    recovery movement, 30, 245, 328, 354
    Temperance movement, 99

Alcott, Bronson, 99, 102
Alcott, Louisa May, 99, 102
Allen, Ethan, 96
*The Alternate #8, xlii*
Altman, Dennis, 45
Altomar Video, *lxi*
Ambush bar (San Francisco), *xxvi, xxvii, lii*
"Ambushed in Manbush: Hair Fetish Confidential, 'Hair Balling'!" (Fritscher), *li, lii*
*American Bear* magazine
  economics of, 293
  fiction, 305-308, 332
    physical appearance of characters, 308-311
    sexual practices in, 311-315
  images, 119, 212, 329
  inclusiveness lacking, 68, 153
  Lurch interviewed, 5
  readers of, 288
*American Grizzly* magazine, 110, 119, 121, 305
AMG studios, *xxx, xli*
Amory, Richard, 287
Amsterdam, Netherlands, *xxiv-xxv*, 51-53
Anal sex (in pornography), 312, 316-317, 318, 322
Anderson, Timothy, *liii*
Annis, Dave, 218-219
Anthony, Susan B., 243
Appearance. *See* Body images; Looksism; Weight
de Arechaga, Frederick, *xxvi*
Argos bar (Amsterdam), *xxiv*
Army, 114-115, 117
Arnett, Chuck, *xxvi*
Art
  exhibitions, *xxxviii*, 9-10, 147-148, 214, 282
  legality, *xxxiii, liii*
  in publications, *xxxiii, lvi*, 118-121
  purpose, 291-292
Art Institute of Chicago, 147

Arteriosclerotic cardiovascular disease, 19, 22-23, 26
Arteriosclerotic peripheral vascular disease, 23
Arthritis, 19, 23
Asian bears, 53, 132, 296-297, 329. *See also* Ethnicity
*Atlanta Knights, xlvii*
Attitudes, in bear identity
  importance of, 111, 127, 208, 212-213, 250, 352
  naturalness, 111, 127, 208, 224
  in otter survey, 84-85, 90
  Wright on, 72, 321, 352
*A&U* journal, 294
Auden, W. H., 267
*Austin Powers: The Spy Who Shagged Me, xxviii*, 46
Australia
  bear movement in, 3, 269, 282-283, 296
  Brisbane, 249-250, 275-276, 282
  Melbourne, 272, 274-275, 276, 279-280, 282
  Mr. Australian Bear and Cub Competition, 279-280, 282
  Sydney, 269-274, 275-278, 281-282

Baldwin, Guy, 164, 165
Baltimore, Maryland, 109, 115, 117, 185-189, 298
Baltimore Eagle (Baltimore), 117, 187-188
Bare Bears club (Portland, Maine), 6
Barracks bar (Sydney), 271, 277
Bars and nightclubs
  clubs and, 229, 230-231, 234, 239, 244-245
  community at, 68, 81, 301, 359
  culture of, *xxxv*, 43, 295
  diversity lacking at, 186, 271
  history of, in Rochester, 243-244

Bars and nightclubs *(continued)*
  rejection feared at, 66, 141, 196, 298-299
  specific listings. *See also* Lone Star Saloon
    Ambush (San Francisco), *xxvi, xxvii, lii*
    Argos (Amsterdam), *xxiv*
    Baltimore Eagle (Baltimore), 117, 187-188
    Barracks (Sydney), 271, 277
    Bear Hollow (San Francisco), *xxvii*
    Block (London), 43
    Boston Boston (Boston), 41
    Cellar Bar at Heaven (London), 42
    Club Houston (Houston), 238
    Coconut Groove (San Francisco), 177
    Coleherne Pub (London), 42
    Eagle (San Francisco), 180
    88s (New York), 179
    Empire (London), 43-44
    Faultline (Los Angeles), 205
    Gallery (Baltimore), 109, 117, 118
    Gold Coast, *xxv*
    Hippo (Baltimore), 109, 115-116
    Josie's Cabaret and Juice Joint (San Francisco), 180
    Keep (Sydney), 270, 271
    Laird Hotel (Melbourne), 272, 274, 279
    Leatherneck (San Francisco), *xxvii*
    My Place (San Francisco), 356
    No Name (San Francisco), *xxvi*
    North End (Chicago), 72
    Old Crow (San Francisco), *xli*
    Pilsner Inn (San Francisco), *xxxv*
    620 (Iowa City), 218

Bars and nightclubs, specific listings *(continued)*
    Sportsman's Hotel (Brisbane), 275
    Stronghold (Sydney), 270, 271
    Tool Box (San Francisco), *xxvi*
    Toolbox (Toronto), 247
    Touché (Chicago), 75
    Town House (St. Paul), 129, 137
    Wheatsheaf Hotel (Adelaide), 280
  youth in, 55-56, 60
Barton, Crawford, *xlii*
Bashford, Kerry, 277
Bathhouses, 19, 30, 255, 272, 355
*Bay Area Reporter,* 175
BBS. *See* Internet
Bean, Joseph, *lvii,* 166
Bear, definition of. *See* Identity
Bear, Paul, 280
*Bear Annuals, xxiii*
*The Bear Book: Readings in the History and Evolution of a Gay Male Subculture* (Wright)
  identity in, *xxix, xxxii,* 51, 70, 149
  information in, 3, 6, 39, 215-216, 269
  prejudice in, 8, 34
  visuals for, 9
*Bear Classic, xxxi*
Bear Club U.K., 44
*The Bear Cult: Photographs by Chris Nelson* (Nelson), *xxvi, xxix, xxxvi, liv, lvii-lviii,* 305
"Bear Deteriorata" (Fritscher), *lvi*
Bear Essentials event (Australia), 272-274, 275-279, 281, 283
*The Bear Facts* newsletter, 215, 219, 221-226, 230
*Bear Fax* magazine, 68, 360
Bear History Project, *xxiii, xxvii, lxii,* 9

Bear Hollow bar (San Francisco), *xxvii*
Bear Hugs
   East Coast Bear Hugz, 185-189
   movement building through, 185, 221, 301, 358
   parties, 121, 361, 362
   San Francisco, 185, 192, 196, 221, 357-359, 364-365
Bear Icons exhibition, 9-10, 214
*BEAR* magazine
   articles in, *xxiii*, 329, 330
   beardom discovered through, 105-106, 108, 109, 111, 116
   *Classic BEAR,* 166, 356
   community created by, 68, 127-128, 187, 233, 354
      Iowa Bear Paws club and, 218, 219, 230
   ethnicity in, 153, 329
   fiction in, 305-308, 329, 332
      characters' appearance, 308-311
      sexual practices, 311-315
   history of, *xxxiii, xxxvi, liv-lviii*
   on identity, 70-71, 303, 352, 355, 356
   images in, *xlii, xlv, lvii,* 118-119, 166, 212
   otters in, 65-67, 68
   predecessors of, *xl, xlix-l, liv,* 288
   publishing industry and, *xliii,* 293, 296
   videos by, *lv, lviii*
Bear Paws of Iowa club, 215-220, 221-227, 230-231
Bear Pride event (Chicago), 17, 130, 150-151
Bear-A-Tones, 175-183
Beards
   bear identity and, 107, 320, 321
   history of, 95-102
   in leather community, 164, 166
   prejudice against, 95-100, 101-102, 131, 255, 299

Beards *(continued)*
   in publications, 289, 308-310, 316, 318, 329
Bearhug club (England), 40, 44, 52
Be(ar)n (of Melbourne Ozbears), 272
Bearpress, 62
Bear's Digest. *See* Bears Mailing List
Bears LA club, 205
Bears Mailing List
   identity issues on, 68, 69, 70, 107
   Mensch on, 192, 194-199, 201
   networking on, 77-78, 143, 196-198
Bears of San Francisco club, 181, 208, 209
Bears Ventura club (California), 205-206, 207-210
BearsCanberra club (Australia), 276, 282
BearsPerth club (Australia), 281
Beauty. *See* Body images
*The Beauty Myth* (Wolf), 10
Behar, Ruth, 335, 348n26
*Ben Hur, xxx*
*Beneath the Skins* (Dominguez), 166
Bergman, David, *liv*
Berkshire Bears club (Massachusetts), 6
*Best of Colt Films, xxxiii*
Betksy, Aaron, 152, 154, 160
Bianchi, Tom, *liv,* 291-292, 294, 295
Bibeault, Mike, 213
Bible, 289, 297
*Big Ad* magazine, 321
Big and Bear Weekend, 51, 52, 233
*Big Bear Trucking Company, xli*
*Big Boys and Buddies* magazine, 44
*Big Bruno, lv*
*Big Hairy Bruno, xxxii*
Bilko, Sergeant, 48-49
Bill (Houston Area Bears), 233-234, 236-237
Bisexuality. *See also*
   Heterosexuality, phase of

Bisexuality *(continued)*
  closeted, *xxiii*, 8, 125, 196, 230, 266
  in Turkey, 255-256, 259
  open, 75, 80
Bjorn, Kirsten, *xlii*
Black bears. *See* African Americans
Blessed, Brian, 266
Block bar (London), 43
Blue Max CC motorcycle club, 218, 219
Blue-collar. *See* Working class
*Blue-Collar Buddies,* 354
Blum, Dean, 219
Bly, Robert, 363
Body hair. *See* Hairiness
Body images. *See also* Clone culture; Stereotypes; Weight
  age and, 60, 135-136
  in contests, 211-214
  health and, *lix,* 35, 333-334
  liberation from, 42-43, 135-136, 182, 227-229, 303, 358-359
  masculinity and, *xxix, xxxi-xxxii, xxxvii, xliv-xlv,* 34, 300-301
  in media
    artwork, 119-122, 147-148
    gay, 68-69, 111, 228-229, 291-295, 297, 300-301
    mainstream, 10, 50, 211, 214
    pornography, *liii,* 8, 211, 289, 292
  oppression by, 9, 72, 304, 327-328
    sizeism, 33, 43, 45-46, 53-54, 126-127, 224
  of otters, 83, 85
  theories of, 148-149, 299
Body lice, 19, 27-28
Body mass index (BMI), 21
Bolick, Frank, 226-227
Bordo, Susan, 10, 334, 342
*Born to Raise Hell,* 165
Boston Boston disco (Boston), 41
Brachiopractic eroticism, 16
Bradshaw, Terry, *xxvii*

Brahma Studios, *lvii*
*Brideshead Revisited,* 339, 356
Brisbears club (Brisbane, Australia), 249-250, 275-276, 282
Brody, Jane, 20
Bronski, Michael, *xxiii, xxx, xxxvii,* 320, 324
Brown, Kerry, 281
Browning, Frank, 149
"The Bruin" (Boomer), 340-341
Bruno (actor), *xxxii-xxxiii, lv*
Brush Creek Media, *xxxvi, xlix, lviii,* 5, 68
BuckcuB (on Bears Mailing List), 69, 93
Buff. *See* Clone culture
Bufkin, Clark, 138
Bulger, Richard, *xxxv-xxxvi, liv-lvii, lix-lxi,* 6
Bulk club (London), 43-44, 49, 52
*Bulk Delivery* newsletter, 44
*Bulk* magazine, 321
*Bulk Male* magazine, 110, 119, 122, 221
Burgoyne, John, 96
Burnside, Ambrose E., 100
Bush, George, 117
Butts, Sonny, *lviii*
Byrnes, Shane, 272, 274, 279


Cabot, Sebastian, 228
Caesar, Julius, 43
Caldera, John, 212
*California Action Guide, l-lii, liv*
Callow, Simon, 266-267
Camm, Rob, 279
Canada, 55-56, 246, 247
Cancers, 19, 23-24
Capitalism. *See* Class; Economics
Carnes, Patrick, 30
Cartier, Jacques, 96
Catalina, 323
Cato, Bob, *xxvii, xlvi-xlvii, lx*
Cellar Bar at Heaven (London), 42

Center for Gay, Lesbian, Bisexual, Transgender Art and Culture (San Francisco), 176
Champlain, Samuel de, 96
Chan, Benny, 75
Chardon Street Convention, 97
Chasers, 40, 42-43, 52, 75, 224, 353. *See also* Admirers
Chesapeake Bay Bears club (Maryland), 110, 117, 189
*Cheyenne*, xxx
Chicago, Illinois
 clubs, 72-76
 events, 17, 130, 150-151, 331
 museums, 147, 163
*Chiron Rising* (CR) magazine, 329, 354
Cholecystitis, 19, 24
Cholelithiasis, 19, 24
Christianity
 Catholicism, 112, 115, 334
 dedication to, 97-98
 homophobia of, 115, 206, 256
Chubbies and Chubby Chasers club (C. and C.C.s) (London), 42-43
"A Chubbies Lexicon" (Brown), 44
Chubby chasers. *See* Admirers
*Cins* magazine, 257
Circumcision, 121
Civil rights, 16-17, 149, 156, 185
Civil War, 96, 100
Clark, Rick A., 58, 62
Class, economic
 American denial of, 11, 304
 identity and, 4, 8, 344-346, 353
 image and, 292, 302-303, 338, 352
 middle-class, 152, 153, 320
 in other countries, 3, 259-260
 in publications, 315, 344-346
 working class, *xlvi*, 108, 153, 304, 354, 358
*Classic BEAR*, 166, 356

Classification
 Natural Bears Classification System, 70, 75
 within bears, *xxxi*, 126, 320
Cleveland, Grover, 102
Clone culture
 blue-collar image of, 352, 355
 body images in, *xxvii*, 149, 327-328
 commercialization of, 152
 exclusion by, 76, 153, 218, 226, 357
 masculinity and, 35-36, 333, 338-340
 in media, 165, 291-295, 303, 327-328
 otter involvement with, 93
 prejudice against, 8, 34
Close, Chuck, 147
Closet. *See* Visibility
Club Houston (Houston), 233
Clubs. *See also* Events
 connection through, 81, 143-144
 critical questioning of, 151-152, 298
 inclusivity and, 8, 66, 122, 166
 membership in, 220-221, 235-236, 244, 250
 motorcycle clubs, *xxvi*, 164, 216-220, 270, 355
 specific listings
  Bare Bears (Portland, Maine), 6
  Bear Club U.K., 44
  Bear Paws of Iowa, 215-220, 221-227, 230-231
  Bearhug (England), 40, 44, 52
  Bears LA, 205
  Bears of San Francisco, 181, 208, 209
  Bears Ventura (California), 205-206, 207-210
  BearsCanberra (Australia), 276, 282
  BearsPerth (Australia), 281

# Index 373

Clubs, specific listings *(continued)*
  Berkshire Bears
    (Massachusetts), 6
  Brisbears (Brisbane, Australia),
    249-250, 275-276, 282
  Bulk (London), 43-44, 49, 52
  Chesapeake Bay Bears
    (Maryland), 110, 117, 189
  Chubbies and Chubby Chasers
    (England), 42-43
  Cougar Leather (Adelaide,
    Australia), 280-281
  Empire Bears (Rochester, New
    York), 21
  Gen-X Bears International, 6,
    56, 72, 75-76, 169-173, 301
  Girth and Mirth, 36, 122, 129,
    177, 245, 321
  Girth and Mirth Belgium, 44
  Girth and Mirth U.K., 43, 52
  Great Lakes Bears-Chicago,
    72-74, 76
  Harbour City Bears (Sydney,
    Australia), 270-274, 276
  Heart of Texas Bears (Austin),
    235
  Houston Area Bears, 233-242
  Kiwi Bears (New Zealand), 69
  Mainely Bears, 6
  Minnesota Bears, 129, 138, 141
  Montreal Bears (Canada), 246
  Monty Bears Group
    (Massachusetts), 6-8
  New England Bears, 6, 213
  New York Metrobears, 31, 32
  North Country Bears
    (Minnesota), 129-130,
    137-139
  Northeast Ursamen
    (Connecticut), 6
  Ozbears (Australia), 269-271,
    272, 275, 276, 280, 281
  Pacific Drill Patrol, *xxvii-xxix,
    xxxii, xlvi, li*
  Rhode Island Grizzlies, 6

Clubs, specific listings *(continued)*
  Sydney Bears (Australia), 277
  The Ursine Group (Iowa), 215,
    217, 220-221, 226-231
  VicBears (Melbourne,
    Australia), 272, 274-275,
    276, 279-280, 282
  WOMBATS (Australia), 281
  for youth, 55-56, 57, 59
COA Films, *lxi*
*Coach,* 332
Coburn, David, 270-271, 273
Coconut Groove (San Francisco),
  177
Coleherne Pub (London), 42, 43
Colt, Rip, *xxxi, xxxiii*
Colt Studios, *xxxi, xxxii-xxxiii, xxxvi*
Columbus, Christopher, 96
"Come Back to the Raft Again, Huck
  Honey" (Fiedler), 288
Comeau, Gary, 7
Coming out. *See* Visibility
"Coming to Terms with
  Sadomasochism: Psychiatry
  vs. Sex Research" *(The
  Advocate),* 16
Commercialization. *See* Economics
Communal living, *xli,* 1-2, 99-100,
  102, 295
Community
  at bars, 68, 81, 301, 359
  *BEAR* magazine creates, 68,
    127-128, 187, 233, 354
  Iowa Bear Paws club and, 218,
    219, 230
  Lopez on, 109, 111, 116
  identity and, 72, 153-154
  inclusivity and, 72, 122, 130-131
  leather, 42, 358
  through events, 189, 213
  through the Internet, 3, 195-196
Computers. *See* Internet;
  Technology; Web sites
Conan the Barbarian, 120
Condoms, 119. *See also* Safer sex

Con-Sociate Family, 99
Constant, John, *xxiv*
Contests, *xxxv,* 68, 117, 211-214, 239
   Melbourne Bear and Cub
      Competition, 274-275, 277,
      279
   Miss Gay Universe AT LARGE
      Pageant, 185
   Mr. Australian Bear and Cub
      Competition, 279-280, 282
   Mr. Bear Pride, 282
   Mr. International Bear, 208-209,
      212, 296, 331
   Mr. New England Bear, 213
   Mr. Southern California Bear,
      205-206, 207-208
Continuous positive airway pressure
   (CPAP), 22
Cooper, James Fenimore, 288
*Cop Faces, xxxii*
Copley, John Singleton, 96
Cornwallis, Charles, 96
Cortes, Hernando, 96
Cougar Leather club (Adelaide),
   280-281
*Country Exchange,* 354
*Cowboy Beards and Mustaches, lii*
Cox, Mike, *lviii*
CPAP (continuous positive airway
   pressure), 22
Crabs (body lice), 19, 27-28
Cruising, 150-151, 249, 259, 302
Cummings, Andy, 220, 221, 224-227
Currier & Ives, 100
Curtis, Richard, 266-267
Custer, George Armstrong, 100


Daddies, 342-344, 353. *See also*
   Fatherhood
   "Big-Bellied Daddy" icon, 47
   media on, *xlvii, xlix*
   nurturance and, 340
   otters as, 82, 87
*Daddy* magazine, 306

*DaddyBear* magazine
   age in, 329
   artwork in, 119
   ethnicity in, 153, 308
   fiction in, 305-307
      appearance of characters,
         308-311
      sexual practices, 311-315
*Daddy's Beerbelly in Bondage, lii*
*Daddy's Tools, lv*
Damon, Matt, 294
*Damron's Guide,* 218
Dannecker, Martin, 1
D'Aurora, Gary, 217
Davis, Jefferson, 100
Day, Greg, *xlii*
De Soto, Hernando, 96
Dean, James, 300-301
Death, in gay culture, 292, 295
DeBlase, Anthony, *xxxvi, xlix, lii*
Definition of bear. *See* Identity
Delay, David, *lii*
*Dellakname-i Dilkusa* (Ottoman
   book), 255
*Demetrius and the Gladiators, xxx*
Depression, 29, 32-33, 34
*Der gewöhnliche Homosexuelle*
   (Dannecker and Reiche), 1
Diabetes mellitus, 19, 24-25
Diamond, Val, 183
DiCaprio, Leonardo, 293
Dicker, Kevin, 279
Didion, Joan, *xxvii*
Dieting, 20, 31
"Dirtiest Blond Contractor in Texas"
   *(Target Album #3), xxxvii*
Divine, 185
Dollwet, Robert, 208, 210
Dominguez, Ivo, 166
Domino (artist), *xxxvii-xxxviii, xl-xli,*
   118
Donahue, Bob, 70
Dooley, Michael, 276
Douglas (artist), *lvi*
Douglass, Frederick, 243

Drag
    fear of, 63, 323
    masculinity and, 34, 36
    popularity of, 107, 185, 239, 241, 249
Drake, Sir Francis, 96
Drugs. *See also* Alcohol; Recovery movement
    addiction to, 185
    health and, 22, 29-31
    lower use among bears, 28, 32, 331, 354
    steroids, *xliv*
    Viagra, 30-31
*Drummer* magazine
    age in, *xlvii*
    bears and, 167, 306, 356
    Fritscher as editor of, *xxxv-xxxvi, xxxix*
    history of, *xxxvi-xxxviii, xlix-l, lii-liii*, 293
    images in, 165, 307, 317-319
        Fritscher on, *xxv, xxxiv, xli-xlii, liv-lv*
    importance of, *xliii-xliv, xlviii*
Drury, S., 139
Duodenal ulcer, 19, 25-26
Dyason, Andrew, 275
Dyer, Richard, 21, 322
Dyer, Steve, 191, 192, 195-196, 201


Eagle bar (San Francisco), 180
Earle, Ralph, 96
East Coast Bear Hugz, 185-189
Eating disorders, 32-33, 34
Economics. *See also* Class
    capitalism, *xlvi*, 150
    consumerism, 152, 157-160, 164
    employment and, 244, 355
    media and, 10, 292-294, 297, 301, 306, 323
    politics and, 9
    resistance to commercialization, 330, 356, 358, 363

Edwards, Jimmy, 265
Effeminacy
    acceptance of, 125, 256
    rejection of, *xxxii*, 264, 323, 338, 340, 343
The 88s (New York), 179
*El Paso Wrecking Company*, *xli*
Embry, John, *xliii*
Emerson, Ralph Waldo, 99, 100
Empire Bears club (Rochester, New York), 244-247
Empire pub (London), 43-44
*Empty Closet*, 244
Enger, Jim, *xxxii, xxxiii, xxxix-xli, xlii*
England
    bars in, 42-44
    bears in, 39-44, 53, 263-268
    clubs in, 39-40, 42-44, 49, 52-53
    ethnicity in, 12n4
    piercings in, 49
Ephebe. *See* Stereotypes
Erotic. *See* Sexuality
Erotica. *See* Pornography
Ersoy, Bulent, 256
Ethnicity. *See also* African Americans; Latinos
    Asian bears, 53, 132, 296-297, 329
    bear identity and, 4-5, 53, 298, 299, 353
    in England, 12n4
    homosexuality and, 125-126
    in media, *lvii*, 50, 153-154, 344-346
    in otter questionnaire, 80, 82
    in pornography, 308, 316, 318, 323, 329
    racism, 9, 53, 110, 299
    sexuality and, 347n4
Etienne (author), *xxxvii*
Europe, *xxiv-xxv*, 1-2, 44, 49, 51-53, 150. *See also* England; Germany
Evans, Paul, 274, 279

Events, *xxxvii*, 28, 81, 106-107, 141, 151-152. *See also* Bear Hugs; Clubs; Contests
   Bear Essentials (Australia), 272-274, 275-279, 281, 283
   Bear Expo/International Bear Rendezvous, 191, 212
   Bear Pride (Chicago), 17, 130, 150-151
   Big and Bear Weekend, 51, 52, 233
   Great Lakes Bear Pride, 331
   Southern Decadence, 238, 239, 242
   Southern Hibearnation (Australia), 279, 282, 283
   Sydney Gay and Lesbian Mardi Gras (Australia), 273, 278
Exercise, 31, 33

Facial hair. *See* Beards
Falstaff, Sir John, 264
*Falstaff Examining the Recruits* (Hogarth), 264
Fantasies
   during puberty, 253-254
   of nurturance, 340
   pastoral, 289-290, 293, 295-296, 304, 341-342, 352
   of prison, *xlvi-xlvii*
   of working class, 304, 317, 354
*The Fat Angel Times* newsletter, 44
Fatherhood, 206-207, 208, 343. *See also* Daddies
Faultline Bar (Los Angeles), 205
Fey Way Gallery, *xxxviii*
Fiedler, Leslie, 288
Fist-fucking, 16
Fitchburg, Massachusetts, 6-7, 95-99, 101, 102
*Flash Gordon*, 266
Fongheiser, Carl, 227
Foucault, Michel, *liv*, 1

*Four Weddings and a Funeral*, 266-267
France, 53
French, Jim, *xxxi, xxxiii, xl*
Friendships, 139-144, 196, 207, 208, 210
Frisch, Fran, *lvi*, 118, 217
Fritscher, Jack, 363
*Frontiers Newsmagazine*, *xlvii*, 175
Fruitlands, 99-100, 102
*The Full Monty* (McNally), *xliv*
Fund-raising, 122, 152
   by Bear-A-Tones, 180, 181-182
   by clubs, 141, 208, 209, 239, 241, 247

Gage Brothers, *xli, xlvii*
Gallery (Baltimore), 109, 117, 118
*Gallery 5* (Colt), *xxxi*
Gallstones, 19, 24
Gannett, Lewis, 101
Garfield, James A., 102
Garrior, Paul, *xxxi-xxxiii, xlvi, li*
Gastroesophageal reflux disease (GERD), 19, 26, 27
Gates, Horatio, 96
Gateway Motorcycle Club, 219
Gay Alliance of the Genesee Valley, 244
Gay liberation movement. *See* Liberation movement, gay
Gay Men's Health Summit (Boulder, Colorado), 11
Gay Men's Press, *xxix*
*Gay Times* magazine, 43, 44
Gaynor, Janet, *xlvi*
Gender, 152-153. *See also* Drag; Effeminacy; Masculinity; Women
Gen-X Bears International club, 169-173, 301
   Chicago chapter, 72, 75-76
   New England chapters, 6
   Toronto chapter, 56
*German Bear* magazine, 305

Germany, 1-2, 263, 273, 363
Gibbons, Billy, 265
Gilligan, Carol, 339
Girth and Mirth, 36, 122, 129, 177, 245, 321
  in other countries, 43, 44, 52
Glamor bears, 54n3, 304
Goethe, Johann Wolfgang von, 255
Gold Coast bar, *xxv*
Goldman, Emma, 243
Gonchar, Frank, *xxvii*
Gonorrhea, 28
*Good Housekeeping* magazine, 332
Goodman, John, 339, 356
Gott, Ted, 273
*GQ* magazine, *lvi*
Grace, W. G., 265
Grant, Ulysses S., 102
Great Lakes Bears club-Chicago, 72-74, 76
*The Great Train Robbery*, *xxx*
Greece, ancient, 41, 211, 361-362
Greene, Nathaneal, 96
Grey, Zane, 287
Griffiths, Richard, 266
Grizz (artist), 110, 118
Grizzly Adams, 224, 228
"Grizzly Fantasies" (Lopez), 119
Group sex, 19, 121, 185-189, 355, 357-359, 361
*The Growler* newsletter, 141
*GRUF* magazine, *lvi*, 305
Guild Press, *xxx*
Guillermo, Padre, 112, 113
Gulf Coast Bears club. *See* Houston Area Bears club

Habermas, Jürgen, 332
HABITAT II conference, 257
Hairiness
  health and, 19
  identity and, 126-127, 320, 321, 328

Hairiness *(continued)*
  in magazines, 309-311, 316, 318, 329
  otters and, 83, 85, 91
Halsted, Fred, *xxxviii*, *xlviii*
"Handballing: High Risk Sport" *(New York Native)*, 16
*Handjobs* magazine, 306
Hannah, John, 267
Harbour City Bears club (Sydney, Australia), 270-274, 276
"Hard Drive" (Macoy), 110
Harding, Don, 276, 279
Hardwick, Carl, *xxxiii*
Harper, Paul, 227
Harris, Daniel, 9, 33-34, 36
Harrison, Benjamin, 102
Harvard University, 101-102
Hay, Bob, 269-270, 275, 276
Hayes, Rutherford B., 102
Heart attack, 19, 22-23, 26, 27
Heart of Texas Bears club (Austin), 235
"The Heavy Bear" (Schwartz), 334
*Heavy Duty* magazine, 329
Held, Virginia, 339
Hell's Angels, 164, 355
Hemming, Tony, 280
Hemry, Mark, *xxxv*, *xlviii-xlix*, *l*, *liv*, *lvii*, *lix*
Hepatitis, 28-29
Hercules, 120
Herpes, 28
Heterosexuality. *See also* Bisexuality
  body images and, 34, 49, 50, 107, 294, 300
  compulsory, *xxxiv*, 255, 328, 336
  masculinity and, *lviii*, 10, 63, 363, 365
  phase of, 106, 113-114, 206-207, 253
  pornography and, 317, 323, 344
  stereotyping and, *xxxii*, *liii-liv*, 115, 299

Heyl, Steve, 212
Hiatal hernia, 19, 26-27
High blood pressure, 19, 21, 27
Hill, Scott, 68
*Him* magazine, 44
Hippo (Baltimore), 109, 115-116
Hirsute Club, li
*The Hirsute Stud Ranch Newsletter,* li-lii
Hispanics. *See* Latinos
*A History of Gay Literature* (Woods), 287
HIV. *See* AIDS
Hocquenghem, Guy, 1, 45
Hodges, Mike, 266
Hoffman, Beardog, *lvii*
Hoffmüller, Udo, 1
Hogan, Hulk, *lii*
Hogarth, William, 264
Hollibaugh, Amber, 337
*Home Improvement,* 121, 228, 332
Homomasculinity, *xxxiv, xli-xlii, xlviii, lvi*
Homophobia, 55, 93, 185, 264, 365
  liberation from, 60, 171
  in media, 288, 336
*Honcho* magazine, *lvi*, 68, 293
hooks, bell, 329, 347n4
Houston Area Bears club, 233-242
"How to Hunt Buckskin Leather Mountain Men and Live Among the Bear" (Fritscher), *lv*
Howard, Tom, *lviii*
Hubel, Durk, 210
*Huckleberry Finn* (Twain), 288
Hughes, Charles Evans, 102
The Hun (artist), *xlv, lvi*
*Hun Video Gallery, xlv, lvi*
Hurles, David, *xli-xlii*
Hurst, Alan, 217, 221
Husky, Jack, *lx, lxi*
*Husky* magazine, *lvi*
Hutter, David, 267-268
Huysmans, Joris-Karl, 160

Hyperlipidemia, 27
Hypertension, 19, 21, 27
Hyslop, Seumas, 279


Identity, of bears
  American culture and, 3, 156-159
  in *The Bear Book, xxix, xxxii,* 51, 70, 149
  body images and, 294, 299, 328
    attitudes and, 72, 90, 126-127, 208, 212-213, 320-321
  class and, 3-4, 8, 344-346, 353
  coming out and, 109, 111, 117
  debate over, 106-107, 221-226, 290-291
  diversity in, 59, 149, 205, 258, 364-365
  ethnicity and, 4-5, 53, 298-299, 353
  Fritscher on, *xxv, xxvii*
  gay liberation movement and, *xlv,* 8, 257
  masculinity and, *xlviii,* 10-11, 300, 321-322
  media and, *xxxiv-xxxv, lvi,* 67-72
  national, 263-264
  of otters, 65-67, 69-72, 77, 82-83, 86-87, 91-93
  theories of, 151-156, 335, 338-342
  Wright on, 351-357
Impotence, 25
*In & Out, liii*
*In Defense of Beauty* (Bianchi), 291
*In Praise of Older Men* (Hutter), 267
*In Praise of Older Women, xlvii*
*In Touch, xlix*
*Inches* magazine, *xlii, lx*
Inclusivity. *See also* Prejudice
  acceptance by bears, 207, 208, 359
  of admirers, 68, 106-107, 130, 171, 221, 228-229
  beauty images and, 126, 304
  at clubs, 8, 66, 122, 166

Inclusivity *(continued)*
  leather community and, 15-17, 42, 59, 110
  of otters, 68-69, 72-77
  outsiders from gay community, 15-17, 110-111, 159, 357
  outsiders within bear community, 66-67, 72, 126
  rejection, 66, 141, 196, 257, 299
*Indulge* magazine, 307, 315-317
International Bear Rendezvous, 191, 212
*International Leatherman* magazine, 167, 317-319
International Mr. Bear contest, 208-209, 212, 296, 331
Internet. *See also* Bears Mailing List; Technology; Web sites
  accessibility, *xliii*, 196-198, 258
  for rural men, 105, 108, 196, 230
  in Turkey, 257-259, 260
  for youth, 56-58, 60, 171
  anonymity of, 62, 108, 198-199
  BBS (computer bulletin boards), 217, 221, 233-234, 244, 301
  fantasies and, *xlv*, 295
  identity formation and, 151, 155-160
  networking through, 3, 93, 169, 187, 250
  Queernet, 193-194
  seeking relationships, 60, 62
  videos on, *xlvii*
Isherwood, Christopher, *xxxix*
Iversen, Ken, 281

*Jack Fritscher's American Men* (Fritscher), *xxv, xxix, xxxii, xl, liv, lx*
Jackson, Janet, 111
Jackson, Stonewall, 100
Jakal (artist), *xlv*
Jay, A., *xxxvii*

Jealousy, 52-53
Jeremy, Ron, 114
Johnson, Ron, *xxvi*
Jones, Grace, 41
Josie's Cabaret and Juice Joint (San Francisco), 180
*The Joy of Gay Sex* (Silverstein and White), 165-166
Judgment of Paris, 211
Julien, Max, *xlii*
*Just Men* magazine, *xxviii, xlii, lii*
"Just Shut Up and Sing!" (Bear-A-Tones), 180, 183
Justice, Robertson, 265


KA (artist), *li*
Kahn, Coppélia, 344
Kane, Jim, *xxv, xxxvi*
Kane, Kate, 153, 154, 155
*Kansas City Trucking Company, xli, xlvii*
Kantrowitz, Arnie, 34, 36
Katt, Tom, *xlvii*
Keen, Sam, 341
Keep bar (Sydney), 270, 271
Kelly, Beth, 153, 154, 155
Kelso, Steve, *xxxiii*
Kerle, Trish, 10
*King of Queens,* 34
*Kit Carson and the Mountain Men, xxxi*
Kiwi Bears club (New Zealand), 69
Klorese, Roger, 193-194, 195
Kloubec, Mike (aka John Muir), *xxxv, li, lv, lvii-lviii, lx*
Knighton, Kevin, 279
Knox, Henry, 96
Koestenbaum, Wayne, 9, 33-34, 35
Kramer, Larry, 17, 294
Kris studios, *xxx*
Kruse, Dale, 282
Kruse, Jerry, 226-227
Kuzak, Pete, *xxxiii*

La Bonté, Richard, *xlvi*
Laird Hotel (Melbourne, Australia), 272, 274, 279
*Lambda Book Report, xxix*
Lambda Istanbul, 257
Lane, Charles, 99
Lane, Laurie, 279
Lankard, Ken, 210
Latinos. *See also* Ethnicity
   gay identity of, 5, 115
   in media, *xlii,* 153, 316, 318, 329
   Puerto Ricans, 109-111, 115
Laur, Bill, 219
LaVey, Anton, *xxvi*
*Leather!* (Willard), *xxx-xxxi*
Leather Archives and Museum (Chicago), 163
*Leather Blues* (Fritscher), *xxv*
Leather community
   bars, 44, 68, 109, 185, 355
   bear community overlaps with, 52-53, 216-220, 245, 270, 280, 353
      leather bears, 320, 323, 357-359, 364-365
   bears contrasted with, 163-167, 213, 225, 364-365
   daddy roles in, 342
   in Europe, 42, 53
   health and, 16
   images in, *xxxiv,* 48, 119, 338, 351, 362
   inclusivity issues in, 15-17, 42, 59, 110
   National Leather Association, 240
   in pornography, 314-315, 319
   sadomasochism and, *xxv,* 48, 166, 353
*The Leather Journal* magazine, 167
*Leather Obsession, xlvii*
*Leatherfolk* (Thompson), *xxvi,* 165
*Leatherman* magazine, *xlix*
Leatherneck bar (San Francisco), *xxvii*

*Leather-Stocking Tales* (Cooper), 288
Leber, Will, 296
Ledermeister (Paul Garrior), *xxxi-xxxiii, li*
Lee, Jim, 118
Lee, Robert E., 100
Lembo, Joe, *li*
Lesbian Gay Bisexual Youth of Durham Region, 55
Lesbians
   aesthetics of, 348n24
   on aging, 343
   friendships and, 139-140
   gay men and, 54, 302, 327, 346
   sexuality and, 332, 337
   weight and, 34
Let Us Entertain You (LUEY), 238-239
Lewinowski, Rich, 7
Leyland, Winston, *xlviii*
Liberation movement, gay. *See also* Politics
   de-radicalizing of, 148-149, 152, 154
   identity and, *xlv,* 8
   inclusivity issues, 8, 15
   masculinity and, *xxxiv,* 135-136
   media and, *xxx, xxxiv,* 324
   progress of, 1-3, 59-60, 135-136, 243-244
   sexuality and, 39, 45-46, 319-320, 324
   technology and, *xxvi*
   in Turkey, 256-257, 260
*Life* magazine, *xxvi, li*
Lile, Tom, 118
Lincoln, Abraham, 96, 100, 102
Linotti, Ed, *xxvii-xxviii*
Literature. *See also* Pornography
   clone look in, 291-295
   Ottoman, 255
   pastoral, 287-291, 295-297
   science fiction, 120

Locke, Philip, 67, 68, 166-167, 321, 323
Locke, Richard, *xxxix, xli, xlvii-xlviii,* 292
Lockner, Clint (Chuck Romanski), *xxxiii, xl*
*Lockner's Key, xxxiii*
Lockwood, Gary, *xxxi*
London, England, 39-40, 42-44, 49, 52-53
Lone Star Saloon (San Francisco)
  Bear-A-Tones and, 177, 179, 180
  community at, 359
  history of, *xxvii, xxxvi, xlv, lvii,* 356, 357
Longone, Chuck, *li, lv*
Longus, 287
Looksism, 9, 72, 304
  sizeism, 33, 43, 45-46, 53-54, 126-127, 224
Lopez, Ali, 188
"Lost Dad" (Mann), 340
*Love and Death in the American Novel* (Fiedler), 288
Lowery, Alan, *xxvii*
Lucie-Smith, Edward, *xxix, liv*
Luisi, Ed, 217
Lurch, 5

*Mach* magazine, 307, 317-319
Macoy, Vince, 110
Maddox, Bob, *xxv*
*Magnum, P.I., liii*
*Magnus* magazine, 363
Mainely Bears club, 6
Mains, Geoff, 165, 358
*The Male Body* (Bordo), 10
*Mandate* magazine, 293, 324
MAN2MAN magazine, *xxv, xxxv, xlviii-l, liv-lv, lviii,* 363
Mann, Anita (John Mata), 239, 241
Mann, William, *xxix*
*Manpower 5* (Colt), *xxxi*
*A Man's Man, li, lv, lx*

Manu, Veet, *li*
"Mapping the Genome of Bear" *(Bear Classic), xxxi*
*Mapplethorpe: Assault with a Deadly Camera* (Fritscher), *xxxix*
Mapplethorpe, Robert, *xxxviii-xli, lvii-lix*
Maritain, Jacques, *xxxiii*
Marketing. *See* Economics
Marky Mark, 294
Marriage
  by closeted bisexual men, *xxiii,* 8, 196, 255-256, 259
  as a phase, 206-207
Martin, Judy, 67
Martin, Mary, *xlvi*
Martin, Tim, 119
Martinez, Jacinto Lopez, 112
Masculinity
  bear identity and, 10-11, 59, 66, 321-322, 332-333
  in clone culture, 333, 338-340, 352
  gender and, 63, 90, 321-322
  homomasculinity, *xxxiv, xli-xlii, xlviii, lvi,* 363
  homosexuality and, *liii-liv,* 59, 136, 291, 364-365
  images of, *liii-liv,* 147-148
  hairiness and, 127
  in media, *xxix, xxxi-xxxii, xxxvii, lvii*
  size, *xliv-xlv,* 34-36, 45
  leather and, 48, 165
  in media, *xlii, lviii,* 65-66, 300-301
  of otters, 84, 86, 92
  theories of, 72, 342, 345-346, 350n47
Masturbation
  pornography and, 312, 317, 322, 331
  sexual compulsion and, 30
Mata, John, 239, 241
Matuszak, John, *xxvii,* 331

Mauerman, Luke, 68
Mazzei, George, 71
McCormack, Garry, 280
McDonald, Glen, 276
McDonald, Michael, 121
McKenzie, Tex, 274
McKinley, William, 102
McNally, Terrence, *xliv*
Meat Loaf, *xxviii*
Media. *See also* Art; Literature; Pornography
  bear identity in, 67-72, 85
  beauty images in, 10
    gay, 228-229, 291-295, 297, 300-301
    mainstream, 50, 211
  economics and, *lxi,* 10, 292-294, 297, 301, 306, 323
  homophobia in, 336
  inclusivity issues in, *lx-lxi,* 43, 66, 119-120, 122, 153
  on the Internet, 198
  leather, 165-167
  masculinity in, *xxxii, xxxv, xxxvii*
  movies, 265-267
  privacy and, *xxxiv-xxxvi*
  significance of, *xliii,* 164-165, 301
  stereotypes in, *xxxvii, xlviii,* 73-74, 108, 111, 214
  in Turkey, 257
  in United States, 296
Melbourne Bear and Cub Competition (Australia), 274-275, 277, 279
Melbourne Ozbears club (Australia), 272
*Melbourne Star Observer,* 279
Melville, Herman, 288
*Men* magazine, 306
*Men on Men* (Bergman), 294
Mentzer, Mike, *xxviii*
Mentzer, Ray, *xxviii*
Mercader, Anthony, 277
Merida, Rolando, *lvi*
*Metropolitan Bear* newsletter, 32

Meyer, Detlev, 363-364
Milk, Harvey, *xxxviii, xlviii,* 2
Miller, Bob, 118
Millivres-Prowler press, *xxix*
Minneapolis, Minnesota, 129-133, 137-138
Minnesota Bears club, 129, 138, 141
Miss Gay Universe AT LARGE Pageant, 185
Mizer, Bob, *xxx, xli*
*Moby-Dick* (Melville), 288
Molestation. *See* Sexual abuse
Monogamy, 80, 82, 195
Montreal Bears club (Canada), 246
Monty Bears Group club (Massachusetts), 6-8
Moscone, George, *xxxviii*
Motorcycle clubs, *xxvi,* 164, 216-220, 270, 355
Movement, bear, *lvi,* 3, 282-283, 290-291, 351. *See also* Liberation movement, gay
Mr. Australian Bear and Cub Competition, 279-280, 282
Mr. Bear Pride contest, 282
Mr. International Bear contest, 208-209, 212, 296, 331
Mr. New England Bear contest, 213
Mr. Southern California Bear contest, 205-206, 207-208
Muir, John (Mike Kloubec), *xxxv, li, lv, lvii-lviii, lx*
Munroe, Dave, *xlvii*
Muren, Zeki, 256
Museum of Contemporary Art (Chicago), 147
My Place (San Francisco), 356
Mykonos Town, Greece, 150-151
Myocardial infarction. *See* Heart attack

Nardi, P., 139
*Nasty Blond Carpenter, lx, lxi*
National Association to Advance Fat Acceptance, 20

*National Enquirer,* liii
National Institutes of Health, 20-21
National Leather Association: Houston, 240
Native Americans
 bear archetype, 31, 297
 experiences of, 109
 in media, 287, 290, 316
Natural Bears Classification System, 70, 75
Nature. *See* Rural life
Nelson, Chris, *xxix, xxxvi, lv, lvii-lviii,* 305
Netherlands, *xxiv-xxv,* 51-53
Neuer, Stephan, 1
New England Bears club, 6, 213
New York Metrobears club, 31, 32
*New York Native,* 16
*New York Times, The,* 20
New Zealand, 69
No Attitude Guys, 274, 279
No Name bar (San Francisco), *xxvi*
North Country Bears club (Minnesota), 129-130, 137-139
North End bar (Chicago), 72
Northeast Ursamen club (Connecticut), 6
Nye, Robert, 264


Obesity. *See* Weight
"Officer Mike: SFPD's Finest" *(Skin), xxviii*
Old Crow bar (San Francisco), *xli*
Old Reliable (David Hurles), *xli-xlii*
Oliver, Albert, 181
*100 percent GL* magazine, 257
Opel, Robert, *xxxviii*
*Opposite Sex: Gay Men on Lesbians, Lesbians on Gay Men* (Miles and Rofes), 327
*Oprah, xxiii*

Oral sex
 in group settings, 19, 357
 in pornography, 311-312, 316, 318, 322
Orgies. *See* Group sex
*Orientalism* (Said), 290
Otters
 admirers of, 78, 80, 81-83, 88
 identity of, 65-67, 69-72
 inclusion of, 68-69, 72-77
 Otter Questionnaire
  on attitude, 84-85
  demographics of, 80-83
  on identity, 85-87
  on physique, 83-84
  on socializing, 88-90
  summary of, 77-79, 90-93
*OUT* magazine, 303
*Out of the Shadows* (Carnes), 30
Outcalt, John, 35
Outsiderhood. *See* Inclusivity
Ozbears club (Australia), 269-271, 275, 277
 Melbourne, 272
 South Australia, 280, 281


Pace, Dan, *xxxiii*
Pacific Drill Patrol, *xxvii-xxix, xxxii, xlvi, li*
Padilla, Dan, *xxxiii*
Palm Drive Video
 history of, *xxxi-xxxii, xxxv, li, lv, lvii-lviii, lxi*
 videos by, *lii, lx*
Palmer, Joseph, 95-102
Palmer, Thomas, 96, 97, 98
Pansies, 264
Parasites, 29
Paris (Greek mythology), 211
Patroclus, 361-362
Pediculosis, 19, 27-28
Perez, George, 118
Perles, Tony, *xxvii*
Perrenet, Nick, *xxiv*

Personal ads
  on the Internet, 198-199
  in publications, *xlix-liii,* 332, 354, 360
    ethnicity in, 329, 345
    heterosexuality in, *xxxiv*
P.G. (letter-writer to *BEAR* magazine), 65-66, 67, 70, 75
*Physique Pictorial, xxx, xlv, liv*
Picano, F., 320
Piercings, 47, 49, 314, 317, 319
Pierrot, Darren, 218-219, 224
Pile, Steve, 151, 152
Pilgrims, 96
Pilonidal sinus and cyst, 28
Pilsner Inn bar (San Francisco), *xxxv*
Pirami, Mario, *xxvi,* l
Pitt, Brad, *xxviii*
Plato, 361-362
*Play It As It Lays* (Didion), *xxvii*
Playfulness, 84-86, 91-92, 224, 341, 351, 352
*Playgirl* magazine, 331
*The Pleasure Principle* (Bronski), 300
Political correctness, 9, 11, 16-17, 212, 363
  Fritscher's dislike of, *xxvii, xxix-xxx, xxxv, xxxvii, xlv-xlvi*
Politics. *See also* Liberation movement
  activism, *xxiv, xlviii,* l, 11, 156, 331
  lack of, in bear clubs, 73, 303
  right wing, *xlvi,* 9, 17
  of weight, 33
Ponce de Leon, Juan, 96
Poole, Wakefield, *li*
*Popular Witchcraft: Straight from the Witch's Mouth* (Fritscher), *xxvi*
Pornography
  analysis of, 305-307, 319-324, 327-332, 340-346
  bear magazines, 307-315

Pornography, analysis of *(continued)*
  gay magazines, 315-317
  beauty images in, *liii,* 8, 211, 289, 292
  heterosexual, 114, 344
  masturbation and, 30, 288
  sadomasochism in, 293, 313-315, 317-319, 322-323
  sexual practices in, *lxi,* 293
  videos, *xxxii-xxxiii, li-lii, lv, lviii, lx*
*Powerplay* magazine, 317-319
Prejudice. *See also* Age; Homophobia; Inclusivity; Looksism; Racism; Sexism; Stereotypes
  against bears, 9, 76, 166
  by bears, 51, 69, 72
  origin of, 110
  in pornography, 324
Preston, John, 324
Pride. *See* Events
Privacy. *See* Visibility
Probyn, Elspeth, 152
Project Athena, 192
Promiscuity, 16, 30
Prophylactics
  condoms, 119
  medications as, 19, 28
Psychiatry, 16, 22, 29-30
Puerto Ricans, 109-115. *See also* Latinos
*Pumping Iron, xliv*
Puritans, 96
Putnam, Israel, 96


*Queen's Quarterly, xxxvii*
*The Queen's Throat: Opera, Homosexuality, and the Mystery of Desire* (Koestenbaum), 33, 35
Queernet, 193-194, 197
*Quo Vadis, xxx*

Racism, 9, 53, 110, 299. *See also* Ethnicity
Radcliffe, Jack, *lviii*
Radical Democratic Green Party (Turkey), 256
*Rainbow Country, xxxv*
Rainbow Motorcycle Club (RMC), *xxvi*
Rainey, Gavin, 272
Raleigh, Sir Walter, 96
*Ramayana,* 297
Rand, John, 68
Rann, Randy, *lviii*
Ream, Rodger, 109-110, 118
*A Rebours* (Huysmans), 160
Recovery movement, 30, 245, 328, 353, 354
Redewill, Rick, *lvii*
Redford, Robert, *xxxix*
Reeves, Steve, *xxx,* 361
Reiche, Reimut, 1
Rejection. *See* Inclusivity
Religion
  Bears Mailing List debates on, 195
  Bible, 289, 297
  Christianity, 97-98, 112, 115, 206, 256, 334
  Hinduism, 297
  Wicca, *xxvi*
Remington, Bob, 110, 118
Renslow, Chuck, *xxv, xxx*
Revolutionary War, 96
REX (artist), *xxviii, xlv*
*RFD* magazine, *xxvi, lvi,* 68
Rhode Island Grizzlies club, 6
Ridinger, Robert B. Marks, 68
Rimming
  health risks of, 29
  in pornography, 313, 317, 319, 322
*The Rise and Fall of Gay Culture* (Harris), 33
Roadhouse, John, 357
*Robert's Rules of Order,* 216, 220, 227

Robichaud, Don, 7
Robinson, Bruce, 266
Rocca, Joe, 282
Rochester, New York, 243-247
Rofes, Eric, 4, 70-71, 72
Romanski, Chuck (aka Clint Lockner), *xxxiii, xl*
Roosevelt, Theodore, 102
*Roseanne,* 339, 356
Rowberry, John W., *lx-lxi*
Rowe, M., 320, 324
Rubens, Peter Paul, 50
Rubin, Gayle, 165, 337-338
Rudnick, Paul, *liii*
Rural life
  fantasies of, 159, 293, 304, 330, 341-342, 352
    in pastoral literature, 289-290, 295-296
  identity and, 8, 320
  isolation helped by media access, 105-106, 108, 196, 230
  more closeted, 364
  in otter questionnaire, 80, 82
Russell, Clay, 1
Russo, Donnie, *xlvii*


Sadomasochism
  health and, 16
  leather and, *xxv,* 48, 166, 353
  in media, 293
  other communities and, 17, 213, 353, 357, 358
  piercings and, 49
  in pornography, 307, 313-315, 317-319, 322-323
Safer sex
  bear community support for, 28, 117, 141, 290
  in media, *lviii,* 119
  at parties, 185, 188, 189
  rhetoric of, 342
Said, Edward, 290
Samson, 292

San Francisco, California
  bear community in, 130-131, 296, 356, 365
  Bear Hugs, 185, 192, 196, 221, 357-359, 364-365
  Bears of San Francisco club, 181, 208, 209
  gay community in, 2-3, 8
  Mr. International Bear contest, 208-209, 212
*San Francisco Chronicle, xxxv*
*San Francisco Examiner,* 177
*San Francisco Sentinel,* 356
Sandland, P. J., 280
Santa Claus, 228, 263
Scabies, 19, 27-28
Schumacher, Scott, 172
Schwartz, Delmore, 334
*Scott of the Antarctic,* 265
Sears, Clara Endicott, 102
*Seattle Gay Times,* 356
*See Dick Cum, li, lv*
Selleck, Tom, *liii*
Sexism, 53, 341, 363, 365
Sexual abuse, 113, 198, 206
Sexual Compulsives Anonymous (SCA), 30
Sexuality. *See also* Bisexuality; Heterosexuality; Lesbians; Pornography; Sadomasochism; Safer sex
  across age, 61-62, 301, 353, 363
  AIDS and, *xlv,* 143, 290, 294, 352
  anal, 312, 316-317, 318, 322
  in ancient Greece, 361-362
  among bears, *liii,* 52, 351
  clubs and, 43, 238, 245
  etiquette of, 360-361
  fear of, 291, 336, 339
  friendships and, 139-140, 142
  in gay liberation movement, 39
  group, 19, 121, 185-189, 355, 357-359, 361
  Internet and, 196, 197-198
  lesbians and, 332, 337

Sexuality *(continued)*
  masculinity and, 34-36
  masturbation, 30, 312, 317, 322, 331
  in media, *xxxvi,* 287-292
  oral, 19, 311-312, 316, 318, 322, 357
  politics and, 212, 337
  sexually transmitted diseases, 28-31, 60-61, 169. *See also* AIDS
  theories of, 292, 297
  women and, 289, 302
Shakespeare, William, 43, 264
Shapiro, Al, *xxxvii*
Shilts, Randy, *xxxv*
Sibal, Jim, 9-10
Siegal, Elliot, *xxxix*
Silvers, Phil, 49
Silverstein, Charles, 165, 320
SIRCO Video, *lxi*
Siward, Earl, 263
620 bar (Iowa City), 218
Sizeism, 33, 43, 45-46, 53-54, 126-127. *See also* Looksism; Weight
Skepsis web site, 155-159
*Skin* magazine, *xxviii, xlii, lx*
*Skinflicks* magazine, *lx*
Sleep apnea, 19, 21-22
Smith, David Grant, *lv, lix-lx*
Smith, John, 96
Smith, Shawn, 137
Smith Brothers cough drops, 100
Smoking, *xliii-xliv, lviii,* 21, 319
"The Sociology of the Urban Bear" (Wright), *lv,* 338, 351-356
*Some Dance to Remember* (Fritscher), *xxxvii, xxxix, xliv, xlix,* 363
*Son of Drummer* magazine, *xxv*
*Song of the Loon* (Amory), 287-290, 291, 301
*Southern Cumfort* magazine, *lvi,* 305

Southern Decadence event, 238, 239, 242
Southern Hibearnation event (Australia), 279, 282, 283
Sparrow, David, *xxv, xxxi, xxxvii, xli*
Sportsman's Hotel (Brisbane, Australia), 275
Spratt, Sir Lancelot, 265
St. Paul, Minnesota, 129, 137-138
Stacey, Clay, *li*
Stafford, Steve, *lvi*
Stark, John, 96
Steele, Jason, *lviii*
Stereotypes, 33-36, 46-50, 320, 338, 362-363. *See also* Clone culture; Prejudice
  class and, *xlvi*
  of effeminacy, *xxxii,* 115, 255, 264, 340
  ephebe, 8, 135-136
  in media, *xxxiv,* 68-69, 324
  twink, *xxvii,* 8-9, 34, 36, 76, 93
Stern, Randy, 169
Stewart, Jim, *xli*
Stompers (New York), *xxxviii*
Stoner, Jeff, 70
Stroke, 19, 22, 23, 27
*Stroke* magazine, *xxv*
Strongest Man competitions, 44, 49-50, 121
Stronghold bar (Sydney), 270, 271
Summer, Donna, 116
Suresha, Ron, 68
Sydney Bears (Australia), 277
Sydney Gay and Lesbian Mardi Gras Festival (Australia), 273, 278, 281-282
Syphilis, 28

T. C. (artist), *lvi*
Taft, William H., 102
*Take It from Here,* 265
"Talking Big" (Brown), 43

*The Target Album #3* magazine, *xxxvii*
Target Studios, *xxxiii-xxxiv, xxxvi-xxxvii*
Tarzan, 120
Tattoos, 42, 47, 49, 53, 329
  in pornography, 314, 317, 319
Taylor, Barry, 279-280
Technology. *See also* Internet
  artifice of, 160
  employment and, 141, 229, 320
  gay liberation movement and, *xxvi*
  modern changes due to, *liv,* 199-201
  in publishing industry, *lv, lviii-lix*
Thomas, Bart (Richard Bulger), 6
Thomas, Joe, 105, 108
Thomas, Lou, *xxxiii-xxxiv, xxxvi-xxxvii*
Thompson, Mark, *xxvi,* 165
Thoreau, Henry David, 99, 100
"Those Dirty Classifieds" *(Just Men), lii*
Thrift, Nigel, 151, 152
Thrombophlebitis, 18-19
Thurman, Bob, 201
Tiffany (in Houston Area Bears), 240-241
*Tight Little Island,* 265
Tim (of Great Lakes Bears-Chicago), 72-74, 76
Tom (of Gen-X Bears Chicago), 75-76, 79, 81
Tom of Finland, *xxxvi, xl,* 119
*Tomorrow's Men, xxxi*
Tony (artist), 118
Tool Box bar (San Francisco), *xxvi*
Toolbox bar (Toronto), 247
Toronto Gay Youth Group, 56
Touché bar (Chicago), 75
Town House bar (St. Paul), 129, 137
*Transcendental Wild Oats* (Alcott), 99

Transsexuality, 34, 256. *See also* Drag
Trask, Reverend George, 97, 101
Tress, Arthur, *xxxviii*
Tronto, Joan, 339
Tuberculosis, 333
Turkey, 253-261
Turtle, 118
Tuttle, H. K., *xxxviii*
Twain, Mark, 288
Twelve-step groups. *See* Recovery movement
Twinks. *See* Clone culture; Stereotypes
*2001: A Space Odyssey*, *xxxi*

Ulcers, 19, 25-26
*Unbearable Weight: Feminism, Western Culture, and the Body* (Bordo), 334
Uncle Sam, 96-97
*Uncut* magazine, *lx*
UnderBear parties, 229-230
*Unfähig zur Emanzipation? Homosexuelle zwischen Getto und Befreiung* (Hoffmüller and Neuer), 1
United States, 3, 52, 156-159, 291, 296-298, 304. *See also* Western culture
University of Rochester, 244
*Urban Aboriginals* (Mains), 165, 358
Urban life, 8, 80, 82, 304, 320
The Ursine Group club (Iowa), 215, 217, 220-221, 226-231
Ursus, Dade, *lvi*
Utopianism, 1-2, 99-100, 295, 335

Verdi, Giuseppe, 264
Vespucci, Amerigo, 96
Viagra, 30-31

VicBears club (Melbourne, Australia), 272, 274-275, 276, 279-280, 282
Vigilante (model), *lviii*
Visibility
  bisexuality and, *xxiii*, 8, 125, 230, 259, 266
  coming out experiences, *xxiv*, 42, 74, 226, 228-229
  ethnicity and, 126
  heterosexuality and, 299-300
  Internet and, 62, 107-108, 156, 197
  in media, *xxxiv-xxxvi*, 317
  rural, 364
  in Turkey, 254-255, 257, 259-260
  of youth, 55-57, 59, 61

Waco, Tex, *lviii*
Wade, Russ, *lviii*
Wagstaff, Sam, *lix*
Walker, Clint, *xxx*, *xxxi*
*The Waltons*, 353
Ward, Bill, *xlv*, 118
Washington, George, 96
Waugh, T., 322, 323, 324
Web sites. *See also* Internet
  *The Advocate* www.Advocate.com, 1
  Bear History Project www.BearHistoryProject.com, *xxv*, *xlv*
  Bear Paws of Iowa, 229-230
  Bear Resources, 258, 259
  Bear Web Ring www.bearring.org, 63
  Bear Youth www.bearyouth.org, 55, 57-58, 59, 60, 61-63
  Greg Day photographs www.ManDreams.com, *xlii*
  Gen-X Bears International www.genxbears.org, 169
  Hairy Chest Page, 258

Web sites *(continued)*
  other sites
    www.BearArchives.com, *xxix*
    www.BearStream.com, *xliii*
    www.BeefyBoyz.com, *xxxvii, xlv, liii*
    www.HuzBears.com, *xliii*
    www.MuscleBear.com, *xlv, liii*
    www.skepsis.com/bears, 155-159
    www.ToughCustomers.com, *xli*
  Youth Resource www.youthresource.com, 63
Webber, Bruce, 291
Webster, John, 69
Weichelt, Chip, *xlvii*
Weight. *See also* Body images
  health and, 19-23, 34
  identity and, *xliv-xlv*, 212, 321, 328, 352
  of otters, 85, 91-92
  in pornography, 309, 310, 316, 318, 323
  sizeism, 33, 43, 45-46, 53-54, 126-127
Welles, Orson, 264
*West-East Divan* (Goethe), 255
Western culture, 211, 287-289, 290, 343
  Turkey influenced by, 256, 257, 260-261
*Whack-O!*, 266
Wheatsheaf Hotel (Adelaide), 280
*Whipcrack* magazine, *xxv-xxvi*
*Whisky Galore!*, 265
White, Edmund, 165
Whites. *See* Ethnicity
Whitman, Walt, 48, 100, 364
"Who's Who in the Zoo? A Glossary of Gay Animals" (Mazzei), 71

Wilde, Oscar, 41, 267
Willard, Avery, *xxx*
Wilson, Woodrow, 102
Windmill Theatre, 265
*Winter* (Hutter), 267-268
*Withnail and I*, 266
Wittke, Chris, 127
Wolf, Naomi, 10
WOMBATS club (Australia), 281
Women. *See also* Lesbians
  as bears, 75, 235-236, 240-241, 250, 302-303
  beauty images and, 10, 228, 291, 295, 327, 333
  in literature, absence of, 288-290
  sexism against, 53, 341, 363, 365
  sexuality and, 347n15
  Suffrage movement, 243
Woods, Gregory, 287
*Worcester Phoenix*, 7
*Worcester Spy*, 98
Working class, *xlvi*, 108, 153, 304. *See also* Class
  Wright on, 354, 358, 363
World's Strongest Man Competition, 44, 49-50, 121
Wrestling, *xliv*, 40, 44, 48-49, 113, 221
Wright, Les
  on clubs, 215-216, 221
  on history, 68, 153-154
  on identity, *lv*, 51, 321, 338-339
  on media, 306

*XY* magazine, 293


*Young Physique*, *xxxi*
Youth, 55-57, 169-173

# *Order Your Own Copy of This Important Book for Your Personal Library!*

## THE BEAR BOOK II
## Further Readings in the History and Evolution of a Gay Male Subculture

_____ in hardbound at $49.95 (ISBN: 0-7890-0636-7)

_____ in softbound at $24.95 (ISBN: 1-56023-165-3)

| | |
|---|---|
| COST OF BOOKS_____ | ☐ **BILL ME LATER:** ($5 service charge will be added)<br>(Bill-me option is good on US/Canada/Mexico orders only;<br>not good to jobbers, wholesalers, or subscription agencies.) |
| OUTSIDE USA/CANADA/<br>MEXICO: ADD 20%_____ | ☐ Check here if billing address is different from shipping address and attach purchase order and billing address information. |
| POSTAGE & HANDLING_____<br>(US: $4.00 for first book & $1.50<br>for each additional book<br>Outside US: $5.00 for first book<br>& $2.00 for each additional book) | Signature _____ |
| SUBTOTAL_____ | ☐ **PAYMENT ENCLOSED:** $ _____ |
| IN CANADA: ADD 7% GST_____ | ☐ **PLEASE CHARGE TO MY CREDIT CARD.** |
| STATE TAX_____<br>(NY, OH & MN residents, please<br>add appropriate local sales tax) | ☐ Visa  ☐ MasterCard  ☐ AmEx  ☐ Discover<br>☐ Diner's Club  ☐ Eurocard  ☐ JCB |
| | Account # _____ |
| **FINAL TOTAL**_____<br>(If paying in Canadian funds,<br>convert using the current<br>exchange rate. UNESCO<br>coupons welcome.) | Exp. Date _____<br><br>Signature _____ |

Prices in US dollars and subject to change without notice.

NAME _____
INSTITUTION _____
ADDRESS _____
CITY _____
STATE/ZIP _____
COUNTRY _____ COUNTY (NY residents only) _____
TEL _____ FAX _____
E-MAIL _____

May we use your e-mail address for confirmations and other types of information? ☐ Yes  ☐ No
We appreciate receiving your e-mail address and fax number. Haworth would like to e-mail or fax special discount offers to you, as a preferred customer. **We will never share, rent, or exchange your e-mail address or fax number.** We regard such actions as an invasion of your privacy.

*Order From Your Local Bookstore or Directly From*
**The Haworth Press, Inc.**
10 Alice Street, Binghamton, New York 13904-1580 • USA
TELEPHONE: 1-800-HAWORTH (1-800-429-6784) / Outside US/Canada: (607) 722-5857
FAX: 1-800-895-0582 / Outside US/Canada: (607) 772-6362
E-mail: getinfo@haworthpressinc.com
PLEASE PHOTOCOPY THIS FORM FOR YOUR PERSONAL USE.
www.HaworthPress.com

BOF00